THE GRAND RESORT HOTELS
of the
WHITE MOUNTAINS

THE GRAND RESORT HOTELS of THE WHITE MOUNTAINS

A Vanishing Architectural Legacy

by

Bryant F. Tolles, Jr.

DAVID R. GODINE · BOSTON

*To Douglas A. Philbrook,
friend and fellow White Mountain collector,
aficionado and historian,
for his invaluable assistance, support and generosity.*

First published in 1998 by
DAVID R. GODINE, PUBLISHER
Box 450
Jaffrey, New Hampshire 03452

Copyright © 1998 by Bryant F. Tolles, Jr.

All rights reserved. No part of this book may be used or reproduced in any
manner whatsoever without permission, except in the case of
brief quotations embodied in critical articles and reviews.

Library of Congress Cataloging-in-Publication Data
Tolles, Jr., Bryant Franklin, 1939-
The grand resort hotels of the White Mountains : a vanishing
architectural legacy / by Bryant F. Tolles, Jr. — 1st ed.
p. cm.
Includes bibliographical references and index.
ISBN 1-56792-026-8
1. Hotels—White Mountains (N.H. and Me.)—History.
2. Resort architecture—White Mountains (N.H. and Me.)—History.
I. Title.
TX909.T58 1995
647.94742'201—dc20   95-35160
CIP

LIST OF ABBREVIATIONS AND FREQUENTLY CITED SOURCES

ATC • *Among the Clouds* (1877-1917), published on the summit of
Mount Washington, New Hampshire

CCRD • Carroll County Registry of Deeds, Ossipee, New Hampshire

DCL • Dartmouth College Library, Hanover, New Hampshire

NHHS • New Hampshire Historical Society, Concord, New Hampshire

HLL • Plymouthiana Collection, Herbert H. Lamson Library,
Plymouth State College, Plymouth, New Hampshire

WME • *The White Mountain Echo* (1878-1927), published in Bethlehem, New Hampshire

Table of Contents

Preface		7
Acknowledgments		9
Introduction		13
Chapter 1	The Precursors: Rosebrooks, Crawfords, Fabyans and the Early Highway Hotels	29
Chapter 2	Railroad Development and the Pre-Civil War Hotels	47
Chapter 3	The Prosperity of the 1860s and Hotel Expansion	77
Chapter 4	The Grand Resort Hotel Concept Is Securely Rooted: The Seventies	109
Chapter 5	The Maturation of the Building Type: From the Eighties to World War I	143
Chapter 6	The Hotel That Blew Down: The Metallak, the Surviving Record, and the Symbol	181
Chapter 7	The Full Evolution of the Building Type: The Second Glen House, the New Profile House, and the Mountain View House	191
Chapter 8	Paragons of Style and Elegance: The Mount Washington Hotel at Bretton Woods and The Balsams at Dixville Notch	213

Appendix A	A List of Pre-1930 White Mountain Hotels Accommodating Fifty or More Guests	239
Appendix B	Lists of Known Pre-1900 Paintings, Printed Views, and Illustrated Maps Depicting White Mountain Hotels	247
Bibliography		251
Index		261

Color sections follow pages 94 and 158

✑ Preface ✑

THE INSPIRATION, thought and planning behind *The Grand Resort Hotels of the White Mountains: A Vanishing Architectural Legacy* originated some years ago. I initially became intrigued with the architecture and associated history of this distinctive and captivating building type during the 1960s and 1970s while on family hiking and skiing expeditions throughout the mountains from our house in Center Sandwich, New Hampshire. My first opportunity, however, to closely and systematically study the hotels of the region came during the national bicentennial era. At that time I was conducting research and field surveys, and taking photographs for my book *New Hampshire Architecture: An Illustrated Guide*, published by the University Press of New England for the New Hampshire Historical Society in 1979. My interest has been further developed as a result of over twenty years of collecting books, pamphlets, periodicals, printed views, photographs, maps, broadsides, view books, hotel ephemera and objects, and other paper items pertaining to the White Mountains area. This rich and varied collection has provided the bulk of the source material for this volume.

From long association with the subject and the region, I was aware that the hotels of the White Mountains were rapidly disappearing and that soon the physical evidence that constituted the best available documentation—the buildings themselves—would largely be a memory from the past. The 1970s and 1980s have seen further additional closings, some accompanied by auctions, of several more of the grand resort hotels (The Waumbek; Crawford House; Sunset Hill House; Forest Hills Hotel; Sinclair House; Mountain View House), so that today only four of the original total of thirty remain open to the public—the Mount Washington Hotel (Bretton Woods); The Balsams (Dixville Notch); and the Eagle Mountain House, and Wentworth Hall and Cottages (Jackson). Today there are few traces remaining of this fascinating building type in the White Mountains.

Despite the large volume of literature that has been published pertaining to the White Mountains since the mid-nineteenth century, nothing is available today (in part due to the lack of manuscript materials) that comprehensively, insightfully and accurately treats the architecture and related social, cultural and economic history of the region's grand resort hotels. Bits and pieces of this story have appeared in general histories, monographic works, regional and local histories, journal and magazine articles, newspapers, and hotel promotional materials; however, none of these sources deals with the subject within the larger framework of general White Mountain history, with references to the origins and development of the hotel building type there, elsewhere in New England, and across the United States. Furthermore, in these sources it is exclusively through illustrations and limited descriptive narrative that the architecture of the White Mountain examples has been critically surveyed, often in a superficial, fragmentary and inaccurate manner. This book represents an attempt to treat this architecture chronologically in relation to broad historical patterns or themes as well as to analyze, in comparative fashion, the history, qualities and features of individual buildings and complexes, and the contributions made by their financiers, architects and builders.

It is with specific purpose that I have exclusively focused on the grand resort hotel building type (see Introduction), its antecedent highway inns and smaller hotels, and other selected hotels of particular architectural significance. While at one time I considered writing a general architectural history of all the inns, hotels and boarding houses in the White Mountains (at the height of the industry in c. 1895 there were well over 200 accommodating 40 or more

PREFACE

The Old Man of the Mountain, Franconia Notch, NH. *Engraving from promotional flyer, "Profile House, Franconia Notch, White Mountains, N.H.," c. 1875. Author's Collection.*

guests each), I quickly dismissed this idea. In doing so I concluded that the grand hotels, the supreme architectural accomplishment in the region between 1860 and 1930, were the subject of primary importance and interest, and that their history, unlike that of the hotels at large, could be related in a far more orderly, coherent and provocative fashion. This I have attempted to do in a manner that relies on all known printed and unpublished sources, with a structure, thematic approach and writing style that is intended to have value and appeal to scholars as well as general readers. The inclusion of extensive illustrations, essential as documents of hotel architecture and history, adds a visual dimension without which the volume could not achieve its objectives (black and white photographs possess figure numbers while color images are identified by plate numbers). The subject itself, however, is the principal fascination; the grand hotel concept, and the architecture and life associated with it, have long captured the public imagination and will likely continue to do so in the future. It is my hope that this book will provide the basis of greater understanding of these grand and vulnerable White Mountain buildings within a regional as well as national context.

BRYANT F. TOLLES, JR.
Center Sandwich, NH
January 1997

Acknowledgments

THERE ARE MANY INDIVIDUALS, as well as institutions and organizations and their staffs, to whom I owe a great debt of gratitude for assistance in the researching and compilation of this book. The major portion of my research, supplementing that accomplished using the resources of my own collection, was carried on in the White Mountain Collection of the Dartmouth College Library, Hanover (Stanley W. Brown, Curator of Rare Books; Kenneth Cramer, College Archivist); the New Hampshire Historical Society, Concord (John L. Frisbee, Director; William N. Copeley, Librarian; Deborah Tapley, Assistant Librarian; Donna-Belle Garvin, Curator of Collections); the New Hampshire State Library, Concord (Stella J. Scheckter, Administrator, Bureau of Reference and Loan); the Mount Washington Observatory Resource Center, North Conway (Guy Gosselin, Director); the Maine Historical Society, Portland (Nicholas Noyes, Librarian; Elizabeth Maule, Manuscript Librarian); the Herbert H. Lamson Library at Plymouth State College (Rick Lilla, Access-Reference Librarian; Gary McCool, Public Services Librarian); the American Antiquarian Society, Worcester, MA (Nancy Burkett, Librarian; Georgia B. Barnhill, Curator of Graphic Arts); the Massachusetts Historical Society, Boston (Peter Drummey; Brenda Lawson); the Hugh M. Morris Library at the University of Delaware; the Appalachian Mountain Club, Boston (Jack Hewitt, Librarian; David Belknap, Chair, Library Committee); the Avery Architectural and Fine Arts Library, Columbia University, New York City (Janet Parks, Curator of Drawings); and, the Registries of Deeds for Carroll (Ossipee), Coos (Lancaster) and Grafton (Woodsville) counties. Of those individuals who offered access to their personal collections and provided valuable advice on the project, I particularly wish to credit Douglas A. Philbrook, Gorham; Earle G. Shettleworth, Jr., Augusta (Director, Maine Historic Preservation Commission); Richard Hamilton, Littleton (Executive Director, White Mountain Attractions, Inc.); Stephen P. Barba, Dixville Notch (President; The Balsams Corporation); and, the late Glen Kidder, Acton, MA. For financial assistance essential to the completion of my research I would like to thank former Dean Helen Gouldner, College of Arts and Sciences, University of Delaware, for three one-year Supplemental Funds Grants in support of the project.

In my search for source materials extending over a three year period I had the pleasure of visiting virtually every community in the White Mountain region and examining collections, most of which are modest but still extremely useful, at a wide variety of local libraries and historical societies. Of these repositories I wish to express my sincere appreciation to the following, whose White Mountain holdings are unusually strong: the Henney History Room, Conway Public Library (Ann Cullahan); the North Conway Public Library (Carrie Gleason, Librarian); the Littleton Public Library (Kathryn Taylor, Librarian); the Littleton Area Historical Society (Frances Heald); the Bethlehem Public Library (Muriel Brown, Librarian); and, the Sugar Hill Historical Museum (Jane Vincent, Curator). In addition to this primary group I also owe my considerable thanks to: the Jackson Public Library (Priscilla E. Bissell, Librarian); the Jackson Historical Society (Alice Pepper); the Bartlett Public Library (Jean Garland, Librarian); the Lisbon Historical Society (Mary Clough); the Jefferson Historical Society (Helen Merrill); the Whitefield Historical Society (Ruth Harris; Ree Fisher); the Conway Historical Society (Marian Putnam; Anne Levesque); the Bethel Historical Society (ME) (Randall Bennett); the Moosilauke Public Library, North Woodstock (Jean Ralph, Librarian); the Upper Pemigewasset Historical Society, Lincoln (Leslie Sargent); the Berlin Public Library (Yvonne Thomas, Librarian); the Gorham Historical Society (Francis

Peabody); the Plymouth Historical Society (Rachel Keniston); the Plymouth Public Library (Patricia Topham, Librarian); the Wolfeboro Historical Society (Harrison Moore); the William D. Weeks Memorial Library, Lancaster (Barbara Roberts, Librarian); the Lancaster Historical Society (Faith Kent); the Tamworth Historical Society (Harriet Atwood); the Cook Memorial Library, Tamworth (Jean Vlitz); the Whitefield Public Library (Sandra Holz, Librarian); the Abbie Greenleaf Memorial Library, Franconia (Amy W. Bahr, Librarian); the Northumberland Public Library, Groveton (Lena Mills, Assistant Librarian); the Dalton Public Library (Doris Mitton, Librarian); the Sandwich Historical Society (Robin Dustin, Director); and, the Twin Mountain Public Library (Anna Evans, Librarian).

Lastly, I would like to acknowledge with gratitude the assistance of these individuals whose help was invaluable: James L. Garvin, Architectural Historian, and Christine Fonda, New Hampshire Division of Historical Resources, Concord; Frank Mevers, New Hampshire State Archivist, Concord; Harland Eastman, book dealer and collector, Springvale, ME; George McAvoy, former co-owner and proprietor of the Crawford House, now living in Littleton; the late Warren Swift, former owner and manager of the Sunset Hill House, Sugar Hill; Frank Schuyler Dodge, Jr., member of the former owning family and onetime proprietor of the Mountain View House, a summer resident of Littleton; the late Charles Whiton, Administrative Assistant, Franconia Notch State Park; Charles Ricardi, Catherine Bedor and Dan Walsh, Mount Washington Hotel, Bretton Woods; John and Benjamin Harrington, H. P. Cummings Construction Company, Ware, MA; Len Reed, public relations consultant, Bethlehem; Elizabeth D. Hengen, historic preservation consultant, Concord; Charles O. Vogel, historian of White Mountain artists, Townsend, MA; David Sherman, formerly of the National Park Service, whose home is in Arlington, VA; William R. Gifford, town historian, Colebrook; Richard N. Johnson, Jackson; Raymond Evans, Twin Mountain; Donald Lapham, Wolfeboro; the late William L. Taylor, Professor of History, Plymouth State College; and, the late Walter W. Wright, former Curator of Rare Books and Special Collections, Dartmouth College Library. My appreciation is also due to Linda Magner, Theresa Horner and Anne Cady, graduate students in art history, Thom Thompson, undergraduate major in photography/geography, and Robert Williams, graduate student in history, University of Delaware, for their excellent photo lab work which produced the majority of the illustrations included in this book.

I would also like to extend my great appreciation to Neil Tillotson, the founding owner of the Tillotson Corporation in Boston and the owner of The Balsams Grand Resort Hotel, for his keen interest in and generous support of the book project. He credits his interest in The Balsams when he was inspired to acquire it to "middle-aged sentimentality." He was aware that his mother's grandfather, David Hodge, and his Native American wife were one of the two original homesteader families on the north side of Dixville Notch where the hotel is located. The other homesteader family was the Parsons, whose house was on the site of the hotel complex. So many of the people who have helped make this book possible share such an attachment to the hotels and to the people of the North Country.

Finally, I would like to thank my wife Carolyn and my daughter Thayer Tolles for the invaluable assistance they rendered in reading and critiquing the manuscript, Stephanie Taylor, graduate student in art history, for her outstanding word-processing skills, Sarah Giffen Rooker for her painstaking copyediting, and Bruce Kennett and Eugene Kuo for their creative design work.

While limitations of space prevent me from listing literally every source of research materials and information, I know that all those in some way associated with the project share with me a belief in the significance of the architecture and history of the White Mountain grand resort hotels, and in the need to further a respect for and knowledge of their rich heritage through this publication.

B. F. T., Jr.

Opposite: White Mountains, c. 1893, with principal railroad routes. *Cartography by Robert T. Holloran, Jackson, NH.*

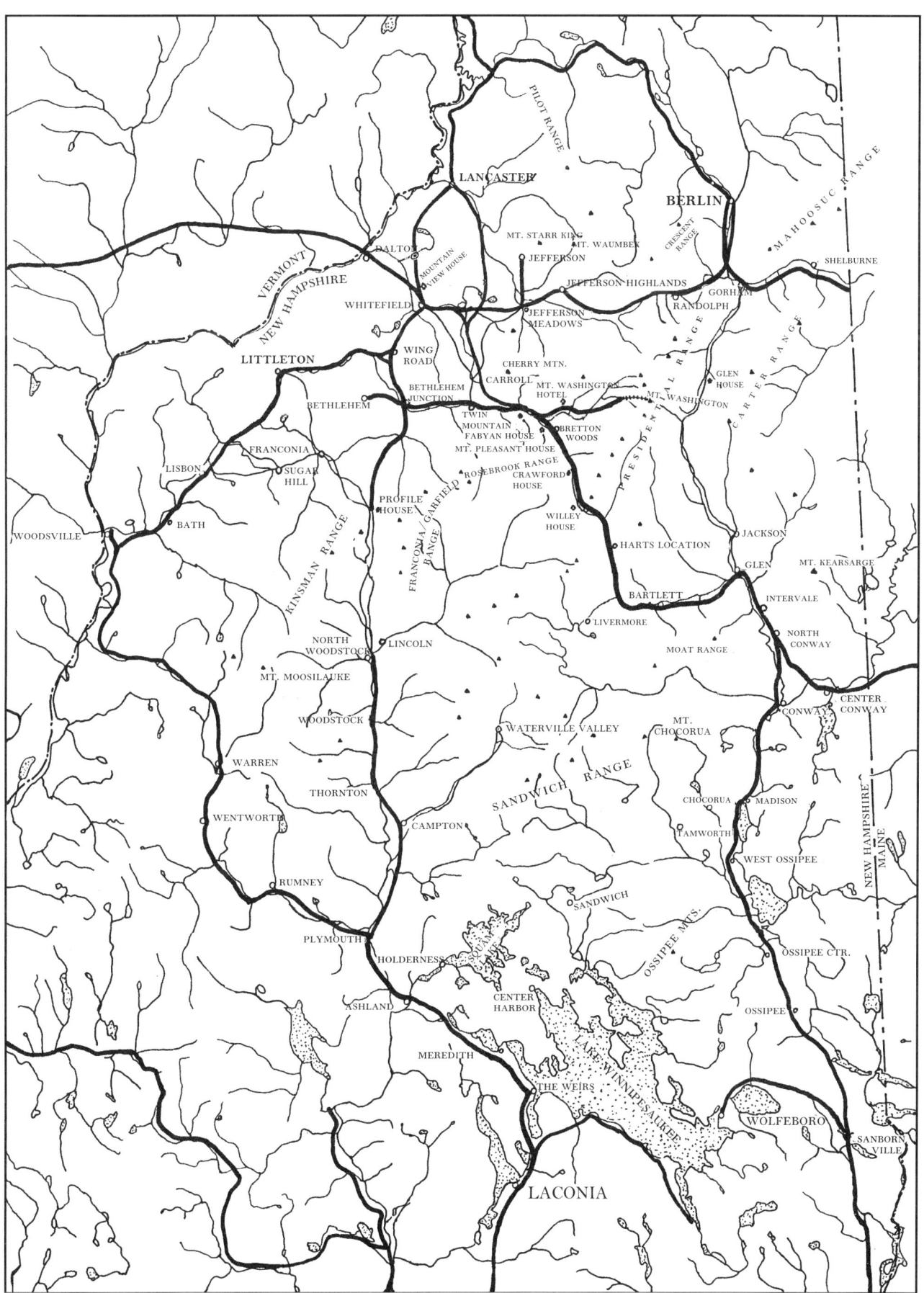

Introduction

AN EXAMINATION of the architectural origins and development of the White Mountain grand resort hotels and their vanishing physical legacy properly begins with consideration of the concept of this unique and fascinating building type as embodied in the descriptive adjective "grand." What do we mean when we use this word? What images does it bring to mind? What does it suggest about the type and its place within the broad sweep of American national and regional history? More specifically how does it apply to this history within the more limited context of New Hampshire's beautiful mountainous North Country?

There are untold variations of the word "grand" with many different connotations. One that seems most appropriate for the subject of this book may be quoted from a recent edition of *Webster's New Twentieth Century Dictionary*:

> That which makes a strong impression because of its great size, dignity and excellence, and is higher in rank or status than others in the same category.[1]

Consulting other modern dictionaries a number of very relevant synonyms appear—large, noble, magnificent, imposing, majestic, sumptuous, grandiose, august, stately, impressive, splendid, comprehensive, pretentious, superb, distinguished, exalted, handsome and luxurious.[2] Given the abundance of these synonyms, with their many nuances, it should be evident that the word "grand," as a modifier for the term "resort hotel," conveys many meanings, each of which tells us something about the building type and the life style it fostered.

Having established a basis of understanding for the grand resort hotel concept, let us now depart the dictionary definition of "grand," and examine the building type within the general framework and amidst the divergent themes of our national history. This may be most effectively done by referencing the published work of Jeffrey W. Limerick, a Boulder, Colorado, architect, who, as a Yale School of Architecture student and instructor in the 1970s, extensively and very productively studied the grand resort hotel in the United States. His 1979 book, *America's Grand Resort Hotels*, coauthored with Nancy Ferguson and Richard Oliver, provides an invaluable background analysis of the significance and place of this building type in American culture and life.[3] This excellent volume in part originated from Limerick's earlier essay, "The Grand Resort Hotel in America," published in *Perspecta 15: The Yale Architectural Journal* (1975).[4] The broad vision provided by these writings, coupled with the scholarship of others, helps one to grasp the full meaning of the grand resort hotel phenomenon as it occurred in the White Mountain region from the mid-nineteenth century until World War I.

The history of resort life and the building type that accommodated it, provides an indelible chronicle of American social, cultural, economic and architectur-

Fig. 1. Hotel Lookoff, Sugar Hill, NH. *Photograph by Rev. Samuel J. Nickerson, c. 1885. Sugar Hill Historical Museum.*

al development. Through study of the grand resort hotel concept one can better comprehend our national system of values, American cultural characteristics and evolutionary patterns in the creation of our nation. In Limerick's words, "by looking at the resorts, one can appreciate the impact of new means of transportation and technological innovations; the American attraction to novelty and fashion; the changes in American attitudes toward nature and the landscape; and the connection between architectural styles and cultural aspirations."[5]

Since the pre-Revolutionary War era, Americans have embraced travel and the ritual of the vacation to provide aesthetic and intellectual stimulation, religious enlightenment, improved physical and mental well-being, social interaction, recreational involvement and change from routine life habits. The resort life to which those with sufficient means were attracted gave people the opportunity to mix with others with similar interests or of the same social status, or to climb the social ladder. The grand resort hotels greatly appealed to the wealthy and the career-accomplished—the captains of business and industry, high political officials, professional leaders, socialites, fortune-seekers and even opportunists of questionable motivation—and provided them with a public, stage-like setting for display of wealth, social standing and fashion, as well as the opportunity to observe their peers performing the same script. Unlike today, when affluent resort patrons often seek anonymity, privacy and tight security in a complex modern world, the typical guest of a century ago aspired to be seen and admired in a social environment where appearances were everything. Also highly prized, as it is by many in today's society, were the aura of exclusiveness and the ambiance of romance. As Limerick has aptly observed, "for participant and spectator alike, resort hotels . . . [provided] an arena for social games of every sort."[6]

As specimens of architecture, grand resort hotels

were like insular worlds unto themselves, conceived to offer all that their patrons desired in a physical setting that emphasized comfort, diversity of experience, aesthetic allure and efficiency. While there were many common qualities, hotels as individual entities were planned "to answer the needs of a particular time and place and to live up to the expectations of a particular clientele."[7] Not surprisingly, grand resort hotels, many of which were hastily erected for quick profit, were highly vulnerable, both financially and physically, to several hard realities—swings in the national economic cycle, the ever-changing tastes and preferences of their patrons, competition from other hotels or attractions such as international expositions, and the great scourge of fire that destroyed so many. Those few that have survived to our time have done so by successfully adjusting to social, cultural and economic change, by retaining the flavor and physical trappings of tradition and history, and by plain good fortune.

Limerick points out quite correctly that grand resort hotels "possess two seemingly contradictory architectural characteristics."[8] On one hand they must offer their guests something different from the everyday urban or suburban existence and, in accomplishing this, satisfy the popular perception of the good life. At the same time they must be run as efficient, machine-like business ventures, bringing consistent profit to their owners, while systematically satisfying a host of demands posed by their clientele. As models of smooth and effective operation the nineteenth-century hotels introduced to the American public several important conveniences and advances in technology—improved fireplaces, steam heat, gas and electric lights, improved sanitation and water systems, elevators, bell and telephone communications systems, and box-spring mattresses—before they were generally available in the American home. In many respects these marvelous innovations were the product of intense competition between the hotels and the desire by their owners and managers to offer the best in service and luxury.

Over the years, the grand resort hotels in this country have had a magnetic attraction for visitors as well as general appreciators and scholars in large part because of their unique character, romantic

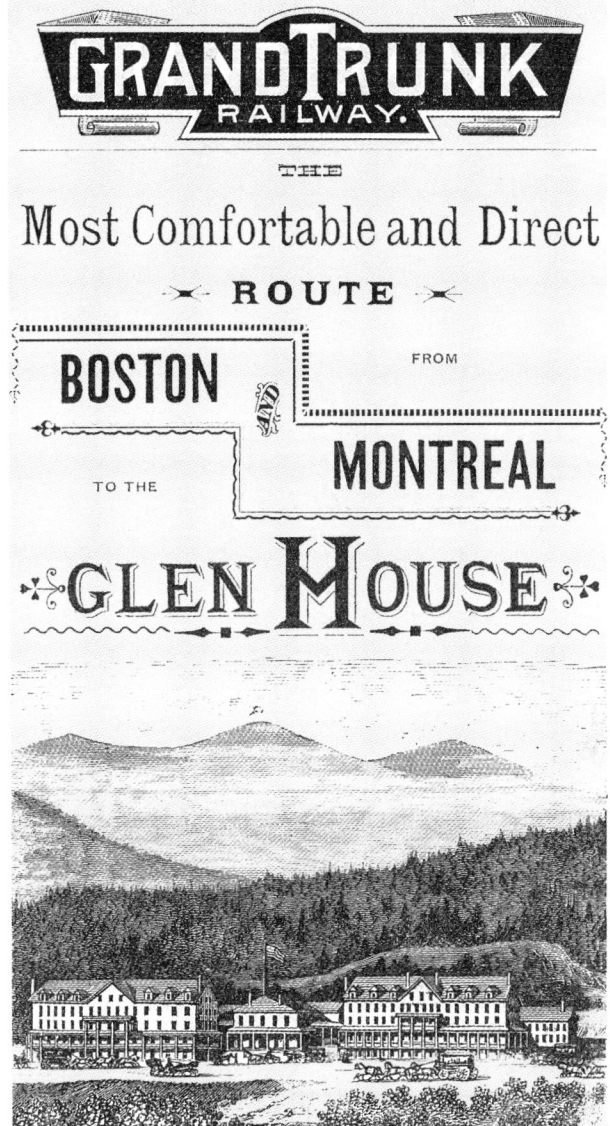

Fig. 2. "White Mountains by the Grand Trunk Railway" timetable (Boston: Grand Trunk Railway, c. 1884). Author's Collection.

ambiance and captivating natural settings. Oftentimes borrowing from foreign cultures, many of these buildings were planned in enticing eclectic styles intended to make distinct architectural statements, but also to relate to the natural surroundings and fit

Fig. 3. Grand Union Hotel, Saratoga Springs, NY. *Advertising engraving from Thursty McQuill (Wallace Bruce),* The Hudson River By Daylight... *(New York: John Featherston, 1874), map view. Author's Collection.*

with local historical traditions. In the White Mountains, hotels were designed in various early revival styles (or combinations thereof) including the Greek, Italian, or Gothic, or in later Victorian eclectic vernaculars such as the French Second Empire (Mansard), Stick, English Queen Anne, Shingle, Italian Renaissance, Spanish Renaissance, Colonial Revival or Rhenish.

Many times landscape strongly influenced the appearance of the hotels, as in the case of the unrealized design (1923) for the third Profile House in Franconia Notch, New Hampshire, which, had it been built, would have taken the form of a huge Swiss chalet, intended to exist in ideal harmony with its American "Alpine" environment (see Chapter 7). In other instances landscape was the raison d'être for hotels and, in the White Mountains, many were constructed to take advantage of spectacular mountain panoramas, lovely valleys or intervales, rapidly flowing rivers and streams, dramatic precipices, enchanting waterfalls or other natural features. At many hotel sites, therefore, there existed a fascinating and occasionally awkward relationship between the natural and the man-made, where the "tourist's experience of nature . . . [was always] tempered by the comfort and luxury of the resort hotel itself."[9]

As conservatively run business enterprises, in which the fiscal "bottom line" determined degree of success, the grand resort hotels, in the great majority of cases, displayed styles that were derived from residential architecture and were not notably innovative; yet they intrigued, satisfied and relaxed their patrons. To be sure there were exceptions where pace-setting architectural and engineering excellence were attained; two prime examples in the White Mountain region are the Mount Washington Hotel (1901-1903) at Bretton Woods (see Plate 15) and Hampshire House (1916-18) at The Balsams in Dixville Notch (see Chapter 8 and Plate 19). For the most part, however, the hotels achieved aesthetic and

Fig. 4. Catskill Mountain House, Catskill, NY. *Advertising engraving from Thursty McQuill (Wallace Bruce),* The Hudson River By Daylight . . . *(New York: John Featherston, 1874), map view. Author's Collection.*

functional impact, with resultant pleasure for their guests, by virtue of their immense size, sensibly arranged and appointed interior spaces, and pronounced visual imagery. In the case of the White Mountains, where only a modest number were architect-designed, the great majority of the hotels were plain, unembellished and highly functional, most likely planned by local contractors or financiers. When times were prosperous and profits generous, such buildings, or major additions to existing complexes, were often erected in extraordinarily brief periods to capitalize on the propitious economic climate, and to develop or further increase guest patronage. In the White Mountains, and in New England at large, many hotels, consequently, were the outgrowth of the same underlying desire for profit and general lack of design interest that produced the textile and shoe factories of the region during mid and late nineteenth century. Bland, unimaginative, vernacular creations, these buildings still form a vital part of the grand hotel tradition. The White Mountains' classic example, the second Fabyan House (1872-73) (see Chapter 4 and Fig. 4-4), while seemingly little more than a sterile collection of connected, cut-out, rectangular shoeboxes, still performed a service role qualitatively the equal of its visually more attractive counterparts.

To further lay the basis for an in-depth discussion of the White Mountain grand resort hotels, it is also essential to briefly trace the origins and development of this building type in a much broader national context. The hotel in the United States initially appeared in the late 1700s as an expanded version of the older highway inn or tavern. With this new building type, spaces for dining halls, ballrooms and assemblies supplemented traditional spaces devoted to food, drink and lodging. Suited to a more formal social regimen, these structures, whether situated in village, town or city, were important centers of community life. As travel became more prevalent and business

Fig. 5. Poland Spring House, South Poland, ME. *Lithograph from George H. Haynes,* Souvenir of New England's Great Resorts *(New York: Moss Engraving Company, 1891). Author's Collection.*

grew, a need arose for larger and more specialized hotels modeled on European prototypes. Historians of American architecture frequently cite New York City's City Hotel (1794) and Asher Benjamin's Exchange Coffee House (1807) in Boston as well-conceived examples of the developing building type. In the White Mountains this first stage commenced in the early part of the 1800s and lasted into the 1840s, when hotels resembling their more modern urban cousins began to appear.

As is so often the case in architecture, one pioneering building provided the impetus and the know-how for more efficient hotel design. With the construction of Isaiah Roger's Tremont House in Boston in 1822, the United States seized the lead from Europe in the development of the modern hotel. Among its many innovations the Tremont featured the world's first self-contained lobby and office area, a separate barroom, a dining room of unprecedented size (seventy by thirty feet), elegant public rooms, a subscription library, private lockable sleeping rooms, indoor privies and bathing rooms, and a garden in place of a stableyard. Soon after the opening of the Tremont, Rogers was hired by fur and real estate magnate John Jacob Astor to build an even larger and more luxurious hotel in New York City; the new Astor House boasted a novel steam pump that permitted water to be raised to privies and bathing rooms on the upper floors. These two buildings were significant in that they "established the arenas for competition among hotels that have lasted to the present: size, fashionable styling and decor, and the latest in technical and convenience gadgetry."[10] In the Tremont and the Astor, and the more modern hostelries that would follow them, style, building technology and site were dynamically related, providing settings for varied forms of human activity.

Although Americans expressed some interest in travel to mineral springs and other rural locales in the Colonial and the early National periods, it was not until the 1820s and 1830s that improved transportation and changed attitudes toward recreation and nature encouraged people to seek the resort experience. It was some time, therefore, before hotels at all comparable to the city hotels began to appear at American mountain, lake and seashore resort locales. Prompted by a new romantic fascination in spirituality, ethical and moral standards, healthfulness and the landscape, tourism grew to such an extent that by the 1830s there were a number of first class hotels located near popular attractions in the Northeast. Prominent among the new resort centers were Saratoga Springs, New York; Cape May, New Jersey; and Nahant on Boston's North Shore. But perhaps the most popular of the early resort hotels was the famed Catskill Mountain House (1822-23) in New York State, which, after substantial enlargements in the Greek Revival mode, became the equal of the finest and most luxuriously fitted city hotels. In this landmark establishment, as well as a few others like it, characteristics associated with the grand resort hotel began to appear—nearly self-contained operation, vast physical size, corporate or partner ownership, wood-frame and clapboard construction, and functionally laid out interiors.

The national interest in resort culture continued to expand during the 1840s and 1850s, due in large part to the development of new forms of transportation and the accessibility that they provided to previously remote areas. In the Northeast, regular steamship service was established from New York City along the New England coast, and on the Hudson River, Lake George, Lake Champlain, the Saint Lawrence River through the Thousand Islands, and other inland waterways. Of greater significance were the railroads, which, over several decades, connected the mountain regions from Maine to the Carolinas with the major Eastern population centers, forging a remarkable symbiotic relationship with the resort hotels. Resort communities continued to grow and became more specialized, attracting increasingly well-defined clienteles—Saratoga Springs became associated with gambling, horse racing and the fast social life; Long Beach, New Jersey, with high living, display and family activity; and Cape May, regarded as the fanciest resort of the era, with bathing, gambling and elite social events. Arranged much like the Catskill Mountain House, hotel complexes became larger and more sumptuous (with ells and wings that created expansive, L, U, E, H or T-shaped floor plans), the most extreme example being Cape May's Mount Vernon (1852-53) with 300 feet in frontage, 500-foot wings, 600 rooms with private baths, and accommodations for 2,000 guests. In the White Mountains the first signs of this new hotel concept were manifested in the first Glen House (1850-52) at Pinkham Notch (see Fig. 2-4), the first Profile House (1852-53) at Franconia Notch (see Fig. 2-25), and the second Crawford House (1859) at Crawford Notch (see Chapter 2 and Fig. 2-10).

During the decade following the Civil War industrialization and urbanization became the principal driving forces in American society. Per capita wealth grew, materialism and power became a popular obsession, and leisure time became increasingly possible. Their confidence in natural progress and the democratic way of life shaken by the war experience, Americans looked to Europe as well as to the idyllic American past for cultural inspiration, ideas and values. Utilizing their new wealth, status and leisure, people sought escape from the new faster-paced and competitive life style and identified with the more satisfying, idealized cultural milieus offered through the new and luxurious resort hotels. Resort architecture of the late 1860s and 1870s, therefore, often emphasized the unusual, the cosmopolitan, the exotic and the picturesque. This was perhaps most obvious at Saratoga Springs, now the United States' most lavish and sophisticated resort, to which a curious assemblage of wealthy aristocrats, industrial and business tycoons, politicians, horse owners and promoters, gamblers, mothers escorting marriageable daughters, and eligible young bachelors freely

Fig. 6. "Golf at the Mt. Pleasant House, White Mountains of New Hampshire." Photograph from Scenic Gems of the White Mountains *(Portland, ME: G. W. Morris, [c. 1900]). Author's Collection.*

flocked. Meeting the needs of their customers were such great hostelries as the renovated, Mansard-roofed Grand Union Hotel (1874), claimed to be the grandest hotel in the country, and the smaller but equally splendid and elaborate United States Hotel, reopened the same year. Similarly celebrating the grand life of self-display in the White Mountains, and surely its best example, was the Maplewood Hotel (1876, etc.) in Bethlehem, conceived in a highly ornate combination of Victorian eclectic styles (see Chapter 4 and Plate 7).

During the immediate post-Civil War years, people's urge to connect with the simplicity and stiff moral fiber of an earlier America also spawned an interest in older resort communities, particularly those situated in the inland and seaport towns and villages of New England. Romanticizing the colonial past and searching for pristine retreats from society's mounting pressures, people gravitated to cottages and hotels of plain vernacular forms and styles that satiated their desire for nostalgia or historicity. Perfectly suited for the period was the revised, American edition of the English Queen Anne, which featured irregularity in plan and massing, active combinations of gables, brackets, turrets, modeled chimneys, towers, dormers, pinnacles, recessed balconies and wide porches, and textural variety fostered by the juxtaposition of shingles, brick, clapboard, stone, and lattice and stickwork. Quick to adopt this new, predominantly residential style for hotel purposes were hotels at Cape May (The Chalfonte, 1867), Long Branch, and Coney Island, New York (J. Pickering Putnam's Manhattan Beach Hotel, 1877, and the adjacent Oriental Hotel, 1879). New Hampshire's White Mountains boasted two sterling examples of the Queen Anne in the Wentworth Hall and Cottages complex (1869, 1880s, etc.) in Jackson (see Plate 4), and in the later and even more magnificent second Glen House (1885-87) in Pinkham Notch (see Chapters 3, 7, and Fig. 7-3).

The acceleration of hotel construction in the late 1870s and the firm establishment of the grand hotel building type initiated the golden era of the American vacation resorts that would last until after 1900. Over the next two decades hotels assumed larger proportions than ever before and displayed new stylistic interpretations. In the period following the 1876 Centennial, the nation witnessed tremendous expansion, increased mobility and major technological advances. All of these changes contributed to greater social stratification and widened differences in ethnic origin, religion and living circumstances. Old money was joined by the wealth of a newly industrialized society, creating a private world to which the grand resort hotel, though inherently public in nature, could successfully cater. Competition in the realm of business soon translated into the game of social one-upmanship, and the hotels, like their Civil War predecessors, continued to be an ideal staging theater. In addition, the concept of resort hotels as retreats persisted in people's minds, as they looked for ways to find respite from the stressful, urban, and less desirable aspects of their lives.

After the economic hard times of the 1870s and a resurgence of prosperity, Americans embraced the grand resort hotels for reasons that went beyond their traditional basis of appeal. The popular enthusiasm for good health and physical fitness through sports, first apparent after the Civil War, was transformed into a popular passion by the 1880s, and the grand resort hotels, particularly those in mountain areas, served as perfect outlets. Responding to the new, romanticized vision of outdoor life and athletic competition, the hotels supplemented the old, well-entrenched practices of the evening promenade, the seeking of cures and other quite sedentary pursuits, with a rich array of sporting activities including hiking, fishing, boating, bicycling, golf, tennis, lawn bowling, croquet, badminton, archery, horseback riding, polo and baseball. When automobiles (a new sporting toy for the rich) appeared around 1900, the hotels (responding as always with a formula for financial success) were quick to grasp the implications by constructing or facilitating access to scenic roads. Three noted White Mountain hotels—the Mount Washington, The Balsams and the second Profile—each maintained their own systems of hiking trails with published guides. The Mount Washington also produced lengthy descriptions of desirable auto routes in its annual guest manuals (see Chapters 7 and 8). All of the White Mountain hotels modified their recreational programs and constructed new facilities to accommodate the outdoor sporting craze.

During the 1880s and 1890s America's grand resort hotels faced increasing competition from each other and largely departed from the Queen Anne and other older styles, seeking differentiation through distinctive new architectural styling. At the same

Fig. 7. Signpost, Sugar Hill, NH. Photograph by the author.

time they maintained their traditional low-rise, horizontal massing, and conventional interior arrangement, with the ground-floor space devoted to public areas, and the floors above to sleeping rooms *en suites* along double-loaded corridors. Limerick has referred to this period as "a visual age,"[11] and indeed it was as owners, financiers, and their architects, with history and character of site uppermost in mind, strived to create unique pleasure-providing hotel complexes that embodied fantasy, glamour, picturesqueness, remoteness and affinity with the natural world.

Taking full advantage of new techniques in graphic reproduction, these enterprises, in their promotional publications, press and advertising, sought to capture the public's imagination by presenting carefully chosen, orchestrated and packaged stylized images. The rhetoric of the printed word and pictorial representation, when combined with the realism of the building and site, proved a convincing and effective educational vehicle, drawing the unconverted to the grand hotel mystique. In telling their story, hotels invariably exposed the technology and techniques that made them possible, adding to their attraction as symbols of "personal achievement and national potential."[12] They spoke strongly of national cultural self-confidence. No better example has existed in the White Mountains than the 150-guest second Summit House (1872-73) perched on the crown of Mount Washington some 6,280 feet above sea level, all its building materials transported aloft on scores of cog railroad cars loaded in the valley far below (see Fig. 4-7).

By the late 1880s, when the American Queen Anne style began to fade from popularity, architects all over the United States, including those in the Northeast who had adhered to it longest, adopted the less parochial, palatial architectural styles of Europe. Reacting to novelty and arbitrary forms, as expressed in the Queen Anne, and seeking "a return to solid fundamentals and timeless principles of beauty,"[13] these same architects, with backing from their financiers, borrowed styles from the European past that they ingeniously adopted to the American scene. Following the lead of Richard Morris Hunt and the Ecole des Beaux-Arts in Paris, they applied the principles of classical academic design on a monumental scale to

Fig. 8. Mountain View House, Whitefield, NH. *Photograph by the author, c. 1976.*

many large building types including office structures, libraries, railroad stations, governmental facilities and hotels. Across the country, many hotels from 1890 onward assumed the form of Italian or Spanish Renaissance palaces, French chateaux, Moorish castles or Mediterranean villas.

Not all hotel architects of this era, however, abandoned their American roots. Many, recalling traditional colonial motifs and moved by cultural pride, exploited these in inventive ways to produce buildings in the equally fashionable Shingle style. Still others embraced the principles of the Colonial Revival, which drew upon the tradition of the Ecole des Beaux-Arts, the Shingle style and the Arts and Crafts Movement to achieve fine proportion, charming domestic forms and a profusion of integrally related classical elements.[14]

Throughout the United States during this period numerous grand resort hotels were planned using imaginative combinations of these styles, and it is important to highlight a small representative selection of them in the East as instructive examples. The massive Poland Spring House (1876-1903) in Maine, largely the work of the Portland firm of John Calvin Stevens and Albert Winslow Cobb (see Chapter 6), brought together features of the Stick, Shingle, Queen Anne and Colonial Revival styles to create a provocative and eclectic medley. Stevens, along with his son John Howard Stevens, was also responsible for alterations (1916-17) to the Queen Anne/ Colonial Revival, largely George M. Coombs-designed Samoset Hotel (1889; 1902), Maine's other major coastal hostelry at Rockland. Henry M. Flagler's ambitious Ponce de Leon (1889) in St. Augustine, Florida, was designed by the New York firm of Carrere and Hastings (see Chapter 3) in the Spanish Renaissance style and was complemented by his Alcazar, a smaller but still impressive hotel, derived from the palaces of Seville and opened the same year across the street. The Tampa Bay (FL) Hotel (1891), owned today by the University of Tampa, was the brainchild of railroad and steamship mogul Henry B. Plant and recalls Florida's romantic Spanish past with its distinctive Moorish-Mediterranean styling. The immense, crescent-shaped Colonial Arms (1903-1904) at Gloucester, Massachusetts, was a superb blend of the Shingle and Colonial Revival styles, while the gigantic Homestead (1901, etc.) at Hot Springs, Virginia, is a purer Neo-Federal, Neo-Greco version of the Colonial Revival, built primarily of brick with wood trim painted white, other embellishments, porticos and porches. Situated high in the Shawangunk Mountains at New Paltz, New York, the retreat-like Mohonk Mountain House (1879-1901) is another enticing collection of many eclectic styles (Romanesque Revival, Queen Anne, Swiss Chalet, etc.) and materials, with an apparently irrational, yet always charming combination of towers, chimneys, balconies, dormers and roof forms.[15] Fitting this "high style" eclectic idiom in the White Mountains were the Mount Pleasant House at Bretton Woods (see Fig. 4-14) and the Waumbek Hotel at Jefferson (see Fig. 3-24), both completely rebuilt in the Colonial Revival between 1888 and 1901 (see Chapters 3 and 4); The Metallak, a highly successful amalgam of the Shingle and Colonial Revival styles, erected in Colebrook in 1892-93 (see Chapter 6 and Fig. 6-1); the Mount Washington Hotel, built in Spanish Renaissance Revival in 1901-1903; the virtually identical third (1903-1904) and fourth (1916-17) Gray's Inns, Shingle Chateauesque creations once present at Jackson (see Chapter 5 and Figs. 5-16 and 5-19); and, Hampshire House, the massive Rhenish eclectic addition to The Balsams, built in 1916-18.

Simultaneous with these new stylistic expressions and increased physical scale, ownership of the grand hotels after the 1870s fell to wealthy investors and management groups, while their clientele became even more affluent and cosmopolitan, with visitors from all around the world. To meet more sophisticated tastes, recreational, social, cultural and other programs and services became more elaborate and specialized, and resorts, in many instances, developed into virtually self-contained cities. Continuing a pattern initiated earlier in the century, the main hotel structures were supplemented by smaller buildings housing a myriad of support functions: guest cottages, dormitories for workers, manager's cottages, kitchen and storage outbuildings, power houses and heating plants, horse and automobile barns, hotel farms, sports clubhouses and other facilities. In the White Mountains, this planning concept can still be seen at the Mount Washington Hotel, The Balsams and the Mountain View House in Whitefield (see Plate 14).

By the first decade of this century, however, American grand resort hotels, particularly those in very rural settings, had already peaked and signs of imminent decline were starting to appear. Ever more professionalized and standardized than a quarter century before, the hotel business was being conducted on an increasingly larger scale, requiring greater management expertise and skill, and vast amounts of capital. As resort hotels became more costly to operate, the burden of this expense was passed to the consumer; over time many hotels priced themselves out of existence, eroding the time-honored myth that they functioned solely for their guests' personal enjoyment. In a curious, almost perverted way the grand hotels were victims of their own fantastic success—as "insulated stagesets for ordered social contacts and the display of wealth"[16] their appeal remained for a selected few, but their broader, largely upper-middle-class clientele gradually slipped away to engage in other leisure-time life patterns and pursuits.

There were several other readily identifiable reasons for this phenomenon, and they have had their impact over a prolonged fifty-year period. By far the most significant of these was the advent of the automobile, which by 1915 became sufficiently wide-

Fig. 9. Aerial view of the Crawford House, Crawford Notch, NH. *Photograph by Douglas Armsden, c. 1965, for the* Littleton Courier, *courtesy of Richard Hamilton, Littleton, NH.*

spread in use that it changed the nature of the tourist trade in ways highly detrimental to the survival of the nineteenth-century-model grand resort hotels. Offering increased freedom, flexibility and mobility, the automobile economically undermined the railroads—long the lifeline of the hotels—reduced the length of people's visits and eliminated the older practice of single-destination stays of weeks' or even months' duration. New and different travel habits, predicated on large distances and many stops en route, required more economical, short-term accommodations and "new building types evolved to replace the grand [resort] hotels, which depended on a captive audience for longer periods of time."[17]

Additional historic factors had adverse effects on the hotel business and the building type. By the end of the nineteenth century, even as the automobile was just making its debut, it became evident that Americans were changing their ideas of how to best use their leisure time. In the White Mountains, as well as along the Maine coast and at other Eastern resort locations, a growing desire for personal and family independence, as well as a permanent commitment to a particular area, led to the cottage movement whereby private seasonal residences were preferred to the frequently quite public, regimented and sociological "fish bowl" existence of the hotels. Further contributing to the demise of the grand resort hotels were the momentous events of World War I, the Great Depression and World War II, each of which altered national economic and social conditions and attitudes in ways that made the hotel experience less popular as well as less feasible.

The few grand resort hotels that have survived to the present day have done so by virtue of excellent business management practices, effective marketing techniques, outstanding facilities maintenance, and flexible, diversified social and recreational programming. In addition, spring and fall convention periods, as adjuncts to the summer social season, have been the saving grace of many of these establishments. Unfortunately in the White Mountain region, the larger hotel operations faded quickly after World War I, and only one complex (Eastern Slope Inn, North Conway, 1926; see Plate 11) with a capacity exceeding 150 has been built until recently. Only four grand resort hotels remain open for business today—The Balsams, the Mount Washington Hotel, Wentworth Hall and Cottages (now Wentworth Hall Resorts), and the second Eagle Mountain House. Therefore, for those still seeking the grand hotel experience—the overt late Victorian expression of American optimism and self-assurance—the opportunity lives on in the White Mountains as well as at a few other older resort areas in the United States.

* * *

As a concluding exercise to the preceding review of the major themes in national and White Mountain area hotel history, it is appropriate to set the stage for the chapters that follow by presenting a list, with pertinent data, of the grand resort hotels in the region that meet the general criteria previously discussed and whose maximum guest capacities exceeded 200. The basis for this list is a published tabulation compiled in 1979 by Randall E. Spalding, the long-time owner/proprietor of the Spalding Inn in Whitefield and one of the best informed on the subject of the White Mountain hotels. In an essay originally read at a Newcomen Society symposium on the enterprise of New Hampshire's North Country, Spalding listed nineteen buildings and complexes that fit his perception of the White Mountain grand resort hotel.[18] While I have no argument with the contents, I have chosen to expand the Spalding list by including eleven additional entries to produce a total of thirty. The selection of the hotels for inclusion in this group, while based on shared characteristics and traditions, is admittedly somewhat subjective; hence, the list may by no means be considered definitive and hopefully will inspire healthy debate, and perhaps additions or deletions, in the future. The hotels on this list are arranged chronologically by earliest building date(s), with information about primary and alternative names, location, maximum estimated capacity and status. All, except The Balsams and the Mount Washington Hotel, were constructed almost exclusively of wood, and hence were highly vulnerable to fire.

INTRODUCTION

White Mountain Grand Resort Hotels

Earliest Building Date(s)	Name(s)	Location	Maximum Capacity	Status
1850-52	1st Glen House	Green's Grant ("The Glen")	500-600	Burned
1850-52	1st Crawford House	Crawford Notch	250+	Burned
1852-53	1st Profile House	Franconia (Franconia Notch)	550-600	Burned
1857	Sinclair House	Bethlehem	350	Burned
1859	2nd Crawford House	Crawford Notch	350-400	Burned
1860	Waumbek Hotel (The Waumbek)	Jefferson	500-600	Burned
1861	Kearsarge House	North Conway	250-300	Burned
1866	Mountain View House	Whitefield	300-350	Extant
1868	Intervale House	North Conway (Intervale)	250-300	Burned
1868-69	Twin Mountain House (Hotel)	Carroll (Twin Mountain)	250-300	Demolished
1869	Wentworth Hall and Cottages (Thorn Mountain House)	Jackson	250	Partially Extant
1872-73	2nd Fabyan House	Carroll (Fabyan's)	400+	Burned
1874-75	The Balsams (Dix House)	Dixville (Dixville Notch)	400+	Extant
1875-76	Goodnow House (Franconia Inn)	Sugar Hill	300	Burned
1875-76	Mount Pleasant House	Carroll (Bretton Woods)	250-300	Demolished
1876	Maplewood Hotel	Bethlehem (Maplewood)	500+	Burned
1879-80	Sunset Hill House	Sugar Hill	300-325	Demolished
1882-83	Forest Hills Hotel	Franconia (Pine Hill)	250+	Demolished
1884-85	1st Gray's Inn	Jackson	250-275	Burned
1884-87	2nd Glen House	Green's Grant ("The Glen")	500	Burned
1886-87	Deer Park Hotel	North Woodstock	200-250	Burned
1886-87	Hotel Lookoff (Tree Top Lodge)	Sugar Hill	200+	Demolished
1890-91	Alpine House (Hotel Alpine)	North Woodstock	200+	Demolished
1892-93	The Metallak (The Nirvana)	Colebrook (Lombard's Hill)	225	Blown down
1901-03	Mount Washington Hotel	Carroll (Bretton Woods)	550-600	Extant
1902-03	2nd Gray's Inn	Jackson	200	Burned
1903-04	3rd Gray's Inn	Jackson	250	Burned
1905-06	2nd Profile House (New Profile House)	Franconia	600	Burned
1915-16	2nd Eagle Mountain House	Jackson	225	Extant
1916-17	4th Gray's Inn	Jackson	225	Burned

THE GRAND RESORT HOTELS OF THE WHITE MOUNTAINS

* * *

With the contents of this list in mind, we turn now to the White Mountain region, which, due to its proximity to the East Coast and major urban districts, became one of the most important and popular tourist and vacation centers in North America—and throughout the Western World—between 1830 and 1930. For purposes of this study the geographical scope of this region will be defined as the area extending south to north, from Plymouth and the northern edge of the Lakes Region to upper Coos County; and, east to west, from the Maine state boundary to a line running from Plymouth up the Baker River Valley north to Warren, then to Lisbon, Littleton, and up the northern Connecticut River Valley to Colebrook. Within these parameters attention will first be directed to the early highway, village and town inns and hotels of the first half of the nineteenth century, and the legacy they established as precursors or antecedents to the later grand resort hotels. Next, with a focus primarily on evolving transportation technology and changing social and cultural patterns, the middle decades of the century will be examined, highlighting the pioneering grand hotel ventures. In the major portion of the book, the era of the grand resort hotel, extending generally from the Civil War to the Great Depression, will be reviewed, with attention to specific examples of the building type. More in-depth treatment will be accorded a small selection of these establishments that carry special architectural and historical significance, are unusually well documented, or are still in operation. The concluding chapters, therefore, will discuss The Metallak in Colebrook, the second Glen House at Pinkham Notch, the second or New Profile House at Franconia Notch, the Mountain View House in Whitefield, the Mount Washington Hotel at Bretton Woods, and The Balsams at Dixville Notch, each in its own way exemplifying the epitome and essence of the grand resort hotel achievement, life spirit and architectural presence in the White Mountains.

Notes

1. Randall E. Spalding, "The Grand Hotels: The Glory and the Conflagration," in *The Enterprise of the North Country of New Hampshire* (Lancaster, NH: White Mountains Region Association, 1983), p. 26.
2. *The American Heritage Dictionary*, Second College Edition (Boston: Houghton Mifflin Co., 1982), p. 571; *The Random House Dictionary of the English Language*, 2nd ed., unabridged (New York: Random House, Inc. 1987), p. 829; *Webster's New Twentieth Century Dictionary*, 2nd ed. (New York: William Collins Publishers, Inc., 1980), p. 793.
3. Jeffrey W. Limerick, Nancy Ferguson and Richard Oliver, *America's Grand Resort Hotels* (New York: Pantheon Books, 1979).
4. Jeffrey W. Limerick, "The Grand Resort Hotels of America," *Perspecta 15: The Yale Architectural Journal* (1975): 87-109. See also, Richard Guy Wilson, "Nineteenth Century American Resorts and Hotels," from Wilson, ed., *Victorian Resorts and Hotels: Essays from a Victorian Society Autumn Symposium* (Philadelphia: The Victorian Society of America, 1990), pp. 10-13.
5. Limerick, et al., *America's Grand Resort Hotels*, p. 12.
6. *Ibid.*
7. *Ibid.*, p. 13.
8. *Ibid.*
9. *Ibid.*, p. 16.
10. *Ibid.*, pp. 17, 19; Diane Maddex, ed., *Built in U.S.A.: American Buildings from Airports to Zoos* (Washington, D.C.: The Preservation Press of the National Trust for Historic Preservation, 1985), p. 144.
11. Limerick, "The Grand Resort Hotels of America," p. 92.
12. *Ibid.*
13. Limerick, et al., *America's Grand Resort Hotels*, p. 52.
14. Many other styles were employed in the construction of American grand resort hotels of the 1880s and 1890s, but I have intentionally chosen not to discuss these because they had no impact on hotel building in the White Mountain region. Certain of them, as outgrowths of the Craftsman or Arts and Crafts Movement, produced buildings embodying images of the English cottage, the Scottish castle, the log cabin, the Bavarian lodge, the Southwest mission or pueblo, or the mountain chalet.
15. Deborah Thompson, ed., *Maine Forms of American Architecture* (Camden, ME: Downeast Magazine for the Colby Museum of Art, 1976), pp. 206-207; J.J. Kramer, *The Last of the Grand Resort Hotels* (New York: Van Nostrand Reinhold Company, 1978), pp. 60-64; Limerick, et al., *America's Grand Resort Hotels*, pp. 52, 54-61, 81-93; Joseph E. Garland, *Eastern Point* (Peterborough, NH: Noone House, 1971), pp. 224-26;

Bryant F. Tolles, Jr., *New Hampshire Architecture: An Illustrated Guide* (Hanover, NH: University Press of New England for NHHS, 1979), pp. 267, 321-22, 327-28.

16. Limerick, "The Grand Resort Hotels of America," p. 101.

17. Deborah Noble, Context Report on Grand Hotels, Division of Historical Resources, New Hampshire Department of Cultural Affairs, Concord, 1988.

18. Spalding, "The Grand Hotels," pp. 26-31.

Fig. 10. Cover of informational prospectus, first Profile House, Franconia Notch, NH, c. 1880. *Author's Collection.*

Fig. 1-1. Rosebrook Place, Giant's Grave, Carroll, NH, *woodblock drawn in pencil by Marshall M. Tidd (1859) for new edition of Lucy Crawford's* History of the White Mountains. *Dartmouth College Library. In about 1803-04, Eleazar Rosebrook erected the first hostelry in the White Mountains, adding several outbuildings over the next decade.*

The Precursors: Rosebrooks, Crawfords, Fabyans and the Early Highway Hotels

During the late eighteenth and early nineteenth centuries, the earliest travelers began coming to the White Mountains in small but significant numbers. Explorers, writers, scientists and adventurers, drawn to the beauty, grandeur and natural curiosities of the region, pursued scientific, spiritual and aesthetic inquiry as well as outdoor activity. As land transportation improved, farmers and merchants settled in the wilderness environment, moving their produce and wares within or through the mountains. By the 1820s, they were joined by "a class whose purpose in coming was entirely one of pleasure and recreation." These early excursionists were the forerunners of the summer tourists and visitors who would populate the grand resort hotels of the region after the Civil War.[1]

The first settlers in the White Mountains, especially those located along the primary travel route through Crawford Notch (known then as "the Notch"), seized upon the economic opportunity afforded them by its natural beauty and resources. Through diligence and ingenuity, they developed the facilities and means to service the rapidly growing tourist clientele. These first entrepreneurs constructed new and better roads, laid out hiking and horse trails on mountain peaks, converted residential buildings into inns and erected new hotels that were rustic but surprisingly comfortable. The pioneers in this formidable undertaking bore the names of Rosebrook, Crawford and Fabyan. These were the figures who established the basis of the White Mountain tourist industry and the grand hotel building type with which it would become inextricably linked. The architectural origins of the grand hotel were humble and unspectacular, but their influence was lasting and widespread. They merit close scrutiny.[2]

The First Hostelry

In 1792 Eleazar Rosebrook (1747–1817), a native of Grafton, Massachusetts, moved his family to Nash and Sawyer's Location, an isolated area in the upper Ammonoosuc River Valley near present-day Fabyan Station at Bretton Woods. He joined his son-in-law Abel Crawford (1776–1851) who was living there alone. Rosebrook soon bought Crawford's land when Crawford, who would become known as the "Patriarch of the Mountains," decided to relocate to Hart's Location, twelve miles to the south in the Saco River Valley. For a number of years the Rosebrooks lived in a small log cabin originally erected by Crawford. Here, they occasionally hosted guests, including the distinguished Reverend Timothy Dwight, the early travel writer and later president of Yale College.

In 1803, the opening of the Tenth New Hampshire Turnpike through Crawford Notch changed the history of the region forever. The new road produced a marked increase in the volume of traffic (teamsters, farmers and occasional tourists) and improved economic prospects for the Rosebrooks and their neighbors.[3] Responding to the need for some type of solid travelers' accommodations, Rosebrook promptly constructed "the first house for summer visitors ever kept in the mountains."[4] Only one known image of this building exists. This idealized sketch depicts a wooden, pitched–roof structure, two stories high, with two "underground" rooms, situated on the western slope of a slight ridge of glacial deposit known as "Giant's Grave" (Fig. 1–1).[5] Apparently, from the second floor chamber there was "an outside door, which opened so that one could walk out on this fine hill, from which, to the stranger, the view was beautiful."[6] Rosebrook reputedly built a substantial barn, stables and sheds adjacent to the dwelling, as well as mills along the Ammonoosuc. On this spot he maintained his small inn and conducted related activities until 1817 when he died at the age of seventy, leaving the property to his grandson, Ethan Allen Crawford (1792–1846). Alas, in July 1818, less than a year after Rosebrook's death, this first hostelry in the White Mountains unexpectedly caught fire and burned to the ground, leaving only the foundations for a host of disappointed tourists.[7]

Crawford's Old Moosehorn Tavern (Mount Washington House)

Despite the great personal and financial setback caused by his loss, Crawford struggled on in the rough mountain surroundings, pursuing several occupations that included "assisting visitors up and down the Notch, guiding people up and down Mount Washington, and building paths. Occasionally he and his wife, Lucy, accommodated guests in their new house, a modest twenty–four–foot–square structure moved by oxen in the fall of 1818 from a location one–and–a–half miles away to the site of the destroyed inn."[8] Some accounts suggest that this structure may also have burned within a year, but this has not been firmly documented. We do know, however, that in the spring of 1824, Ethan Allen Crawford erected a thirty–six–by–forty–foot, two–story frame as an addition or a new building; he completed the exterior siding, roof and interior finish during the following spring. Supposedly the tavern was painted red and displayed distinctive moose horns over the door, giving rise to its popular name. Ultimately it proved too small to meet the demand presented by the increasing numbers of travelers to the region.[9]

In late 1831, to provide larger accommodations and meet competition posed by a new neighboring hotel venture (the White Mountain House, see below), Crawford assumed further financial risk and mortgaged his entire property to a Concord bank to fund another expansion project. In the spring and summer of 1832, he constructed a two–story, sixty–by–forty–foot wooden wing with two verandas; one extended up both stories across the entire east side and faced the grand panorama of Mount Washington and the Presidential Range. Opened the following spring, this enlarged complex (with space for twenty to thirty guests) was well patronized for the next few years. In 1837, Crawford vacated the hotel and returned for a time to his birthplace in Guildhall, Vermont.[10]

Operation of the Crawford property passed in 1837 to a man whose name was to become synonymous with the White Mountain hotel industry in its infant stages. With experience gained as a Conway, New Hampshire, innkeeper, Maine native Horace Fabyan (1807–1881) employed funds generated by his former Portland provisions business and made quick repairs to his new hostelry, renaming it the "Mount Washington House." Although he initially rented the property from the bank holding the mortgage, he acquired the title outright by 1841. Four years later he started construction on barns, service buildings, and a new wing to his hotel.[11] *The White Mountain and Winnepissiogee Lake Guide Book*, published in 1846, offers the following description of the growing complex:

> During the past and present season, the whole interior of the old house has been entirely new modeled and repaired, and a superb dining room 60 feet in length, beautifully carpeted and curtained, with full length tables, and every article of luxury and convenience, are only a few of the improvements. The chambers above (12

in number) are all beautifully arranged and furnished... A new building, 140 feet by 40, and three stories high, is nearly finished, and is attached to the first... house with an attic hall the whole length. This, when completed, will form a building 200 feet in length, and furnish about fifty additional rooms, the whole forming the largest and one of the best establishments in the country.[12]

The expanded hotel contained an impressive 100 rooms and must have accommodated over 150 guests when fully occupied. Piazzas—a common feature of the later grand hotels—ran the entire length of both long sides.[13] After its completion in 1848, Fabyan successfully operated the hotel for several years. Unfortunately, the hotel succumbed to fire on 19 April 1853 before it could reap the profits from the coming of the railroad (see Chapter 2). Although Fabyan intended to rebuild in 1854, this project never occurred, due to a long–term legal controversy over the property's ownership.[14]

Unfortunately, it is impossible to fully and accurately reconstruct the exterior appearance of the Mount Washington House because no identifiable views of it have been discovered. It seems reasonable to conclude, however, that this important early hotel prototype closely resembled its smaller neighbors—the Mount Crawford House and the Willey House Hotel (see below). Sketches, engravings and photographs of these two inns suggest that the Mount Washington was likely capped by a pitched roof, possibly with dormers, and sheathed with plain flat–board siding pierced by simple doorways and double–sash windows. The Mount Washington possessed no identifiable style in its architectural detail. As one historian of the White Mountains has aptly pointed out, virtually all other hotels of the era were represented in published woodcut engravings, but the Mount Washington was not, which might very well imply that "the building possessed all the charm of an army barracks starkly thrust and imposed upon nature."[15] Nevertheless, the significance of this early vernacular building type as a progenitor of the grand hotel should not go unrecognized.

Abel Crawford's Mount Crawford House

Following the sale of his land near Giant's Grave to his father–in–law Eleazar Rosebrook in 1792, Abel Crawford re–established himself at the southern end of the Notch in an open wilderness area on the Saco River. Here, under the mountain later known as "Mount Crawford," Abel, his wife, Hannah, and his sons first occupied a rough log cabin until he built a farmhouse, barns and a sawmill. Over the next fifteen years, Crawford, like Rosebrook, witnessed an increasing number of travelers and responded to the demand for overnight facilities by operating the family abode as a modest inn. He also provided guide service through the Notch. Though the exact year cannot currently be determined, the appellation "Mount Crawford House" likely came into use soon after 1800.[16]

According to White Mountain historian Frederick W. Kilbourne, sometime "previous to 1820" a new inn bearing the same name took the place of the farmhouse on the Crawford tract.[17] Ironically, while pictorial images of it have survived, far fewer details are known of its history than of the Mount Washington House. In fact, it may have existed as early as 1800, but its initial appearance remains a mystery. The first published reference to the building appears in an 1848 guidebook and notes a new addition:

This establishment, 70 by 40 feet, has been enlarged one third of its length, and another story added, which gives a large number of sleeping apartments, and a fine dining and sitting room; the whole building has been completely painted and repaired inside and out, and furnished in the best style.[18]

By this time, Crawford's son–in–law Nathaniel T. P. Davis was running the Mount Crawford House. After 1856, when Dr. Samuel A. Bemis gained ownership of the inn and the 100–acre Crawford farm, he used it as a residence. Operated only sporadically for the summer season, its last recorded openings were in 1872 and 1876. There is some question as to when the inn was torn down—Kilbourne cites the year 1900.[19]

Fig. 1-2. "Old Crawford's, Notch, White Mtns.," pencil and watercolor sketch of the Mount Crawford House by James Elliot Cabot (1821-1902). New Hampshire Historical Society. This sketch (c. 1845-46) is one of twelve drawings Cabot made during two visits to the White Mountains after his graduation from Harvard Law School.

Fortunately, several architectural views of the Mount Crawford House are available for close study. The earliest of these, a rare and revealing pencil and watercolor sketch on paper drawn around 1845–46 by James Elliot Cabot of Boston,[20] provides a panoramic vista of the Crawford farm, with the inn (a plain pitched–roof, two–and–one–half–story, five–bay wooden structure) prominently situated amongst the barns and outbuildings (Fig. 1–2). Plate 2 of William Oakes' *Scenery of the White Mountains* shows the building after 1848 in its enlarged form of six bays with two dormers.[21] Later photographs, such as the one in the 1887 edition of Thomas Starr King's *The White Hills*, illustrate a larger, fully developed building of nine bays and three dormers with a west–end porch (Fig. 1–3).[22] Given the arrangement of the fenestration and the known presence of public rooms on the first floor, it is likely that sixty or more guests could have been housed for the night. In every respect the Mount Crawford House was a statement of conservative functional simplicity, in keeping with other early White Mountain highway inns of its era.

The Willey House and Hotel

The twelve–mile distance between the Mount Crawford House and Ethan Allen Crawford's inn north of the Notch was sufficiently long to justify the establishment of another stopping place for travelers making the weary and still arduous journey through the

THE PRECURSORS: ROSEBROOKS, CRAWFORDS, FABYANS AND THE EARLY HIGHWAY HOTELS

Fig. 1-3. The Old Crawford House, Crawford Notch, NH, *photograph from Thomas Starr King,* The White Hills . . . *(1887), p. 216. Author's Collection. This view shows the hotel at its maximum size situated beside the Portland & Ogdensburg Railroad route through the Notch. Residential in appearance, it originated as a farmhouse, was subsequently opened to travelers, and then expanded.*

rough mountain terrain. According to John H. Spaulding, in his classic *Historical Relics of the White Mountains* (1855), this need was met by the construction of the first structure to be built in the Notch—the old Notch House—"in the year 1793 by a Mr. Davis."[23] Sources suggest that Davis, a Mr. Henry Hill, and others (including Ethan Allen Crawford who rented it in 1823) managed the house for brief periods before it was abandoned.[24] In October 1825, Samuel Willey, Jr. moved his family into the small one-and-a-half-story, wood-frame structure. Less than a year later, on 28 August 1826, the oft-described tragic episode occurred: a great deluge and landslide destroyed the entire family, their hired help, several farm animals and the barn, while miraculously sparing the house from demolition.[25] A sketch executed by James Elliot Cabot in 1845 shows

Fig. 1-4. "The Willey House, Sept. 5, 1845," *pencil and watercolor sketch by James Elliot Cabot. New Hampshire Historical Society. The artist depicts the old Notch House and new barn after the disaster, and well before the construction of the Willey House Hotel.*

[33]

Fig. 1-5. "The Willey House, Crawford Notch, White Mts.," *stereo view, c.1875, Kilburn #657. Author's Collection. The 1845 hotel to the left was typical of the vernacular residential architecture of the day, but its newly enlarged scale and floor plan suggest the beginnings of a new regional building type.*

the old Notch House and a replacement barn, along with evidence of the 1826 disaster (Fig. 1-4).[26] Almost immediately, the site became the major tourist attraction in the area, drawing many new visitors to the mountains.

In 1844 Horace Fabyan, with experience gained from his Mount Washington House venture, purchased the dilapidated and tenantless building, now known by its popular historic name of the "Willey House." After repairing the former hostelry and barn, he built a new seventy by forty-foot, two-and-one-half-story hotel the next year. The structure faced east on the Notch road toward Mount Webster and was just south but physically connected to the Willey House.[27] After completing and furnishing the hotel, Fabyan, playing the role of real-estate speculator, sold it to John Davis of Conway.[28] Several owners and proprietors successfully operated the Willey House Hotel for much of the remainder of the century; both the hotel and the legendary old house burned to the ground on 24 September 1899.[29]

Old stereographic views and *cartes de visite* produced by Kilburn and other photographers reveal that the hotel was of the same vernacular building type as the two built by the Crawfords (Fig. 1-5). Painted white early in its history and set into the mountain side,[30] the Willey House Hotel was seven window bays long, with an off-center front doorway (flanked by vertical lights) opening out onto a long veranda. It possessed little hint of architectural individuality until 1891, when proprietor J. T. Dutton created fourteen additional bedrooms in the attic story by adding dormers (with returns) topped by steep-pitched roofs reflecting a Gothic Revival influence.[31] The eclectic nature of this otherwise very plain building was reinforced by small Italian Revival brackets under the eaves at each end. A photograph showing these modifications was reproduced many times over by G. W. Morris and Chisholm Brothers, Portland, Maine, publishers of turn-of-the-century tourist viewbooks (Fig. 1-6). Early hotel developers, like their successors, were primarily concerned with profit and hence built frugally. Yet the successful form, proportions and aesthetic detail of the Willey House Hotel also suggest a respect for sound construction and orderly, modestly creative design.

Fig. 1-6. Willey Hotel and Willey House, Crawford Notch, NH, photograph from Holman D. Waldron, With Pen and Camera thro' the White Mountains *(1896). Author's Collection. Note the 1891 alterations that included the addition of several eclectic stylistic elements.*

Tom Crawford's Notch House

The most well–known early forerunner of the grand hotels and the one most frequently depicted by artists was the new Notch House, formerly situated on a small plateau at the northern end of the Notch at the "Gateway" formed by Elephant Head and the east shoulder of Mount Willard. Sensing a need for additional accommodations for the growing numbers of travelers, Ethan Allen Crawford and his father Abel designed and erected this two–story, 36–by–120–foot building in 1827–28; it opened in January 1829 with Ethan's brother, Thomas J. Crawford, as proprietor. The new inn quickly prospered, servicing commercial traffic as well as visitors to the Willey House. These visitors reached the many natural features of the Notch and Mount Washington by a horse trail behind the hotel, later known as the famed "Crawford Path." Tom Crawford assumed ownership and remained as proprietor until 1852. When he overextended his financial resources by commencing construction of a new hotel across the Notch road (see Crawford House, Chapter 3), Crawford was forced to sell out to a company headed by Major Joseph L. Gibb of Littleton. Fire leveled the structure in 1854.[32]

While printed sources reveal little about the appearance or interior layout of the Notch House, certain guidebooks published during the 1840s and 1850s do offer some useful facts. George W. Brigg's Railway Manual (1849) mentions a new addition in a brief descriptive passage:

> The Notch House, kept by Thomas J. Crawford, is finely situated in respect to scenery, and presents strong inducements to the tourist to make it his mountain home. Here is the post–office; and from this point the ascent of the mountains is the most interesting, though not, perhaps, the easiest. The house has recently been enlarged and newly furnished, affording ample accommodations for its numerous guests, and all the comforts and conveniences of which its situation will admit. The establishment is supplied with good horses and carriages for the road, and with intelligent and obliging Guides and sure–footed saddle–horses for the ascent of the mountains.[33]

J. Disturnell's *The Eastern Tourist* (1848) describes this "most romantic spot, at the very source of the Saco River [Saco Lake] . . . where the mountains are rent asunder" and states that the capacity of the Notch House had been increased to seventy–five guests.[34] The 1846 edition of *The White Mountain and Winnepissiogee Lake Guide Book* provides clarifying details about the new c. 1845–46 addition:

> During the present season the stables on the premises have been removed further down the road, and the main building has been lengthened one–third, and an additional story [a remodeled attic with dormers] added to the whole house, thus making a great number of sleeping apartments; another sitting–room, and extensive office, and a large airy dining–room, finely completed. The whole has been newly painted and firnished [sic].[35]

Tripp and Osgood's 1851 guide remarks on the advantages of the Notch House and its location, as well as pointing to the recently completed physical improvements.[36]

For a well–detailed view of the Notch House early in its history, we may consult a c. 1860 Currier and

Fig. 1-7. "The Gate of the Notch of the White Mountains, with the Notch House" lithograph, Plate 5 from William Oakes, Scenery of the White Mountains *(1848). Author's Collection. Artist Isaac Sprague illustrated the Notch House after its c. 1845-56 enlargement.*

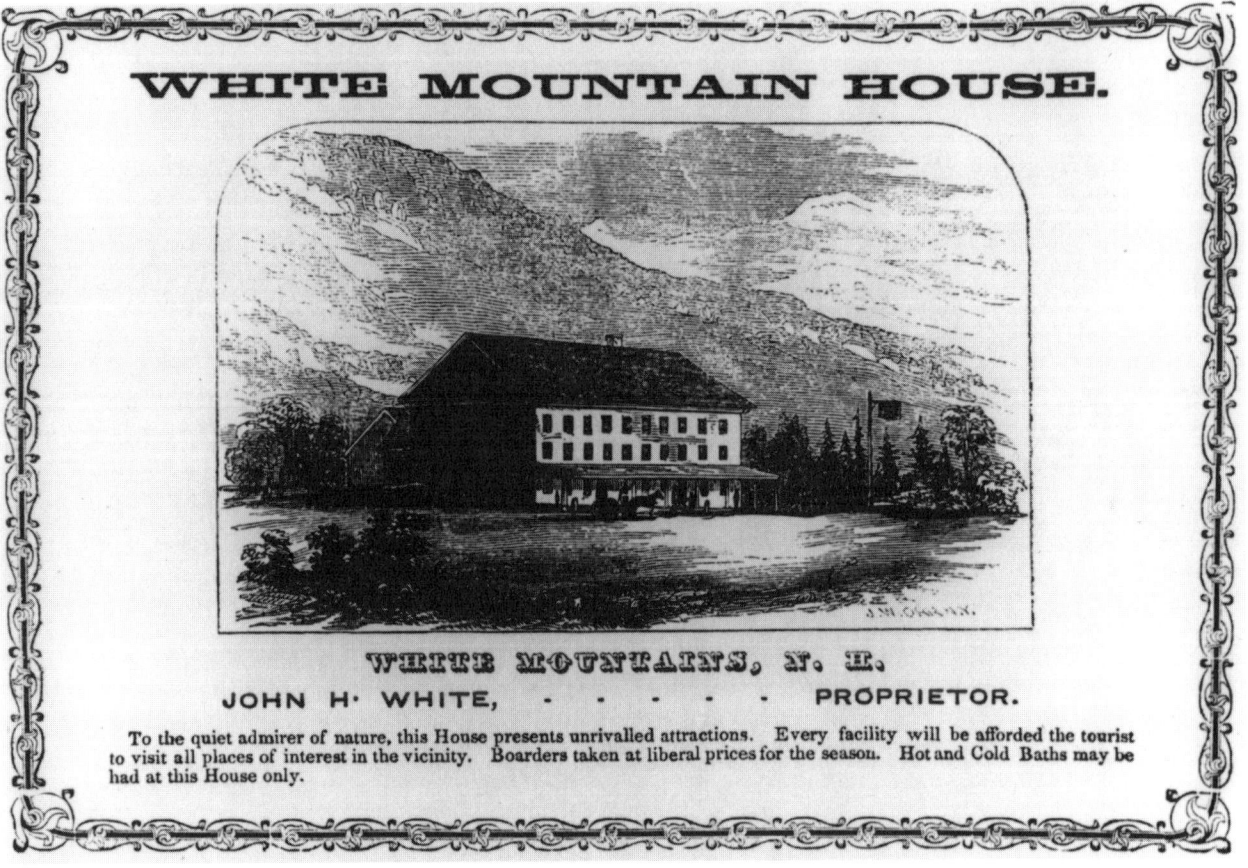

Fig. 1-8. White Mountain House, Carroll, NH, *c. 1853 advertising cut, source unknown. New Hampshire Historical Society. In this rare engraving, one may see the hotel as Abel Crawford knew it before his death in 1846. It housed up to 150 patrons.*

Ives colored lithograph, derived from William H. Bartlett's c. 1836 sketch for the *American Scenery* volumes published between 1838–40 (see Plate 1).[37] Here the enlarged domestic architectural form is similar to the other early hotels in the vicinity of the Notch, except for the presence of an attached barn and the incorporation of a two–portal carriage house in the rectangular mass of the hotel. In a detail from plate 5 of Oakes' *Scenery of the White Mountains* (1848), artist Isaac Sprague depicted the Notch House after the c. 1845–46 enlargement (Fig. 1–7). Evident alterations include the extended length, a new front veranda and added doorway, roof dormers lighting the new attic guest rooms, and new detached stables slightly to the south.[38] The last owner, Major Gibb, is known to have made some further modifications prior to the destruction of the complex, but it is primarily the 1845–46 form that was remembered by visitors to the Notch in the pre–Crawford House era.

The White Mountain House

Of the early highway hotels on the west side of the Presidential Range, the White Mountain House was the only one to last into this century. For many years it was the oldest in the region. It had its origins in an earlier building on the same site, located approximately three–quarters of a mile west of Giant's Grave overlooking the Ammonoosuc River, where today the Cherry Mountain Road joins the main route between Bretton Woods and Twin Mountain. Existing sources are confusing as to when and by whom this structure was erected, although Lucy Crawford referred to the small inn several times in her *History of the White Mountains* (1846). The Crawford history further records that by 1831 the inn was operated as the "White Mountain House," and that it had been purchased the previous year by "a man from Jefferson," New Hampshire.[39] The English traveler and writer E. T. Coke noted that it displayed "a gaily painted sign of a lion (like a snarling cur) and an eagle, looking unutterable things at each other from opposite sides of the globe," and that it "attracted numerous guests."[40] For a time this establishment proved an irritating rival to Ethan Allen Crawford and his Old Moosehorn Tavern. Ironically, after a few years the inn was closed, and in 1843 Crawford himself occupied it, renting what he describes as "the large three–story building" where he lived until his death on 22 June 1846.[41]

Crawford's reference is noteworthy since it implies that at some time prior to 1843, the first inn was either added on to or supplanted by a more commodious wooden structure under the direction of a member of the Rosebrook family.[42] The result was the better–documented White Mountain House, housing up to 150 patrons, that was to pass into the modern hotel era under a succession of proprietors, beginning with Colonel John White in the 1850s, continuing with G. T. Brabrook in the 1860s, and later with the well–known R. D. Rounsevel and the Sheehe–Seymour family.[43] It was destroyed by a disastrous fire, on 8 October 1929, that razed the building in less than two hours. Although rebuilding was considered, this never occurred.[44]

Fortunately, many outstanding engravings and photographs exist of the White Mountain House that give an excellent idea of its appearance after 1850. An advertising cut (c. 1853) depicts Crawford's "large three–story building" as five–window–bays–wide by nine–bays–long, with two front doorways, a full–length front veranda, and a pitched roof with closed gable ends containing a semi–elliptical attic light and three windows[45] (Fig. 1–8). A c. 1875 business card engraving of the hotel (also used in several editions of *Snow's Handbook of Northern Pleasure Travel*) reveals an extended rear ell, new dormer windows on the front roof plane, and an added two–story porch with square–paneled support columns, seemingly inspired by the Italian Revival[46] (Fig. 1–9). A later photograph, taken after the new windows were installed and other alterations made in 1879–80,[47] shows the hotel with its fine front porch stripped away and replaced by a wrap–around veranda, a new extended front roof dormer, a new

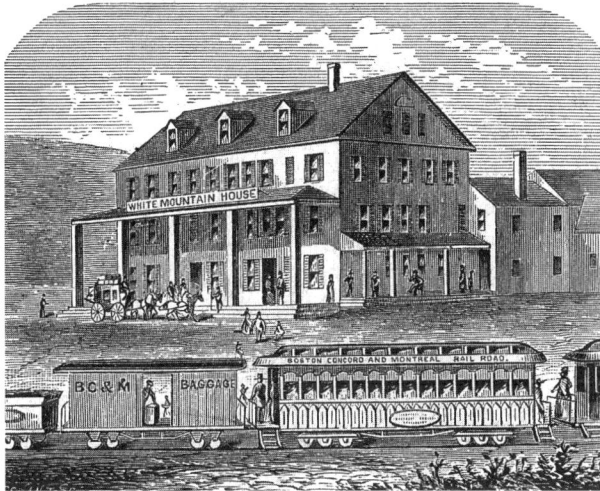

Fig. 1-9. White Mountain House, Carroll, NH, *c. 1875 engraved business card view. Author's Collection. This pleasant view, also used in several contemporary guidebooks, presents the hotel after expansion with new decorative details.*

one–story west wing and an enlarged rear ell (Fig. 1–10). A substantial three–and–one–half–story addition, appended to the east side of the ell, added a new dining room and fifty guest rooms, but little architectural merit, to the complex in 1921–22.[48] To its end the White Mountain House perpetuated the tradition of unsophisticated, functional, but commendable design established by the first group of White Mountain hotels.

Fig. 1-10. White Mountain House, Carroll, NH., *photograph after 1880, photographer unknown. Douglas Philbrook, Gorham, NH. This building maintained the tradition of plain vernacular design established by the earliest White Mountains highway inns.*

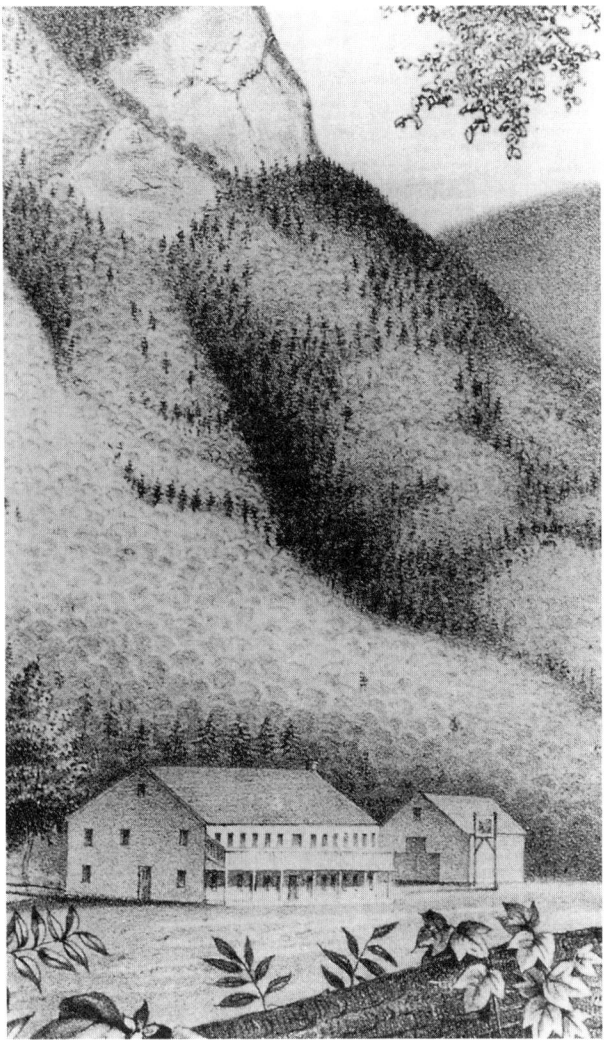

Fig. 1-11. "The Franconia Notch with the Lafayette House," lithograph, plate 8 from William Oakes, Scenery of the White Mountains *(1848). Author's Collection. In enlarged form this early hotel was similar in appearance to Crawford's Old Moosehead Tavern, the Mount Crawford House and the White Mountain House.*

The Lafayette House in Franconia Notch

The earliest origins of the White Mountain grand resort hotels may be traced not only to Crawford Notch and the area immediately west of the Presidential Range but also to Franconia Notch on the far western edge of the mountains. At this spectacular location several small inns helped set the stage for the later development of the regional hotel industry. Kilbourne initially refers to a "house of entertainment" known as Knight's Tavern, built in the first part of the nineteenth century and formerly situated on the east side of the modern highway a few hundred feet south of the entrance to the present Flume parking lot. He also mentions the Lafayette House as "the first hotel of any consequence" erected in or near the Notch at the location that today is roughly 500 feet southeast of the Cannon Mountain Aerial Tramway base station (once the site of the Profile House) in Franconia Notch State Park.[49]

The building and opening of the Lafayette House (also known as Gibbs' Hotel) may be dated to 1835, based on an account of a visit made in that year to Franconia Notch by the renowned English traveler and diarist Harriet Martineau. While there she alluded to the inn as "the solitary dwelling of the pass, called the Lafayette Hotel" and remarked that it "had been growing in the woods thirteen weeks before, and yet we were far from being among its first guests."[50] The first owners and operators were Stephen C. Gibb and Major Joseph L. Gibb, who had been associated with the Notch House (and subsequently the Crawford House, see Chapter 2). In an 1845 pencil and watercolor sketch by James Elliot Cabot,[51] the Lafayette House during the Gibbs' ownership appears first and foremost as a private farmhouse and secondarily as a tavern, with space for only a few guests. The adjoining barn serviced horses and carriages (see Plate 2).

Sometime before 1852, when the Gibbs sold the property to Richard Taft, George T. Brown and Ira Coffin (the developers of the first Profile House, see Chapter 2), this modest hostelry was substantially enlarged.[52] A detail from plate 8 in *Scenery of the White Mountains* shows the inn, barn and stables nestled in the Notch with Eagle Cliff rising dramatically above and just to the east (Fig. 1–11).[53] Both widened and lengthened (from five to fourteen window bays), this building, with its two–story veranda, must have closely resembled the Crawford's Old Moosehorn Tavern. In overall form, it was not dissimilar to the Mount Crawford House or the White Mountain House as they appeared about 1850. After expansion it was said to accommodate the impressive total of a hundred guests,[54] although fifty, as other sources estimate, would seem a more logical total figure.

During 1853, in conjunction with the construction of the first Profile House, the Lafayette House was moved across the Notch road to the rear of the new hotel. There it served as a "work room" and laundry until it was reconstructed and modernized for use as a dormitory for waitresses.[55] A C. P. Hibbard cabinet view (c. 1880) shows the building, minus its veranda, on its new foundations; new features included 2/2 Victorian windows, shutters, dormers, brick chimneys and a square cupola piercing the roof surfaces (Fig. 1–12). The old Lafayette House underwent a final transformation in 1897 when it was "converted into a new and attractive cottage"[56] for both male and female help. "Lafayette Cottage," as it was renamed, had an added third story, altered fenestration and a new hipped roof similar to those of the New Profile House (see Chapter 7). When fire destroyed this great resort hotel complex, including its outbuildings, on 2 August 1923, the last remnants of the original Lafayette House were also lost.[57]

The Major Feeder Hotels to the South

Two famous old establishments—the first Pemigewasset House in Plymouth and the first Senter House in Center Harbor—pre–dated the coming of the railroad to the area. They served as important stopover points in the southern portion of the region for travelers on the main routes to and from the heart of the mountains. After the arrival of the railroads in the 1850s, visitor traffic flow greatly increased, and longer stays became more common. Over the years both buildings grew in size to accommodate a greater number of guests, but in pure architectural terms they adhered to the same general form as the first hotels to the north, save for some variations in roof configuration and decorative detail.

The first Pemigewasset House was one of three hotels by that name to exist in Plymouth over a period spanning more than a century. The Pemigewasset appears to have had its origins in a log structure

Fig. 1-12. "Old Profile House" (Lafayette House), Franconia Notch, NH, *cabinet view, c. 1880, C. P. Hibbard, Lisbon, NH, photographer. Douglas Philbrook, Gorham, NH. The Lafayette House was incorporated into the new Profile House complex of buildings in 1853 by virtue of a move to a new location nearby its original site. Here it served as the dormitory for the hotel's help.*

Fig. 1-13. First Pemigewasset House (c. 1800, 1841, etc.), Plymouth, NH, *daguerreotype, c. 1860. Plymouthiana Collection, Herbert H. Lamson Library, Plymouth State College.* The hotel originated with Webster's Tavern, and was enlarged three times, incorporating a railroad station stop with adjacent dining room on the route north to the mountains.

erected in the 1760s by Colonel David Webster as a tavern. By 1800 Webster and his son, William, replaced this primitive building with a much larger two–and–one–half–story, gambrel–roofed wooden edifice that was operated for several decades under the name "Webster's Tavern." Kilbourne tells us that in 1841 Denison R. Burnam purchased the building, put on an addition and changed the name to "Pemigewasset House."[58] Indicative of its flourishing patronship, the hotel was enlarged two times in the 1850s to house up to 150 guests.[59] By 1859 a wing approximately 40 by 100 feet was added; situated parallel to the new Boston, Concord and Montreal track, it combined a new dining room and railroad station stop. The dining room, said to be the largest of its kind in New Hampshire, was intended to conveniently service railroad travelers who could enter it directly from cars across a level platform. The best surviving illustration of the enlarged complex is a marvelous 1860s daguerreotype (Fig. 1–13) that shows the original tavern (left), the first addition (right center) and the second addition (left center), with its distinctive cross–gable roofs, eaves brackets and extended verandas. Fire, the all–too–common scourge of the old hotels, leveled the Pemigewasset House in 1862, but it was soon rebuilt on the same site (see Chapter 3).[60]

The first Senter House in Center Harbor, the earliest large hostelry in New Hampshire's Lakes Region, was placed in an equally advantageous location for attracting the business of visitors to the White Mountains. Situated on the main street of the town overlooking Lake Winnipesaukee, it was the constant beneficiary of the extensive travel between the mountains and the cities of Portland and Boston. This included both the overland carriage and stage trade, as well as the steamboat traffic on the lake that connected with The Weirs, Laconia, Alton Bay and railheads farther to the south (see Chapter 2). Built in 1825 by Colonel Samuel Senter, with extensive additions by the Coe family in the 1830s and later owner James L. Huntress in 1872, the Senter House, in its final stage, had an overall length of 120 feet and possessed an 80–foot dining room ell (Fig. 1–14).[61] The site had many positive features, as a statement from *Bradlee's Pocket Guide . . .* (1860) attests:

> The house itself occupies a fine position, with a double piazza facing the lake, between which and the wharf is a neat garden of two acres, intersected by a walk, with flights of steps leading to the shore.[62]

During the 1860s and 1870s, it became as much a single destination resort as an important feeder of tourists to the mountains, boasting "charming drives in all directions," "a thoroughly equipped Livery Stable," "music for dancing," a "Billiard Room and Bowling Alley," and fishing, boating, lawn tennis and croquet amongst its many recreational and social offerings.[63] Virtually all of the guidebooks of the era, though prone to promotional over–enthusiasm, commended the hotel as "one of the best in the mountain region, . . . commodious and well furnished, and . . . long and favorably known for the convenience of its arrangements, the perfections of its table, and the courtesy of its proprietors."[64]

With a maximum capacity of 200 guests,[65] the first Senter House was without question the most architecturally interesting of the early grand hotel prototypes. Late Federal, Greek Revival and Italian Revival features were discretely combined to create a rich panoply of forms across the front elevation. The many published engraved and photographic views reveal several doorways, flanked by sidelights and topped by entablatures, opening onto the veranda and porch roof above. Also adding a classical feeling to the three–and–one–half–story building were block square veranda columns, a veranda balustrade and gable moldings. Touches of the Italian Revival were evident in the eaves and gable brackets as well as the octagonal cupola centered on the cross–gable roof, topped by a bracketed flat roof. In quality of design, the first Senter House was surely the equal of the sec-

Fig. 1-14. "Senter House, Centre Harbor," *stereo view, c. 1860, "American Scenery, New England Series," photographer unknown. Author's Collection. Erected in 1825, and later substantially enlarged, the Senter House was the best known hotel in the Lakes Region, and accommodated people traveling to and from the mountains by stage, steamboat and railroad routes.*

ond Crawford House, the first Glen House and the first Profile House (see Chapter 2), and of similar hotel structures that would be built as a product of railroad development during the 1850s and later. Its loss to fire, on 16 July 1887, was a serious, albeit temporary setback for tourism in the White Mountains and for a brief time eliminated a vital link to the northern district. But like the first Pemigewasset House, another hotel of the same name would soon rise from its charred ruins to recapture the tourist market (see Chapter 5).[66]

The Village Inns

Prior to 1850, numerous smaller inns or taverns existed throughout the White Mountains region in or near village and town centers. While these originated largely to serve local customers and travelers conducting business, they also accommodated tourists and people from distant locations visiting the mountains for other purposes. Only a very few of these buildings, however, should in any way be considered architectural precursors to the grand hotels

Fig. 1-15. Lary House *(c. 1837), Gorham, NH, photograph, n. d., by unknown photographer. Dartmouth College Library. This well-known village inn was architecturally similar to the early highway hotels of Crawford and Franconia notches.*

of the later century. Exhaustive treatment of this group of hostelries, therefore, will not be undertaken in this study.

Virtually all the early village inns were domestic in form and thus possessed characteristics of regional residences rather than hotel architecture. Many, in fact, were built as single family houses, only to be expanded later to serve commercial purposes. A case in point was the Granite Hotel (1840, and later) in Littleton. Other comparable early establishments could once be found in the mountains at Littleton (Union House), Woodstock, Campton (Blair's Hotel; Sanborn's Inn), Plymouth, Upper Bartlett, Lower Bartlett (Pendexter House; East Branch House), Bethlehem (Woodbury's Tavern; Turner's Tavern), Conway (Pequawket House) and North Conway (Washington House; McMillan House; Moat Mountain House; Orient House). A rare exception to the norm was the Lary House (c. 1837; burned, 1907) in Gorham; in terms of size, scale, and decorative detail, this hostelry had much more in common with the first highway inns and hotels that were the legitimate forerunners to the grand hotels (Fig. 1–15).[67] It would take the railroads, however, to open the area to further economic development, spurring the growth of the tourist industry and the creation of a new and immensely appealing regional building type for which the White Mountains would become justly renowned in this country and abroad.

∽ Notes ∾

1. Frederick W. Kilbourne, *Chronicles of the White Mountains* (New York: Houghton Mifflin Company, 1916), p. 155.
2. *Ibid.*, pp. 155-156; R. Stuart Wallace, "A Social History of the White Mountains," in Catherine H. Campbell, et al., *The White Mountains: Place and Perceptions* (Hanover, NH: University Press of New England, 1980), pp. 24, 26.
3. Kilbourne, *Chronicles*, pp. 70, 72-73.
4. *ATC* 5, No. 11 (27 July 1881), p. 3; [Georgia Drew Merrill], *History of Coos County, New Hampshire* (Syracuse, NY: W. F. Fergusson & Co., 1888), p. 437.
5. In the *History of Coos County* . . . the building is described as "a rude inn, a teamsters' tavern" (p. 437). The image, of questionable accuracy, was prepared by Marshall Tidd for a new edition of Crawford's *History*, which Lucy compiled in c.

1860, but never published. After its rediscovery in family hands many years later, it was finally published in 1966 by Dartmouth Publications, but without nine Tidd illustrations. The illustrations ultimately surfaced, were donated to Dartmouth College by William Crawford Wheeler and were reproduced in a 1978 edition of the *History*, published by the Appalachian Mountain Club.
6. John H. Spaulding, *Historical Relics of the White Mountains...* (Boston: Nathaniel Noyes, 1855), p. 17.
7. Lucy Crawford, *History of the White Mountains from the First Settlement of the Upper Coos and Pequawket* (White Hills, 1846), pp. 20-21; Kilbourne, *Chronicles*, pp. 73, 75, 77.
8. Kilbourne, *Chronicles*, p. 77.
9. Crawford, *History*, pp. 71-72, 76; Kilbourne, *Chronicles*, pp. 79-80.
10. Crawford, *History*, pp. 148-49, 154-56; Kilbourne, *Chronicles*, pp. 79-82. Kilbourne indicates that Crawford was forced to give up his hotel and farm due to ill health and financial difficulties.
11. Kilbourne, *Chronicles*, pp. 163-64; Peter B. Bulkley, "Horace Fabyan, Founder of the White Mountain Grand Hotel," *Historical New Hampshire* 30, No. 2 (Summer 1973), pp. 55-58. The exact date of Fabyan's acquisition is unknown due to the lack of a proper deed, likely lost during the great fire of 1886 in Lancaster, which gutted the Coos County Registry of Deeds.
12. *The White Mountains and Winnepissiogee Lake Guide Book*, 1st ed. (Boston: Jordon & Wiley, 1846), pp. 67-68.
13. *Guide to the White Mountains and Lakes of New Hampshire...*, 2nd ed. (Concord, NH: E.B. Tripp & R.C. Osgood, 1851), p. 67. In his pamphlet *Mount Washington House* (New York: Baker, Godwin & Co., 1852), Fabyan stated that the hotel "contains some hundred and fifty rooms" (p. 15), but this is inconsistent with the figure cited in the contemporary regional guidebooks. On the main floor were "several long parlors" which were "connected with sleeping rooms for the convenience of those unable to ascent to the upper apartments" (pp. 15-16). Curiously, this unusual and enlightened floor plan was uncommon in later White Mountain hotels.
14. Bulkley, "Horace Fabyan...," p. 65; F. Allen Burt, *The Story of Mount Washington* (Hanover, NH: Dartmouth Publications, 1960), p. 70. It is possible also that Fabyan was ruined financially by the fire, though it is unknown whether or not the property had been insured, and a claim filed for losses.
15. Bulkley, "Horace Fabyan," pp. 60-61. Fabyan's *Mount Washington House* (see note 13), the first of many promotional booklets published for the White Mountain hotels, displays a building illustration on its front cover, but the civilized, finely detailed structure depicted in no way resembles the Mount Washington House from what is known about it from other published sources.
16. Florence Morey, "Abel Crawford and his Mount Crawford House," *Appalachia* 30, No. 1 (15 July 1954), pp. 1-3; William Oakes, *Scenery of the White Mountains with Sixteen Plates from the Drawings of Isaac Sprague*, reprint ed. (Somersworth, NH: New Hampshire Publishing Co., 1970), Plate 2 commentary by Sherman Adams.
17. Kilbourne, *Chronicles*, p. 73.
18. *The White Mountain and Winnepisseogee Lake Guide Book*, 2nd ed. (Boston: Henry Marsh, 1848), pp. 45-46. *The Guide to the White Mountains and Lakes of New-Hampshire*, 1st ed. (Concord, NH: Tripp & Morril, Printers, 1850), known as the first edition of Tripp's guide, mentions enlargement by "one addition after another," but is unspecific about dates.
19. Burt, *The Story of Mount Washington*, p. 50; Morey, "Abel Crawford...," p. 4; Kilbourne, *Chronicles*, p. 158; *WME* 2, No. 1 (28 June 1879), p. 7. Nathaniel T. P. Davis was the husband of Abel's only daughter Hannah. In 1845 he opened the path up Mount Washington that still bears his name.

Later known as "Notchland" or "Bemis Station" (Hart's Location), the Mount Crawford House site was located opposite to where the stone house built by Dr. Samuel A. Bemis, a Boston dentist, remains in use today as an inn. While citing the demolition date, Kilbourne states in a footnote that timber from the inn was used to construct a cottage at the Bemis railroad station. The 1876 opening, under the lease proprietorship of Charles W. Morey, is documented by a letter (27 June 1876) to Morey from owner Samuel A. Bemis (Dartmouth College Archives). The third edition (Concord, NH: Edson Eastman, 1863) of *The White Mountain Guide Book* states that the inn closed in 1862.
20. This fine pictorial document, labeled "Old Crawford's Notch, White Mts.," is one of twelve White Mountain drawings prepared by Cabot on a trip taken after his graduation from Harvard Law School.
21. William Oakes, *Scenery of the White Mountains...*, 1st ed. (Boston: William Crosby and H.P. Nichols, 1848), Plate 2. The plates in this large folio volume are large uncolored lithographs.
22. Thomas Starr King, *The White Hills; Their Legends, Landscape, and Poetry*, (Boston: Estes and Lauriat, 1887), op. p. 216. See also the photos in *WME* 27, No. 10 (10 September 1904), p. 20; *ATC Souvenir Edition* No. 2 (1897), p. 43; and *Appalachia* 30, No. 1 (15 June 1954), op. p. 4 (by T.E.M. White, North Conway). In her *Appalachia* article Florence Morey states that a full inventory of the contents of the Mount Crawford House, made when Dr. Bemis assumed title in 1856, does exist, although its exact whereabouts today are unknown.
23. Kilbourne, *Chronicles*, p. 89; Burt, *The Story of Mount Washington*, p. 32; Spaulding, *Historical Relics of the White Mountains*, p. 55. There is some disagreement as to the precise building date, as some sources, such as Eastman's *The White Mountain Guide Book*, 1st ed. (Concord, 1858), claim that the old Notch House was not raised until around 1820. Kilbourne's explanation of the 1793 date is the most convincing yet.

24. Burt, *The Story of Mount Washington*, p. 32. Ethan Allen Crawford's venture at the old Notch House failed in less than two years, ironically because of competition from his own inn at Giant's Grave northwest of the Notch and his father's hotel to the south.
25. This legendary event in White Mountain history is described in great detail in Benjamin Willey's *Incidents in White Mountain History* (Boston: Nathaniel Noyes, 1856), and in numerous printed sources published since. See particularly Kilbourne, *Chronicles*, pp. 85-100, and Burt, *The Story of Mount Washington*, pp. 32-37.
26. The Cabot sketch (NHHS) is inscribed, "the Willey House, Sept. 5, 1845." Cabot intentionally omitted an addition that had been put onto the house. Among other excellent printed views are William H. Bartlett's, "The Willey House," (c. 1836) from Nathaniel P. Willis, *American Scenery*, 2 vols. (London: George Virtue, 1838-40), Plate 3 ("The Notch of the White Mountains, with the Willey House") of William Oakes, *Scenery of the White Mountains*, and an illustration from Thomas W. Parsons, *The Willey House and Sonnets* (Cambridge, MA: John Wilson and Son, 1875).
27. Bulkley, "Horace Fabyan," p. 60; Kilbourne, *Chronicles*, p. 164.
28. *The White Mountain and Winnepisseogee Lake Guide Book*, 2nd ed. (1848), p. 47.
29. *The Littleton* (NH) *Courier*, 27 September 1899, p. 6. Leonard & Mayfield of Whitefield, NH, were proprietors at the time of the fire. The cause was said to be a defective chimney, and the loss, covered by insurance, was $5,000. The owner was George H. Moran, also the owner of the late Dr. Bemis' estate.
30. William Guild, *New York and the White Mountains* (Boston: Bradbury & Guild, 1852), p. 78.
31. *ATC* 15, No. 2 (11 July 1891), advertisement, p. 6.
32. Crawford, *History*, p. 114; "Notch House," *ATC* 24, No. 48 (6 September 1900), p. 1; Kilbourne, *Chronicles*, pp. 161-62; Burt, *The Story of Mount Washington*, p. 41.
33. *A Railway Manual Containing Railway Maps of the Entire Route from Boston North . . . to which is added a Complete Guide to Lake Winnipiseogee and the White Mountains* (Boston: George W. Briggs, 1849), p. 44.
34. *The Eastern Tourist; Being a Guide . . .* (New York: J. Disturnell, 1848), p. 99.
35. *The White Mountain and Winnepissiogee Lake Guide Book*, 1st ed. (1846), pp. 57-58.
36. *Guide to the White Mountains and Lakes of New Hampshire*, 2nd ed. (1851), p. 30.
37. The Bartlett plate is entitled "The Notch House, White Mountain, New Hampshire." See also, note 26. The Currier & Ives view was in turn copied, inadvertently in reverse, by Kellogg and Bulkeley of Hartford, Connecticut, some time after 1867.
38. For a comprehensive discussion of views of the Gateway to the Notch, many of which include the Notch House, see Catherine H. Campbell, "The Gate of the Notch," *Historical New Hampshire* 33, No. 2 (Summer 1978): 91-122.
39. Crawford, *History*, pp. 150-54; Kilbourne, *Chronicles*, pp. 80-81.
40. E. T. Coke, *A Subaltern's Furlough: Descriptive Scenes in Various Parts of the United States, Upper and Lower Canada, New-Brunswick, and Nova Scotia, During the Summer and Autumn of 1832* (New York: J. & J. Harper, 1833), Vol. 2, p. 149. The new hotel proprietor, identified by Burt (*The Story of Mount Washington*, p. 44) as William Denison, made use of Ethan Allen Crawford's Mount Washington carriage road without securing permission, and later constructed a new path closer to the mountain that intersected with the road, after Crawford fenced off his land to protect his rights. Apparently this act, and the presence of the White Mountain House, however, did not severely hurt Crawford's hotel business.
41. Crawford, *History*, p. 186; Kilbourne, *Chronicles*, p. 83. In a footnote Kilbourne claimed that a portion of the first inn on the site formed a section of the later White Mountain House.
42. Kilbourne, *Chronicles*, pp. 165-66. *The History of Coos County* (1888), whose accuracy may be legitimately questioned, notes that Phineas Rosebrook, Jr. moved into the first inn in 1827 and "finished it," and that it was "a square, two story house, plastered on the outside" (p. 439). The Crawford history (p. 151) implies that a man named William [Denison] bought it from Rosebrook. *The Guide to the White Mountains and Lakes of New Hampshire*, 2nd ed. (1851) refers to the White Mountain House under Col. John H. White as "a new and neat House" (p. 31).
43. *The White Mountain Guide Book*, 1st ed. (Concord, NH: Edson C. Eastman, 1858), p. 70; Frank W. Rollins, *The Tourists' Guide-Book to the State of New Hampshire*, 2nd ed. (Concord, NH: The Rumford Press, 1902), p. 302; *ATC* 33, No. 20 (5 August 1911), advertisement. A letter dated "1865" in the Sylvester Marsh papers at the Mount Washington Observatory Resource Center (North Conway) indicates that Brabrook agreed to sell the White Mountain House to Marsh, the developer of the Mount Washington cog railroad, in that year. It is not known, however, if a property transfer actually occurred.
44. *The Littleton Courier*, 10 October 1929, p. 1; *The Coos County Democrat* (Lancaster, NH), 16 October 1929, p. 2. The total loss was estimated at $50,000 to $100,000. A nearby cottage, barn and other outbuildings survived the blaze.
45. Contained on what appears to be a proof sheet, NHHS (Hotel and Inns file). J. W. Orr of New York was the engraver.
46. Snow's *Handbook of Northern Pleasure Travel, to the White and Franconia Mountains . . .* (Boston: Noyes & Snow, 1876), p. 138. Used in annual editions of this guide through 1880, this view erroneously shows three instead of two front dormers.
47. *The Idler* (No. Conway, NH) 1, No. 1 (22 June 1880), p. 4.
48. *WME* 45, No. 4 (22 July 1922), p. 4; *The Littleton Courier*, 10 October 1929, p. 1.
49. Kilbourne, *Chronicles*, p. 166.
50. *Ibid.*, pp. 145-46, 167.
51. The sketch is entitled "Lafayette House, Franconia Notch, Sept. 1, 1845."

52. Sarah N. Welch, *Franconia Notch: History and Guide* (Littleton, NH: By the Author, 1981), p. 25.
53. Plate 8 from Oakes' *Scenery of the White Mountains* is titled "The Franconia Notch with the Lafayette House."
54. *Ammonoosuc Reporter* (Littleton, NH) 2, No. 6 (27 August 1852), p. 2.
55. *Ibid.*; Frederick W. Kilbourne, "A Closed Chapter of White Mountain History: The Franconia Notch as Summer Resort," *Appalachia* 16, No. 3 (February 1926), p. 308.
56. *ATC* 21, No. 7 (26 July 1897), p. 4.
57. Two other inns in the Franconia Notch region are often confused with the Lafayette House. The oldest of these, the Mount Lafayette House, was a small hostelry (erected, 1850s; burned, spring, 1861) of undetermined description. It was located about two-and-one-quarter miles below the Profile House site, at the present-day Lafayette Place Campground near the heads of the Old Bridle Path and the Falling Waters Trail up Mount Lafayette. The second building, also operated under the name of Mount Lafayette House (erected, 1882; burned 27 May 1911), was a converted residential structure situated about three miles from the Profile House site at the base of "Three Mile Hill" where the road to Franconia intersects with the Gale River road (Kilbourne, *Chronicles*, pp. 168-69).
58. Kilbourne, *Chronicles*, p. 173; exhibition label copy, HLL; *Manchester [NH] Union*, 29 July 1935; Eva A. Speare, *Twenty Decades in Plymouth, New Hampshire, 1763-1963* (Plymouth: Bicentennial Commission, 1963), p. 76. Mr. Burnham was the father-in-law of Charles Greenleaf, later proprietor of the Flume and Profile houses, and the Hotel Vendome in Boston. Burnham ran the hotel as a "temperance house," and specialized in an excellent livery stable for the provision of stagecoach transportation north into the mountains. It was located near the present railroad station on a rise overlooking the Pemigewasset River, just south of the "T" intersection of Highland and Main Streets.
59. *Guide to the White Mountains and Lakes of New-Hampshire*, 1st ed. (1850), p. 42.
60. *The White Mountain Guide Book*, 2nd ed. (Concord, NH: Edson C. Eastman, 1859), p. 137; *Manchester Union*, 29 July 1935; advertising broadside, "Pemigewasset House," (1 June 1862), HLL. Henry Greeley, formerly the proprietor of Greeley's Mountain House in Waterville Valley (see Chapter 5), was the proprietor of the Pemigewasset House at the time. In 1862 the hotel contained a telegraph office.
61. *Weirs [NH] Times and Tourist Gazette*, 20 July 1887, p. 4; *WME* 10, No. 4 (23 July 1887), p. 13; D. Hamilton Hurd, *History of Merrimack and Belknap Counties, New Hampshire* (Philadelphia: J.W. Lewis & Co., 1885), p. 728.
62. *Bradlee's Pocket Guide for the Use of Travellers to the White Mountains and Lake Winnipiseogee* (Boston: John E. Bradlee, 1860), p. 27.
63. John H. Bachelder, *Popular Resorts, Routes to Reach Them...*, 1st ed. (Boston: John H. Bachelder, 1873), advertisement, p. 55.
64. *The White Mountain Guide Book*, 1st ed. (1858), p. 128. Eastman's series of guides included this statement, without alteration, through fifteen editions until 1879!
65. *Laconia [NH] Democrat*, 22 July 1887, p. 1.
66. *Ibid.*; *ATC* 11, No. 9 (20 July 1887), p. 1; *WME* 10, No. 4 (23 July 1887), p. 13; *Weirs Times and Tourist Gazette*, (20 July 1887), p. 4. The fire was caused by a defective chimney, and, because it burned for one-and-one-half hours, many of the interior contents were saved. It threatened but only slightly damaged the much smaller Moulton House (c. 1834; enlarged, 1860), the town's other hotel next door. The loss to owners Henry L. Huntress & Son was estimated at $26,000, $10,000 of which was covered by insurance.

    Another large hotel of the pre-railroad era in the Lakes Region was the Pavilion Hotel (later the Kingswood Inn) in Wolfeboro. Erected in 1849-50, it was substantially enlarged in c. 1860 and in 1871-72 to accommodate over 250 guests. For purposes of this study, however, it will not be treated in the text as it was largely a single destination resort facility rather than a stopover for people moving to and from the mountains to the north.
67. The Granite Hotel was located in the center of Littleton on the north side of Main Street on the site of the later Northern Hotel. The Lary House was situated near the junction of the Berlin and Jefferson roads, about one mile west of the center of Gorham.

Fig. 1-16. "Washington House, No. Conway, N.H.," *stereo view, c. 1865, #453, "New Series, American Scenery," J.W. and J.S. Moulton, Salem, MA. Author's Collection. This early hostelry opened about 1812.*

Fig. 2-1. "Alpine House, Gorham, N. H.," *engraving from Capt. Charles A. J. Farrar's* Illustrated Guide Book to the Androscoggin Lakes . . . *(1884). Author's Collection. In 1876 the second Alpine House succeeded the White Mountain Station House on the same site.*

CHAPTER 2

Railroad Development and the Pre-Civil War Hotels

It was the coming of the railroad to the White Mountains that opened the once inaccessible wilderness area to tourism and encouraged the development of hotel entrepreneurship. Without the railroads, the dramatic era of the grand resort hotel would not have been possible—the railroads literally drove the industry to unpredicted levels of success and prosperity. Conversely, once the hotels became well established after the Civil War, they in turn fostered the further growth of the railroads. For several decades the hotels and the railroads enjoyed and benefited from this delicate, vital, interdependent relationship. However, as the relationship began to break down late in the century, and new outside forces (see Introduction and Chapter 8) imposed themselves on the regional economy, both industries underwent a lengthy and dramatic decline. Despite this depressing but in many ways inevitable phenomenon in the historical cycle, the glory of the hotels and the railroads that sustained them will forever remain etched in the annals of White Mountain history.

Early Rail Routes to the Mountains

During the 1840s and 1850s the railroads began to reach into the White Mountains. The earliest of these routes originated in Boston, connected with Portland, and then shifted toward the northwest, touching the east side of the region. Also beginning in Boston, a second major rail route ran northward to Concord, New Hampshire, continuing beyond while skirting the mountains to the west. Once these two routes were established, others emerged, all terminating on the fringes of the mountain district.[1]

From early travel guides we know the first railroad between Boston and Portland was completed in 1842, which made connections between land and water transport to the White Mountains faster and more comfortable. Stagecoaches made the arduous fifty-mile trek between Portland and Conway in a single day; after an overnight stay, they then proceeded northward to Crawford Notch. A variation on this route included a stage trip from Portland to Sebago Lake, followed by a delightful twenty-eight mile ride in the little steamer "Fawn" on Sebago Lake, the Songo River and Long Lake to Bridgton, Maine, and concluded with a stage link to Conway.[2]

A highly significant event in White Mountain history occurred when the first railroad reached the region, supplanting the older stage transportation routes. On 4 July 1846, ground was broken in Portland for the Atlantic and St. Lawrence Railroad (later called the "Grand Trunk Railway"). After construction delays and an expenditure of $2,800,000, it finally reached Gorham, New Hampshire, in July 1851. Ultimately connecting with Island Pond, Vermont and Canada, this scenic road enabled a traveler to go from Boston, via Portland, to the mountains in just nine hours, for the reasonable price of $4.50. Such a revolutionary development provided a much needed stimulus to the burgeoning hotel industry.[3]

The advance of the railroads from the south was a much slower process, and, unlike the Atlantic and St. Lawrence line, the southern lines touched but did not initially penetrate the White Mountains. Although the Boston to Concord route was developed quite early (there were several possible connections by the 1840s), stagecoach lines to points north (Center Harbor, Plymouth, Conway, North Woodstock, Franconia, Littleton, etc.) remained active until after 1844. At that time the Northern Railroad and the Boston, Concord and Montreal Railroad (B., C. & M.) were chartered to extend routes into northern New Hampshire. The completion of the Northern in 1848 created a second means of one-day travel to the mountains. The new track between Concord and White River Junction, Vermont, connected with the Connecticut and Passumpsic Rivers Railroad to Wells River, Vermont, where travelers could then take a stagecoach to the heart of the region. In 1853 the B. C. & M., rival of the Northern, created a third, more direct all-rail route to the mountains. This route ran northward through Laconia and Plymouth to Woodsville, New Hampshire. By 1858 the company had leased the White Mountains Railroad (purchase followed in 1873), which extended the line through to Littleton.[4]

A direct product of the construction of the B., C. & M. was the establishment of the Lake Winnipesaukee route to the mountain region. From The Weirs, a station stop on the lake just beyond Laconia, passengers could continue their trip via Center Harbor by steamboat. The famed "Lady of the Lake," built in 1849, was the first steamboat to take passengers to meet stagecoaches for the final leg of their journey on to Conway and the mountains. In 1851, the establishment of the Cocheco Railroad (later the Dover and the Winnipiseogee) between Dover and Alton Bay allowed for the development of a route that ran thirty miles across the lake to Wolfeboro and then on to Center Harbor and points north. Travelers preferring an all-land alternative to the Winnipesaukee route could travel on the B., C. & M. to Plymouth and then take a stage on through Franconia Notch to the northern towns, or over to the Crawford Notch area.[5]

The extensive transportation network that developed between New York and New England during the 1840s and 1850s supported these various routes to the White Mountains. Perhaps the most popular routes north from New York were those combining water and rail transit—the three major companies conducting such business were the Fall River Line, the Norwich Line and the Stonington Line. Also competing for the tourist trade were the all-rail routes, such as the New York and New Haven Railroad, which linked with the New York, Hartford and Springfield Railroad. Passengers could either travel east from Springfield to Worcester and Boston, and then make connections for the north, or they could travel on a series of small railroads directly up the Connecticut River Valley to White River Junction and the mountains. Travelers could also leave from the tourist mecca of Saratoga Springs on a much slower and less direct two-day journey to the White Mountains that included trains, a steamboat ride across Lake Champlain and stagecoaches.[6]

By 1860 the three major rail routes to the White Mountains, their offshoots and other travel options were in place. Although greatly augmented because of consolidations (with some resulting name changes) these first routes were to remain much the same into the twentieth century. These extensive railroad lines put the White Mountains literally at the back door of Boston, New York and the other major cities of the Northeast. In addition, the railroad development encouraged travel from many other areas of North America and Europe, while bringing people to the mountains from greater distances and in greater numbers than had ever been imagined by the early highway innkeepers. During the decade before the Civil War, the bond between the railroads and the hotels was strongly forged—the railroads needed the tourist industry to generate business, while the hotels needed the railroads to transport visitors, supplies, luxury items and the mail to the mountains. The near-perfect balance and dynamism created by this symbiotic relationship resulted in pressure for the construction of more and larger hotels. At the same time, new forms of architecture as well as social

Fig. 2-2. "Mount Madison House, Gorham, New Hampshire," *advertisement with photograph from* Among the Clouds *34, No. 3 (12 July 1912), p. 5. Author's Collection. In 1907 the second Alpine House was moved across Gorham Common and became part of the Mount Madison House.*

and recreational alternatives needed to be created in order to successfully meet the demands imposed by the rapidly mushrooming White Mountain tourist trade.[7] The expansion of the railroads after 1848 and the resulting proliferation of hotels brought the region into "a predominant and enviable position among the nation's resorts."[8]

The First Rail Hotels at Gorham

With the arrival of the Atlantic and St. Lawrence Railroad in 1851, the previously small and sleepy Androscoggin Valley town of Gorham became the first White Mountain rail terminus and was transformed into an important tourist center for the entire region. Immediately the railroad company contributed to Gorham's economic awakening by constructing the $20,000 White Mountain Station House in the same year (see Plate 3).[9] Serving the dual purpose of hotel and railroad station, like the Pemigewasset House in Plymouth, this imposing three-story wooden block with a large rear ell was 100 feet in length by 50 feet in depth (the ell had roughly the same dimensions). It possessed a respectable 165 rooms and a guest capacity of 250. Beckett's *Guide Book of Atlantic and St. Lawrence* (1853) described the interior of the stately edifice as having "broad and lofty halls, and ample parlors, sitting and withdrawing rooms, fitted and furnished with corresponding elegance—a noble dining room, eighty feet by thirty, and sleeping rooms...."[10] Situated in an advantageous spot on the town common (facing Railroad Street between Park and Glen streets), on the site of the current tennis courts, the hotel could boast only limited mountain views from its broad front and side piazzas.

Fig. 2-3. "Gorham House, Gorham, N. H.," *stereo view, c. 1865, Kilburn # 2975. Douglas Philbrook, Gorham, NH. This modest town center hotel was spawned by the coming of the railroad to Gorham, and for a time, was run jointly with the Alpine House.*

Fortunately, from the research of local historian Nathaniel T. True, much is known about the origins and early history of the White Mountain Station House. In an 1882 article, one of a series written for the Gorham newspaper, *The Mountaineer*, True identified the chief contractor (and presumably the designer) as Captain Edward Merrill of nearby Bethel, Maine.[11] The railroad company hired Ezra Beal of Norway, Maine, as "master builder and finisher of the house" (Beal is also credited with the building of the U. S. Hotel and the Falmouth House in Portland).[12] Opened in July, 1851, the hotel was run for two years by N. C. Woodward and Mrs. S. A. (Margaret) Hayes, until Colonel John R. Hitchcock, later to manage the Summit and Tip-Top houses on Mount Washington, assumed a twenty-year proprietorship. Hitchcock renamed this finely detailed Italian Revival structure "Alpine House" and ran it until the building succumbed to fire on 21 October 1872.[13]

In 1875-76 the managers of the railroad, now owned by the Grand Trunk, replaced the first Alpine with a smaller hostelry on the same site and under the same name.[14] The second Alpine House accommodated 75 to 100 guests and featured the same T-shaped floor plan, but had an additional story in the main front section (Fig. 2-1). The rear ell section was considerably shorter than that of the older building and was two-and-one-half as opposed to three stories tall. The new structure lacked the marvelous Italian Revival eaves brackets, corner pilasters, and square, paneled piazza columns of the first Alpine, but the same stylistic spirit, augmented by traces of the Gothic Revival, was expressed in comparable, though more subdued design elements. Particularly noteworthy were the closed gable dormers in the ell, the delicate, canopied balconies at each front and side-wall floor level, and the seemingly fragile balustrades and support columns of the front and side piazzas. Clearly, in both buildings every effort was made to offer the latest style embellishment in a manner that contrasted sharply with the plain White

Mountain area highway inns and hotels of the 1830s and 1840s.

Weston F. and Charles R. Milliken (also proprietors of the first Glen House) and Guilford D. Stratton, successfully operated the second Alpine House for thirty years, until 1905 when declining profits forced its closure. At the beginning of the next year the Grand Trunk sold the property to Charles W. Gray, the owner/manager of Gray's Inn in Jackson (see Chapter 5), who kept it open through the summer season, selling it to Charles A. Chandler of Gorham in 1907. Chandler promptly detached and moved the front portion of the building across Gorham Common to the north side of Main Street. There he appended it, as a new east wing, to his Mount Madison House, which had been operating on the site since c. 1870. Despite its relocation, which afforded mountain vistas far superior to those of the old site, the Alpine remained essentially unchanged on the exterior, with interior space rearrangements only on the first floor. The new Mount Madison House, with its over 300 feet of piazzas, was operated as a hotel until after World War II; it then served as a school until it was demolished around 1967 (Fig. 2-2).[15]

Like the original White Mountain Station House and its successor hotel, the Gorham House was also the direct result of the coming of the railroad. Erected in 1853 by local merchant Hazen Evans, this modest yet significant building, remarkably little changed from its original appearance, still stands on Main Street opposite Exchange Street in the center of Gorham (Fig. 2-3). Over the years and a succession of owners, the hotel experienced some structural modifications, including the addition of stores in the lower story, a large public meeting hall above and an ell off the east wing. A rambling, nicely proportioned structure with pleasant Greek Revival-inspired decorative details, the Gorham House closely resembled many of the older White Mountain village inns that were more domestic than commercial in form. While it was less an architectural precursor to the grand hotels than the two Alpine Houses, it contributed to the conditioning of the area's economy and psyche for the remarkable hotel expansion that was soon to come.[16]

The First Glen House, Joseph M. Thompson, and Charles R. Milliken

The opening of the Atlantic and St. Lawrence Railroad to Gorham and increased trade, particularly in the hotel industry, stimulated the economy for miles around. As a result, better transportation links with towns to the south were needed and these lead to the establishment in 1851 of a stage line to Conway through Pinkham Notch on the east side of Mount Washington. The presence of this line, Gorham's improved fortunes, and growing tourist interest in the mountains combined to provide the stimulus for the construction of a major hotel in Green's Grant at the "Glen."[17] Located eight miles south of Gorham at an open clearing over 1,600 feet above sea level, this spectacular site revealed the scenic beauty of the upper Peabody River Valley and offered unsurpassed views of Mount Washington and the Northern Presidential Range. These and other natural attractions, such as Tuckerman's Ravine, the Emerald and Garnet pools, Crystal Cascade, and Glen Ellis Falls made the Glen an ideal place for hotel development.

A wonderfully entertaining, unsophisticated verse by Franklin Leavitt, the well-known mountain guide and mapmaker from Lancaster, provides a highly suitable introduction to a discussion of the first Glen House, the earliest of the White Mountain grand resort hotels:

Eighteen hundred and fifty-one
  The Glen House was begun,
They worked upon it 'til they got it done,
  'Tis the nearest house to Mount Washington.
Thompson built it and named it Glen.
  And it is kept now by a man named Milliken.
    FRANKLIN LEAVITT (1885)[18]

The first Glen House originated with Bellows' Farm House, a small inn opened in 1850 by Exeter land speculator John Bellows who made additions to an old dwelling previously on the property. During 1851, Bellows took in some guests, but he then sold

Fig. 2-4. The First Glen House, Pinkham Notch, NH, *photograph, c. 1870, photographer unknown. Douglas Philbrook, Gorham, NH. Erected in c. 1850 and greatly enlarged over the next twenty years, this structure was one of the earliest grand resort hotels in the mountains.*

the inn, along with 700 acres of land, the following spring to Joseph M. Thompson, a native of nearby Shelburne and former Portland hotel-man, for the impressive sum of $11,000. Renaming the inn "Glen House," Thompson completed an unfinished ell and opened between twenty to thirty rooms of his new hostelry to the public for the 1852 season. That summer's tourist patronage proved to be so steady that as soon as he closed the hotel in the fall, Thompson built what was then known as "the old front, 120 feet in length by 44 in width and three stories in height."[19] It was ready for the 1853 season.

Features of the enlarged building and its magnificent surroundings are described in early editions of Eastman's *White Mountain Guide Book*:

> There is a grand portico to the principal entrance. Over this is a balcony upon which the second story windows open, from which may be had an uninterrupted view of the five highest mountains in New England. From this balcony, also, the guests of the hotel can watch with a glass the progress of the horseback parties ascending or descending the rugged ledges of Mount Washington. The dining room is a noble hall calculated to seat two hundred persons, and the withdrawing rooms . . . are spacious, airy, and exceedingly pleasant.[20]

A long piazza extended across the front and around each end, in which there were doors opening outside from a hallway running the full length of the structure.[21] Confirming this description are early stereo and cabinet views that corroborate many of the same Greek and Italian Revival stylistic details present in the hotels of Gorham and at other regional hostelries of the same period (Fig. 2-4).

Encouraged by consistently good profits and the opening of the Mount Washington Carriage Road from the Glen to the summit in 1861, Thompson committed his resources to further expansion in 1865-66 and doubled the hotel's size. In doing so, he moved his mountain establishment one step closer to the status of a grand resort hotel. Again, Eastman's *Guide* offers a valuable account of this momentous undertaking:

> The Glen House has been enlarged this past season, so that it is now one of the largest and grandest hotels of the White Mountain region. In fact, a new hotel . . . has been built and attached to the old house. The office and receiv-

ing hall [and dining room] occupy a spacious apartment between the old and the new. The parlor is a magnificent room, 100 by 50 feet, elegantly furnished. The dining room is a fine hall [of identical dimensions] in which all the 600 guests, which the hotel will now easily accommodate, may dine at once....[22]

Set into the hillside on the north end of the old building, the addition, with the exception of its two-level piazza, was nearly identical to the 1852-53 portion in size, form, floor plan, roof configuration and window placement. With approximately 200 rooms, a parlor claimed to be the largest in the United States, and an imposing front measuring 414 feet,[23] the enlarged, white, wood-framed Glen House quickly gained a reputation as the eastern White Mountains' most impressive and comprehensive resort hotel complex.

After Joseph Thompson's untimely drowning in the Peabody River freshet in October 1869, the hotel was run by his son-in-law, Stephen Cummings, for a year and then sold by heirs to Weston F. and Charles R. Milliken in 1871. It passed to the sole control of Charles Milliken in 1874.[24] Under Milliken's direction, the Glen House became a bona fide grand resort hotel, with all the desired amenities provided within and proximate to its commodious physical plant. Early stereo views of the gas-lit dining room and the sumptuous drawing room show the discreetly ornate quality of the interior architectural detail and furnishings (Figs. 2-5 and 2-6). Guidebook advertisements describe the elaborate social, cultural and recreational opportunities made available to guests, most of which were not offered by the earlier highway and village inns and other early hotels. Milliken's Glen House featured lavish meals, dancing, and musical and dramatic performances amongst its social and cultural amenities. Recreational offerings included carriage rides to local natural attractions, wagon rides up to the top of Mount Washington, fishing, hiking, horseback riding, lawn tennis, croquet, bowling and billiards.[25]

These advertisements and illustrations, similar to the image adorning the sheet music "Glen House Galop" (1868), reveal the almost Alpine village quality of the Glen, with the hotel, stables, barns and other outbuildings surrounded by timber lands, orchards and fields for horses and other livestock and

Fig. 2-5. "Dining Hall, Glen House, N. H.," *stereo view, c. 1870, "American Views" series, John P. Soule, Boston, #499. Author's Collection. Reputed to be one of the largest in New England, the dining hall could accommodate 600 people at one meal sitting.*

Fig. 2-6. "Glen House Drawing Room," *stereo view, c. 1870, Kilburn #39. Author's Collection. This view shows one corner of the 100-by-50 foot parlor, claimed to be the largest hotel room of its kind in the United States at the time.*

Fig. 2-7. "Glen House Galop" *sheet music cover, lithograph, 1868, by G. D. Russell & Company, Boston. Author's Collection. The scene of the first Glen House and outbuildings suggests an almost Alpine village quality of what was virtually a self-sufficient community.*

crops (Fig. 2-7).[26] Also present in the complex were a printing office, harness shop, carriage shop, blacksmith shop, library, and great kitchen and laundry. As with many of the grand hotels that would follow, the first Glen House with its adjacent farm was a nearly self-sufficient economic unit—a vibrant community of 500 to 600 people when at full capacity. In a short time it had progressed from "a country tavern to a first-class hotel,"[27] and when it was lost to fire at the end of the 1884 season the event was greatly regretted by former clientele and the entire White Mountain hotel industry. Milliken, however, vowed to build again at the same location, and history would not deny him (see Chapter 7).[28]

The Crawford House

Up the Notch to Crawford's we ride.
Over Frankenstein Trestle by Willey Slide.
Through the Gateway the train will go.
Crawford House is quite a show.
The columns out front are very large,
and a man named Merrill is in charge.
BY THE AUTHOR, *with deep respect for the talents of* FRANKLIN LEAVITT (1991)

On the west side of Mount Washington and the Presidential Range additional hotel development and expansion, similar to that of the Glen, were also occurring. These would build on the earlier successes of the Mount Washington House, which burned in 1853, and Thomas J. Crawford's Notch House, located just above the Gateway to Crawford Notch (see Chapter 1). In 1850 Crawford made a major business commitment that proved ill-fated. Instead of expanding the Notch House, he plunged into the construction of a new and much larger hotel on flat ground across from the Notch road northwest of Saco Lake.[29] Thus at the watershed between the Saco and Ammonoosuc rivers began the creation of the first Crawford House, which, alas, remained under Crawford's ownership for only a short time. Overextended, Crawford was forced to sell the unfinished structure and all his real estate holdings near the Notch (including the Notch House), and on 9 October 1850, he and his wife, Mary, transferred all their land and buildings to businessman Ebenezer Eastman of Littleton for $8,000.[30] Soon thereafter Major Joseph L. Gibb (see Chapter 1) became the hotel's first manager. The Grafton and Coos County histories mention Eastman (Cyrus), Tilton (Frank) & Co. of Littleton, in association with E. J. M. Hale and James H. Carleton of Haverhill, Massachusetts, as hotel owners in 1852. Instead of purchasing the hotel from Crawford, as these sources indicate, they apparently bought it from Ebenezer Eastman before his death in 1853.[31] It is Gibb's name, however, that is most often associated with the early history of the Crawford House. In the fall of 1858, Charles Hartshorn and William H. Witt assumed the management of the hotel under lease arrangement, only to lose it to a disastrous fire just a few months later on 3 April 1859.[32]

Small engraved views, the earliest a corner detail on Franklin Leavitt's 1852 "Map of the White Mountains, N. H.," offer a good general impression of the first Crawford House. Facing south toward the Notch, it was initially T-shaped in plan, with a central, three-and-a-half-story pavilion with a fine Greek Revival portico. Identical five-bay, two-and-a-half-story wings were topped by pitched roofs with

Fig. 2-8. "Crawford House. At the Notch of the White Mountains. New-Hampshire.," *woodblock engraving, billhead detail, c. 1861. Author's Collection. Erected in 1850-51, the first Crawford House received additions to its east and west wings in 1852-53 but burned in 1859.*

Fig. 2-9. "Crawford House, White Mountains, N. H.," *c. 1853 advertising cut, source unknown. New Hampshire Historical Society. In this nicely conceived engraving, the first Crawford House is depicted with a new west wing that, so far as is known, was never constructed.*

dormer windows. The supplement (June 1853) to Tripp's 1852 *White Mountain Guide Book* informs us, though, of the need for more "sufficient accommodations," and that "the enterprising landlord of the Crawford House, Maj. Gibb, has extended the wings of his house."[33] An illustrated advertisement appeared in the same guide as well as in other guides, maps and hotel letterheads and billheads (Fig. 2-8).[34] In this view the wings have each been enlarged to eight bays; at least one wing, comparable in size to the front wings, was added to the east side rear of the central pavilion. Together the wings provided some 200 sleeping rooms, as touted in the advertisements. Clearly then, as the dating of the publicity indicates, this growth must have taken place in 1852-53.

It is possible that the owners contemplated and even planned for additional expansion later during the 1850s because of the existence of an unidentified, yet beautifully rendered, engraved advertisement view (Fig. 2-9).[35] However, there is no documentary evidence to affirm that such a building project was realized. The thought and energy behind such an ambitious scheme demonstrates the optimistic and resourceful entrepreneurship of the early White Mountain hotel developers as they persevered in satisfying the rapidly growing tourist market.

It would be difficult to find better evidence of this spirit than in the response to the burning of the first Crawford House. Within two days of the fire, Cyrus Eastman and his partners were laying plans for the prompt replacement of the hotel. What ensued was a construction effort that must stand as one of the most impressive building feats in American hotel history. In just under two weeks, Eastman completed the rough overland move of the necessary lumber from Littleton, over twenty miles away, and amassed on-site a work force of 175 men and 75 oxen and horses.[36] An old sawmill nearby was reactivated to prepare the framing members and finishing wood for the structure. With rough plans prepared by East-

Fig. 2-10. "Crawford House," Crawford Notch, NH, *stereo view, c. 1865, "American Scenery, White Mountains," unidentified photographer. Author's Collection. The largest hotel in the White Mountains at the time of its completion in 1859, the second Crawford House was built in the amazingly short period of just over two months.*

man (a heretofore unidentified architect was sent the plans for modification, or "arrangement"), work proceeded at a feverish pace in order to honor Eastman's pledge that the "new house [would be] ready to receive guests in sixty days, with a three day's grace." With his master builder, Charles Richardson,[37] Eastman was "everywhere present, superintended everything, averted disaster and prevented delays, and opened the new Crawford House to travelers July 13, 1859, when 40 received dinner, and 100 were entertained for the night."[38]

At the time of its whirlwind completion the second Crawford House was noted in the press as being "the most spacious hotel about the mountains" (Fig. 2-10).[39] With a front elevation width of about 200 feet, the building had a nearly square E-shaped floor plan with a two-and-a-half-story center section flanked by two-and-a-half-story wings each possessing ell frontages of 200 feet.[40] Eastman's 1859 *White Mountain Guide Book* provides additional details about the layout, amenities, and general flavor of the establishment:

> The Crawford House is a large and new edifice, very commodious and agreeable for a summer hotel. There are pleasant piazzas on the outside, and five halls, much used in the evening for promenading, run the entire length of the house within. The parlor is large and well furnished, the dining room ample in its proportion, and its tables always supplied with the delicacies of the metropolitan markets, as well as such substantial articles of mountain production, as delicious berries, and the richest milk and cream. The office is situated in the central part of the house.... Here also is the post office of this wild region. Portraits of two of the Crawfords, patriarchs of these mountains, adorn the wall. The lodging rooms of the house are well furnished, and pleasant, especially those which have windows toward the Notch. Connected with the hotel are a bowling-alley for rainy-day and evening amusement, and extensive stables, furnished with a large number of horses.... Last summer two tame bears ... afforded guests much amusement.[41]

The structure, while stark and awkward in scale, did come to acquire a certain aesthetic charm, with slight suggestions of the Gothic Revival in its narrow mul-

Fig. 2-11. "Crawford House Parlor," Crawford Notch, NH, *stereo view, c. 1865, Kilburn # 1779. Author's Collection. Gas-lit public rooms such as this one featured mass-produced Victorian eclectic furniture and fine decorated wool carpeting.*

lioned windows and later steep pitched-roof dormers, as well as traces of the Colonial Revival in its Doric posts and corner pilasters, boxed cornices, balustrades and white painted exterior. Its public interior spaces and many of its bedrooms boasted mass-produced but noteworthy Victorian eclectic wooden furniture, much of it used well into this century (Fig. 2-11).

In 1870, after a dozen years of ownership, the Littleton group sold the Crawford House property to Asa T. Barron. Barron then went into partnership with C. H. Merrill and his brother Oscar F. Barron, forming the operating company "Barron, Merrill, and Barron" that would administer the Crawford complex from 1872 to 1908. Under their proprietorship, the complex grew to cover over an acre of land and to accommodate up to 400 guests.[42] In 1875, the opening of the Portland and Ogdensburg Railroad through the Notch brought a new, greater influx of tourists to the area. A panoramic engraved view from an 1880 guidebook[43] shows the long two-and-a-half-story bedroom wing that was appended to the original west wing in c. 1876 to meet the needs of these new tourists (Fig. 2-12).[44] For the 1879 season they built a new kitchen, expanded the dining room and converted the attic space into sleeping rooms by adding dormers.[45] Expansion continued in 1881 with the further conversion of attic space into bedrooms and in 1883 with the addition of a northwest piazza.[46] Newspapers such as *Among the Clouds* and the *White Mountain Echo* reported on these improvements as well as interior renovation and redecoration

Fig. 2-12. "The Crawford House, White Mountains." *advertisement engraving from Thursty McQuill,* From New York to the Summer Resorts of New England . . . *(1880), p. 44. Author's Collection. Advertising cuts such as this are often the best pictorial sources for the White Mountain hotels.*

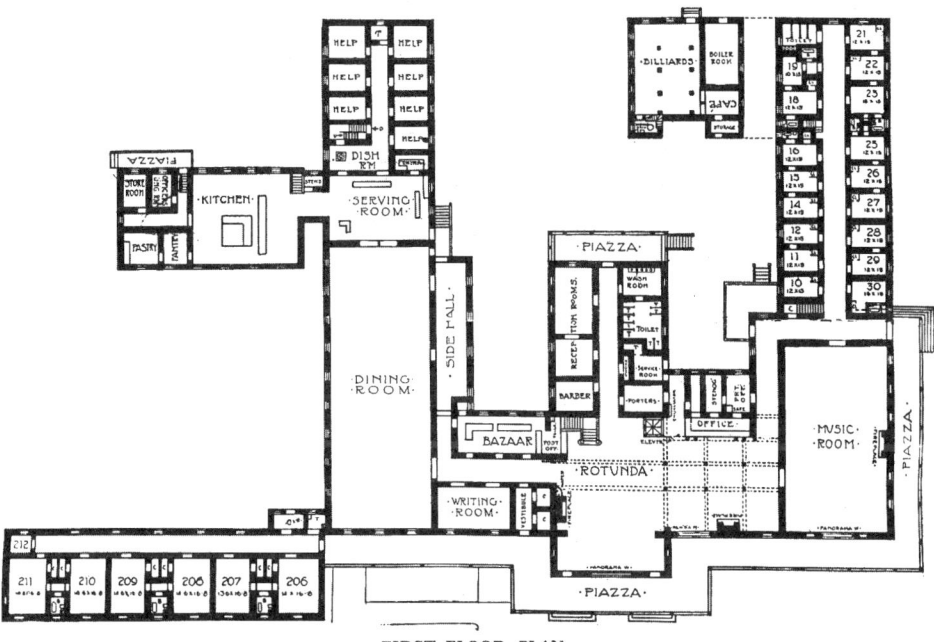

Fig. 2-13. First Floor Plan, Crawford House, Crawford Notch, NH, *c. 1930. Barron Company Collection, New Hampshire Historical Society. One of a series of floor diagrams made for the hotel, this rendering shows that few changes were made to the Crawford House during the twentieth century.*

projects. Such projects reflect the owners' interest in maintaining the hotel in the best possible condition, while decorating the interior in the most fashionable manner. A 1930s plan, showing a layout of the first floor similar to that of a half century before, indicates that the hotel remained essentially in this form until the modern era (Fig. 2-13).

The second Crawford House, ultimately one of America's most historic grand resort hotels, remained open for 116 years until it no longer became financially feasible to operate (Figs. 2-14 and 2-15). Despite the efforts of several organizations and private individuals to save the hotel, it closed in October 1975. At a spectacular, highly emotional four-day

Fig. 2-14. Crawford House, Crawford Notch, NH, *photograph, c. 1960. Richard Hamilton, Littleton, NH, from the* Littleton Courier. *At the peak of its popularity this hotel was regarded as one of America's finest and most historic grand hotels, in operation for 116 years until it burned in 1977.*

Fig. 2-15. Dining Room, Crawford House, Crawford Notch, NH, *photograph, c. 1960. Richard Hamilton, Littleton, NH, from the* Littleton Courier. *A close inspection of this spacious, unbroken space will reveal at each place setting the special commemorative plate issued to mark the 100th anniversary of the second Crawford House in 1959.*

auction in July 1976 the contents of the hotel, including fixtures and architectural fragments, were sold. For a time the hotel, stripped of virtually everything of value, sat silently, a hollow shell of a building surrounded by the stunning landscape of the bowl formed by the Gateway of the Notch, the Southern Presidential Range, and mounts Field, Avalon and Tom.[47] Over a year later, on 20 November 1977, a fire of undetermined origin destroyed the vacant and desolate 165-room hotel. The twenty-seven acre tract on which it had stood passed to the Appalachian Mountain Club in 1979 for guardianship and recreational use.[48] An important early example of the grand hotel building type and an attraction to thousands, including American presidents, professional leaders and captains of industry, the Crawford House had continued and left a significant historical legacy that merits more extensive examination and analysis in decades to come.

The Early Mount Washington Summit Buildings

The construction and enlargement of the inns and hotels in the Pinkham and Crawford Notch areas during the 1850s resulted in increased determination by tourists to reach the summit of Mount Washington.[49] New walking paths and plans for a carriage road created a need for overnight accommodations on the summit more elaborate and civilized than the "three stone cabins" Ethan Allen Crawford had erected there in 1823.[50] Although the resulting buildings had no direct design relationship to the White Mountain grand resort hotels, they still merit attention. The resulting Mount Washington hostelries served as guest annexes to the great hotels, and their tourist appeal aided the development of the hotel industry throughout the region.

In 1852-53 Lucius M. Rosebrook and Joseph S. Hall of Lancaster, and Nathan R. Perkins of Jefferson built the first "hotel" on Mount Washington's summit at an elevation of 6,280 feet. Immediately dubbed the "Summit House," this rude, but substantial one-story structure, constructed in two stages, was sixty-four feet long, twenty-four feet wide, and had outer blasted stone walls eight-feet high and four-feet thick (Fig. 2-16). To prevent its demolition by high winds, the building was literally bound to the rock summit by four two-inch wire cables that extended over the roof and were attached to iron rods cemented into the ledge on each side. Inside the building was a stove, a dining table for thirty to forty guests, a small kitchen and a row of beds separated from each other by curtains. The roof, initially quite flat, consisted of wooden members brought up from the Glen at the base of the mountain on the backs of men and horses. In 1853, new part-owner Nathaniel Noyes, a restaurant manager from Boston, replaced this roof with a pitched one, which gave the building a second attic story for sleeping rooms. With the completion of the Tip-Top House, the Summit House was devoted solely to lodging rooms. It was torn down in the spring of 1884 when a wooden dormitory for the staff of the second Summit House (1872-73) was built on the site (see Chapter 4).[51]

In the same year that the first Summit House was completed, rival firm Samuel F. Spaulding & Co. financed and built the Tip-Top House, also on the top of Mount Washington. Samuel Spaulding served as chief contractor and orchestrated the moving of all the building materials up the mountain except the stone, of which there was clearly no real shortage. With massive six-foot walls of rough boulders similar to those of the Summit House, Tip-Top measured twenty-eight by eighty-four feet. It was at first protected by a low-pitched almost deck roof, held down by iron rods and bolts, upon which visitors could

Fig. 2-16. "Top of Mt. Washington 6285 Feet Above the Level of the Sea," *frontispiece engraving from John H. Spaulding,* Historical Relics of the White Mountains *(1855). Author's Collection. Tip-Top House, built in 1852-53, is at the left of the scene, topped by an American flag. The first Summit House is to the right with the true summit of Mount Washington, and its observation tower, between them.*

Fig. 2-17. "Tip-Top House, Mount Washington, N. H.," *stereo view, c. 1860, Kilburn #153. Author's Collection. Built in 1853, Tip-Top originally had a nearly flat roof, but was equipped with the pitched roof and attic story shown here in the 1860's.*

stand to enjoy unobstructed mountain views in good weather. In 1861-62, lessee John R. Hitchcock commenced a series of alterations, arranging for the construction of a new wooden pitched roof with skylights that provided additional sleeping quarters in the attic story (Fig. 2-17).

Between 1877 and 1884 the Tip-Top House served as the founding office of *Among the Clouds,* the first summer daily newspaper to be printed on a mountain summit. Subsequently, the versatile little structure lay unused and neglected, despite many public pleas in the press to restore it. On 8 June 1908, a disastrous fire leveled every building on the summit except the Tip-Top House. This catastrophe drew renewed attention to the building, and it was soon repaired and reopened as an overnight lodging house and cafe—an annex to the new Summit House. Just eight days after opening to the public, on 29 August 1915, fire again struck the wooden interior and roof leaving only the outer walls standing and its historic sign, saved by a Summit House employee.

The following year the Mount Washington Railway hired famed hotel builder Sylvanus D. Morgan of Lisbon as contracting supervisor to rebuild the Tip-Top as it had first appeared in the 1860s. The restored building had a rearranged, modern interior and a stone passageway with a woodframe roof connecting it to the Summit House. But for a few minor modifications such as extended roof dormers, the building remained in this condition until it was restored as a museum in 1980 by the State of New Hampshire White Mountain Commission; it was placed on the National Register of Historic Places in 1982.[52] The Tip-Top House served a variety of functions over the years as an eating establishment, small hotel, Summit House annex, late-season facility, hiker dormitory, hotel employee dormitory, observatory, workshop, laboratory, storage building, contractor's office and *Among the Clouds* headquarters. Legend and romance have always been associated with this remarkable structure. Approaching its 150th anniversary, it stands as a symbol of survival in a harsh environment, mountain hospitality, idealized outdoor recreation, scientific endeavor, the economic success of tourism, and concern for the natural environment.[53]

Hotels at Town Centers

In addition to the hotel development in Gorham, on Mount Washington, and in the adjacent notches during the 1850s, other neighboring White Mountain towns also witnessed the growth of the hotel industry. Each of these communities could be reached directly by the railroad or by easy stage connections from nearby railheads. Most notable of these was North Conway, on the east side of the mountains, where several small hotels had already originated (see Chapter 1). In the 1850s two more hostelries went into business. The earliest of these was the Kearsarge Tavern, created by Samuel W. Thompson

Fig. 2-18. North Conway House, North Conway, NH, *photograph, 1992, by the author. Relocated to Pine Street, east of Main Street, some years ago, this former hotel building was an important forerunner to the later grand resort hotels.*

around 1840 when he enlarged his farmhouse to accommodate thirty to forty guests. This tavern became famous as a haven for landscape artists such as John F. Kensett and Benjamin Champney.[54] The Kearsarge House, a grand hotel, replaced this modest establishment in the 1860s (see Chapter 3). The North Conway House also began as a small farmhouse. Opened in 1858 by Nathaniel R. Mason at the corner of Main and Mechanic Streets, it soon expanded into a hotel accommodating 100 guests (Fig. 2-18).[55] This substantial wooden building was three-and-a-half-stories with a pitched roof. Like the earlier highway inns, it possessed a rectangular box-like form making it a logical forerunner to the later grand hotels.

In Conway, a few miles to the south, Samuel Thom and partners Hiram C. and Nathaniel Abbott built the 100-room Conway House in 1850-51 (Fig. 2-19). Perhaps the most stylistically interesting of the early White Mountain region village or town hotels, the hotel was adorned with many handsome Greek Revival motifs. A magnificently proportioned double portico with Doric square and round columns on its south-facing front created an unusually distinguished entrance. Other noteworthy Greek Revival features included flat Doric corner and wall pilasters beneath a wide, plain entablature, heavily molded pavilion and dormer gables, and a long veranda supported by Doric square columns. Not surprisingly, considering the sophistication of the design, newspaper sources disclosed that the hotel was planned by architects, apparently from Portland, but their names remain unidentified. The same sources suggested, however, that Charles Hall of Portland acted as fore-

Fig. 2-19. Conway House, Conway, NH, *photograph from* Morris' Scenic Guide . . . Great Summer Resorts . . . *(1901-02). Author's Collection. Planned by unknown Portland architects and erected in 1850-51, Conway House was one of the finest Greek Revival commercial buildings in northern New Hampshire.*

man of the construction, and that the frame was fabricated and raised by one Jacob Berry of unknown origins.[56] Centrally situated at the focal point of transportation systems, the Conway House attracted over the years many notable visitors who were able to enjoy its pleasant surroundings, fine food, natural springwater, and recreational opportunities. By the turn of the century, the establishment had begun to lose business to the larger hotels in the north as the railroads and automobiles allowed people easier and quicker access to the center of the mountain district.[57] The building burned to the ground on 7 April 1912, leaving a "gruesome sight" in the middle of town were it had stood; to this day a portion of the site is still vacant.

To the north of Conway, the serene village of Jackson took longer to emerge as a significant summer resort, but when it did, it became a major center (two of its nineteenth-century hotels are still in operation).[58] With the 1858 opening of the Jackson Falls House, the town entered the hotel business (Fig. 2-20). Joseph B. Trickey erected the building, and his family managed the business continuously for over ninety years. Like the Conway House, this long, rectangular, two-and-a-half-story structure was a clear precursor to the grand hotels. In 1885-86 it was jacked up off the ground so that a new first story could be inserted underneath, raising the capacity to 100 guests; its planar front elevation then resembled that of the first Pemigewasset House (see Fig. 1-13). The later addition of bay windows, projections for bathrooms and a second-floor porch above the first-floor veranda resulted in a cluttered but still provocative main facade. Devoid of high architectural style, this highly functional, vernacular building was demolished in 1978, and its remnants were burned.[59]

Established as the White Mountain House in 1850, Thayers Hotel (or Inn as it has been more recently titled) has long been an institution in Littleton and is one of the best known early town center hotels in the mountains (Fig. 2-21). The inn is as much domestic as commercial in appearance and, in terms of scale and proportion, bears no direct resemblance to the larger hotels of the 1850s. It does, however, possess certain eclectic mid-Victorian features that were present in these other buildings—most

Fig. 2-20. Jackson Falls House, Jackson, NH, *cabinet photograph by C. P. Hibbard, Lisbon, NH, #236, c. 1886. Douglas Philbrook, Gorham, NH. Constructed in 1857-58, this hotel, Jackson's first, was jacked up off the ground and given a new first story in 1885-86.*

common among these is the Greek Revival front Doric portico. The portico of Thayers Hotel displays fluted columns and corner pilasters, an eaves entablature, closed, heavily molded front-end gable cornices, and ornate pierced balcony balustrades. Thayers also has details that were unusual for regional hotel architecture such as an end gable Gothic Revival window, enormous front balcony scroll consoles, a large Italian Revival octagonal cupola on the roof ridgepole with a concave spire roof, corner pilasters, and round-arch "Siamese twin" windows. The principal landmark on Main Street, this modest Greek temple structure—imbued with classical bilateral symmetry and formalism, and yet Victorian frivolity—was recognized for its architectural excellence by the National Register of Historic Places, which listed it in 1982.[60]

Conceived and financed by Littleton storekeeper Henry L. Thayer in anticipation of the coming of the railroad, Thayers Hotel, unlike many of the other White Mountain hotels of its period, is reasonably well documented. James R. Jackson's *History of Littleton* provides ordinarily rare information about its builders, local carpenters Jonathan Nurs and Andrew Scott.[61] From other sources and physical evidence of the building itself we know that the exterior has been altered very little since it was built. The most pronounced changes occurred around 1885 when the side oriel windows were added, about 1907 when the two connected wings were attached on the east side, and between 1927 and 1947 when under the Eames ownership the wings were enlarged. Able to house up

Fig. 2-21. Thayers Hotel (Inn), Littleton, NH, *photograph, 1991, by the author. Endowed with striking mid-Victorian eclectic style features, this town center hotel has been a locus of social life in Littleton since its opening in 1850.*

to 100 guests, Thayers Hotel has played a vital role in Littleton's social and civic life for almost a century and a half, serving as a popular public house for dinners and receptions, political gatherings and business occasions. It has never lost the "home-like character" first ascribed to it by nineteenth-century promotional pieces and advertisements.[62]

Like Thayers Hotel, the first Lancaster House, situated some twenty miles northeast in the town of Lancaster, was more significant for its stylistic elements than for any precedent-setting architectural form (Fig. 2-22). This richly embellished Italian Revival building was also the product of railroad development into the North Country but with an ironic twist. Erected in 1857-58 by John Lindsey, the first owner and manager, the Lancaster House was financed by a $20,000 settlement paid the town by the Atlantic and St. Lawrence Railroad for failure to honor a previous commitment to lay its track through Lancaster. Thus, instead of fostering hotel development by its presence, the railroad inadvertently achieved the same result through its absence.[63]

Enlarged over time to accommodate 150 guests, the first Lancaster House consisted of a four-square three-story block, with a long ell to the rear. The building had a flat roof with generous overhangs and was crowned by a cubical cupola (itself with a flat roof and tall finial) from which could be seen superb views of the Presidential Range, Stratford Peaks, the Pilot Range and Vermont's Green Mountains. Most outstanding of its Italian Revival decorative details were heavy paired eaves brackets with drop pendants, flat window caps, a front pavilion with arched windows and console-supported balconies, and flanking, delicately fabricated two-story verandas held up by thin clustered columns. When fire destroyed the hotel on 28 September 1878, the White Mountain region lost one of its most important examples of the pure Italian Revival vernacular, but its impact and influence would be evident in the stylistic adornment of other hotel buildings later in the century.[64]

Richard Taft and the First Flume House

On the west side of the White Mountains, Franconia Notch became yet another significant locus of early hotel development. Following the opening of the Lafayette House in 1835, growth in the tourist trade warranted construction of two additional hostelries within just three years of each other. The earliest of these was the first Flume House (Fig. 2-23), erected at the south end of the Notch (today just east of Route 3 opposite to and above the entrance to the Flume Reservation). There is some question in published literature as to when and by whom this hotel was built, but there is strong reason to believe William Kenney and Ira Coffin constructed the building around 1847-48.[65] In 1848 they sold out to Richard A. Taft (1812-

Fig. 2-22. "Lancaster House," Lancaster, NH, *stereo view, c. 1870, Miller & Wilson, Lancaster. Author's Collection. The first Lancaster House, built in 1857-58, was distinguished by its outstanding Italian Revival style form and embellishment.*

1881), originally from Barre, Vermont, who was at the time managing the Washington Hotel in Lowell, Massachusetts. Under his firm name, the "Flume and Franconia Hotel Company," later builders of the Profile House, Taft operated the Flume House from 1849 to 1866 when Colonel Charles H. Greenleaf (1841-1924) became his business partner. In 1871, the hotel burned to the ground, taking with it an associated small white chapel across the road.66

With its rectangular box mass, pitched roof and extensive verandas, the first Flume House must have looked very much like other early regional forerunners to the grand hotels. A few years following its opening, Taft enlarged the hotel, as described in the 1852 edition of Tripp's *White Mountain Guide Book*:

> Since last season [the Flume House] . . . has been entirely remodeled and refurnished. Additions have been made to it, so that it is superior to any among the Mountains, for size. It is two hundred and sixty feet in length, fronting the road; three stories high with a double piazza,—and can accommodate two hundred people. The lower floor is divided into offices, parlors, a dining hall, etc. Parlors and parlors with bedrooms attached occupy the second story. The third flight consists of sleeping compartments exclusively.67

Its large mass, augmented by the presence of a long row of square Doric columns supporting the piazzas on the main east facade and south end, on the first and second story levels, gave the hotel a commanding presence. From these strategically placed protective promenades, the views of Cannon Mountain to the north, the Pemigewasset Valley to the south, and Mount Lafayette and the Franconia Range to the east must have been superlative. The first Flume House also attracted visitors with its proximity to such fascinating natural wonders as the Basin, the Flume, and the Pool. Its placement, therefore, was quite calculated; every effort was made here, as at the other White Mountain hotels of the era, to provide people

Fig. 2-23. "Flume House, Franconia Mountains," *c. 1853 advertising cut, source unknown. New Hampshire Historical Society. Surely the best early view of the first Flume House, this engraving shows the long piazzas and rows of square Doric columns for which the hotel was widely recognized.*

with varied social and recreational options as well as opportunities to intimately relate to nature and immerse themselves in religious contemplation.

The First Profile House

The Profile House is in Franconia Notch,
  And is a good place to stop.
And when you see the Profile you will laugh,
  And the house is kept by Greenleaf & Taft.
FRANKLIN LEAVITT (1885)
Stanza from a poem about Franconia Notch[68]

Fig. 2-24. "Profile House," Franconia Notch, NH, *stereo view, c. 1860, "White Mountain Scenery" series #111, John P. Soule, Boston. Author's Collection. Built in 1852-53, the first Profile House offered guests direct access to the mountain wilderness.*

Spectacularly situated almost 2,000 feet above sea level in a generous bowl formed by Cannon Mountain, Eagle Cliff and Bald Mountain, the first Profile House possessed an ambiance even more conducive to the kinds of programs, activities and experiences possible at the Flume House. In 1852 the Flume and Franconia Hotel Company acquired the Lafayette House and substantial land adjacent to it at the northern end of Franconia Notch (see Chapter 1). Here the partners promptly constructed a new T-shaped 110-room hotel, which they opened the following year under the highly appropriate name of "Profile House" (it being within easy distance of the wonderful craggy visage known today as the "Old Man of the Mountain").[69] In its initial form the building had the barn-like quality of the first Glen House and the White Mountain Station House (Alpine Hotel) in Gorham (Fig. 2-24). The three-and-one-half story hotel was marked by a visually dominant front central pavilion with a portico consisting of four tall square Doric columns topped by a moderately pitched roof with dormers. The presence of the portico, facing south toward Profile Lake, endowed the first Profile House with an almost institutional character in much the same fashion as the first Glen House, both Crawford Houses, Conway House, and Thayers Hotel.

In 1866 Taft, Tyler & Greenleaf commenced a series of expansions that would ultimately give the

Fig. 2-25. "Profile House, Franconia Notch, N. H.," *cabinet photograph, c. 1885, C. P. Hibbard, Lisbon, NH. Richard Hamilton, Littleton, NH. The first Profile House evolved over a thirty-year period, and is illustrated here in its fully mature form.*

Fig. 2-26. "Profile House Drawing Room," *Franconia Notch, NH, stereo view, c. 1875, Kilburn # 58. Author's Collection. Such a fashionable Victorian parlor was expected by the wealthy East Coast clientele that visited the hotel each summer.*

Fig. 2-27. "Dining Room, Profile House, Franconia Notch, N. H.," *cabinet photograph, c. 1885, C. P. Hibbard, Lisbon, NH. Richard Hamilton, Littleton, NH. This expansive room, with its 23-foot-high ceilings, was one of the additions made in 1872 and had a capacity of 500 people.*

building the proportions of a grand hotel.[70] The 1866 edition of Eastman's *White Mountain Guide Book* precisely describes the first of these changes:

> The Profile House has been enlarged the past year by the addition of a new [east] wing, containing a parlor nearly 100 by 50 feet, with fine rooms in the second and third stories; by an addition to the dining room, and by a new kitchen wing and a new landing. The house is now nearly twice the size of the former house, and is excelled by no hotel in the state.[71]

Then in 1872, Taft & Greenleaf, Mr. Tyler having retired from the partnership, proceeded ahead with a second major addition, as announced in the Littleton newspaper, *White Mountain Republic*:

> The new dining room at the Profile House will be 132 feet long by 60 feet wide with 23 feet ... [high], having a capacity for 500 people. This will be the largest dining hall in New England. There is an addition of sixty first-class rooms to be made to the house [matching west wing]; also a large and well arranged billiard hall.[72]

The partners continued the expansion by adding an open octagonal cupola (a trademark of the hotel) in 1880, a fifty-room extension of the ell in 1882, a new piazza in 1893, and front bay window towers with pyramidal roofs around 1903.[73] Stereo and cabinet photographs dating from the mid-1880s and earlier illustrate the sum total of alterations completed to that time, both on the exterior of the complex (Fig. 2-25), as well as the interior, which boasted the sumptuously appointed parlor (Fig. 2-26) and immense dining hall (Fig. 2-27) with their lavish late-Victorian eclectic architectural detailing and furnishings.

The changes made at the Profile House did not exclusively entail building additions and modifications; more often they involved interior decorating or modernizing such as the updating of heating, lighting and mechanical systems. In order to stay competitive with their rivals and continue to attract a large enough clientele, all the hotels in the region regularly devoted portions of their profits to these improvements and aggressively promoted them in guidebook and serial advertising. For instance, an article in *Among the Clouds* describes the preparations for the 1885 season made by the Profile House:

> Great improvements have been made at the Profile House this season. A hard wood floor has been laid in the office, the walls have been tastefully painted and decorated, the ceiling paneled and elegantly papered, the colors all harmonizing and producing an exceedingly pleasing

effect. Turkish rugs and new Wakefield furniture add to the luxury and comfort of the apartment. A fine hard wood floor has been laid in the northern end of the parlor, and that portion of the room is divided off by heavy portieres, to serve as a dancing hall or for theatricals. Besides the ornamental additions, new steam heating apparatus has been put in to heat the rooms in one wing and in the front of the hotel.[74]

Because most of the guests at the Profile House and the other large White Mountain hotels were from affluent social backgrounds, it was expected that the amenities and decor at these establishments would be absolutely nonpareil.

Until the late 1870s the Profile House was accessible only by stage road from North Woodstock to the south and Littleton and other points to the north. In 1878-79, in response to mounting tourist demand, Richard Taft and the parent Franconia and White Mountain Notch Company completed the construction of a short nine-and-a-half-mile, narrow-gauge railroad from Bethlehem Junction, which the Boston, Concord and Montreal had reached in 1872. This line was routed directly to a special station in Franconia Notch directly next to the hotel (Fig. 2-28). Acquired in 1892 by the B., C. & M. (and rebuilt as a standard gauge line in 1897), the Profile and Franconia Notch Railroad, as the little spur was called, opened the expanding Profile House property to even greater development until it became a grand resort community, more extensive in size and scope, but markedly similar to the first Glen House.[75]

From the late 1860s to the end of the century, the resort, with the large hotel structure as its nucleus, evolved into a nearly self-sufficient settlement, which seemed to constitute an almost separate world (Fig. 2-29). Commencing in 1868, the first two of an eventual total of twenty cottages were constructed adjacent to the Profile House, increasing guest capacity to 600 by 1905. These cottages were terraced into the east slope of Cannon Mountain and connected to the

Fig. 2-28. Rear of the first Profile House, Franconia Notch, NH, with the Profile and Franconia Notch Railroad. *Photographer unknown. New Hampshire Historical Society. This c. 1895 scene reveals the spectacular setting of the first Profile House, positioned on a plateau in a bowl formed by the surrounding mountains. A narrow-gauge railroad line routed guests directly to a special station next to the hotel.*

main house, many by enclosed walkways. They were initially rented and then sold to prominent families from eastern cities who occupied them for entire summers, providing the hotel with a permanent clientele. Of varying mid and late-Victorian eclectic styles—one was modeled after George Washington's "Mount Vernon" in Virginia—the cottages were likely built by local contractors, who perhaps employed published design books. It is also conceivable some cottages may have been designed by architects from Boston, New York, Philadelphia or other cities from which their owners originated.[76]

Other outbuildings, some of considerable size and functional importance, added to the village character of the Profile House complex. Supplementing the cottages were the railroad station, the relocated Lafayette House, a boathouse on Echo Lake, other small buildings and a large red stable constructed by Taft. This stable accommodated 350 horses and a fleet of carriages, coaches and mountain wagons used for recreation, guest transit, supplies and other purposes.[77] During the off-season of 1888-89, a nicely scaled Shingle style livery stable joined the group (Fig. 2-30). Planned by the firm of Loring (George F.) and Phipps (Stanford) of Boston and erected under the supervision of S. F. Simpson of Littleton, this interesting structure was one of the few pre-1900 architect-designed outbuildings associated with the White Mountain hotel resorts.[78]

Much like the Glen House and the Crawford House, the Profile House, through its facilities, personnel, and programs, offered a tremendous variety of ways for guests to spend their leisure time and satisfy their divergent interests. In addition to the stables there was a billiard hall, bowling alleys, music room, post office, telegraph office, barber shop and souvenir store. Recreational opportunities in the 1890s included hiking, tennis, badminton, croquet, golf (at a course three miles away), fishing, boating (on Echo and Profile lakes), horseback and wagon riding, and indoor games. Dining at the Profile House, as at so many of the grand hotels, was in itself

Fig. 2-29. First Profile House and Cottages, Franconia Notch, NH, *photograph from* Scenic Gems of the White Mountains *(c. 1904). Author's Collection. The Profile House resort, with the hotel as the centerpiece, constituted an isolated, nearly self-contained village.*

STABLE FOR PROFILE HOUSE, WHITE MOUNTAINS.

Loring & Phipps, Architects, Boston, Mass.

Fig. 2-30. "Stable for Profile House, White Mountains," *plate based on sketch by Loring & Phipps, Architects, Boston.* Inland Architect *(Chicago), September 1890. Avery Architectural and Fine Arts Library, Columbia University, New York, NY. This interesting Shingle Style structure was one of only a few architect-designed outbuildings associated with the White Mountain grand resort hotels.*

a pleasant adventure with vegetables, fruit, meat, milk, flowers and other produce obtained from Profile House Farm a few miles distant from the Notch, other area farms, or from outside suppliers (shipped in by road or rail).[79] The following seemingly hyperbolic claim from a c. 1903 "Profile House and Cottages" brochure may, therefore, be quite truthful:

> The hotel . . . offers all that is desirable in spacious apartments, comfortable furnishings, grand scenery, hygienic conditions, delicious cuisine, fine music, unusual facilities for land and water sports, excellent service and a well-known high class of patronage.[80]

Despite its great popularity and its success as a business venture, the first Profile House was deemed by the owners to be physically deteriorated and outmoded by the turn of the century. A new, modern main edifice, it was determined, would take the place of the venerable structure, so steeped in history and tradition, but worn out by nearly five decades of hard use. After careful study the hotel management and the cottage owners reached the difficult decision to replace the entire hotel structure, but to retain virtually all outbuildings. Accordingly, during the autumn of 1905 the old house, amidst much nostalgia, was torn down. Work immediately began on a new Profile House, which would eclipse the old in size and functional efficiency (see Chapter 7).[81]

The founding editor of *Among the Clouds*, Henry M. Burt, in his 1874 *Guide Through the Connecticut Valley to the White Mountains and the River Saguenay*, gives a moving sense of the visitor's experience at one of the earliest of the grand resort hotels in the White Mountains:

> A welcome sight indeed, is the Profile House to the weary traveler, as it greets his vision at the twilight hour. Fatigued by an all-day's ride, he

leaves the coach and enters this magnificent hotel, surprised at its extent and the strange wildness of the scene around it. Having satisfied the wants of an appetite that had been sharpened by the ride, he strolls down the carriage road, which is overshadowed by the dark walls above. All nature seems hushed in repose, and naught for the sighing of the wind in the tree tops far above disturbs his meditation. How vast and how mighty seem the everlasting mountains, whose summits are lost to him in the darkness of the night! Retracing his steps, he enters the hotel and joins, perhaps, in the merry-making in the parlor, where a gay and bewitching scene presents itself. Merry voices mingle with sweet music, and joy seems unconfined.[82]

With their almost unavoidable interplay of the human and natural worlds, whether at the Glen, Crawford or Profile, the visitors of the 1850s must have enjoyed similar experiences at all these truly grand hotels.

❧ Notes ☙

1. Peter B. Bulkley, "A History of the White Mountain Tourist Industry, 1818-1899" (M.A. Thesis, University of New Hampshire, 1958), p. 18. Bulkley's thesis is the most reliable and best single account of the economic history of White Mountain tourism and of the hotels.
2. *Ibid.*, pp. 19-20.
3. *Ibid.*, pp. 20-21; Kilbourne, *Chronicles*, pp. 220-22.
4. Bulkley, "History," pp. 21-24; Kilbourne, *Chronicles*, pp. 223-24. The Northern Railroad became part of the Boston and Maine Railroad system in 1890. Railroad expansion north of Littleton did not take place until the 1870s. By 1895 virtually all of the White Mountain lines were consolidated under the aegis of the Boston and Maine.
5. Bulkley, "History," pp. 24-25.
6. *Ibid.*, pp. 25-27.
7. *Ibid.*, p. 28; Wallace," A Social History of the White Mountains," in Campbell, et al., *The White Mountains*, p. 28. The railroads responded to the bustling business provided by the hotels by expanding train schedules; building their own, oftentimes quite ornate railroad stations; investing in tourism by erecting hotels; and printing and distributing, for tourist consumption, White Mountains maps, guidebooks and viewbooks illustrating the major hotels and favorite scenic attractions.
8. Bulkley, "History," p. 30.
9. *Coos County Democrat*, 30 July 1851, p. 2.
10. Samuel B. Beckett, *Guidebook of the Atlantic and St. Lawrence, and St. Lawrence and Atlantic Rail Roads including . . . the White Mountains* (Portland, ME: Sanborn & Carter, and H. J. Little & Co., 1853), pp. 63-64; *Tripp's White Mountain Guide Book, or, Guide to the Mountain and Lake Scenery of New-Hampshire*, 4th ed. (Boston: Redding & Company, 1852), pp. 29-30.
11. Nathaniel T. True, "History of Gorham, N. H.," *The Mountaineer* (Gorham), 7 July 1882, p. 1.
12. *Ibid.*, p. 1; Guy Gosselin, "Zadoc and Ezra—Two Journals," *Mount Washington Observatory News Bulletin* 25, No. 2 (Summer 1984), p. 27. With references to Beal's published diary (Don C. Seitz, ed., "Journal of Ezra F. Beal—Diary Kept by a Distinguished Son of Norway," published serially in the Norway (ME) Advertiser, 1926), Gosselin recounts Beal's many associations with the Atlantic and St. Lawrence Railroad—as director, builder of many of its railroad stations, builder of the White Mountain Station House, and possible company engineer for the road from Gorham to the Glen House site (Bellows). The diary contains several references to the Gorham hotel project.
13. True, "History," *The Mountaineer*, 7 July 1882, p. 1; *White Mountain Republic* (Littleton), 24 October 1872, p. 2. It was asserted at the time that the fire was caused by a defective chimney.
14. True, "History," *The Mountaineer*, 7 July 1882, p. 1.
15. *Ibid.*; *The Mountaineer*, 27 September 1905, 31 January 1906, 27 February 1907, 2 October 1907; *ATC* 27, No. 2 (13 July 1903), p. 4; *ATC*, 31, No. 1 (13 July 1907), p. 4. Accommodating 100 guests, the enlarged Mount Madison House originated with the east end, erected as a store and dwelling by B. C. Flanders, and later (c. 1870) added to and opened as the "Eagle Hotel" by Sargent & Jewett. Mr. and Mrs. Charles Chandler acquired the Eagle in 1902, remodeled it, and changed the name to "Mount Madison House." When the second Alpine House was attached to it in 1907 (Webber & Wellman of Augusta, ME, were the movers), a large dining hall served as the physical linkage. In 1946 Mr. and Mrs. Edward Bredeau (Chandler's daughter) sold the complex to the Sisters of the Presentation of Mary, and it was used as a boarding and parochial school (Academie Notre Dame des Monts) until closing in the 1960s (Gorham Historical Society exhibit labels).
16. D. B. Wight, *The Androscoggin River Valley: Gateway to the White Mountains* (Rutland, VT: Charles E. Tuttle Company, 1967), p. 508; True, "History," *The Mountaineer*, 7 July 1882, p.1; Gorham Historical Society exhibit labels. Evans sold the Gorham House to Parris Lathem, who in turn sold it to Walter Buck. After additional transfers, in 1881 it passed to Guilford D. Stratton, who ran it in conjunction with the Alpine House. The creation of stores on the first floor eliminated the

lower portion of a two-story porch under a third-story overhang, but the upper portion remains intact today. The building possesses an incorrect date marker ("1858") under the eaves on its front elevation. The impact of the Greek Revival may be seen in the corner pilasters, eaves molding, plain side wall entablatures and square-paneled porch columns.

17. Bulkley, "History," p. 31.
18. David Tatham, "Franklin Leavitt's White Mountain Verse," *Historical New Hampshire* 33, No. 3 (Fall 1978), p. 227.
19. True, "History," *The Mountaineer*, 7 July 1882, p. 1.
20. *The White Mountain Guide Book*, 1st ed. (1858), pp. 23-24.
21. Beckett, *Guide Book of the Atlantic and St. Lawrence*, p. 82.
22. *The White Mountain Guide Book*, 6th ed. (Concord, NH: Edson C. Eastman, and Boston: Lee & Shepard, 1866), p. 37.
23. True, "History," *The Mountaineer*, 7 July 1882, p. 1.
24. *Ibid.*
25. Advertisement, Hugh J. Chisholm, *Chisholm's White Mountain Guide Book* (Portland, ME: Chisholm Brothers, 1882); advertisement, Lucy Crawford, *The History of the White Mountains, From the First Settlement of the Upper Coos and Pequawket*, 2nd ed. (Portland, ME: Hoyt, Fogg & Donham, 1883), p. 216; advertisement, *WME* 1, No. 10 (14 September 1878), p. 10.
26. *ATC* 4, No. 6 (23 July 1880), p. 4.
27. Charles R. Milliken, *The Glen House Book, White Mountains* (Cambridge, MA: John Wilson and Son, 1889), p. 23.
28. *Ibid.*, pp. 23-24; *Concord (NH) Monitor*, 2 October 1884, p. 1; *White Mountain Republic* (Littleton), 4 October 1884; Wight, *The Androscoggin River Valley*, pp. 294-95. Fanned by a strong wind, a fire on October 1 destroyed the hotel complex and stable in two hours. Nothing survived from the burned buildings other than a few hotel records, and all the horses, cows and carriages. Several barns and other outbuildings escaped the blaze. Originating in the kitchen the fire occurred at 8:00 p.m. on the day the hotel closed for the season. Only a few staff members were present, the last guests having departed that morning. The loss was assessed at $200,000, with one half covered by insurance.
29. Bulkley, "History," pp. 32-33; George E. McAvoy, *And Then There Was One; A History of the Hotels of the Summit and West Side of Mount Washington* (Littleton, NH: The Crawford Press, 1988), p. 26.
30. Agreement between Thomas J. Crawford, of the Notch, and Ebenezer Eastman of Littleton, County of Grafton, State of New Hampshire, 9 October 1850. Mount Washington Observatory Resource Center, North Conway, NH.
31. (Merrill), *History of Coos County*, p. 437; Hamilton Child, *Gazetteer of Grafton County, N. H., 1709-1886* (Syracuse, NY: Syracuse Journal Co., 1886), p. 493. Though unnamed in available sources, Gibb may also have been a member of the owning consortium.
32. McAvoy, *And Then There Was One*, pp. 29-30; *White Mountain Banner* (Littleton), 7 May 1859, p. 3; *People's Journal* (Littleton), 6 May 1859, p. 2. The piece in the *Journal* noted:

The fire is supposed to have originated by sparks from the chimney. The house was owned principally by E. J. M. Hale of Haverhill, Mass., and Messrs. Eastman, Tilton and Co., of this village—the furniture by Charles Hartshorn and J. L. Gibb of this village. The whole property was valued at some 28,000; insured for about 16,000 dollars. A new house will probably be immediately erected.

33. *Tripp's White Mountain Guide Book, or Guide to the White Mountain and Lake Scenery of New-Hampshire*, 5th ed. (Boston: Redding & Company, 1852), supplement (Concord, June 1853).
34. *Ibid.*, advertising section. The same view was used in the 1858 (1st) and 1859 (2nd) editions of Eastman's *White Mountain Guide* (text and advertising section), and in the 1858 edition of Harvey Boardman's "Map of the White Mountains, New Hampshire...."
35. The Crawford House advertisement is paired with one for the first Flume House on one side of the same undated broadside sheet (consult "Hotels and Inns File," NHHS). So far as I am aware the advertisement was never published.
36. [Merrill], *History of Coos County*, p. 438.
37. *Manchester Weekly Mirror*, 16 July 1859. Old hotel folders ("Early Stories of Crawford House," c. 1960) point to the wide span of the dining room and the ballroom as being quite unusual. Survivor of many intense storms during its existence, the hotel was extremely solid in its construction, with its major frame risers mortised and tenoned into large sills, and reinforced diagonally. Every piece of the building was said to fit perfectly when assembled on-site. The "attic hand-hewn beams formed a box construction and reportedly was the reason that the dining room did not have a support pillar showing. The weight of the building was carried by the outer walls, a unique mode of construction since there were two stories of rooms above the dining room." The large brass key to the first Crawford House was placed in the face of the lobby fireplace of the second when it was built. Originally there were two semi-circular staircases in the lobby, but one was later removed to permit installation of an elevator (1883).
38. [Merrill], *History of Coos County*, p. 438. See also *White Mountain Banner*, 14 May 1859, p. 2.
39. *White Mountain Banner*, 28 May 1859, p. 2.
40. *Ibid.*; [Merrill], *History of Coos County*, p. 437.
41. *The White Mountain Guide Book*, 2nd ed. (Concord, NH: Edson C. Eastman, 1859), pp. 54-55. The building consumed about 2,000,000 feet of lumber, and, with furniture, cost approximately $40,000. It was lit entirely by gas from a works expressly built for this purpose (*Manchester Weekly Mirror*, 16 July 1859). See also *The People's Journal* (Littleton), 7 June 1861.
42. "Early Stories of Crawford House" (c. 1960); *The White Mountains: A Handbook for Travelers* . . . (Boston: James R. Osgood and Co., 1876), p. 148; Florence Morey, "One Hundred Years of Crawford House," *Appalachia* 32, No. 3 (15 June 1959), p. 422. Gibb, Hartshorn & Co. managed the hotel for

the Littleton ownership in the mid-1860s, and upon the death of Col. Gibb, was succeeded by Walcott and Hartshorn who operated it for several years (see Eastman guides, 1863 to 1872). The Barron's hotel interest grew dramatically over the years until they owned or leased the Twin Mountain House, the Fabyan House, the Mount Pleasant House and the Summit House on Mount Washington, in addition to Crawford's. For a period of seventy-two years Asa's sons—Oscar G., William A. and Hal—were resident managers of these popular hostelries (see Chapters 3-5). The Barron ownership of the Crawford House lasted until 1947 when it passed to new owners.

43. Thursty McQuill (Wallace Bruce), *From New York to the Summer Resorts of New England . . .* (New York: New York News Company, 1880), op. p. 44.

44. *Northern New England and Canada Resorts: A Handbook for Tourists and Travelers . . .* (New York: Taintor Brothers, Merrill & Co., 1877), p. 62. This guide published the same view as in figure 2-12, which therefore provides an approximate building date.

45. *ATC* 3, No. 1 (9 July 1879), p. 1; *WME* 2, No. 1 (28 June 1879), p. 1. Steam heat was also added in 1879.

46. *ATC* 5, No. 1 (9 July 1881), p. 1; *ATC* 7, No. 9 (20 July 1883), p. 1. Over the years other modifications were made to the main building and new outbuildings were added. Only two of the latter remain on the property today, the studio of resident painter Frank H. Shapleigh, erected in 1881, and a large garage with second-story dormitory completed in 1911. Adjacent to the hotel site is the marvelous Victorian eclectic Boston and Maine Railroad station for Crawford's, which, based on the dating of the original plans at the Maine Historic Preservation Commission (Augusta), was erected in 1891 or soon thereafter.

47. Paul Doherty, "Auction of the Contents and Furnishings of the Crawford House," *Appalachia* 41, No. 13 (December 1976): 84-86. *Manchester* (NH) *Union Leader*, 5 August 1976, p. 1.

48. *Littleton Courier*, 23 November 1977, p. 1; *Manchester Union Leader*, 21 November 1977, p. 1; Richard Hamilton, "Crawford House—1859-1977," *Appalachia* 43, No. 1 (15 June 1980): 113-114; Peter Crane, "Crawford House Property Update," *Appalachia* 44, No. 3 (June 1983): 214-15; Janet M. Hounsell, "Auction, Flames Ended Crawford House's 183-Year Life," *The Valley Visitor* (North Conway, NH), 23 July 1988, p. 5.

49. Bulkley, "History," pp. 34-35.

50. Crawford, "History," p. 61.

51. A. J. Coolidge and J. B. Mansfield, *A History and Description of New England: New Hampshire* (Boston: Austin J. Coolidge, 1860), pp. 693-94; *ATC* 24, No. 5 (13 July 1900), p. 1 (Nathanial Noyes' recollections of the first Summit House); *The White Mountain Guide Book*, 1st ed. (1858), p. 66; *ATC* 12, No. 17 (28 July 1888), p. 1; Benjamin G. Willey, *Incidents in White Mountain History* (Boston: Nathaniel Noyes, 1856), pp. 264-66; Kilbourne, *Chronicles*, pp. 230-31; Burt, *The Story of Mount Washington*, pp. 66-67, 96; *ATC* 3, No. 8 (18 July 1879), p. 1.

52. *ATC*, Illustrated Souvenir Edition, 15 July 1902; "Tip-Top House," *Mount Washington Observatory News Bulletin* 4, No. 2 (June 1963), pp. 8-9; C. Francis Belcher, National Register of Historic Places Nomination Form for Tip-Top House, State of New Hampshire, Department of Resources and Economic Development, Concord; "The Fire On Mount Washington," *ATC* Magazine Number (1908); *ATC* 32, No. 1 (5 July 1910), p. 3; "Burning of the Old Tip-Top House," *ATC* 37, No. 36 (30 August 1915), p. 1; *ATC* 38, No. 1 (10 July 1916), p. 1, and No. 48 (14 September 1916), p. 1; "Tip-Topless," *Mount Washington Observatory News Bulletin* 25, No. 3 (Fall 1984), p. 57. Samuel F. Spaulding & Co. consisted of Samuel F. Spaulding, John H. Spaulding (the author of *Historical Relics of the White Mountains*, 1855), Abraham Bedell, and Anson Stillings. When plans were materializing for the restoration of the Tip-Top House during the 1980s, a debate raged over the configuration of the roof, but the "flat roofers" prevailed, and the building was returned to its original appearance. At the same time the interior was restored as closely as possible to the decade of the 1860s, based on old written accounts and stereo views.

53. Additional early summit buildings were constructed in the White Mountains, but these are beyond the scope of this study, and therefore will not be discussed in the text. However, they possess significance similar to that of the first Summit and Tip-Top houses and deserve brief mention. Most comparable in appearance and function was the Summit House on Mount Lafayette, which was erected around 1880 but burned in 1910 (its stone foundation walls are still visible). A plain two-and-a-half-story, wood-frame hotel with cupola stood on the summit of Mount Kearsarge in Lower Bartlett from c. 1848 until its destruction by a wind storm in November 1883. From 1860 to 1942 the Tip-Top House (also known as "Prospect House") stood on the summit of Mount Moosilauke near Warren. Until enlarged in 1881, this little stone structure with wooden pitched roof, was, in form and proportions, a near duplicate of the Mount Washington and Mount Lafayette buildings. Small hostelries were also constructed on the summits of Mount Hayes (c. 1866) and Mount Moriah (c. 1855) near Gorham.

54. "North Conway," *ATC* 18, No. 41 (30 August 1894), pp. 1, 4; Georgia D. Merrill, *History of Carroll County, New Hampshire* (Boston: W. A. Fergusson & Co., 1889), p. 884; Carl B. Garey, "The Kiarsarge [sic] House," (Unpublished typescript manuscript, n. d., Conway Public Library). The Kearsarge Tavern is also often referred to as the Kearsarge House.

55. "North Conway," *ATC* 18, No. 41 (30 August 1894), p. 4; Merrill, *History of Carroll County*, pp. 884-85. After it ceased service as a hotel, the North Conway House was moved to Pine Street. It originated from a one-story farmhouse of ten rooms.

56. "Conway House Burned," *The Reporter* (North Conway), 11 April 1912, p. 1; *ATC*, 7 August 1902, p. 4; Merrill, *History of*

Carroll County, p. 878; *Guide to the White Mountains and Lakes of New-Hampshire...*, 2nd ed. (1851), p. 18. The construction cost was $50,000 and there was space for 75-125 guests. The first proprietor was Horace Fabyan (see Chapter 1); his successors included Samuel C. White, Leavitt H. Eastman, A. C. Fowler, L. L. Blood & Son, and John Shorey. In 1895-96 the hotel was repaired and refurnished, and the dining room was expanded.

57. *Conway New Hampshire. Its Attractions for the Tourist, and its Facilities for Business* (Conway: S. A. Evans, 1889), p. 10; *Waterville* (ME) *Morning Sentinel*, 9 April 1912; "Conway House Burned," *The Reporter*, 11 April 1912, p. 1. The fire was apparently caused by a faulty chimney. The hotel burned to the ground, but the adjacent stable and garage survived. The loss was estimated at $30,000 of which $10,000 was covered by insurance.

58. Wentworth Hall and Cottages, and the Eagle Mountain House (see Chapters 3 and 4) are the only two nineteenth-century hotels still in operation in Jackson.

59. Kilbourne, *Chronicles*, p. 171; Margaret B. Garland, *Yesterdays: Lodging Places of Jackson and their Recipes* (Jackson, NH: Jackson Historical Society, 1978), pp. 45-46; Janet Hounsell, "Gone 10 Years, Jackson Falls House Still Recalled," *The Valley Visitor*, 8 December, 1988, p. 5; *ATC* 9, No. 34 (28 August 1885), p. 4; *WME* 9, No. 5 (31 July 1886), p. 15; "Jackson Falls House: An Era Ends, Another Begins," *Lewiston* (ME) *Evening Journal*, Magazine Section, 22 September 1979, p. 8A. The Jackson Falls House was located in the center of the village where the U. S. Post Office and a small, one-story shopping block are now situated. The hotel barn still stands to the east of this site. After the 1885-86 reconstruction an annex was built and ells were added to it.

60. *Guide to the White Mountains and Lakes of New-Hampshire*, 2nd ed. (1851), p. 47; National Register of Historic Places Nomination Form for Thayers Hotel, State of New Hampshire, Department of Resources and Economic Development, Concord.

61. James R. Jackson, *History of Littleton, New Hampshire* (Cambridge, MA: Published for the Town by the University Press, 1905), Vol. I, pp. 141-42, and Vol. III, p. 364.

62. "'Dad Thayer's' Tavern," *White Mountain Republic Journal*, 20 April 1894, p. 5; brochure, "A Walking Tour of Main Street, Littleton, NH," (1983); John H. Colby, ed., *Littleton: Crossroads of Northern New Hampshire* (Canaan, NH: Phoenix Publishers, 1894), pp. 420-24. Thayers was also known briefly as the St. Andrews Inn, but this name was dropped in 1982 when the hotel returned to Eames family ownership. In the 1930s Henry Ford attempted unsuccessfully to acquire the front portico and other parts of the hotel for installation in his tavern restoration at Greenfield Village (Edison Institute), Dearborn, MI.

63. Exhibition label, Lancaster (NH) Historical Society; Rev. A. N. Somers, *History of Lancaster, New Hampshire* (Concord, NH: The Rumford Press, 1899), pp. 514-16. A railroad route was later pushed north to Lancaster by the Boston, Concord & Montreal Railroad. Lancaster House was situated near the center of town on the west side of Main Street on the site of the present Lancaster Motel.

64. John B. Bachelder, *Popular Resorts; and How to Reach Them*, 2nd ed. (Boston: John B. Bachelder, 1874), pp. 111-12; *Coos County Democrat*, 31 March 1954, p. 1; *White Mountain Republic*, 3 October 1878, p. 3; Bonnie Isham, "Disasters of Lancaster," Lancaster Academy English course paper (11th grade), 1964, Lancaster Public Library. The fire, which started in the ell, caused a loss of $30,000 for which there was $14,000 in insurance protection. The burning of the hotel resulted in a brief depression in the town until the second Lancaster House, a similar-sized Queen Anne structure, was erected in 1881-82 by John Lindsey of N. A. Lindsey & Co. Fire gutted this building (on the same site) on 31 March 1954 and it was not replaced (see Chapter 5).

65. *Bicentennial Commemorative Booklet of the Town of Lincoln, New Hampshire, 1764-1964* (Lincoln: n. p., 1964), p. 20. Other newspaper and book sources are less specific about the building date; there is even less clarity concerning the builders.

66. *Ibid.*, pp. 21-22; *Coos County Democrat*, 18 July 1849, p. 2; Kilbourne, "A Closed Chapter of White Mountain History," p. 308; *The White Mountain Guide Book*, 2nd ed. (1859), p. 101. The chapel, fifty feet square and crowned with a spire and balustrade, was an important adjunct to the first Flume House. It was used for both Sunday religious services and social gatherings.

67. *Tripp's White Mountain Guide Book*, 4th ed. (1852), p. 108.

68. David Tatham, "Franklin Leavitt's White Mountain Verse," p. 225.

69. Kilbourne, "A Closed Chapter of White Mountain History," p. 309; George H. Haynes, *Souvenir of New England's Great Resorts* (New York: Moss Engraving Company, 1891), "Franconia Notch..." section; *WME* 15, No. 8 (20 August 1892), p. 2. According to Jackson's *History of Littleton* (Vol. II, p. 142), the same Jonathan Nurs who helped build the White Mountain House (Thayers Hotel) also assisted in the construction of the first Profile House.

70. *ATC* 29, No. 53 (12 September 1905), p. 1. Mr. Taft gradually bought out the other partners in the company and became sole owner after 1863 until his death in 1881.

71. *The White Mountain Guide Book*, 2nd ed. (1866), p. 121.

72. *White Mountain Republic*, 29 March 1872, p. 2.

73. *The Idler* (North Conway) 1, No. 1 (22 June 1880), p. 4; *ATC* 6, No. 1 (10 July 1882), p. 1; *ATC* 17, No. 1 (17 July 1893), p. 4; *ATC* 29, No. 53 (12 September 1905), p. 1. In 1881 when Richard Taft died, his wife became owner, and Colonel Greenleaf became sole manager. Greenleaf was also the proprietor of the Hotel Vendome in Boston. In 1898 the business was placed under a corporation, the "Profile and Flume Hotels Company," with Greenleaf as president and Charles F. Eastman of Littleton as treasurer. At this time the corporation owned over 6,000 acres of land in Franconia Notch.

74. *ATC* 9, No. 2 (14 July 1885), p. 8.
75. Bulkley, "History," pp. 61-62; Diane M. Kostechke, ed., *Franconia Notch: An In-Depth Guide* (Concord: Society for the Protection of New Hampshire Forests, 1975), pp. 12-13. Two steam engines, the "Profile" and the "Echo," were used on the line, each pulling one baggage car and one passenger car. The railroad was discontinued in 1921 because of its inability to compete with the automobile. At the time it was owned by the Boston and Maine Railroad, which had absorbed the B., C. & M.
76. Gary N. Chamberlain to E. A. Farnsworth, typed letter, 30 March 1972, NHHS; Kilbourne, "A Closed Chapter of White Mountain History," p. 309; *ATC* 25, No. 3 (15 July 1901), p. 1. Fourteen cottages had been built by 1901, and nineteen by 1903.
77. Frances Ann Johnson Hancock, *Saving the Great Stone Face: the Chronicle of the Old Man of the Mountain* (Canaan, NH: Published for the Franconia Area Heritage Council by Phoenix Publishing, 1984), p. 26.
78. *ATC* 13, No. 3 (15 July 1889), p. 8; Henry F. and Elsie R. Withey, *Biographical Dictionary of American Architects (Deceased)* (Los Angeles: Hennessey & Ingalls, Inc., 1970), pp. 380-81. The stable was 150-by-75 feet and contained horse stalls, carriage rooms, harness rooms, a blacksmith shop, and storage areas.
79. Charles Pollock, *White Mountain Scenery* (Boston: Charles Pollock, 1895), "Profile House" entry (cover title, "White & Franconia Mts."); *The White Mountains*, 1st ed. (1876), p. 260.
80. "Profile House and Cottages, White Mountains, New Hampshire" brochure (Franconia Notch, NH: The Profile & Flume Hotels Co., c. 1903), p. 1.
81. *ATC* 29, No. 53 (12 September 1905), pp. 1, 8; *ATC* 30, No. 7 (19 July 1896), p.1.
82. Henry M. Burt, *Burt's Guide Through the Connecticut Valley to the White Mountains and the River Saguenay* (Springfield, MA: New England Publishing Company, 1874), p. 232.

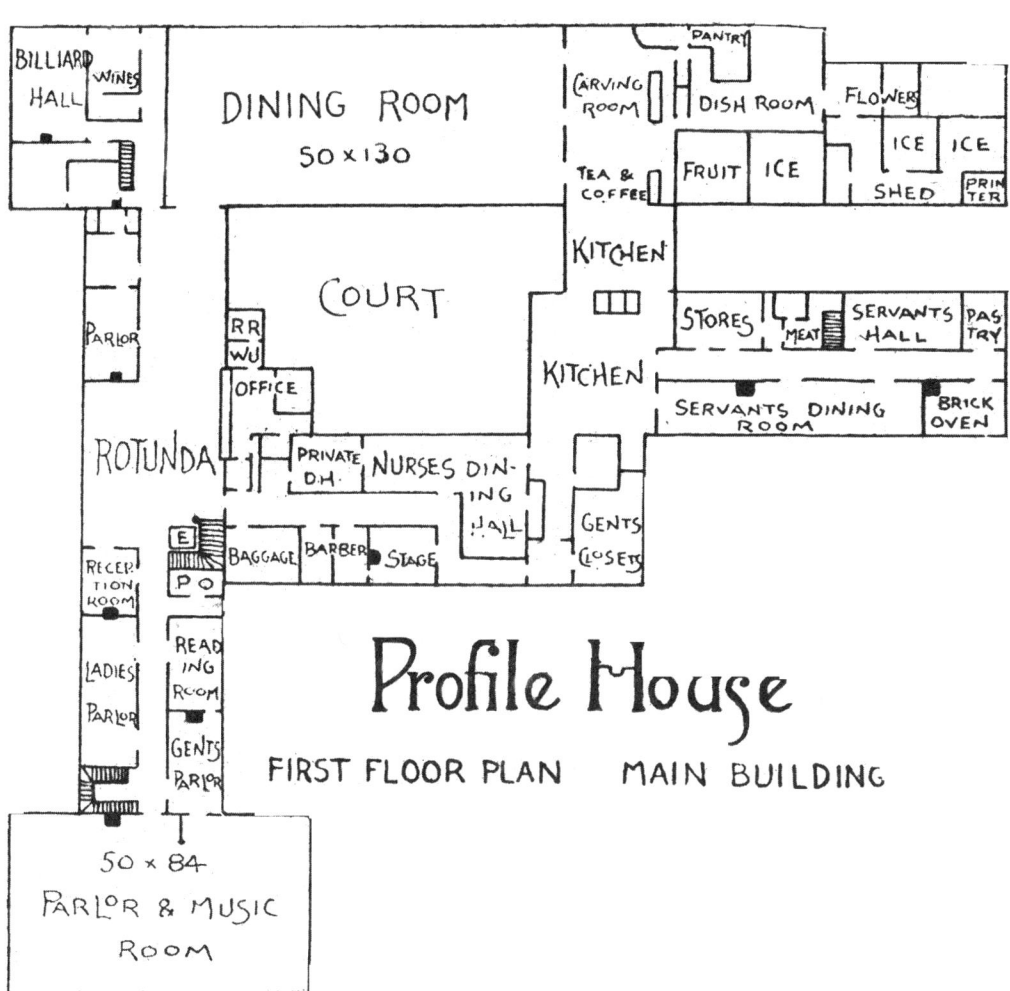

Fig. 2-31. First Profile House, Franconia Notch, NH, *"First Floor Plan, Main Building," from booklet,* Profile House, Taft & Greenleaf, Props. *(c.1890). Author's Collection. This seemingly random collection of interior spaces was, in fact, representative of careful functional planning.*

Fig. 3-1. "Kiarsarge [sic] House, North Conway, N.H.," *stereo view,* "White Mountain Scenery" *#77, c. 1865, John P. Soule, Boston. Author's Collection. Erected in 1861, this building became the south wing of the full Kearsarge House complex after 1872.*

CHAPTER 3

The Prosperity of the 1860s and Hotel Expansion

During the 1860s, the White Mountain hotel industry continued to grow at an impressive rate. Despite the national discord and dislocation produced by the tumultuous Civil War, the decade was one of unprecedented prosperity in which the tourist trade reached new levels of stability and maturity. Even in the immediate post-war years, in the face of a national cholera scare and impending economic depression, the hotels continued to report full capacities and generated considerable profits. It was not until 1868 that the hotels of the region began to show signs of declining business, but even this was a short-lived phenomenon.

The 1860s experienced many of the catalysts that had influenced the expanding hotels in the previous decade. National bursts of economic activity, characterized by advancing industrialization and the growth of the railroads, influenced the Northeast and its resort areas more than any other region of the country. The intense industrial development created improved living standards and generated new disposable income and leisure time for the social elite and the burgeoning middle class. In seeking ways to spend their extra dollars and free time, people looked to the expanding mountain and seacoast resorts of the Northeast. The pressures on the existing hotels provided an incentive for further development of the resort industry and all related tourism.

Tourism has traditionally benefited from people's desires to escape or gain relief from the stressful aspects of their lives. This concept of escape came to fruition during the 1860s in the White Mountains. Rapid economic growth, in creating more opportunities for professional, monetary and social advancement, also intensified competition; the quest for success, while embraced by many, became an all-consuming preoccupation that large numbers of people sought to avoid through the new summer vacation ritual. Ironically, for many the selection of a vacation site, in turn, constituted a form of competition in itself. The dramatic expansion of American cities, particularly in the Northeast, produced more crowded and less healthy living conditions, as well as increasingly hectic and pressured life styles. Such conditions also fostered an interest in visiting White Mountain resort areas and their hotels (some "roughed it" on extended hiking and camping trips), with stays ranging from a few days to the entire summer "social season." Not surprisingly, the Civil War also impelled people, particularly Union military officers and political leaders, to leave their concerns behind and seek rest, relaxation and intimacy with nature. Whatever their motivation for coming to the mountains, these visitors sought new outlets and pleasures through unusual curiosities and attractions, as others had in the previous three decades. The latest enticement was the new

Fig. 3-2. "Kearsarge House, North Conway, N. H.," *stereo view, c. 1875, N. W. Pease, North Conway, #36. Author's Collection. An early grand hotel, it was distinguished by its tall central tower with Italian Revival details.*

Mount Washington Summit Road, opened with much fanfare in 1861. Thus, it was "this chain of social, economic, and psychological happenstances" that unleashed a flood of visitors to the White Mountains and other resorts throughout the United States in the middle years of the nineteenth century.[1] Not surprisingly, resort hotel architecture, commencing in the 1860s, often expressed the sophisticated, the exotic, the extraordinary, and the picturesque.

North Conway Blossoms as a Hotel Center

While only limited hotel expansion occurred in Crawford, Pinkham and Franconia notches in the 1860s, the primary White Mountain region towns became more securely established as centers for the growing hotel industry. One of the most important was North Conway, traditionally the financial and commercial locus for the Eastern Slope Region. There, three noteworthy hostelries, two of them grand resort hotels, commenced operation during the decade.

Perhaps the most historic and best known was the Kearsarge House (also called "Kiarsarge" in its early years), arguably the "largest and best appointed hotel in North Conway" while it stood.[2] Located west of Main Street, just south of the town common (where the playground is today), this great rambling wooden structure was raised on the spot originally occupied by Samuel W. Thompson's Kearsarge Tavern (see Chapter 2). In 1861, Thompson, the pioneer promoter and entrepreneur of local tourism, added to the old building and erected what would later become the south wing of the fully developed complex.[3] Taking the formal name of "Kearsarge House," this hotel was a three-and-one-half-story, pitched-roof, rectangular structure with later ell additions (Fig. 3-1). Because of its similarity in appearance and size, the Kearsarge fit the same specifications as other grand hotel antecedents in town—Washington House, North Conway House, and the Sunset Pavilion.

In response to the arrival of the Eastern Railroad in North Conway, Thompson greatly enlarged his establishment in 1871-72, at a cost of $130,000, to absorb the increased flow of visitors. In doing so he created a 300-guest grand hotel whose exterior remained little altered until its destruction by fire in October 1917. Operated by the newly formed firm of Thompson, Sons, & Andrews, the new Kearsarge House was lauded in guidebooks for its spacious, comfortable, gas-lit interiors, its new furnishings and other advantages (Fig. 3-2).[4] One of its most visible and appealing features was its tall frontal tower, from which could be seen:

Fig. 3-3. The Foyer, Kearsarge House, North Conway, NH, *photograph*, The Kearsarge, North Conway, N.H. *(North Conway: Kearsarge Hotel Company, [c.1903]). Author's Collection. This illustration reveals the spaciousness of the hotel's public areas.*

> ... the grand old peaks of the White Mountains range—Mount Washington, bathed in clouds and light, upheaving its massive head in the distance; to the right Kiarsarge [sic] and to the left the Mote [sic] range, Cathedral Peaks and White Horse Ledge; while in the foreground the lovely Conway intervale spreads out like a field of emerald velvet, threaded by the sparkling sheen of the Saco river.[5]

The Kearsarge further benefited from its central location, which ensured easy access from the nearby railroad station. A plank walk connected the two buildings and likely steered people toward the hotel as they disembarked from trains.[6]

Upon first viewing the front elevation new arrivals would have been struck by the asymmetry of the Italian Revival-inspired complex, with the lofty tower positioned off-center to the right of the center pavilion. Long piazzas, supported by frail, vertical timbers, extended across the front and around the sides, providing an excellent venue for the ritual of promenading, a popular past-time for women during this era. Other prominent stylistic features included bracketing under the roof eaves and on the tower stages, truncated dormers, and a cut-off pyramidal roof with round-arch dormers atop the tower. Together these details created a superbly unified architectural composition, the horizontality of the building mass perfectly balanced by the verticality of the tower.

Upon passing through the main entrance of the Kearsarge House guests would no doubt have been impressed by its grand hotel ambiance, as was surely the intention of Thompson and other owners:

> The interior ... is fitted up with every modern improvement; and the house throughout is furnished with especial reference to the comfort and convenience of guests. On the first floor is the office, parlor, reception room, dining-hall, gentleman's reading room, billiard hall, barbershop, and wash-rooms. The rotunda, in the centre of the building, is forty feet square, and well lighted, with an entrance from the front and rear, affording such perfect ventilation, that in the warmest day one is here sure of a cool retreat. The parlor is an elegant room, forty by sixty; and here, during the season, one may listen for six nights in the week to the best concert and dancing music.
>
> The dining-hall is a well-lighted and cheerful room, with ... an admirable view of the White Mountain groups.

Fig. 3-4. The Music Room, Kearsarge House, North Conway, NH, *photograph, The Kearsarge, North Conway, N. H. (North Conway: Kearsarge Hotel Company, [c. 1903]). Author's Collection. Late Victorian decor and gaslight fixtures refitted with electric lights are visible in this photograph.*

All the public rooms, including the ladies' parlor, on the second story, have been richly frescoed . . . to meet the increasing autumn patronage, steam has been introduced into the sleeping-rooms, arranged singly and in suites. They are high, airy, and thoroughly ventilated; and all have bells connecting with the office.[7]

Photographic views of the foyer (office) (Fig. 3-3) and the music room (Fig. 3-4), published in a promotional booklet about 1903, show late-Victorian decor from earlier decades and provide an accurate impression of the interior during the hotel's prime years.[8] For recreational and social activities, the Kearsarge offered baseball, croquet, golf (on a course behind the hotel), lawn tennis, pool and billiards, riding, dancing and musical performances.

While the Kearsarge House was very well situated, the Intervale House, North Conway's other grand hotel, possessed a location considered to be one of the most spectacular in the mountains. From its spacious verandas at Intervale, a small village on the Jackson road almost two miles north of town, guests could enjoy the view made famous by John Frederick Kensett and other White Mountain artists—an uninterrupted panorama of the entire Presidential Range and adjacent peaks rising dramatically above their foothills and the open, unspoiled Saco River intervale. This magnificent vista, the main attraction of the hotel, has remained largely intact to this day. The building site, now occupied by the Intervale Motel, is little changed from over a century ago when it formed the center of a small summer hotel, inn and cottage community, serviced by its own railroad stop.[9]

The development of the Intervale House was an eventful episode in the saga of the White Mountain hotels. In 1868 (some sources say 1860) W. H. H.

THE PROSPERITY OF THE 1860S AND HOTEL EXPANSION

Trickey erected the first portion of the hotel on the site of the former tavern and homestead of Captain Elijah Dinsmore. Little information is available today about its initial appearance and early years. The property passed to Frank A. Mudgett and Alfred Eastman in 1871 and, in 1874, came under the ownership of Mudgett, his brother Herbert S., and their father, Stephen, who had bought out Eastman's interest. The new firm, S. Mudgett & Sons, enlarged the building in 1873 and may have expanded it again during the off-season months of 1879-80, but this has not yet been concretely documented.[10]

Fortunately the subsequent history of the hotel is far less sketchy. On 6 September 1883, *Among the Clouds* was more specific about what the owners planned for the ensuing season:

> The proprietors of the Intervale House have completed their plans for the enlargement which will probably be ready for another year. The dining-room wing of the house is to be removed and an ell, 100 x 60 feet, put on at right angles to the main house, running towards the road. The new part will contain the dining-room and from 30 to 50 new rooms. The hotel and cottages will then have accommodations for about 300 guests. The house will be thoroughly modernized, and its popularity cannot fail to be largely increased.[11]

The frontispiece to *The Intervale, New Hampshire*, printed in 1887, illustrates the expanded Intervale House with its new northeast side addition (Fig. 3-5). Though the building is simpler and more austere, exterior features found on the Kearsarge House, such as expansive connected piazzas and truncated roof dormers, were carried over to the Intervale. That this project was completed in a matter of months is quite remarkable; in November 1883 a great gale blew down the frame of the addition soon after it had been raised, and the Mudgetts had to begin construction again. The new ell, three-and-a-half-stories high, virtually doubled the size of the original house.[12]

With the tourist business expanding, the Mudgetts continued to enlarge their hotel. In 1887 they further improved the complex with a new office and lobby, billiard room, toilet rooms, and large, open fireplaces.[13] They also attached a final addition at right angles to

Fig. 3-5. "The Intervale House," North Conway (Intervale), NH, *frontispiece engraving from Winfield S. Nevins*, The Intervale, New Hampshire *(1887). Author's Collection. The hotel, with one of the best panoramic views in the White Mountains, is depicted after an addition put on in 1883-84.*

Fig. 3-6. Intervale House, North Conway (Intervale), NH, *postcard view, c. 1900. Author's Collection. The complete complex shown here was burned in 1923, depriving North Conway of the last of its grand resort hotels.*

the southwest side of the building in 1888-89, providing twenty-two more bedrooms, "all finished in hard wood, the rooms large and airy, and richly furnished."[14] It was this sprawling complex, long sustained by its own farm and fresh springwater supply, that succumbed to fire on 22 May 1923, depriving the town of its last early grand resort hotel (Fig. 3-6).[15]

North Conway's third notable hotel of the 1860s, while not of grand hotel proportions or elegance, did closely resemble other local precursors. The Sunset Pavilion, or simply "The Sunset," originated as a small forty-guest expanded farmhouse. It was opened in 1867 by Mahlon L. and Frank L. Mason, later to become co-owners of Mason's Hotel. In the fall of 1869 the Masons made plans to build a wing at either end of the existing structure. However, a sudden flood on the neighboring Saco River destroyed the saw mills from which the lumber was to be obtained and delayed work. After finally completing one wing, they constructed a rear ell in 1873 and added a new kitchen in 1888. These projects created a wooden L-shaped structure, three-and-a-half-stories tall, with a pitched roof and dormers, and broad twelve-foot piazzas across the front and rear elevations, and north end (Fig. 3-7). Capable of accommodating 150 overnight guests, the building was plain and functional and bore a close resemblance to the 1861 Kearsarge House and the Intervale House after its enlargement in 1883-84.[16]

Late nineteenth-century promotional literature and advertising, though inclined toward overexuberance, offer useful information about the grounds, setting and interiors of the Sunset Pavilion. On the

Fig. 3-7. "Sunset Pavilion House, North Conway, N. H.," *stereo view, c. 1875, Kilburn #990. Douglas Philbrook, Gorham, NH. Very plain and functional, this building resembled other grand hotel precursors of its time and earlier.*

Fig. 3-8. "The Sunset, North Conway, N. H.," *advertisement engraving from* North Conway and Vicinity *(c. 1891). Author's Collection. Evident in this view is the fully developed Sunset Pavilion, along with the 1887 ballroom and music hall (interior insert to the right).*

front, or east side of the hotel, reached by a semi-circular entrance driveway, was a "lawn, of unusual size and beauty, which . . . [made] a wide distance between the house and the road, . . . [and was] furnished with pretty trees—elm, maple, balm of gilead, birch and lombardy poplars."[17] From this location at the north end of Main Street, on "Sunset Bank," a bluff overlooking the Saco River intervale:

> . . . the visitor . . . [had] a fine view of Mt. Kearsarge, and Mt. Bartlett and the Rattlesnake range of hills [from the front] . . . while from the rear piazza the eye is carried across the valley of the Saco to the White Horse Ledge, and to the north the summit of Mt. Washington and the Presidential range . . . [were] plainly visible.[18]

The interior of the hotel sounded equally appealing in an 1886 advertisement essay:

> Inside are modern conveniences, electric bells, pure running spring water on each floor, and fine, large, bathrooms. The chambers are large, light and pleasant, and well and prettily furnished. The lower story, including office, parlors, dining, drawing, reading and smoking rooms, is wonderfully attractive, with its oriental-looking portieres, tasteful window draperies, and pleasant-tinted, harmonious paints and wall-papers, and an immense open fire-place with cosy great corners and ponderous coping-stone in the long, south parlor.[19]

Although they were more modest in size, and often more restrictive in their culinary, social and recreational offerings, many White Mountain establishments of the same operational scale as the Sunset Pavilion provided an atmosphere and milieu comparable to that of the grand hotels.

Closely associated with the Sunset was a ballroom and music hall built in 1887 from plans by Walter T. Winslow of the Boston firm of Winslow, Wetherell and Bradlee.[20] It is shown, along with an interior insert view to the right of the hotel, in an advertisement from a c. 1891 North Conway Board of Trade

[83]

booklet (Fig. 3-8).²¹ A hotel promotional publication from the 1920s describes this unusual little building:

> The ballroom and music hall is the finest of its kind on the East Side, being finished of yellow pine in its natural state and color. It is thirty by sixty feet in size, open to the roof (which is arched and twenty-five feet at the ridge) and has a perfect floor for dancing. There are twelve large, square windows with colored panes, huge trusses on the roof which remind one of the timbers of a ship, and a great brick and granite fireplace at the west end, which rises fifteen feet from floor to ceiling, is ten feet wide and two and a half feet deep, pyramidal in form with a great granite coping, making a most picturesque interior. The hall is placed at the northwest corner . . . under a separate roof and connected with the hotel by a piazza. . . .²²

In 1917 Harry H. Randall purchased both the hotel and the ballroom/music hall to be run as an adjunct of the Hotel Randall next door (later the site of the Eastern Slope Inn).²³ Fire destroyed much of the Sunset Pavilion on 22 June 1940 and it was subsequently demolished. But the hall survived to become the remodeled and enlarged headquarters of the summer Eastern Slope Theater.²⁴

From Thorn Mountain House to Wentworth Hall and Cottages

Wentworth Hall and Cottages in Jackson is unique amongst White Mountain grand resort hotels; at its height the collection of main, service and dependent residential units was aesthetically bound together and operated under principles of "cottage system" hotel management then employed in Great Britain. Under this system, the complex was designed as a group of buildings, rather than as a single unit, allowing guests privacy in separate cottages and social interaction in the public spaces of the main hotel.

Though nearly all its buildings were constructed during the 1880s and after, the Wentworth traces its beginnings to the decade of the 1860s when Joshua Trickey built a country inn for his daughter Georgia

Fig. 3-9. Thorn Mountain House, Wentworth Hall and Cottages, Jackson, NH, *advertising cut*, White Mountain Echo *11, No. 6 (4 August 1888), p. 18. Author's Collection. Opened in 1869, this building operated independently for several years until it was modernized and absorbed into the Wentworth Hall complex in the 1880s.*

prior to her marriage to General Marshall C. Wentworth of Jackson. Opened in 1869 as "Thorn Mountain House," it occupied the site upon which Wentworth Hall would later be situated, just west of the Wildcat River near the center of the village.²⁵ While there is no published information about the initial physical appearance of this structure, several illustrations post-dating 1880 exist that indicate its basic configuration. An advertisement in the 1888 *White Mountain Echo* shows the old hotel garbed in Queen Anne-style decor after the first of many renovations were undertaken during the development of the Wentworth Hall complex (Fig. 3-9).²⁶

Sometime around 1880, General Wentworth commenced the ambitious task of realizing his vision of an English-inspired mountain resort community. To perform the master planning and execute the separate building designs, he contracted New York City architect William A. Bates (1853-1922), known for his residential, country club, and hotel commissions in and around the metropolis.²⁷ Working exclusively in the popular Queen Anne vernacular, of which he was a nationally known proponent, Bates launched Wentworth's grand project with the completion of Arden Cottage in 1881.²⁸ A comparison of his front elevation perspective (likely based on a presentation drawing) (Fig. 3-10) with a recent photograph (Fig. 3-11) reveals marked differences as well as similarities. The cottage was conceived "in true old English

Fig. 3-10. "Cottage for M. C. Wentworth, Esq., Thorn Mt. House, Jackson, N. H.," *engraving,* American Architect and Building News 9, #262 (1 January 1881), op. p. 7. Morris Library, University of Delaware. *This reproduced perspective sketch by architect William A. Bates shows Arden Cottage, the oldest of the cottages in the Wentworth Hall complex.*

Fig. 3-11. Arden Cottage, Wentworth Hall and Cottages, Jackson, NH, *photograph, 1990, by the author. A comparison of this recent photo with the perspective sketch in figure 3-10 reveals differences in detail but the same Queen Anne-style spirit.*

style from the old-fashioned knocker on the 'Dutch' door to the very peak of its gable roof" (see Fig. 3-10). In its first years this building was regarded as functionally innovative, while also a model of traditional artistic excellence.[29] The current cottage incorporates the layout, front elevation format and Queen Anne spirit of the original plan, but lacks some of the details initially called for (see Fig. 3-11).

In 1882-83 Bates gave further form to General Wentworth's ideal hostelry by designing Wentworth Hall, in which he attempted to reproduce "the solid comfort, artistic effects, and picturesque beauty of an English memorial hall of Queen Anne's days" (see Plate 4).[30] An assessment from the *White Mountain Echo* corroborates the architect's success:

Wentworth Hall, in the style of architecture, finish and adornment, is in hotel building a new departure . . . of noticeably symmetrical

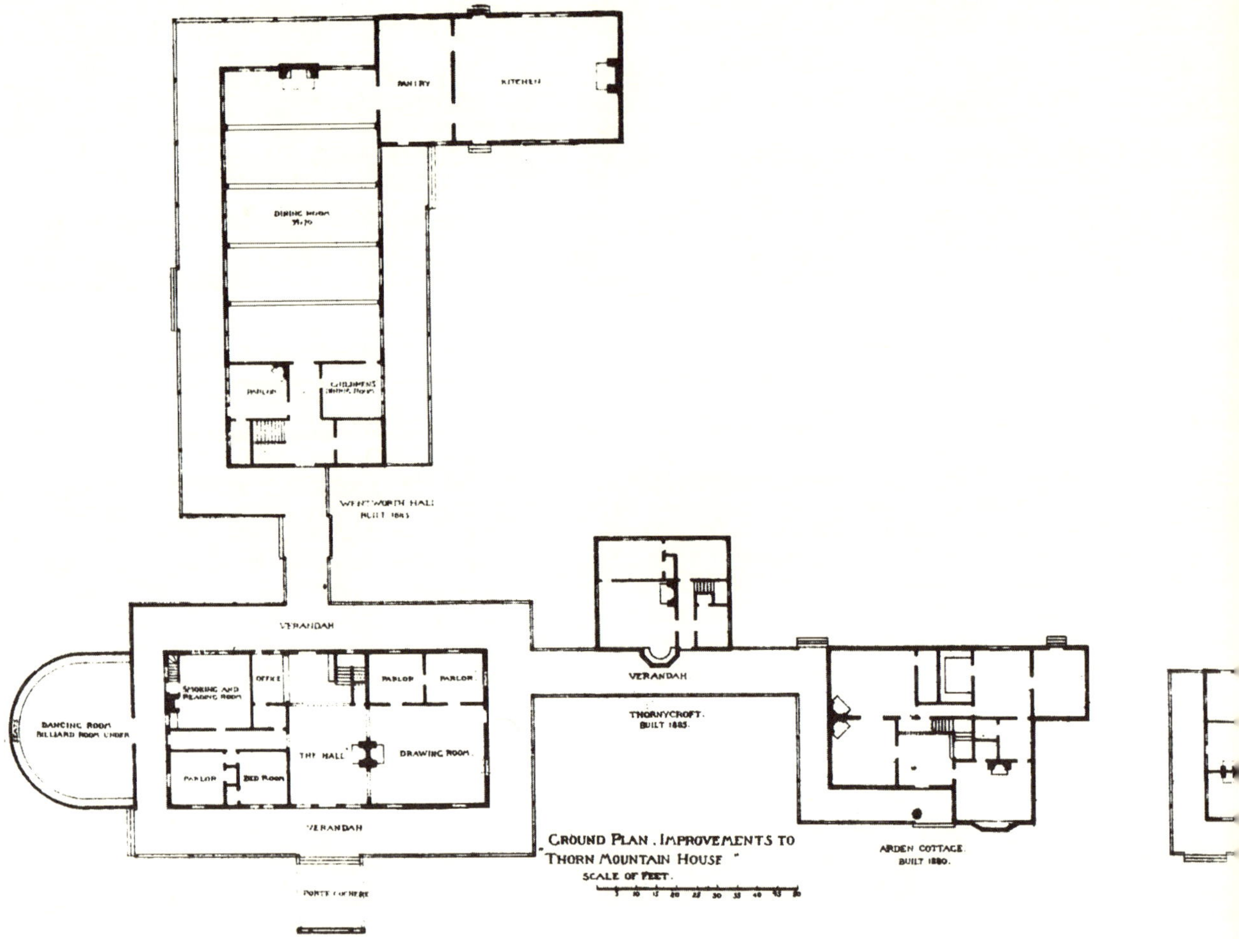
PANTRY
KITCHEN
DINING ROOM
PARLOR
CHILDREN'S DINING ROOM
WENTWORTH HALL
BUILT 1885
VERANDAH
SMOKING AND READING ROOM
OFFICE
PARLOR
PARLOR
DANCING ROOM
BILLIARD ROOM UNDER
PARLOR
BED ROOM
THE HALL
DRAWING ROOM
VERANDAH
PORTE COCHERE
VERANDAH
THORNYCROFT.
BUILT 1885.
ARDEN COTTAGE.
BUILT 1880.
GROUND PLAN. IMPROVEMENTS TO
"THORN MOUNTAIN HOUSE"
SCALE OF FEET.
5 10 15 20 25 30 35 40 45 50

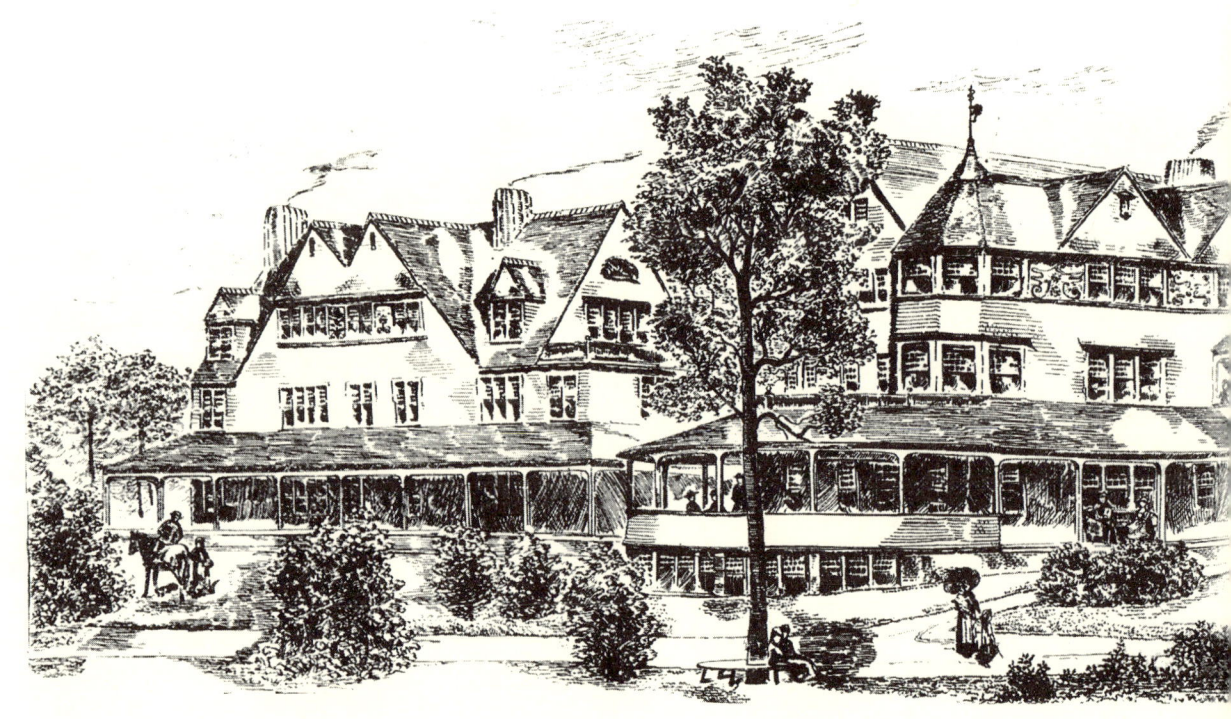

Fig. 3-12. "Thorn Mountain House and Cottages, Jackson, N. H. for Gen. M. C. Wentworth," *engraving*, American Architect and Building News *18, #520 (12 December 1885), Supplement, op. p. 3. Morris Library, University of Delaware, Newark, DE. This perspective sketch of the Wentworth Hall complex, with floor plans, was executed by architect William A. Bates of New York City.*

outlines and harmonious tints. Approached from Glen Station [to the south], we first descry the pyramidal roof of the tall central turret, which is lighted by stained windows and surmounted by a brass bannerette, graven with initials and date of erection. Then we see the proportionate gables, the red and gold and pale green of the exterior, and the lofty chimney. As we draw nearer we observe the fancy-cut belts of shingles, the long large windows and broad piazzas.[31]

Another observer, writing at the same time, takes us inside the new building, as well as to the remodeled Thorn Mountain House next door:

Approaching . . . by wide drives one enters a spacious hall finished in oak, with heavy wainscot and paneled ceiling. This room has a fine large fireplace. Opening from the hall are the parlors finished in white and gold, of delicate modeling. On the other side of the hall are the billiard, reading and dancing rooms. The dining-room will seat three hundred and fifty guests, and with kitchens, etc., occupies a building [Thorn Mountain House] by itself to the west of the hall. It is finished in mahogany, with a high wainscot and open-timbered ceiling, richly moulded; the west end of the room being occupied by a huge brick fireplace of the olden time with andirons and swinging crane. The decoration throughout has been carefully studied with the endeavor to obtain yet rich results.[32]

Wentworth Hall served as the principal service building for the growing complex; it contained a smoking room, children's and nurses' dining room, and thirty sleeping rooms—painted in robins-egg blue and furnished with the latest Queen Anne furniture. Outside, guests enjoyed tennis, horseback riding, golf, swimming and croquet typical of Victorian-era White Mountain resorts.[33]

The building of "Thornycroft," and "Glenthorne" in 1885 brought Wentworth's scheme one step closer to full realization. These are shown together with the three older buildings, in a ground plan and front elevation perspective sketch published in *American Architect and Building News* in December of that year (Fig. 3-12).[34] Designed by Bates, these cottages possessed the broken asymmetry and ornamental playfulness of detail so characteristic of the Queen Anne style. "Elmwood," added to Wentworth's "miniature cottage city" in 1885, increased guest capacity to 250.[35] The next year "Wildwood Cottage" was constructed and the Casino, distinguished by its conical-roofed cylindrical tower, and arched apertures, was erected and attached to the south side of the Thorn Mountain House.[36] It was at this point that the full complex was retitled "Wentworth Hall and Cottages."

Floor plans (Figs. 3-13 and 3-14), bearing Bates' name and professional address, validate his authorship and appear for each building in promotional materials published by the hotel between 1880 and 1900. These plans, often used by prospective guests to select their rooms, provide valuable documentation of the floor layouts both in the main house and several of the cottages. This fine architecture was supplemented by a new stable (1886), also by Bates (Fig. 3-15); a hydroelectric plant (1894); and other structures. By century's end, the complex comprised over twenty buildings.[37] Virtually all these, some to a greater extent than others, exhibited features closely associated with the Queen Anne style—variety in wall color and texture, fancy-cut and arranged shingles, bay windows, polygonal turrets, elaborate chimneys, intersecting pitched roofs, small-paned windows and balconies. Linked together by covered piazzas and open walkways, the various buildings achieved a unity in harmony with the beautiful natural surroundings of the Wildcat and Ellis River valleys and enclosing hills.[38]

Thanks to the concern and interest of recent owners, Wentworth Hall and Cottages (now known as Wentworth Resort Hotel) remains as one of only four grand resort hotels still operating in the White Mountains. In the 1920s it was owned by Nathan Amster, who made his fortune in mining, railroads and as a founder of New York's famous Third Avenue El. Harry Schiener and E. M. Lowe, the movie theater mogul, held title to the hotel from the 1930s to

THE PROSPERITY OF THE 1860S AND HOTEL EXPANSION

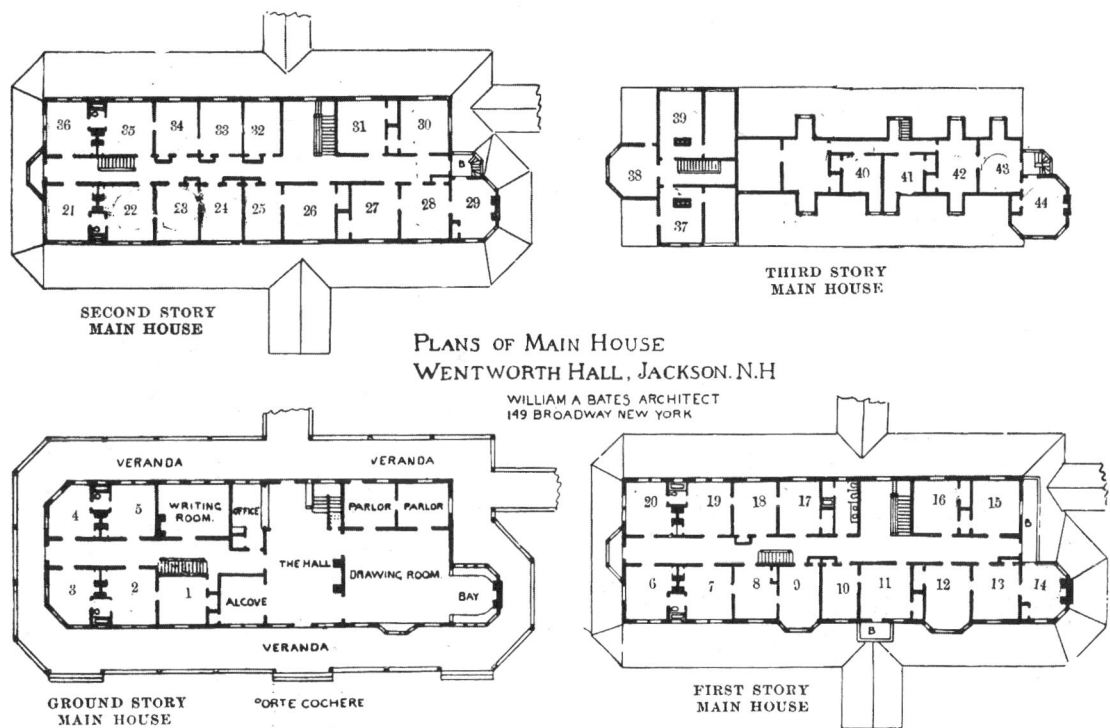

Fig. 3-13. "Plans of the Main House, Wentworth Hall, Jackson, N. H.," *from* Wentworth Hall and Cottages *promotional booklet, c. 1900. Author's Collection. Prepared by architect William A. Bates, these floor plans for Wentworth Hall (1882-83) allowed guests to select their rooms sight unseen.*

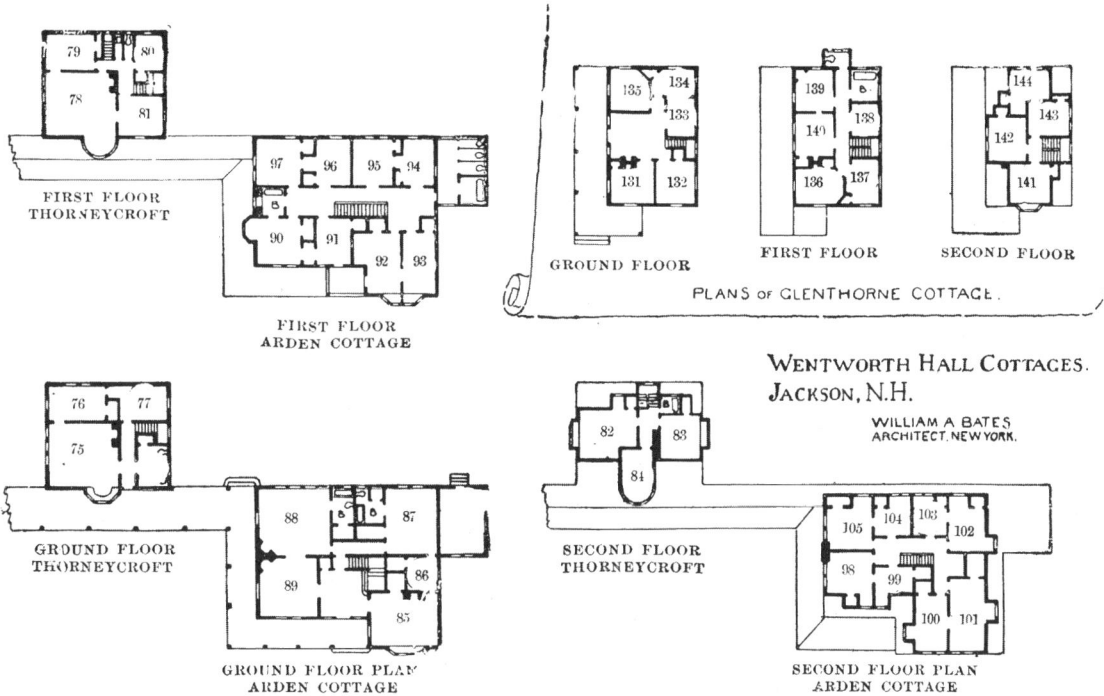

Fig. 3-14. "Wentworth Hall Cottages, Jackson, N. H.," *floor plans from* Wentworth Hall and Cottages *promotional booklet, c. 1900. Author's Collection. Arden, Thornycroft and Glenthorne Cottages composed the central part of the cottage village conceived by General Wentworth.*

Fig. 3-15. "A Stable at Wentworth Hall, Jackson, N. H.—W.A. Bates, Architect," *engraving,* The Sanitary Engineer and Construction Record, *27 August 1887, p. 346. Maine Historic Preservation Commission, Augusta, ME. This was the largest and most impressive outbuilding in the Wentworth Hall complex.*

1971 when it was temporarily closed, only to sit boarded up and dilapidated for the next decade. Purchased in 1982 by developer Ernest J. Mallett, Jr., the structurally unsound and functionally unusable buildings were removed until just nine of thirty-nine remained. Seven underwent total restoration and now serve as the core of a modern condominium community. Reopened in 1983, the remnants of the original Wentworth now accommodate over 125 guests in structures revitalized with painstaking care using replicas of old building elements, original materials and historically accurate paint selections. The result of this preservation effort is a convincing reflection of White Mountain village hotel life in the late Victorian period.[39]

The Barrons and Twin Mountain House

While the Thorn Mountain House was taking form at Jackson, plans were also developing for another major hotel on the west side of the Presidential Range. Anticipating the opening of the Mount Washington Cog Railroad (see Chapter 4), Asa T. Barron of Quechee, Vermont, in partnership with his brother Oscar F., purchased the Neal farmhouse and lands at Twin Mountain (Carroll) in 1867-68. Situated on a bluff above the Ammonoosuc River at the intersection of the Whitefield and Bethlehem roads, the roomy cottage took in boarders for a brief period.

The next year the partners built a new, and much more substantial hostelry christened "Twin Mountain House" in recognition of two 4,000 foot peaks to the south (Fig. 3-16). This large wooden L-shaped building was the first large hotel in the mountains topped with the fashionable hipped-on-Mansard roof with dormers. Otherwise it was architecturally bland, displaying a few Italian Revival features such as flat door hoods with brackets, eaves bracketing, and paneled square support columns and balustrades on its front veranda.

To help manage the new venture Asa brought in his son Oscar G. Barron, then just nineteen years old, who would become one of the White Mountains' most distinguished hotel entrepreneurs. For a brief time the young Barron worked under C. H. Merrill, but soon became sole proprietor in 1872 when Merrill went to the Crawford House. Initially housing 200 guests the hotel experienced immediate success, in large part due to the arrival of the Boston, Concord & Montreal Railroad the next year. The Barrons promptly responded with additions to the west end and rear ell in 1873-74, increasing the capacity to nearly 300 (Fig. 3-17). Perhaps its greatest attraction was its central location, allowing easy access to Franconia Notch and the Profile House, Crawford Notch and the Crawford House, Jefferson and the Waumbek House, Mount Washington, Beth-

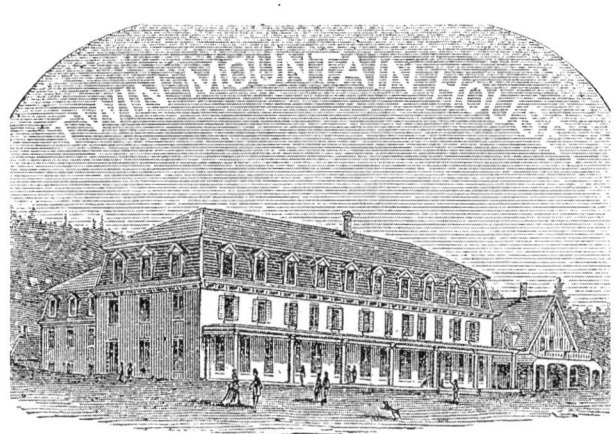

Fig. 3-16. "Twin Mountain House, A. T. & O. F. Barron, Proprietors," *Carroll, NH, engraving from Thursty McQuill,* The White and Green Mountains . . . *(1872), p. 2. Author's Collection. The earliest portion of the hotel was built in 1868-69, and was attached to the original Neal farmhouse to its right.*

Fig. 3-17. Twin Mountain House, Carroll, NH, *photograph, c. 1890, by J. C. Blake, Littleton (successor to C. P. Hibbard, Lisbon). Douglas Philbrook, Gorham, NH. The hotel is illustrated in its fully developed state after additions of 1873-74. The famous Brooklyn, NY, theologian, Henry Ward Beecher, summered here for many years.*

lehem and its many hotels, as well as nearby mountains, streams and cascades.[40]

Steeped in history and frequented by many famous political, literary and social personages, the Twin Mountain House, like the Crawford House nine miles away, always possessed a certain aura. Of the many notable guests who visited during the height of its fame, presidents Grant, Hayes, Arthur, Harding and Coolidge stand out. Tragically, President Garfield was en route to the hotel when he was unexpectedly assassinated in 1881.

A haven for sufferers of hay fever or "autumnal catarrh," the hotel attracted many seeking relief including the noted theologian Henry Ward Beecher, pastor of Plymouth Congregational Church in Brooklyn, New York, who came to Twin Mountain in 1872 and returned with his sister, authoress Harriet Beecher Stowe, for the next seventeen seasons. A dynamic and eloquent preacher of national repute, Beecher literally transformed the hotel into his summer parish, drawing up to 1,000 people to his Sunday services—some came by special trains from as far away as Plymouth. To accommodate the throngs the Barrons first pitched a huge tent beside the hotel and ultimately built a special six-sided assembly pavilion. Beecher's magnetic appeal apparently did not prove distasteful to either himself or the Barrons—during the critical early phase of their ownership the Barrons had in residence their exclusive showman and marketing agent, and Beecher's presence could only have been a boon for business![41]

The Twin Mountain House successfully lived up to its billing, as evidenced by Rev. George W. Gile's account of his visit in the mid-1870s:

> In the parlors, elegantly furnished, wild flowers and ferns were arranged in exquisite taste and beauty. From the chandeliers in the dining hall were suspended little log-cabins and canoes, filled with wild moss and roses, while miniature flags of all nations, placed in the drinking glasses at each plate on the table, gave the whole scene an indescribable loveliness and charm. The entertainment was complete, a lavish rich-

Fig. 3-18. "Dining Room, Twin Mountain House, White Mts., N. H.," photograph #167, c. 1880, C. P. Hibbard, Lisbon, NH. Douglas Philbrook, Gorham, NH. Though relatively austere and simply furnished, this room possessed its own special charm, enhanced by unusual decorations and excellent cuisine.

ness of everything that was palatable and tempting was set before you; waiters neat, prompt, and polite, anticipated your every want.[42]

Photographer C. W. Hibbard of Lisbon created a fine cabinet view (c. 1885) of the dining hall, capturing the atmosphere Gile sensed when there (Fig. 3-18).[43]

Remarkably the Twin Mountain House remained in the possession of the Barrons and their managing company for seventy-eight years, one of the longest periods of continuous ownership in White Mountain hotel history. Finally, in April 1946 hotelman George Nichols of New York acquired the hotel; his firm, S. G. Riesner Company, Inc., continued summer operation through 1959. The hotel was then permanently closed, exactly ninety years after it opened. Raymond S. Johnson of Groveton, New Hampshire, then purchased the structure and tore it down during the following year to make way for a site development project that never materialized.[44] But the Twin Mountain House, at least, escaped the all too common fate of destruction by fire and passed into memory as one of the grand hotels with the longest operation under one ownership.

Sinclair House and the Origins of Bethlehem as Hotel Center

During the 1860s, at the same time the Twin Mountain House was becoming established, Bethlehem, eight miles to the west, began its rise to prominence as the White Mountain's largest hotel center. Situated on a long ridge nearly 1,500 feet above sea level, the town possessed natural advantages that few other mountain communities in the eastern United States could match. Among these were superb panoramic vistas, cool and refreshing breezes, abundant spring and stream water, and a "pure, dry atmosphere" providing a healthful climate for people suffering from asthma, hay fever or other maladies. Bethlehem's central location north of the major notches provided ready access to stage and eventually rail transportation. As the Civil War approached the town was poised for the development of the tourist industry.[45]

One of the first to recognize the possibilities of the "summer boarding business" was John H. Sinclair, a prominent politician and native of Barnstead, New Hampshire, who lived in Bethlehem from 1847 to

1869 and again from 1875 to 1879. Continuing the local tavern tradition, but also anticipating the coming influx of vacationers, Sinclair built a small hostelry of "eight or ten rooms" in 1857. This building was the earliest in Bethlehem to house guests on a long-term basis. In an interview conducted by Frank H. Burt, editor of *Among the Clouds*, Sinclair recounted an amusing episode involving a local citizen and his reaction to the new venture:

> Sir Isaac Newton Gay, the old hermit who lived down near the Maplewood [a later hotel] so many years, came by one day while I was building. I well remember how the old man drew himself up, leaning on his cane, and looking at me in a commiserating manner, said, 'Squire, do you think a house of this magnitude will ever pay in a town like this?' The old man lived to see my modest little house grow to ten times its original size, and a hundred times as many visitors coming to town.[46]

The fruit of Sinclair's initial labors was a small two-and-a-half-story, gable-roofed house on Bethlehem Street (known locally as "the Street") at the intersection with the road that went over the west shoulder of Mount Agassiz from Franconia.[47]

From 1861 until well into the twentieth century, expansion of this unpretentious building continued in earnest as its owners tried to keep pace with the seemingly insatiable need in Bethlehem for more hotel space. Sinclair enlarged his house in 1861, putting on what later became the center section of the hotel. He also added a west wing, a virtual mirror image of the original structure. The resulting three-unit facade had a perfectly balanced symmetry; the Greek-temple-form central portion with square cupola was flanked by identical wings (Fig. 3-19). Clearly Sinclair and his contractors were influenced by the popular Greek Revival style that had inspired so many residential, institutional and public buildings in New England from the 1830s to the 1860s. These schemes, like the Sinclair, tended to be arranged according to the three-unit axial plan (with either joined or detached buildings), recalling Ammi Burnham Young's "Old Row" at Dartmouth College in

Fig. 3-19. "Sinclair House, Bethlehem, N. H.," *stereo view, Kilburn #113, c. 1870. Douglas Philbrook, Gorham, NH. Viewed from the northwest, the hotel was enlarged by owner John Sinclair in 1861 to create a perfectly symmetrical three-unit complex.*

Hanover, perhaps the best example of the plan in northern New Hampshire.[48]

In 1866-67 Sinclair enlarged the new hotel a second time, giving it "rank among the larger mountain houses."[49] Stereo views, often the only reliable source of architectural information, reveal the form of the full complex starting to take shape. A large five-story rectangular box of a building appears, covered by a hipped-on-Mansard roof, and displays a full-length, two-story piazza on the long east elevation. With its great mass and Mansard roof, the new addition, while a functional success, destroyed the simple, pleasant symmetry of the original building composition, creating an aesthetic dilemma for future owners and builders.

It took new owners and several more years to resolve this design problem. After contracting E. R. Abbott to manage the hotel for a time, Sinclair sold the property in 1870 to J. A. Durgin and D. W. Ranlet. Ranlet's interest soon passed to A. B. Richardson and then to Warren Fox. The partnership of Durgin & Fox, which maintained ownership until 1888, created the next large expansion, implementing a staged building program between 1875 and 1878. Guest capacity first surpassed 250 and soon reached 300.[50] Newspaper advertisements and guidebook engravings supply the sole basis of architectural description and analysis (Fig. 3-20). During the expansion the original wings of the old hotel were raised to four stories, creating one continuous roof line, broken inten-

Fig. 3-20. "Sinclair House, Bethlehem, N. H.," *engraving from* Summer Saunterings by the B. & L. *(1885), p. 128. Author's Collection. After additions in 1866-67 and 1875-78, the hotel assumed this appearance on its main facade, and remained relatively unaltered until the time of its burning in 1978.*

Fig. 3-21. Dining Room, Sinclair House, Bethlehem, NH, *photograph from* The Sinclair Hotel, White Mountains, Bethlehem, N.H. *(Bethlehem: n.p., [c.1910]). Author's Collection. This new dining room was included in a large 1900-01 addition to the hotel.*

tionally by the old cupola-topped pavilion facing the main street. Also added were many Italian Revival trappings typical of the era, such as flat hoodmolds over windows and doors, heavy, paired eaves brackets, dormers with ornamented jambs, and paneled brick chimneys. The massive L-shaped complex, thanks to the vision of Durgin & Fox, appeared as a logical, unified whole, its various elements successfully conveying the essence of mid-Victorian cultural taste.

Daniel W. Harrington and William McAuliffe purchased the Foxes' share of the Sinclair in 1888 and ran it under the name Durgin & Company. In 1908 they formed the Sinclair Hotel Company, with Harrington as president and McAuliffe as treasurer.[51] Durgin & Company completed two more additions. In 1891 they appended a small ell containing an enlarged office and card rooms with new bedrooms above.[52] A decade later they attached a considerably larger ell to the rear corner of the east facade, increasing guest capacity to 350. Fitted with square corner towers punctuated by wide bay windows, it was described in the annual hotel improvements article in the *White Mountain Echo*:

> The Sinclair House at Bethlehem has been enlarged by a very handsome addition, which increases the capacity of the hotel by fifteen elegant and sightly rooms, most of them en suite with bath. The furnishings of these rooms are of the daintiest and harmonize perfectly with the decorations of the rooms. The handsome new dining-room . . . is winning unstinted praise. It is so spacious that it affords ample room for more than four hundred to dine at one time. Three large plate glass scenery windows provide a superior outlook toward Mount Washington. At night the room is brilliantly lighted and all the beauties of its decoration are displayed to the best advantage.[53]

A c. 1910 promotional booklet for the hotel contains an interior view of this new dining room, with its polished hard-wood floors, ample windows, delicate electric light fixtures, and classical molding and vertical support column details (Fig. 3-21).

Passing to additional owners and experiencing minor alterations since 1901, the Sinclair House ended its long period of service in 1975, after 118 seasons. Its contents were sold at auction in August 1976. For the next two years the building sat derelict and deteriorating, a nostalgic remembrance of the grand resort hotel legacy it had helped to establish and perpetuate (see Plate 5). Preeminent among Bethlehem's few surviving hotels, the Sinclair was destroyed by a fire of undetermined origin on 24 October 1978. As the final remaining wall collapsed, one newspaper account of the emotional event noted, it was like "the last gasp of an old lady."[54]

Plate 1. "The Notch House, White Mountains, New Hampshire," *colored lithograph, c. 1860, by Currier & Ives, New York. Douglas Philbrook, Gorham, NH. This scene, derived from William H. Bartlett's c. 1836 engraving, shows the Notch House as it was originally built in Crawford Notch. It would later grow to accommodate seventy-five guests.*

Plate 2. "Lafayette House Franconia Notch, Sept. 1, 1845," *pencil and watercolor sketch by James Elliot Cabot. New Hampshire Historical Society. Opened in 1835, this modest highway inn was the first in Franconia Notch. Like other early White Mountain hostelries, it was built as a farmhouse, but also served as a tavern and accommodated overnight guests.*

Plate 3. "White Mountain Station House, By J. R. Hitchcock & Co. Gorham, N. H.," *lithograph (c. 1855) by John H. Bufford's Lith., Boston. Douglas Philbrook, Gorham, NH. Built in 1850-51 and later named "Alpine House" by Hitchcock, this fine Victorian eclectic structure was the first of the hotels in the White Mountains to include a railroad station.*

Plate 4. Wentworth Hall, Wentworth Hall and Cottages, Jackson, NH, *photograph, 1990, by the author. Erected in 1882-83 from plans by New York architect William A. Bates, this structure is the centerpiece of the Wentworth Hotel and condominium village today. It still serves as the main service facility for several cottages that were part of the original nineteenth-century complex.*

Plate 5. Sinclair House, Bethlehem, NH, *photograph, c. 1976, by the author. The Sinclair House was situated at the center of the White Mountains' largest tourist community. The hotel was closed in 1975, and sat unused and deteriorating until it burned in 1978.*

Plate 6. "*Pemigewasset House, Plymouth, N. H.,*" *lithograph by John H. Bufford, Boston, c. 1855. Douglas Philbrook, Gorham, NH. This lyrical scene from east of the hotel illustrates the intimate relationship that existed between the White Mountain hotels and the railroad systems that penetrated the region.*

Plate 7. "The Maplewood, White Mountains, Bethlehem, N. H.," *lithograph by William H. Brett Engraving Co., Boston, c. 1878. New Hampshire Historical Society. This magnificent view portrays the Victorian eclectic architecture of the complex and the opportunities for pleasure and relaxation available to guests.*

Plate 8. The Maplewood Casino, Maplewood, Bethlehem, NH, *photograph, 1991, by the author. Designed by Littleton architect Edward Thornton Sanderson in c. 1887, this pleasure pavilion for Maplewood Hotel patrons is an outstanding regional example of Shingle Chateauesque style architecture.*

Plate 9. The Upland Terrace Hotel (formerly the Uplands), Bethlehem, NH, *photograph, c. 1976, by the author. In this close view of the west wing (1912), unusually fine and delicate late Victorian eclectic detail is visible.*

Plate 10. Sunset Hill House, Sugar Hill, NH, *photograph, 1973, by the author. Built between 1879 and 1903, the Sunset Hill boasted an impressive 375-foot facade and distinctive corner towers. The hotel is shown just days after its final closing as it awaited demolition.*

Jefferson and the Waumbek Hotel

The small village of Jefferson, eighteen miles northeast of Bethlehem, possessed many of the same natural inducements for tourists but rested undiscovered until just before the Civil War. Early visitors to that region of the White Mountains were impressed by its elevation (1,400 feet), panoramic views, beautiful scenery, pure air, agreeable climate, and excellent drainage and water supply. Perhaps the most influential of these people was the Reverend Thomas Starr King. His widely acclaimed book, *The White Hills; Their Legends, Landscape and Poetry* (1859, and subsequent editions), drew national attention to the charms and opportunities of the mountains, fostering its tourist industry.[55] King recognized the potential of Jefferson and in his characteristically florid writing style, made this telling pronouncement in his book:

> Jefferson . . . may without exaggeration be called the ultima thule of grandeur in an artist's pilgrimage among the New Hampshire mountains, for at no other point can he see the White Hills themselves in such array and force.[56]

King went on to observe prophetically:

> There is as yet no large public-house in Jefferson. If a good hotel should be erected there, the village would soon become one of the most popular resorts among the mountains, . . . and would need no further introductions of its advantages and claims.[57]

Through the solicitous urgings of Reverend King speculation became reality. While on his travels through the mountains King often stayed at the Plaisted family's wayside inn in Jefferson, known as the Red Tavern. Here, he became acquainted with proprietor Benjamin H. Plaisted and, pressing him with his vision for the town, encouraged him to build a hotel; he even selected a location and suggested the

Fig. 3-22. "Waumbek House, Jefferson Hill, N. H., B. H. Plaisted Proprietor," *letterhead engraving, c. 1863. Author's Collection. The first portion of what would eventually become the great Waumbek Hotel was erected by Benjamin H. Plaisted in 1860 after strong urging by theologian and writer Thomas Starr King.*

Indian name of "Waumbek," meaning "White Hills."[58] Plaisted promptly responded, and in 1860 he erected the first portion of what would ultimately become the great Waumbek Hotel—"a three-story building 40 x 60 feet, with an ell for culinary purposes and necessary attachments" (Fig. 3-22).[59] Grateful to King for his assistance, Plaisted then proceeded to name the peak rising 3,913 feet behind the hotel, Mount Starr King—making King one of the few theologians in the United States to have a mountain named after him.[60]

The new hotel venture was an immediate success, which is hardly surprising when one takes into account the primary attraction of the site:

> This house being situated on the north side of the mountains, the scenery from its verandas is perfectly lovely and picturesque. Overlooking the beautiful Jefferson intervales, commanding an uninterrupted view of the White, Franconia, Starr King and Cherry Mountains, the Green Mountains in Vermont, Whitefield and Randolph Hills, Mt. Washington House [on the summit of Mt. Washington], and trains on the Mt. Washington Railway, [they] can all be distinctly seen from the piazza; in fact, there is no spot about the White Mountains where one can see so much mountain scenery as from the broad verandas of the Waumbek.[61]

Upon learning of this vista and other advantages, visitors flocked to Jefferson in greater numbers. Business prospered, and Plaisted met the challenge by adding a southeast wing, 40 by 100 feet, to his house in 1865.[62] This created an asymmetrical, T-shaped edifice, its only suggestions of architectural style being Greek Revival-inspired doorways with side windows, lights and moldings, and eaves brackets most commonly associated with the Italian Revival (Fig. 3-23).

Plaisted sold the majority of his interest in the hotel to William Merrill a few years later and built the adjacent Plaisted House around 1872. J. R. Crocker then acquired the Waumbek and enlarged it

Fig. 3-23. "Waumbek House, Jefferson, N. H., Merrill & Plaisted, Proprietors," *advertising engraving from* The Summer Excursionist of the Central Vermont Railroad Company... (1874), p. 122. Author's Collection. Benjamin H. Plaisted added a southeast wing (right) to his original hotel in 1865, responding to the increased numbers of visitors to Jefferson.

Fig. 3-24. "The Waumbek and Cottages, at Jefferson, in the White Mountains," *photograph from* Scenic Gems of the White Mountains *(c. 1905). Author's Collection. Consisting of two spliced sections, this photo shows the full Waumbek complex in all its Colonial Revival grandeur.*

around 1879 to hold a capacity of over 200 guests with the addition of a fourth story under a Mansard roof.[63] In this form, the building closely resembled other smaller neighboring hotels constructed at the time (Maple and Grand View houses in Jefferson; Mount Adams, Pliny Range, E. A. Crawford's and Highland houses in Jefferson Highlands). Striking similarities in floor plans, proportions and roof forms suggest that a locally distinctive building mode momentarily became dominant, perhaps the product of a single contractor or group of contractors.

With the acquisition of the property in 1888 by the concern of Plumer & Porter (formally incorporated as the "Jefferson Hotel and Land Company"), the Waumbek entered its grand era.[64] At the instigation of the new owners, the old hotel underwent a total visual metamorphosis; it dramatically increased in size over the next fifteen years to become one of the largest and most luxurious grand hotel complexes in the White Mountains, if not the entire United States. To launch such an ambitious plan of expansion the services of a major architectural firm were required, and the company directors did not think small-scale. In 1888, and possibly earlier, they hired the recently formed partnership of Carrere (John Mervin, 1858-1911) and Hastings (Thomas, 1860-1929) of New York City, who later achieved international recognition, to transform their ideas into reality.[65] Establishing an office in 1884, this firm had made an auspicious debut, signing on as a major client Henry M. Flagler, the wealthy American capitalist and Florida railroad and property developer. Carrere and Hastings planned several notable buildings in the St. Augustine area for Flagler before 1890, including the Hotel Ponce de Leon and the Alcazar Hotel (see Introduction), both in a modified version of the Spanish Renaissance Revival vernacular. Hence, when the firm took on the Waumbek project it had already established a track record in hotel design.[66]

The first phase of the expansion program, Carrere and Hastings' only documented commission for the Waumbek, resulted in an extension—100 feet long by 32 feet wide—to the front of the original 1860 building.[67] The *White Mountain Echo* described this wholesale alteration in July 1889:

> The old [front] facade has been removed and replaced with an elegant new one in the colonial style, while additional space given to the interior increases the capacity of the hotel by new offices, parlors and sleeping rooms. The exterior of the house is painted in yellow and white.[68]

Fig. 3-25. Main Dining Room, Waumbek Hotel, Jefferson, NH, *photograph from* The New Waumbek Hotel and Cottages at Jefferson, N. H. *(Jefferson: n.p., [c. 1920]). Jefferson Historical Society. This view, made after the dining room had been expanded into the piazza areas, shows an interesting combination of Colonial Revival architectural detailing and furnishings.*

Conceived with seemingly playful Victorian whimsy, the addition displayed, in harmonious relationship, such familiar Colonial Revival features as Ionic wall pilasters, small-paned, double-sash windows, and dormers (see Fig. 3-24). There also were corner towers with French ogee roofs, a Dutch profile main roof line, a semi-circular veranda, and a corner rotunda with a conical roof and two-story, columned loggia. A driveway penetrated the northwest end of the extension through a segmental arch opening. Although asymmetrical almost to the point of distraction, the building was a testament to good design and managed to hold together aesthetically, its diverse parts balancing each other to create a unified whole.[69]

As this project was being completed, proprietors Plumer & Porter were contemplating another large wing to be added before the 1890 season. An article in *Among the Clouds* (July 1889) notes "plans have already been drafted," raising the possibility that Carrere and Hastings may have also been responsible for this phase of the expansion.[70] While such an attribution for the design has yet to be proven, the results, on the exterior and interior, were very reminiscent of the firm's 1888-89 work. Perhaps awaiting the arrival of the Concord and Montreal Railroad spur (1892) to the center of town, hotel officers deferred construction of the new wing until 1891-92.

Among the Clouds, in characteristically thorough fashion, provided the salient details:

> The old barns and other buildings west of the hotel were removed last year and an extension was made to the west 112 feet in length, and upwards of forty feet in width. The first floor... is given up to the new dining room [Fig. 3-25] and the upper stories to guests' rooms, about 40 in all. A large barn on the street east of the hotel, 200 feet long, has been built, and a new laundry and other buildings have also been added.[71]

The basement was devoted to children's play rooms and billiard rooms. Forming what would soon become the center portion of the complex and marked by a center hexagonal tower and two-story piazza, the addition increased guest capacity to 300.[72] Further expansion continued unabated throughout the 1890s until nearly 600 guests could be accommodated.

By 1901, as a result of additional building and the absorption of most of the other local hotels and boarding houses, Jefferson had become both a one-industry and one-company town. The Jefferson Hotel and Land Company purchased the Starr King House (c. 1879, 80 guests) in 1890, followed by the Jefferson Hill House (later called "The Jefferson") (1872, 100 guests) in 1895, the Plaisted House (later titled "Waumbek Hall") (c. 1872, 125 guests) in 1899, and Sunset Inn (40 guests) and Mountain View House (20 guests) at other times in the decade.[73] During the same period the company's land holdings were increased to 900 acres. Five new cottages out of an eventual total of eleven were built east of the main house, six of which still stand. In 1897-98 the hotel itself received another major wing angled obliquely on its northwest end, enlarging the dining room, incorporating a music room, and adding forty more sleeping rooms to the structure. The presence of two additional round corner towers with French ogee roofs on the new end wall again suggests that Carrere and Hastings were the probable designers.[74] Additional expansion (dining room, office, piazza and porte cochere) was carried out in 1900 and 1901.[75] All this development was visually chronicled in an outstanding bird's eye view of the building and adjacent lands published in hotel promotional booklets during the 1910s and 1920s (Fig. 3-26).

The Jefferson Company properties remained unchanged throughout the early part of this century although unrealized plans were laid in 1902 to upgrade the hotel and reconfigure the building arrangement. At that time George L. Theobald, a Concord, New Hampshire, contractor and a Boston architect named Gray completed studies to increase the room capacity of the hotel, improve office and dining space, relocate some of the smaller outbuildings and roadways, and install new landscaping. It was also proposed that the old southeast wing be extended to provide fifty more guest suites.[76] These modifications were not completed, indicating a possible slackening of business and reduced demand for hotel space just after 1900. In 1916, however, manager A. W. Hodgdon completely refurbished the hotel inside and out, at a cost of over $100,000, and for marketing purposes renamed it "New Waumbek Hotel & Cottages."[77] This occurred under the new ownership of O. H. Brown and F. F. Shute of Spring Lake, New Jersey, with Shute subsequently becoming the sole owner in 1920.[78]

In just two hours, on 9 May 1928, fire, the curse that has befallen so many of the White Mountain hotels, completely leveled the great main building along with four cottages and other outbuildings. This catastrophic episode, literally and figuratively, left a huge hole in the middle of the village of Jefferson. The headline in the *Coos County Democrat* (Lancaster) edition reporting the fire read quite simply and poignantly, "What Was Once the Pride of the White Mountains Now in Ruins." But the owner Shute demonstrated resilience by opening the resort for business the following summer, using the remaining buildings, with Waumbek Hall as the centerpiece, to accommodate guests and service functions (Fig. 3-27).[79] From the 1930s through the 1970s the property continued to be operated in this manner, changing hands many times. In 1971 it was pur-

Fig. 3-26. "New Waumbek Hotel & Cottages, Jefferson (White Mountains) N. H.," *booklet cover*, The New Waumbek Hotel and Cottages at Jefferson, N.H. *(Jefferson: n.p., [c. 1920]). Jefferson Historical Society. This marvelous panorama depicts the main hotel with the affiliated Starr King (left edge, middle), Plaisted (lower left) and Jefferson Hill (right center, lower edge) houses, and several cottages behind.*

Fig. 3-27. The Waumbek Hotel (Waumbek Hall), Jefferson, NH, *photograph, c. 1980, by Richard Hamilton, Littleton, NH. After the destruction of the main hotel by fire in 1928, this building (formerly Plaisted House) was the centerpiece of the remaining portions of the hotel complex until it was razed in 1980.*

chased by a private investment and conservation trust in which the Gregg family of Nashua had primary interest.[80] The hotel struggled for a few more years, but finally closed in 1980. Following an auction of its contents, Waumbek Hall was demolished in the fall of that year. Of the buildings comprising the Jefferson Hotel and Land Company properties, only the Jefferson Hill House survived, a reminder of the Waumbek's once glorious past, but even it finally fell to the wrecking ball in the spring of 1993 (Fig. 3-28).[81]

The Second Pemigewasset House

Of the smaller White Mountain hostelries originating in the 1860s, the second Pemigewasset House in Plymouth is by far the most significant, both historically and architecturally (see Plate 6). After the first Pemigewasset House burned in 1862 (see Chapter 1) the property was sold to the Boston, Concord and Montreal Railroad, and in 1863, a new hotel rose on top of the old foundations, under the aegis of the Pemigewasset Hotel Company. Not surprisingly, the railroad was the major stockholder, recognizing the need to maintain a hotel facility in Plymouth to serve as a stopping off point for those traveling on the B., C. & M. into the northern mountains. Over the years many people did just that, and the hotel hosted many famous individuals including former President Franklin Pierce and the renowned novelist Nathaniel Hawthorne. It was at the Pemigewasset in May 1864 that Hawthorne, accompanied by Pierce, unexpectedly passed away, giving the hotel an honored place in American literary history.[82]

The 1863 edition of Eastman's *White Mountain Guide* offers a comprehensive, first-hand description of the second Pemigewasset House:

> The new hotel, which is without exception the finest in the State, is 230 feet in front [facing Main Street], with a wing of 80 feet, and is

Fig. 3-28. Jefferson Hill House (The Jefferson), Jefferson, NH, *photograph, 1991, by the author. Built beginning in 1872, the Jefferson Hill House was the last surviving hotel unit from the original Waumbek community before its demolition in 1993.*

Fig. 3-29. "Dining Hall of the Pemigewasset House," Plymouth, NH, *engraving from Rev. George W. Gile,* Excursions to the White Mountains with Dr. Ordway's Parties of '75 and '76 *(Lawrence, MA: George S. Merrill and Crocker, 1877), p. 7. Dartmouth College Library. This room was noted for its spacious, unobstructed space and tall windows.*

Fig. 3-30. Lobby and Main Desk, Pemigewasset House, Plymouth, NH, *photograph, c. 1900. Plymouthiana Collection, Herbert H. Lamson Library, Plymouth State College. The office, or lobby, displays fine dark wood classical detail on the columns, doorways and main desk. It was connected to a stairway leading from the railway platform below.*

four stories high. There are . . . [150] sleeping rooms, all of which are lighted by gas, and are large and commodious. There are also many suites of rooms, for families. The parlor is a large and spacious room, elegantly furnished, fronting the south. The dining room [Fig. 3-29] is a noble hall, on the main floor, lighted by large windows and without a single column or pillar to mar its symmetry. The office [Fig. 3-30] is also a spacious hall in the centre of the house, with a stairway leading from the Railway platform below. On the roof is a large observatory from which may be had a fine view of the valleys of the Baker and Pemigewasset Rivers, and also of Lafayette, Osceola, and almost the entire range of the Waterville and Franconia Mountains . . . the Passenger Depot of the Boston, Concord & Montreal Railroad is in the basement, rendering it very convenient for those passing through Plymouth to dine.[83]

Travelers who patronized the little restaurant off the platform were serviced with style and efficiency as is apparent in a wonderfully vivid photograph dating from around 1900 (Fig. 3-31). Often when trains arrived at the station villagers would greet the passengers, along with a quadrille band "playing with ambition and irrepressible enthusiasm."[84]

With its T-shaped floor plan and stepped down the hillside toward the Pemigewasset River, the hotel

Fig. 3-31. Diner, Pemigewasset House, Plymouth, NH, *photograph, c. 1900. Plymouthiana Collection, Herbert H. Lamson Library, Plymouth State College. This small restaurant, seemingly poised to receive patrons, serviced railroad passengers during train stops at the hotel station.*

must have been an imposing presence in the town center. Embellished with a profusion of architectural details, all beautifully articulated and interrelated, it was without qualification one of the best pure examples of the Italian Revival style in New England and possibly the nation. Among its striking features were Doric corner pilasters, plain entablatures, eaves brackets, single and paired ("Siamese") round-arched windows, dormers with ornamented jambs, and side and rear verandas with square column supports, console brackets and pierced balustrades. Atop a moderately pitched roof at the center intersection of the planes was perched the "observatory" (or cupola), octagonal in form, with round-arched windows and a pyramidal roof cap with finial. But perhaps most impressive about the building was the front central open pavilion with its closed bracketed gable, and square, paneled columns, broken by a second story balustrade (Fig. 3-32). Behind the column screen was a Palladian window at the second floor level and an unusual first-floor, round-arched main doorway flanked by vertical round-arched lights. A forceful, nicely proportioned "high-style" architectural statement in small town rural surroundings, the Pemigewasset possessed aesthetic attributes that only a few of the grand hotels of the same period or later could boast.

On 12 May 1909, while under J. R. Elliott's proprietorship, the second Pemigewasset House fell victim to fire and was replaced three years later by another hotel of the same name on a new but nearby site.[85]

Fig. 3-32. "Pemigewasset House, Plymouth, N. H.," *stereo view, c. 1870, Kilburn #194. Author's Collection. The facade fronting the main street of Plymouth possessed a nicely scaled and articulated Italian Revival central pavilion with an octagonal cupola or "observatory" above.*

Like the other White Mountain hotels suffering the same fate, it had effectively served its public in ways that had become quite characteristic of the small community, highly rural, and in some cases nearly wilderness-based tourist economy of the region. It had offered a guest life style that urban or suburban hotels elsewhere in the Northeast could not hope to match. An 1888 article in *Among the Clouds* captured the essence of the visitor experience at the Pemigewasset:

> For those who wish to get away from the bustle and swelter of the metropolis, and yet who do not care to go beyond the borders of civilization and cannot find solitude in the charms that sages have seen in her face, the Pemigewasset is a model hostelry. Here you can get all the rest that you want, while there is sufficient life and excitement to rout monotony and destroy all tedium . . . an ever shifting panorama of human activity is presented that exhibits typical America in its fullest measures.[86]

Here, as at other White Mountain hotels of the 1860s, people could seek peace of mind, healthfulness of body, and relaxed conviviality. They were able to temporarily free themselves from the stresses of war and post-war recovery as well as social and economic pressures produced by a nation undergoing unprecedented industrialization and urbanization. Fortuitously, the decade ahead would accelerate these tendencies, and the White Mountain hotel industry would continue to respond with energy, vision, and determination.

Notes

1. Bulkley, "History," pp. 44–46, 47, 49–52.
2. Moses F. Sweetser, *Chisholm's White Mountain Guide Book* (Portland, ME: Chisholm Brothers, 1887), advertisement, p. 28.
3. At the time of the final large addition to the Kearsarge House in 1871-72, the Kearsarge Tavern, or first Kearsarge House, was split into two sections and moved to separate sites in North Conway. One half was relocated to a side street and converted to a residence (it later became the rectory for the Episcopal Church), while the other half was repositioned across Main Street to form part of Kearsarge Hall, a rooming house. See Kilbourne, *Chronicles*, p. 160, and Ruth B.D. Horne, *Conway Through the Years and Whither* (Conway, NH: Conway Historical Society, 1963), p. 67.
4. Moses M. Sweetser, *Among the Mountains* (Boston: Passenger Department, Boston & Maine Railroad, 1889), p. 20; *The White Mountain Guidebook*, 10th ed. (Concord, NH: Edson C. Eastman; and Boston: Lee & Shepard, 1872), p. 160; *Faxon's Illustrated Handbook of Travel...*, rev. ed. (Boston: C.A. Faxon, 1874), p. 179; Merrill, *History of Carroll County*, p. 884; *The Reporter* (North Conway), 24 May 1923, p. 1. The Andrews of the new firm (1873) was I. N. Andrews, formerly of the staff of the Profile House. This partnership was succeeded by S. W. & S. D. Thompson who ran it until 1881, S. W. Thompson from 1881 to 1883, Thompson & Schoff until 1887, and then Alfred Schoff, F. L. Porter, Arthur Taylor, and L. J. Richer after that date. An unusual feature of the hotel was that it was open all year long until 1878. After that time it took guests only during the summer months.
5. George F. Field, *Field's Handbook of Travel...* (Boston: Passenger Department of the Eastern & Maine Central Railroad Line, 1873), p. 27.
6. *Chisholm's All Round Route and Panoramic Guide of the St. Lawrence ... ; The White Mountains ...* (Montreal: C.R. Chisholm Bros., 1875), p. 190.
7. Bachelder, *Popular Resorts; and How to Reach Them* (1874), p. 14. Electric lights were installed in 1887 (*ATC*, 15 August 1887, p. 5).
8. During the 1880s and 1890s, and particularly after 1899, under the aegis of the Kearsarge Hotel Company, the hotel was recurrently remodeled and upgraded, with some minor changes to the layout of the physical plant (for example, see *ATC*, 10 August 1899, p. 4; *WME*, 11 July 1908, p. 13; and, *ATC*, 11 July 1916, p. 1). Sadly, the names of the designer and chief contractor of this interesting building remain unknown to date.
9. Other nineteenth-century hotels and inns at Intervale (bisected by the Conway-Bartlett town line) were the Bellevue House (1871-72, etc.), the Idlewild, the Clarendon House (1890-91), Pendexter House, Langdon House, Pendexter Mansion and Cottage (c. 1874, etc.) and Fairview Cottage.
10. Winfield S. Nevins, *The Intervale, New Hampshire* (Salem, MA: Salem Press, 1887), p. 37; Horne, *Conway Through the Years*, p. 70; *ATC* 18, No. 41 (30 August 1894), p. 8; Merrill, *History of Carroll County*, p. 880; *ATC* 3 No. 42 (4 September 1879), p. 1.
11. *ATC* 7, No. 50 (6 September 1883), p. 1. This expansion program supplemented the construction of the adjacent Intervale Cottage, a thirty-guest annex erected in c. 1879. It is possible that this was the "enlargement" referred to in *ATC* 3, No. 42 (4 September 1879), p. 1. See also, *ATC* 6, No. 18 (5 August 1882), p. 4, and *ATC* 8, No. 1 (12 July 1884), p. 1.
12. Merrill, *History of Carroll County*, p. 889; Nevins, *The Intervale*, pp. 37-38; *ATC* 18, No. 41 (30 August 1894), p. 8. This *ATC* article indicates that there were actually two parts to the addition—a large three-story wing, forty by eighty-five feet, and a smaller one-story wing, forty feet square. Twenty bedrooms were included as well as a new parlor. This information updates that provided in the article in *ATC* 7, No. 50 (6 September 1883), p. 1. See also, *WME* 7, No. 3 (12 July 1884), p. 8, and *ATC* 8, No. 41 (6 September 1884), p. 4.
13. *ATC* 11, No. 33 (17 August 1887). p. 5.
14. *ATC* 13, No. 12 (25 July 1889), p. 1. See also, *ATC* 13, No. 2 (13 July 1889), p. 5, and No. 7 (19 July 1889), p. 5.
15. *The Reporter*, 24 May 1923, p. 1. The loss from the blaze was estimated at $200,000, with less than half compensated from insurance. The hotel had just been purchased by Fred A. Jones of Brookline, NH.
16. *ATC* 18, No. 41 (30 August 1894), p. 4; Merrill, *History of Carroll County*, p. 885; Horne, *Conway Through the Years*, p. 69; *WME* 1, No. 4 (3 August 1878), p. 1. After 1871 the Masons divided their hotel holdings, Frank L. taking Mason's Hotel, and Mahlon L. becoming sole owner of the Sunset Pavilion.
17. *ATC* 22, No. 42 (2 September 1888), p. 3.
18. *WME* 1, No. 4 (2 August 1878), p. 1.
19. Lucy Crawford, *The History of the White Mountains, From the First Settlement of the Upper Coos and Pequawket*, 3rd ed. (Portland, ME: B. Thurston & Co., 1886), advertisement, p. 15.
20. *WME* 10, No. 5 (30 July 1887), p. 15; Withey, *Biographical Dictionary of American Architects (Deceased)*, p. 666. Designer of business and commercial buildings in Boston, Winslow (1843-1909) was a partner in the firm with George H. Wetherell (1854-1930) and Nathaniel J. Bradlee (1829-1888). This firm, in particular Wetherell, was commissioned to design several of Boston's large hotels, including the famed Parker House.

    The carpentry work for the new building was superintended by Henry Towle of North Conway, and the masonry construction was completed under the direction of Joseph Johnson of Fryeburg, ME.
21. *North Conway and Vicinity* (North Conway, NH: North Conway Board of Trade, c. 1891), advertisement.
22. *The Sunset Inn, North Conway, New Hampshire* (North Conway, n. p., c. 1925). For additional data about this structure,

see *WME* 10, No. 5 (30 July 1887), p. 15, and *ATC* 11, No. 16 (28 July 1887), p. 4.

23. *ATC* 39, No. 2 (24 July 1917), p. 1; Horne, *Conway Through the Years*, pp. 68-69. The hotel, known as the "Sunset Inn" after the Randall purchase, passed to Manufacturers Trust Company of New York in 1937, when the company bought the Hotel Randall. The president of the bank, local native Harvey Dow Gibson, took a particular interest in the care and management of the properties. The Hotel Randall (the third hostelry to bear this name), erected in 1926, was renamed the "Eastern Slope Inn" soon after this acquisition (see Chapter 5).

24. *The Reporter*, 27 June 1940, p. 1; *Boston Post*, 1 July 1940, pp. 1, 3; Horne, *Conway Through the Years*, p. 69. After the remnants of the hotel had been removed, the owners of the Eastern Slope Inn erected a ski lodge on the site. The damage from the loss was assessed at more than $75,000.

25. Garland, *Yesterdays*, p. 71; *ATC* 37, No. 2 (13 July 1915), p. 2; Merrill, *History of Carroll County*, p. 961. Based on logic and on supposition, I believe that the Thorn Mountain House may have been located where the building named "Wentworth Hall" stands today. In 1882-83, when Wentworth Hall was constructed, the old structure may have been moved back to its more recent location behind, but attached to, the namesake building. It had rooms for fifty guests.

26. *WME* 11, No. 6 (4 August 1888), advertisement, p. 18.

27. Withey, *Biographical Dictionary of American Architects (Deceased)*, p. 42.

28. Merrill, *History of Carroll County*, p. 961; *ATC* 5, No. 25 (13 August 1881), p. 2. This building had space for thirty guests.

29. *ATC* 6, No. 14 (1 August 1882), p. 8.

30. Merrill, *History of Carroll County*, p. 961.

31. *WME* 6, No. 3 (14 July 1883), p. 10.

32. *American Architect and Building News* 18 (12 December 1885), p. 282. It is my belief that at this time the old Thorn Mountain House (connected to the main building by a covered walkway) was totally remodeled inside and out in the Queen Anne style. Bates' plan identifies the two buildings as "Wentworth Hall, Built 1883," lending credence to this possibility (see Fig. 3-12). Thus far no evidence has surfaced to suggest that the Thorn Mountain House was torn down and replaced by a new structure. See also *WME* 6, No. 3 (14 July 1883), p. 10.

33. *WME* 6, No. 3 (14 July 1883), p. 10; Crawford, *History* (1883 ed.), advertisement, p. 221; Merrill, *History of Carroll County*, p. 961. Amenities included running stream water in guest rooms, excellent natural lighting, telephone and telegraph service, electric bells, open fireplaces in all public rooms, and well-engineered sanitation.

34. *American Architect and Building News* 18 (12 December 1885), p. 282, and drawing #520, Supplement, op. p. 3. In 1885 the name of the full establishment was changed from "Thorn Mountain House" to "Wentworth Hall and Cottages."

35. *WME* 8, No. 1 (27 June 1885), p. 8; *ATC* 9, No. 1 (11 July 1885), p. 8.

36. *WME* 9, No. 1 (3 July 1886), p. 12; *ATC* 16, No. 14 (26 July 1892), p. 1. The Casino was apparently not completely finished on the interior until 1892 when it was dedicated at a special leap year ball.

37. *WME* 8, No. 12 (12 September 1885), p. 8; *ATC* 18, No. 4 (18 July 1894), p. 4; *WME* 19, No. 1 (4 July 1896), p. 2.

38. At various times other buildings were added to the complex, including Sunnydale Cottage (1915), Hurlin Cottage, and Fairlawn and Amster cottages, which still stand. In addition to these, Wentworth Hall, and Arden, Thornycroft, and Wildwood cottages comprise the rest of the buildings in the current establishment. Above the site on a hill to the north is "The Castle" (1891-92), a double-towered fieldstone structure, formerly the residence of General and Mrs. Wentworth. In 1916 the Glen Ellis House (1875-76), a medium-size, Mansard-roofed wooden building, was acquired and used as a 100-guest annex (it was called "Fairview" for a time) to the complex until it was demolished in 1982. With the Glen Ellis House, the collective capacity of Wentworth Hall and Cottages peaked at 350.

39. Plan, Wentworth Hall and Cottages (Harry F. Kittredge, Surveyor [1931], Glen, NH), Jackson, planbook 4, pp. 382-83, CCRD; Garland, *Yesterdays*, p. 73; *NHHS Newsletter* 20, No. 4 (July 1983), p. 7; *New Hampshire Profiles* 33, No. 12 (December 1984), p. 31; *White Mountain Reporter* (North Conway), 22 September 1982, p. 1, and 20 October 1982, p. 1; *The Valley Visitor* (North Conway), 23 June 1988, p. 3; *Magnetic North* 3, No. 3 (Winter 1985), pp. 36, 38; Plan, subdivision, Wentworth Hall Estates (White Mountain Survey & Engineering [3 November 1981], West Ossipee), planbook 58, p. 22, CCRD. The hotel buildings were recently acquired by Fritz and Diana Koeppel who have continued the Mallett restoration work.

40. Frederic Lehr, *Carroll, New Hampshire: The First Two Hundred Years* (Carroll: Carroll Bicentennial Commission, 1972), p. 33; McAvoy, *And Then There Was One*, pp. 40-43; Kilbourne, *Chronicles*, p. 335; *The White Mountain Guide Book*, 9th ed. (Concord, NH: Edson C. Eastman & Co., and Boston: Lee and Shepard, 1870), p. 236; *The White Mountain Guide Book*, 13th ed. (Concord, NH: Edson C. Eastman & Co., and Boston: Lee and Shepard, 1876), p. 116; *Faxon's Illustrated Handbook of Travel*, p. 167; *ATC* 6, No. 7 (11 August 1883). The Neal house was first used as the Barron home and guest house. Advertising cuts and stereo views of the hotel from 1873 on do not show the house, suggesting that at or before that time it was moved behind the hotel and converted to a dormitory for the hired help. One of the additions may possibly have been built as early as 1870, but this has not been concretely ascertained.

41. *Faxon's Illustrated Handbook of Travel*, pp. 169-70; Lehr, *Carroll, New Hampshire*, pp. 35-36; Thursty McQuill [Wallace Bruce], *The Connecticut by Daylight...*, (New York: American News Company, 1874), pp. 77-78.

42. Rev. George A. Gile, *Excursions to the White Mountains with*

Dr. Ordway's Parties of '75 and '76 (Lawrence, MA: George S. Merrill & Crocker, 1877), p. 37.

43. Gas lighting was introduced at the Twin Mountain in 1881 (*ATC*, 19 July 1881, p. 1); given the presence of gas fixtures in the dining hall, it is possible to reasonably date the photograph.
44. Lehr, *Carroll, New Hampshire*, p. 36; Burt, *The Story of Mount Washington*, p. 110; Newspaper Scrapbooks, Special Collections, DCL; *Littleton Courier*, 4 August 1960, p. 1. The sale to Johnson included the 110-room main house, the garage, dormitory, recreation hall, swimming pool, observatory, repair shop and fifty acres of land. After the hotel was demolished, Route 3 to Whitefield was relocated through the Twin Mountain House site, and a new intersection was created where it crossed Route 302 just to the south. The necessary regrading so altered the site that today it is difficult to visualize the original setting.
45. William C. Gage, *"The Switzerland of America:" A Popular Guide to the Scenery of New Hampshire . . .* (Manchester, NH: C.F. Livingston, 1875), p. 76; Child, *Gazetteer of Grafton County, N. H.*, pp. 158-59; Kilbourne, *Chronicles*, p. 332; Gregory C. Wilson, *Bethlehem, New Hampshire: a bicentennial history* (Bethlehem: By the Town, 1974), p. 31; George H. Moses, "A Lost Town: A Sketch of Bethlehem," *Granite Monthly* 17, No. 1 (July 1894), p. 20.
46. Frank H. Burt, "A History of Bethlehem," *ATC* 17, No. 35 (25 August 1893), p. 4. John H. Sinclair was a Democrat and ran for Governor of New Hampshire in 1866, 1867 and 1868, as well as for U.S. Senator in 1876.
47. Kilbourne, *Chronicles*, p. 332.
48. *ATC* 17, No. 35 (25 August 1893), p. 4. See Bryant F. Tolles, Jr., "The Evolution of a Campus: Dartmouth College Architecture Before 1860," *Historical New Hampshire* 42, No. 4 (Winter 1987): 328-82, illustrated.
49. *The White Mountain Guide Book*, 7th ed. (Concord, NH: Edson C. Eastman, and Boston: Lee & Shepard, 1867), p. 237.
50. *ATC* 17, No. 35 (25 August 1893), p. 4. *Snow's Handbook of Northern Pleasure Travel, to the White and Franconia Mountains* (Worcester, MA: Noyes, Snow & Company, 1878), p. 95; *ATC* 1, No. 2 (21 July 1877), advertisement, p. 4; *ATC* 2, No. 1 (9 July 1878), advertisement, p. 3; *WME* 1, No. 1 (13 July 1878), p. 3. Contemporary guidebooks and other printed works supply only inconclusive evidence as to the dates and details of this project, so that we must again turn primarily to pictorial images for answers.
51. *ATC* 17, No. 35 (25 August 1893), p. 4; "Daniel Webster Harrington," *ATC* 37, No. 4 (15 July 1915), p. 1.
52. *ATC* 15, No. 2 (11 July 1891), p. 5.
53. *WME* 24, No. 2 (13 July 1901), p. 14. It has been asserted that Sylvanus D. Morgan (see Chapter 7), the well-known contractor from Lisbon, planned and supervised the construction of an addition to the Sinclair (see Paul A. Williams, "The Saga of 'S.D.' Morgan, Master Hotel Builder of the North Country," *New Hampshire Echoes* 1, No. 4 [Winter 1970], p. 13), but it is not known when this occurred. It is possible, however, that Morgan was responsible for the 1900-01 addition. The square corner towers of this were similar to one integrated into an addition Morgan built on the Upland Terrace, Bethlehem (see Chapter 4) in the late 1880s or early 1890s.

Sometime after 1920 the Mt. Agassiz House (1870, etc.), to the east across Mount Agassiz Street from the Sinclair, was acquired by the Sinclair Hotel Company. It subsequently was used as an annex under the name "Villa West," adding over 100 rooms to the hotel's guest capacity.
54. *Manchester* (NH) *Union Leader*, 28 October 1978. See also, *Littleton Courier*, 25 October 1978, p. 1. For many years in this century the hotel was owned by the Barbador Hotels Corporation, of which David Spiwack and Myron Herrman were the principal officers. In 1976 it was sold to its final owners, Merle Straw of Seabrook, NH, and True Glidden of Portsmouth.
55. *Historical Memories of the Town of Jefferson, New Hampshire, 1796-1971* (Jefferson: Anniversary Committee, 1971), p. 45.
56. Thomas Starr King, *The White Hills; Their Legends, Landscape, and Poetry* (Boston: Crosby, Nichols, Lee and Company, [1859]), p. 389.
57. *Ibid.*, p. 385.
58. [Merrill], *History of Coos County*, p. 420; *Historical Memories of the Town of Jefferson*, p. 45; Andrew Hepburn, *The Great Resorts of North America* (New York: Doubleday & Company, Inc., 1965), p. 35; George C. Evans, *History of the Town of Jefferson, New Hampshire, 1773-1927* (Manchester, NH: Granite State Press, 1927), pp. 193-94.
59. Evans, *History of the Town of Jefferson*, p. 194.
60. Hepburn, *The Great Resorts of North America*, p. 35; *The A. M. C. White Mountain Guide*, 22nd ed. (Boston: Appalachian Mountain Club, 1979), p. 355.
61. "Waumbek Hotel, Jefferson, N.H.," promotional flyer (1879), p. 2.
62. Evans, *History of the Town of Jefferson*, p. 194.
63. *Ibid.*, "Waumbek Hotel, Jefferson, N.H.," p. 2. The major impetus for this expansion was the 1879 completion of the Whitefield & Jefferson Railroad spur to the Jefferson Meadows, just three miles from the hotel.
64. "Hotels and Boarding Houses," *WME* 11, No. 1 (30 June 1888), p. 7; Evans, *History of the Town of Jefferson*, p. 195.
65. *ATC* 13, No. 4 (16 July 1889), p. 1. See also "The Works of Carrere & Hastings," *The Architectural Record* 27, No. 1 (January 1910): 1-120. In an alphabetized list of clients at the end of this article under "W" appears the notation, "Waumbek Hotel, Jefferson, N. Y.," with no date or other information. Clearly, there was a misprint, and an "H" should be substituted for the "Y."
66. Withey, *Biographical Dictionary of American Architects (Deceased)*, pp. 109-111, 269-71. This distinguished firm is particularly well known for its large mansion-type residences and public buildings. Examples of its work include

the New York Public Library (1911), and the House and Senate Office Building, Washington (1905-1906). Carrere and Hastings also designed the Hotel Laurel-in-the-Pines, Lakewood, NJ, which opened in the early 1890s, and had as its partners individuals associated with the Jefferson Hotel and Land Company. Both hotels featured French Renaissance Revival decorative elements. Furthermore, proprietors Plumer & Porter of the Waumbek were also proprietors of the Laurel House in Lakewood, run by the same company as Laurel-in-the-Pines.

67. *ATC* 13, No. 4 (16 July 1889), p. 1.
68. *WME* 12, No. 2 (6 July 1889), p. 7.
69. *ATC* 13, No. 4 (16 July 1889), p. 1. In this lengthy piece Manasah Perkins is identified as superintending contractor, and Moses McDonald as head carpenter. Eugene Gale, later a famed hotel and house builder in his own right, was contracting assistant. The work was completed in 1890 with the further expansion of the main office and the construction of a cottage to the east of the hotel. See *WME* 13, No. 2 (11 July 1890), p. 5.
70. *ATC* 13, No. 4 (16 July 1889), p. 1.
71. *ATC* 16, No. 1 (11 July 1892), p. 4. The barn was later converted to a garage when automobiles supplanted horses.
72. *WME* 15, No. 2 (9 July 1892), p. 2.
73. *ATC* 14, No. 5 (16 July 1890), p. 4; *ATC* 19, No. 11 (25 July 1895), p. 4; *WME* 22, No. 1 (8 July 1899), p. 14; *Historical Memories of the Town of Jefferson*, p. 47.
74. "Beautiful Jefferson," *White Mountain Life* 1, No. 2 (2 September 1897); *ATC* 22, No. 1 (18 July 1898), p. 4; *WME* 22, No. 1 (8 July 1899), p. 14.
75. *WME* 23 No. 1 (7 July 1900), p. 12; *WME* 24, No. 1 (6 July 1901), pp. 11, 16; *The Waumbek's Penny Daily* 2, No. 1 (20 July 1901); *ATC* 25, No. 2 (13 July 1901), p. 4.
76. *ATC* 26, No. 51 (9 September 1902), p. 1.
77. *ATC* 38, No. 5 (15 July 1916), p. 4. The complex was also occasionally referred to as "The Waumbek Colony."
78. Evans, *History of the Town of Jefferson*, p. 196; *Waumbek Hotel and Cottages, Jefferson, White Mountains, New Hampshire* (Jefferson: n.p., [1916]).
79. *Littleton Courier*, 10 May 1928, p. 1; *Manchester Union*, 10 May 1928, pp. 1, 10; *Coos County Democrat*, 16 May 1928, pp. 1, 10. The loss was figured at $600,000 replacement value, with insurance covering roughly one third.
80. *Historical Memories of the Town of Jefferson*, pp. 46-48; *Littleton Courier*, 23 December 1971, pp. 1A, 8A. The combined buildings could house 225 people.
81. *Haverhill* (MA) *Gazette*, 22 November 1976; *Coos County Democrat*, 10 September 1980, p. 1; *Sunday News* (Manchester), 14 September 1980, pp. 1A, 24A; *Littleton Courier*, 17 September 1980; *North Country Weekly*, 8 October 1980; *Coos County Democrat*, 5 November 1986, pp. 1, 2.
82. Exhibition label copy, HLL; Speare, *Twenty Decades in Plymouth, New Hampshire*, p. 96. Other moderate-size hotels dating from the 1860s were the Parsons House (1862, burned 1890) and the first Monadnock House (late 1860s, burned 1895) in Colebrook; Russell Cottages (c. 1863, etc., extant) in North Conway; the Chocorua Inn (Hotel) (1863, etc., razed 1945) in Tamworth; and the Sumner House (c. 1860, burned c. 1900) in Dalton.
83. *The White Mountain Guide*, 3d ed. (Concord, NH: Edson C. Eastman; and Boston: Lee & Shepard, 1863), pp. 203-204. The hotel was able to take up to 300 guests and was open throughout the year.
84. Percy Curtis (Mrs. William N. Cox), *The Profile House* (Boston: Andrew F. Graves, 1872), p. 137.
85. *Plymouth Record*, 15 May 1909, p. 1; *Manchester Union Leader*, 12 May 1909, p. 1. The fire started at the end of the south wing on the east roof plane. A strong west wind fanned the flames and spread the blaze to fields and farm buildings across the river to the east. The hotel was being renovated when the fire occurred. The property was valued at over $80,000 and was insured for $75,000.

The third Pemigewasset House was built on Highland Street just above the town common land where the Herbert H. Lamson Library of Plymouth State College stands today. Erected in 1912, etc., the rambling woodframe-and-clapboard complex was rather uninteresting and disjointed. Lacking distinctive style, the hotel was formed from the former Amos Kidder House, a building acquired from Plymouth Normal School (later P. S. C.) and moved across the street, and a new connector unit. It remained open into the 1950s, suffered fire damage, and was torn down in 1958.

86. *ATC* 12, No. 10 (20 July 1888), p. 1.

Fig. 4-1. The Fabyan House, Carroll, NH, *advertisement engraving from* Hand-Book of Travel Over the Eastern & Maine Central R. R. Line . . . *(1874). Author's Collection. Built in 1872-73, this massive, rambling structure remained largely in this form until it burned in 1951.*

CHAPTER 4

The Grand Resort Hotel Concept Is Securely Rooted: The Seventies

DURING THE FIRST PHASE of the Gilded Age, particularly after the country's recovery from the economic recession of the mid-1870s, the concept of the grand resort hotel became securely rooted in the White Mountain region. Again, as in the early 1850s, it was the symbiotic relationship between the hotel industry and the railroads that proved to be the primary impetus for progress. From 1869 to 1882 the last great burst of railroad construction in the region brought routes into the heart of the mountains. Stimulated by the prosperity of the late 1860s and the opening of the Mount Washington Railway in 1869, railroad financiers saw an opportunity to reap benefits from the flourishing tourist trade. At the same time, once the new lines were announced or actually in place, the hotel industry was also prompted to further expand. As a consequence significant new hotel complexes and major additions to existing ones were planned and built.

Although the railroads were the principal motivating factor behind the continuing tourism boom, the national socio-cultural and economic forces that had worked to the advantage of the hotels during the 1860s (see Chapter 3) persisted in attracting people to White Mountain vacation locales in the 1870s. In their search for romanticized vacation environments, hotel guests were attracted to architecture, both plain vernacular as well as stylized, that conjured images of a pressure-free and uncomplicated American past. New money, and the competition it engendered, led to a popular enthusiasm for leisure and good health, and to the rich menus of social and recreational opportunities offered so splendidly by the mountain resort hotels.

Historian Peter B. Bulkley's scholarship, and the guidebook and newspaper citations upon which his work is based, help trace the next phase of railroad expansion and the implications for the grand resort hotel phenomenon. It is generally conceded that the most important rail expansion of the decade was orchestrated by the Boston, Concord and Montreal Railroad. Initially the B., C. & M. leased the White Mountains Railroad to Littleton in 1863. This line was subsequently extended five miles farther to the east to Wing Road in 1869, and then in a northerly direction to Whitefield during the following year. By 1873, the route had pushed on to Lancaster and the vicinity of Jefferson where travelers disembarked for stays at the Waumbek Hotel and other recently opened local hostelries. From Wing Road a spur was also laid out three miles to the southeast to the Bethlehem Junction in 1872, then six miles farther to the Twin Mountain House in 1873 (see Chapter 3). By 1874, the new extension reached Fabyan House and two years later made the seven-mile connection with the base of the Mount Washington Railway. This created an all-rail route from Boston to the summit of the tallest peak in the Northeast.[1]

While tourist traffic on the west side of the White Mountains was greatly augmented through the efforts of the B., C. & M., this was matched by the construction of two new routes in the eastern region. The earliest of these, the Portsmouth, Great Falls and Conway Railroad (later acquired by the Eastern), was completed to Milton, New Hampshire, by 1852. Due to financial constraints, it was not until spring 1872 that this line was built through to North Conway—just in time to deliver guests to the new Kearsarge House. The other route, the Portland and Ogdensburg Railroad (P. & O.), chartered in 1867, arrived in North Conway in 1871. It then pushed on to Bartlett and through Crawford Notch, reaching Fabyan House in August 1875 (see Chapter 2). The herculean engineering feat of laying track through the Notch received national exposure, provided the Crawford House and other hotels to the northwest with an infusion of business, and created the second all-rail route connecting directly with the Mount Washington Railway.[2]

The two railroads, the Eastern and the Portland and Ogdensburg, inevitable competitors, had a stimulating effect on the Lake Winnipesaukee travel route to the White Mountains. Area hotels and boarding houses, such as the Senter House in Center Harbor, benefited from this competition. In the 1860s the Eastern's steamboat "Chocorua" (the former "Dover") and the B., C. & M.'s "Lady of the Lake" added Wolfeboro as a stop between Alton Bay and Center Harbor (see Chapter 2). In 1872 the Boston and Maine Railroad built the famed steamer "Mount Washington" and commenced service on the lake. Consequently visitors had several options for traveling by water to Center Harbor, and could then complete the journey to the northern mountains by stage route and then railroad. An additional choice permitted tourists to travel by steamer from Alton Bay or The Weirs to Wolfeboro, where, after possible stays at the Pavilion Hotel or the Glendon House, they could pass by rail farther north.[3]

To supplement the completed B., C. & M., Eastern and P. & O. routes to the mountains, three short intramountain railroads were built from 1878 to 1882. The first, the Profile and Franconia Notch Railroad (see Chapter 2), was established in 1878, inaugurating service between Bethlehem Junction and the Profile House in Franconia Notch for the following summer season. In response to the need for direct rail service to the town of Bethlehem and its burgeoning hotel industry, a branch of this railroad was opened in 1881. The second of these lines (see Chapter 3) was the eight-mile Whitefield and Jefferson Railroad, which connected Whitefield with Jefferson Meadows and stage service to the Waumbek Hotel in 1879. The third intramountain railroad, the Pemigewasset Valley, was completed from Plymouth to North Woodstock in 1882, but never reached the Profile House to the north as originally intended. However, it did serve as a major stimulus for hotel development in the North Woodstock area and resulted in the town becoming a major center for tourism by the end of the 1880s.[4]

Fabyan House

Of the many hotels built in direct response to railroad expansion, the largest was the renowned Fabyan House. It stood on the site of Horace Fabyan's former Mount Washington House at Giant's Grave on the Ammonoosuc River in Carroll (see Chapter 1). The hotel's early history is to this day shrouded in mystery. After the 1853 fire that destroyed the Mount Washington, a prolonged legal stalemate ensued involving title to Fabyan's ruined hotel tract. Prevented from rebuilding for several years, Fabyan permanently departed New Hampshire. In 1861, he officially transferred the land to abutter Isaac Dyer, a major White Mountain land speculator and farmer from Baldwin, Maine. In 1864, Dyer sold all his real estate (including the original Rosebrook farm) to Sylvester Marsh, developer of the Mount Washington cog railway. Some sources suggest that Marsh contemplated constructing a hotel on his newly acquired lands to service the patrons who flocked to his novel mechanized route up the mountain.[5]

Was a successor to the Mount Washington House built as early as 1865 or 1866 on or near the site of the old hostelry?[6] Other weightier or more reliable sources indicate the contrary. Most convincing is a letter signed "R. J. L." and dated "Glen House, July 24, 1868," published in *The Germantown* (PA) *Tele-*

graph, describing a ride up Mount Washington on the stage road from the Glen. This revealing account alludes to guests from the Crawford House who had ascended to the summit "from the new railroad [the Portland & Ogdensburg] now nearly completed from the site where the old Fabian House [Mount Washington House] once stood, and where a new hotel is in progress which is to cover an acre in extant."[7] Added to this are references stating that fire had destroyed a hotel on the site that same year.[8] Apparently a hotel, which may be properly termed the "first Fabyan House," was in the process of construction in 1868 when it burned. While its existence is thus confirmed, no printed or photographic images have been found depicting an incomplete building. We have no information, therefore, about the size, appearance or interior plan of this still mysterious hotel.

The story of the so-called second Fabyan House (Fig. 4-1) is much better documented, thanks to historian Peter Bulkley's extensive research on Horace Fabyan's role as a White Mountain hotel developer, and other printed sources. Following the 1868 fire the site remained unoccupied until 1872 when Marsh formally deeded the property to the new Mount Washington Hotel Company. This syndicate consisted of Marsh and his business colleagues, including Charles Hartshorn and T. Walcott. Formed to purchase the former Fabyan tract and to build a new hotel, the company issued $200,000 in shares of capital stock to finance the venture. They contracted John Lindsey, a former stage driver, to superintend the construction and E. D. Dunn of Littleton as the chief builder. Work commenced in the summer of 1872, and they completed the hotel in time for a gala opening in August of the following year.[9]

To create a level site for the new edifice, the 300-foot long alluvial mound known as Giant's Grave, a local landmark, was removed. This drew controversy, largely prompted by an ancient Indian tradition that a curse would befall any white man who would dare to take deep root at the spot.[10] The predicted curse, however, failed to take effect and the new building, projected to accommodate 500 guests, quickly rose. It immediately drew the attention of the tourist guide publishers, evidenced by this thorough description from the 1874 edition of Bachelder's *Popular Resorts:*

Fig. 4-2. "Fabyan House Parlor, White Mts.," *stereo view, c. 1875, Kilburn #1788. Author's Collection. This grand room was 145 feet long and occupied the entire ground floor on the east end of the building.*

The present Fabyan House was built in the form of the letter T inverted, thus: ⊥. The top of the letter represents the main building, which is three hundred and twenty feet long by forty-five feet wide. In the centre is a rotunda sixty feet square, which is gained by projections front and back from the main building. The rotunda forms a very attractive feature, and is the common rendezvous of guests. The hotel and telegraph offices occupy two of its corners: from a third leads a broad, massive stairway to the two stories above.

The parlor [Fig. 4-2], which is one hundred by forty-five feet, occupies the entire eastern end of the building, and is very handsomely furnished. The remainder of the ground-floor is occupied by reception and reading rooms, and private parlors, each thirty by twenty feet. From the rear centre of the rotunda extends an ell in which is the dining-room [Fig. 4-3], one hundred and thirty by forty-five feet, seating comfortably four hundred guests. Carving and serving rooms, culinary offices, and kitchens, arranged with all modern appliances, are located in the rear wings of the building. There are two hundred and fifty sleeping-rooms, high, airy, light, and newly and handsomely furnished. The entire house is lighted by gas, and warmed by steam. It has a billiard and bath

[111]

Fig. 4-3. "Fabyan House Dining Hall, White Mts.," *stereo view, c. 1875, Kilburn #686. Author's Collection. Located in the rear ell, this festively decorated room seated an impressive total of 400 patrons and was supported by carving and serving rooms, culinary offices, and kitchen.*

rooms, an excellent livery, and the complete convenience of first-class hotels.[11]

Situated after 1874 at the vital and active terminus of the P. & O. and B., C. & M. railroads, the sprawling complex offered ample space and amenities to meet the needs of the heavy seasonal tourist traffic.

While the second Fabyan House may have been functionally satisfactory, this did not necessarily imply that it was aesthetically pleasing. Osgood's 1876 White Mountain guide characterized its external architecture as "unattractive," while Ernest Ingersoll, writing in *Down East Latch Strings* (1887), disparagingly referred to it as "a big, dun-colored hotel, of no more architectural presence than a cotton factory. . . ."[12] The analogy to an industrial building type was not totally inappropriate, for the hotel, like many factories, was built for quick profit and efficient operation, with little intended pretense to being good architecture. Nonetheless the Fabyan House did illustrate some late influence of the Italian Revival in its heavy paired eaves brackets, molded veranda supports, nearly flat roofs, and cube-shaped cupola with finial, atop a four-story central box section (Fig. 4-4). Plans to add an additional story under a French Mansard roof in 1880 never materialized; hence, it

Fig. 4-4. The Fabyan House, Carroll, NH, *photograph from Holman D. Waldron,* With Pen and Camera thro' the White Mountains *(1907). Author's Collection. Built for quick profit and efficient operation, the hotel resembled a factory or industrial building, but did display some pleasant Italian Revival decorative details.*

Fig. 4-5. "Mt. Washington from the Fabyan House," *stereo view, c. 1875, Kilburn #1247. Author's Collection. Set in an open area the hotel offered spectacular views of the west side of the Presidential Range. The building is seen from the rear.*

was largely in its c. 1876 form that the building passed into this century without ever receiving a major addition.[13]

To be sure there were some noteworthy improvements to the physical plant during the 1880s, but these did not alter the basic form of the main building.[14] This pattern of regular maintenance, redecoration, upgrading of utilities and occasional adding of new outbuildings continued during the ensuing decade. Under the aegis of the Barrons, the complex, as *Among the Clouds* informed its readers, was the beneficiary of several significant alterations in preparation for the 1896 season:

> The old guests of the Fabyan House will hardly recognize their summer home when they reach it. The somber colors have given place to lighter shades, which are in pleasing contrast with the dark green blinds, which now adorn the house; but the exterior is only a slight indication of what has taken place within. New floors, elegant carpets, and tastefully selected papers, have taken the place of the old, and blending harmoniously make the interior appear quite like an entirely new house.... Private baths, and steam heating apparatus have been placed in many of the rooms, making the house equal in these special features to the demand of the times. In the rear, where the practical work of the hotel is done, there have been many changes. A new laundry building, a boiler house, and a refrigerator building, have been constructed since last year, while driven wells have given an additional water supply. The house has been completely overhauled from top to bottom, and it was never before in such excellent condition.[15]

With guest satisfaction of uppermost concern, the owners of the Fabyan House, like those of other grand resort hotels, made every effort to gain advantage in the highly competitive White Mountain hotel industry. The renovation demonstrates how far owners would extend themselves and their purse strings to survive in the often unpredictable and unforgiving tourist market.

Foremost amongst the owners of the Fabyan House was the famed Barron family. At the height of its holdings, the Barrons controlled all the hotels on Mount Washington and the Ammonoosuc plain to the west, with the sole exception of the White Mountain House. The family's ties with the hotel began in 1879 when Asa T. Barron, with his son Oscar G., left the Twin Mountain House and leased the Fabyan House, displacing the first proprietorship of Lindsey, French & Company. As the Barrons had previously purchased the Crawford House in 1872 and leased the second Mount Washington Summit House in 1873, this action further consolidated their interests in the area. The securing of the Fabyan House lease, to which would be added the Mount Pleasant House lease in 1882, commenced an astounding uninterrupted Barron association with the old wooden hostelry that would eventually exceed fifty years. In 1913 the Barron family firm, in partnership with John N. Conygham, bought the Fabyan House from the Boston and Maine Railroad and continued to operate it for over twenty years until they sold it in the 1930s. Although it never received rave reviews for its beauty, the building satisfied the demands of thousands of visitors for nearly eighty years. When it burned to the ground on 19 September 1951, the White Mountain region was deprived of one of its best examples of highly functional, eminently practical hotel design (Fig. 4-5).[16]

The Second Mount Washington Summit House

The second Mount Washington Summit House, with which the Barrons would be long connected, became a dream in the minds of many after the construction of the Tip-Top and first Summit houses in the early 1850s. Offering a highly unusual mountain experience, these modest and rustic hostelries proved such popular tourist attractions that within a short time it became clear a larger and more comfortable hotel would be needed. Consequently, during the 1850s and 1860s architectural ideas abounded such as that illustrated in the engraved view published in Ben-

Fig. 4-6. "Summit of Mount Washington," *engraving from Benjamin G. Willey,* Incidents in White Mountain History . . . *(1856), p. 89. Author's Collection. This view represents an imaginative scheme, never fulfilled, for a new summit hotel, including an astronomical observatory on one corner.*

jamin G. Willey's 1856 classic *Incidents in White Mountain History* (Fig. 4-6). Here, in addition to ingeniously engineered carriages, is a fortress-like hotel with corner astronomical observatory, envisioned but never built by the summit road company.[17] The enterprising and inventive spirit embodied in this scheme, however, would bear fruit a decade and a half later.

Upon the completion and opening of the Mount Washington Railway in 1869, pressure increased to provide improved accommodations on the summit. The inspiration, and the impetus for such a move, came a few years later when Walter Aiken, the manager of the railway, lodged at Tip-Top one night. Disturbed by rain beating on him through the antiquated and dilapidated roof, he quickly took action, declaring he would build a hotel on the summit where people could sleep in dry beds. Aiken promptly joined forces with James E. Lyon, acting for the Boston, Concord & Montreal Railroad, to finance and erect a suitable establishment. Soon thereafter, in 1872-73, the second Summit House assumed final form at a cost of about $70,000. This achievement prompted proud claims that it was the largest hotel in the United States on top of a mountain as tall or taller than Mount Washington. Considering the ambitious nature of the undertaking, this pride was justifiable—people were awestruck to learn that it took

Fig. 4-7. Second Summit House, Mount Washington, *photograph from Moses F. Sweetser,* Views in the White Mountains, *quarto "omnibus" edition (1879). Author's Collection. While it was under construction in 1872-73, building materials were hauled to the summit in 250 round trips (one car per train) on the Mount Washington Railway.*

freight trains (one car per train) 250 trips up and down the cog railway to transport the required 596 tons of building materials to the summit.[18]

Although it was an unadorned, wholly functional wooden structure reminiscent of many older grand hotel precursors, the new Summit House possessed several interesting characteristics (Fig. 4-7). Designed by architect Edward Dow (1820-94) of Concord and raised under the direction of John Bailey of Littleton,[19] the hotel was 220 feet long and 40 feet wide, with an ell of 80 feet (added a year after the opening). It housed 150 to 200 patrons. Particularly remarkable was the substantial construction; the framework was secured to solid ledgerock by cables, iron rods and bolts, enabling the building to withstand winds of over 180 miles per hour. Facing southeast to ensure maximum sun exposure, an innovative steam heating system, centrally regulated, theoretically circulated heat evenly throughout the sleeping rooms. The interior spatial arrangement was a traditional one with sales counter, office, dining room, barroom, parlors, telegraph office and other public areas on the first floor. The dining room, which occupied a large percentage of the first floor, was able to seat 150 persons, many of whom were day trippers on the stage road or the railroad and were present only for lunch (Fig. 4-8). Overnight guests were accommodated in the story and a half above.[20]

Throughout its eventful history the second Summit House was associated with numerous notable

Fig. 4-8. "Mount Washington Summit House, Dining Hall," *stereo view, c. 1875, Kilburn #1790. Author's Collection. Occupying most of the first floor, this room could seat 150 persons, many of whom were day travelers to the summit. Here, meals were served on china, just as they were at the base.*

people who were both its proprietors as well as its guests. Initially leased to the cog railroad and then to other parties, the hotel was managed by Captain John W. Dodge, his widow Harriet D. Dodge, Charles G. Emmons and after 1886 by the firm of Barron, Merrill and Barron Company, with Miss Mattie A. Clarke as the on-site hostess and administrator. Attracted to the cog, the stage road, the novelty of the building and the spectacular 360-degree views, nationally prominent figures and their entourages—often recorded on the summit in stereos or cabinet views—made their way up the mountain. Culled from the pages of *Among the Clouds* are such names as poet Lucy Larcom, President and Mrs. Rutherford B. Hayes, Ulysses S. Grant, author and traveler William B. Prime, naturalist and author Bradford Torrey, entomologist and author Annie Trumbull Slossen, Rev. and Mrs. Henry Ward Beecher, author Harriet Beecher Stowe, entertainer and entrepreneur Phineas T. Barnam, Union Army generals Joseph Hooker and George McClellan, as well as dignitaries from abroad.[21] A place of pilgrimage and a haven for those trapped on the summit by severe weather, the second Summit House went out in a literal blaze of glory when on 18 June 1908 the great Mount Washington fire obliterated every structure on the summit except the venerable Tip-Top House.[22]

The Mount Pleasant House and its Architects

The Mount Pleasant House, formerly situated on one of the most spectacular sites west of the Presidential Range, now in the town of Carroll (Bretton Woods), is documented more extensively than any other grand hotel built in the White Mountains before World War I. This building's fascinating architectural history reveals distinct transforming phases of development, attributes consistent with the grand hotel building type, and an association with two notable architects from the state of Maine. During its foremost period of activity, from the 1880s to 1939, when it was demolished for structural and economic reasons, it was generally regarded as one of the most elegant and desirable of New England's seasonal resort establishments.

Fig. 4-9. "Mt. Pleasant House, White Mts.," *stereo view, c. 1878, Kilburn, unidentified. Author's Collection. Erected by John T. G. Leavitt in 1875-76, this modest rectangular-box structure formed the core of the grand resort hotel that would follow.*

The Mount Pleasant was largely the product of economic circumstance. With the 1875 completion of the P. & O. Railroad through Crawford Notch to Fabyan's, the existing hotels—Crawford House, Fabyan House and Twin Mountain House—became so taxed by the new influx of tourists that potential investors saw possibilities for another profitable hotel in the area. First to seize this opportunity was Henry L. Tilton of Littleton, a director and treasurer of the Mount Washington Hotel Company, the builder of the Fabyan House a few years before. In 1875-76 Tilton, supplying the vision, energy and financial wherewithal, contracted John T. G. Leavitt, a local builder and lumbering entrepreneur, to erect the new hostelry.[23] For this purpose land was acquired at Bretton Woods on the Ammonoosuc plain, one-half mile southeast of Fabyan's. This property had a breath-taking panoramic vista of Mount Washington, flanked by mounts Clay, Jefferson and Adams to the north, and mounts Monroe, Franklin, Pleasant, Clinton (Pierce), Jackson and Webster to the south.

Here Leavitt built a three-story, rectangular hotel, roughly 40 by 120 feet (including verandas), with a flat roof and small rear ell (Fig. 4-9). Described as "cosy and home-like" this modest fifty-guest hostelry immediately offered recreational opportunities found at much larger resort hotels such as hiking, fishing, bowling, croquet, billiards and carriage riding.[24] In form and detail it was unimaginative, in fact almost identical to one of the wings of the Fabyan House, sharing such conventional Italian Revival features as paired eaves brackets, wide corner boards and molded veranda supports. But the location was prime from the aesthetic point of view, and later it assumed importance as a transportation hub. The hotel became a stop for Maine Central main line trains at the rear of the building and for Concord & Montreal trains to the Mount Washington cog base station at the front.[25]

On 9 July 1881, *Among the Clouds* announced that the hotel had been sold to the newly formed Mount Pleasant Hotel Company in which Oscar V. Pitman of Concord and Joseph Stickney, a coal and railroad magnate originally from Wilkes-Barre, Pennsylvania, had controlling interest. The wealthy Stickney, who viewed hotel ownership as an avocation, would figure prominently in the later development of the Mount Pleasant House and in the formation of the company that would build the grand Mount Washington Hotel nearby in 1901-1903 (see Chapter 8). Immediately Pitman and Stickney enlarged the Mount Pleasant (Fig. 4-10). They created a fourth story under a hipped-on-Mansard roof, extended the north end by one-third to provide a larger dining room and additional sleeping rooms, and attached a new wing off the northwest corner to house a new kitchen, service areas and quarters for the hired help (Fig. 4-11). All totaled they added over 100 new rooms (with space for 150 patrons) in the summer and fall of 1881, the majority of them upstairs sleeping rooms. At the same time steam heat, electric bells and new gas fixtures were introduced. Crowning the main roof towards its south end was an unusual rectangular-box observatory, capped by a truncated pyramidal roof with cast-iron cresting and a flag pole. The company then leased the expanded Mount Pleasant House to various managing interests, the Barron group having the longest tenure.[26]

In 1894, Joseph Stickney became sole owner of the Mount Pleasant House. He promptly determined to

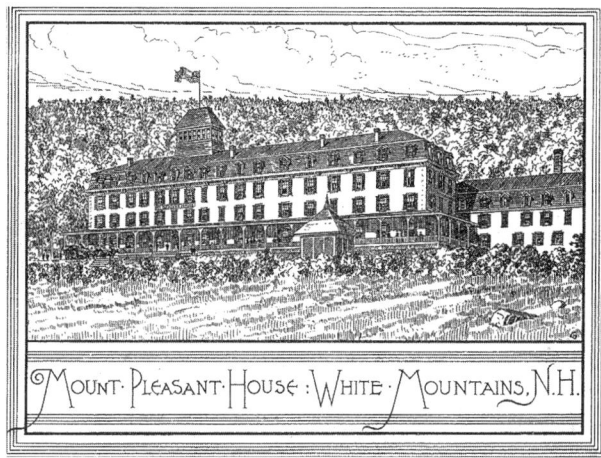

Fig. 4-10. "Mount Pleasant House, White Mountains, N. H.," *engraving from 1885 menu, by the Heliotype Printing Co., Boston. Author's Collection. In 1881-82 new owners Oscar Pitman and Joseph Stickney enlarged the hotel, increasing the guest capacity to 150.*

endow the complex with a spaciousness, grace and beauty that it had never known.[27] The idea and motivation behind this second major expansion had its origins a decade before when Stickney was first associated with the Mount Pleasant Hotel Company. In July 1884, *Among the Clouds* disclosed that such a project was being contemplated,[28] and the following month it reported:

> We have seen the plans for the enlargement of the Mount Pleasant House, work upon which will begin in October. The hotel when enlarged will be one of the most elegant in the mountains, and will be larger than the Fabyan House, having 210 sleeping rooms for guests.[29]

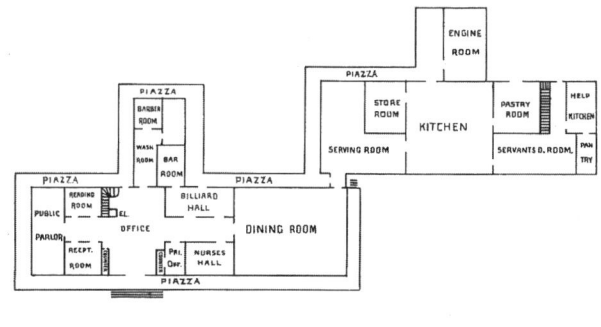

Fig. 4-11. First Floor Plan, Mount Pleasant House, Carroll, NH, *from booklet,* Mount Pleasant House *(Bretton Woods, NH: n. p. [c. 1885]). Author's Collection. Typical of most hotel architecture of the era, all service facilities were concentrated on the first floor level.*

Apparently the plans were the product of John Calvin Stevens (1855-1940) who, as a young junior partner in the Portland architectural firm of Fassett & Stevens, prepared several sketches that served as the basis for the final realized design. These valuable renderings and a beautifully executed rear elevation perspective (likely a presentation drawing) appear in a small sketchbook covering the years 1880-84 when Stevens was associated with the firm (Fig. 4-12).[30] For some reason, possibly financial, the expansion project was not executed on schedule as planned; nonetheless, Stevens' work later would influence the exterior form and interior layout of the Mount Pleasant.

Stickney's undertaking began in earnest in fall 1894 when he augmented his Bretton Woods land holdings to include a large parcel east of the Ammonoosuc River (later to be the site of the Mount Washington Hotel). He also contracted with the highly respected architect, Francis H. Fassett (1823-1908), Stevens' former partner, to prepare the plans for the new addition (Fig. 4-13).[31] Fassett worked in the popular Queen Anne, Richardsonian Romanesque, and Colonial Revival styles, "employing systems of restrained polychromy and surface ornament that he had developed in the 1870s."[32] Certainly one of his finest Queen Anne designs was for the second Glen House (1885-87) in the White Mountains (see Chapter 7). Fassett's formal commitment to Stickney and details of the 1894-95 construction period are documented in an extremely rich and enlightening collection of letters by Fassett and his son Edward F. Fassett (d. 1924) to Stickney and company treasurer Robert I. Jenks (recently acquired by the New Hampshire Historical Society).[33]

As for Fassett and his credentials, it would not be an exaggeration to say that he was Portland's most prominent architect of the nineteenth century. After working first in Boston and New York City, Fassett set up an architectural practice in his native Bath, Maine, in the late 1840s, completing building commissions there and up the Kennebec River to Augusta. In 1864 he then settled in Portland where he would head his own office until his death. As a consequence of the disastrous Portland fire of 1866, which destroyed one-third of the city, Fassett had the opportunity to rebuild many commercial, public and residential structures. Two of his major commissions there were the Congress Square and Lafayette hotels. During his most productive period in the 1870s, he developed a personalized vision of the High Victorian Gothic style, applying it to numerous civic buildings in and around Portland.

The Fassett-Stickney firm correspondence is rare documentation of a representative piece of White Mountain hotel history. A letter dated 30 August 1894 from Payson Tucker, vice president and general manager of the Maine Central Railroad, to Joseph Stickney answered Stickney's letter requesting suggestions for an architect. From Tucker's recommendations of Portland architects John Calvin Stevens, Francis H. Fassett and Frederick A. Tompson, Stickney chose Fassett.[34] With a tentative working agreement apparently reached, Fassett wrote Stickney on September 6 and referred to previously prepared plans, probably those completed earlier by John Calvin Stevens (see above).[35] On September 24 Fassett stated to Stickney that he would "agree to perform all services usually required of an architect, including all plans, drawings, specifications and proper supervision of the work, in making the contemplated additions, alterations, etc. . . . for four per cent of the cost of the work, and necessary travel expenses in supervising the work." He also wrote that he had assigned his son Edward the task of drafting plans.[36] This turned out to be a fortunate decision—the elder Fassett became ill for much of the late fall and early winter, and Edward had to assume primary responsibility for the project.

The letters capture the Fassetts' careful attention to detail, as well as their efforts to keep Stickney fully informed, and involved in all the major decisions. Throughout the fall and into December the two Fassetts conveyed to Stickney sketch plans and elevations, final blueprints and specifications, and working drawings. Excavations and foundation work began, and father and son commented extensively about their routine site visits, their relationships with contractors, and their negotiations with the Maine Central over track location and crossings. The letters further reveal engineering details such as the use of steel as opposed to wood trusses above the first

Fig. 4-12. Mount Pleasant House, Carroll (Bretton Woods), NH, *rear elevation perspective, c. 1880-84, by John Calvin Stevens of the firm of Fassett & Stevens, Portland, ME. Stevens Collection, Maine Historical Society, Portland. This sketch, presumably one of several by Stevens, served as a basis of the 1894-95 transformation of the building to a grand resort hotel.*

floor level. Design sources are also noted—the architects adopted Carrere and Hastings' pavilion at the Waumbek Hotel as a model for the one planned for the south end of Mount Pleasant. The architects discussed other matters with Stickney such as provisions for artesian well water, and new systems for electricity and steam heat. The year 1894 closed with optimism when they sent the final drawings for the superstructure of the building to Stickney on December 31.[37]

During the winter, the Fassetts and Stickney corresponded about delays due to severe weather, contractors' proposals, securing "pictures of the house," engineering questions and the general progress of the construction. On January 19, Francis Fassett wrote to Stickney suggesting June 1 as a date for the project's completion (the date was later pushed forward to June 15). In February, carpentry work was finally started under the direction of Portland chief carpenter John W. Burrowes. All above-ground work was moving ahead.

During the spring the Fassetts wrote to Stickney about a host of subjects including the new covered

Fig. 4-13. Portrait of Francis H. Fassett *(1823-1908) from* Men of Progress... State of Maine *(Boston: New England Magazine, 1897). Maine Historic Preservation Commission, Augusta, ME. A well-known Portland architect, Fassett had commissions for the enlargement of the Mount Pleasant House, as well as for the planning of the second Glen House.*

Fig. 4-14. Mount Pleasant House, Carroll (Bretton Woods), NH, *photograph from* Scenic Gems of the White Mountains *(c. 1904).*
Author's Collection. The "New Mount Pleasant House," reopened in 1895, was the product of a reconstruction
project that took less than one year to complete.

bowling alley, the boiler house plans, relocation of the stables, new grading and landscaping, the employees' barracks, the new laundry, an iron bridge over the Maine Central track, a water tank, paint contracting, the dining room extension, plastering and wallpapering work, and elevator installation. Writing on May 25, Francis Fassett assured Stickney that the old renovated portion of the building would be "finished ready for guests ... during the next ten days." Edward followed with a letter on June 13 containing the exciting news that all major construction would be completed within the week and that smaller jobs would be finished soon afterwards, including the installation of new silver-plated numbers on the bedroom doors! Remarkably, the "New Mount Pleasant House" was ready to take guests less than one year after the beginning of construction, catching the major portion of the 1895 summer social season (Fig. 4-14).[38]

Work continued to the end of the year with unfinished tasks in the "main house." Letters refer to the water system, plumbing needs, steam heat installation, gas piping, elevator repairs, floor planing, telephones, painting and wallpapering. There was also extensive work to be done on the outbuildings. The contractors built a new laundry building (replacing one torn down), a pump house, a blacksmith shop, a relocated and renovated stable, a stablekeeper's house, and a new Shingle-style guest annex called "The Cottage" designed by the Fassett firm (Fig 4-15). As the vast undertaking wound down, Edward complained openly in late October to company treasurer Robert Jenks about delaying the last work phase. By December, he altered his posture, speaking optimistically about its near completion. That fall correspondence also addressed the payment of bills and settlements for claims made by contractors. One particularly annoying and wearing problem the Fassett's dealt with was the unsatisfactory work performance of chief painter, M. H. Higgins, which prompted a legal compromise on payment for con-

Fig. 4-15. "The Cottage" (1895), Mount Pleasant House, Carroll (Bretton Woods), NH, *photograph from Mount Pleasant luncheon menu, 15 August 1906. Author's Collection. This Shingle-style guest annex was also designed by the Fassett firm.*

tracted services. These final letters elaborate on the demanding and complex role played by the architectural firm. Although only related to the Mount Pleasant construction, they document a building process common to all the large White Mountain hotels of the period.[39]

The Fassett-Stickney collaboration resulted in a visually disjointed but still markedly improved, palatial and provocative Queen Anne/Colonial Revival edifice. It was able to accommodate up to 300 people and was intended to attract the wealthiest clientele. The Maine Central Railroad published a quite comprehensive description of the renovation in progress in its guide *Gems of the Northland*:

> . . . the New Mount Pleasant House . . . is going to be one of the most magnificent public houses in the mountains. The old part will be entirely remodelled and an extensive addition [100 feet long] will be made. The new building will be ornamented with towers, gables, and dormers, besides having wide porches and verandas. It will have a frontage of 315 feet, not including verandas and colonnades. It will be three stories high and will cover an area of 18,000 square feet, exclusive of bay windows and verandas. The interior of the building will be arranged for pleasure and comfort [Fig. 4-16]. From a porte-cochere on the east side, there will be a rotunda fifty-five feet long and thirty-nine feet

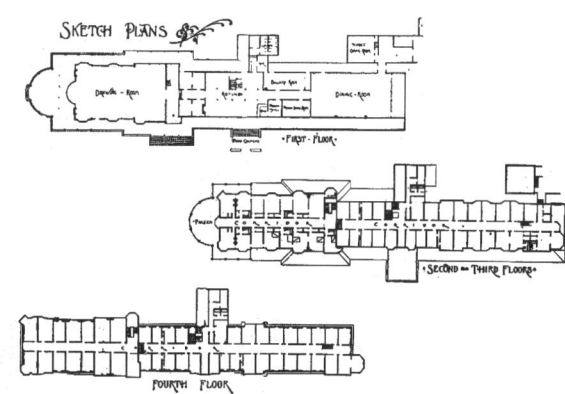

Fig. 4-16. Sketch Floor Plans, Mount Pleasant House, Carroll (Bretton Woods), NH, *from booklet*, Mt. Pleasant House *(Bretton Woods, NH: n. p., [c. 1896]). Author's Collection. The enlarged hotel boasted an eighty-foot-long drawing room opening out onto a semi-circular piazza with a classical colonnade.*

Fig. 4-17. Lobby (Rotunda), Mount Pleasant House, Carroll (Bretton Woods), NH, *photograph from* Bretton Woods Hotels *(Bretton Woods, NH: The Bretton Woods Hotel Company, c. 1919), p. 5. Author's Collection. This fine Colonial Revival interior was particularly noted for its well articulated Ionic columns.*

wide [Fig. 4-17]; on the right will be the office, on the left a large and ornamental fire-place, and the centre the main stairway and elevator. On the right also will be found the great dining-room, lighted by large plate glass windows. From the left of the rotunda the corridor leads to the drawing-room—forty-eight feet wide and eighty-one feet long [Fig. 4-18]. There will also be on the first floor reception, conversation, card and billiard rooms.[40]

The sleeping rooms were to be single, or in suites of two to five rooms, many having private baths with hot and cold running water.

Appended to the south end of the new addition, and surely the most pronounced architectural feature of the hotel, was a two-story semi-circular pavilion with side extensions, all supported by tall, smooth Doric columns. Adjacent to the new building were a new powerhouse, the repositioned barn converted to a laundry, and a new bowling alley and tennis courts. Work continued during the next two years with the erection of a new annex for guest overflow. The contractors also graded land for the future Mount Pleasant Golf Course, created an artificial lake and carried out additional landscaping. Rumors circulated that an electric railroad might be constructed connecting the hotel to the summit of Mount Pleasant, but this incredible scheme never transpired. Sparing no expense, Stickney brought in Anderson (John) & Price (John D.), known widely for their excellent management of the lavish Hotel Ormand at Ormand Beach, Florida, to run the transformed hotel.[41]

Despite its grandeur and extended popularity into this century, the Mount Pleasant House was systematically dismantled during the spring and summer of 1939. Unable to make a profit during the Depression years and simply worn out from heavy use, it had lost its competitive position amongst the remaining White Mountain grand resort hotels. The difficult decision to terminate its operation was reached by parent Bretton Woods Company owner F. Foster Reynolds, who was said to have remarked to Colonel William A. Barron, "I won't have it bothering me any longer." Suffering the fate of so many of its hotel counterparts, the Mount Pleasant had lost a game

THE GRAND RESORT HOTEL CONCEPT IS SECURELY ROOTED: THE SEVENTIES

Fig. 4-18. Music Hall, Mount Pleasant House, Carroll (Bretton Woods), NH, *photograph from* Among the Great White Hills *(Bretton Woods, NH: Mount Pleasant Hotel Co., [c. 1900]). Author's Collection. Considered the loveliest space in the hotel, it was used as a drawing-room and music room.*

battle to fiscal and operational realities. Ironically, the two men charged with razing the hotel and outbuildings, Dana Leavitt and son, Dudley, though of no relation, bore the same surname as the original builder John T. G. Leavitt.[42]

The Eastern Towns Achieve Further Prominence

While the 1870s witnessed astonishing growth in the hotel industry on the Ammonoosuc plain and Mount Washington, profits generated from hotels in North Conway, Bartlett and Jackson in the Eastern Slope Region were actually greater. North Conway developed so dramatically during the decade that it alone became a close economic rival of the Barron family holdings.[43] With the completion of the railroad to the town in 1872, and the economic stimulus it brought, major additions were made to the larger hotels—the Kearsarge, Intervale House and the Sunset Pavilion. New, more modest establishments were also built including the Artist's Falls House (pre-1874), the first Hotel Randall (Randall House) (1864,

c. 1878, etc.), Eastman House (Hotel Eastman) (c. 1872, etc.), Mason's Hotel (1871), Pendexter Mansion (Region House) (c. 1874), and the Bellevue House (1871-72, etc.).

The town of Jackson to the north, while lagging behind North Conway, continued to emerge as a hotel center, with the Glen Ellis House and the first Eagle Mountain House joining the Jackson Falls House and Thorn Mountain House as substantial hostelries. The first Eagle Mountain House was the precursor to a much larger grand resort hotel built in the twentieth century on the same hillside site and under the same family ownership (see Chapter 5). Opened as a twelve-guest inn in 1879 by Cyrus E. and Marcia P. Gale, this simple wood-frame and clapboard, two-and-a-half-story building was immediately successful in attracting a clientele (Fig. 4-19). Its popularity necessitated a complete remodeling of the hostelry, including the addition of a north wing. The owners also relocated and reconstructed the adjacent livery barn in 1881-82. In 1889-90, the Gales built a large annex (enlarged in 1900) just to the south called "Eagle Hall" and connected it to the main house with

[123]

Fig. 4-19. The First Eagle Mountain House and Annex, Jackson, NH, *photograph, c. 1905, by Clifton Church. Jackson Historical Society. Built in 1879, and subsequently enlarged, this complex was the precursor of the grand hotel that operates on the same site today.*

a covered walkway. This annex was three-and-a-half stories in height, with ample piazzas and decorative suggestions of the Queen Anne style. It featured a large ballroom and rooms for billiards, music, reading and cards on the first floor, with thirty-three sleeping rooms above. This increased the maximum capacity to 125 guests. Blessed by its lovely bowl-like natural setting 200 feet above the village, the first Eagle Mountain House prospered for over three decades, only to be destroyed by fire on 12 May 1915. While set back by this disaster, the resilient Gales rebuilt on a more ambitious scale and shortly were back in business (see Chapter 5).[44]

Bethlehem, Isaac Cruft and the Maplewood

During the Civil War and afterwards, the town of Bethlehem continued its development as a summer resort—a process successfully initiated by John Sinclair and his small inn in the 1850s (see Chapter 3). According to local lore, a single occurrence and its aftermath woke up the townspeople to their community's potential as a center of tourism. In 1863 the Honorable Henry Howard of Providence (later to serve as governor of Rhode Island), while visiting the area with family and friends, was involved in a serious runaway coach accident, which took place while his party was descending Mount Agassiz. As a consequence the trip to Bethlehem was extended until the injured had recuperated enough to return home. While convalescing at the Sinclair House, Howard became acquainted with the assets of the town and became convinced of its resort potential. Subsequently he made extensive local land investments. Returning for many summers, he further expressed his faith in the possibilities of development by selling building lots on credit and by lending money to those interested in going into the hotel business. Howard's contribution to the town and its future, coupled with its later adoption as the headquarters of the American Hay-Fever Association, were to assure Bethlehem a national reputation as a place of healthful and pleasant summer sojourn.[45]

The systematic growth of the town during the 1870s was truly remarkable, considering that it predated the arrival of direct rail service from Bethlehem Junction. This curious sequence of events ran counter to the pattern throughout the White Mountains where hotel development normally followed railroad expansion. Despite this circumstance, at least seventeen new hotels, most with space for 50 to 100 guests, were constructed in Bethlehem before 1880. The Sinclair House was also enlarged so that its capacity exceeded 200 during this time. Included on this impressive list are: the Mount Agassiz House (1870); Turner House (expanded in 1864 and 1873-74 from an older tavern); the first Howard House (c.

1870); Hillside House (Inn) (1874); Bethlehem House (Sunset House) (1874); Strawberry Hill House (1874); Bellevue House (1875); Park House (Ranlet's Hotel; The Altamonte House) (1876); Centennial House (Arlington Hotel) (1876); Avenue House (The Gramercy; Maplehurst) (1876); the second Howard House (the "New Howard") (1878); the Alpine Hotel (House) (1876-77); Mount Washington House (Hotel) (The Perry House) (1877); the Highland Hotel (House) (1879-80); and The Broadview (c. 1880). These buildings were highly residential in character and employed a variety of Victorian eclectic forms and ornamental details, but were not on the same scale as the grand hotels. Two additional hotels stand out: the Maplewood built in 1876 and the Uplands erected in 1877. The Maplewood was an exemplar of the grand hotel building type and Victorian splendor, while the Uplands was perhaps the region's finest example of Victorian eclectic taste—so dominant in much of Bethlehem's late nineteenth-century architecture.

Joining John Sinclair and Henry Howard on the roster of Bethlehem's early leaders was Isaac S. Cruft, a transplanted Boston merchant who arrived in the village in 1871. Impressed by Howard's successful vision of Bethlehem's future he promptly acquired a large tract of land known as "Maplewood Farm." Located over a mile east of the center of town on the road to Twin Mountain (at the intersection with the route north to Whitefield), this advantageous site offered an expansive and moving vista of the entire Presidential Range. Cruft launched into the summer resort business by converting a comfortable 1816 farmhouse on the property into a modest inn. In no time tourists discovered the new establishment, which soon gained such favor that the ambitious and enterprising Cruft decided to substantially enlarge his initial venture.[46]

What transpired over the next few years constitutes one of the most extraordinary chapters in the history of the White Mountain grand resort hotels. In few other instances was so much trust placed in the prospect of profit or was the rate of physical growth so rapid. Cruft's first step, sometime before 1874, was to construct a new hipped-on-Mansard roof hotel entitled "Maplewood House" on the road in front of the original farmhouse (Fig. 4-20). He then moved the farmhouse across the main road to the corner of the Whitefield road and supplied it with a new sixty by thirty-four-foot ell. In 1879, Cruft raised the structure to three-and-a-half stories. "Maplewood Cottage," as it was named, would soon serve as a 150-guest annex to the great hostelry that was to come (Fig. 4-21).[47]

In 1875-76, a progression of additional steps unfolded, leading to the formal opening of the Maplewood Hotel. First Cruft cut the Maplewood House in half and moved one section slightly west, in

Fig. 4-20. "Maplewood House, Bethlehem, N. H.," *engraving from John B. Bachelder,* Popular Resorts; and How to Reach Them *(1874), p. 113. Author's Collection. Erected by Isaac Cruft before 1874, this building became part of the large and luxurious Maplewood Hotel in the following decade.*

Fig. 4-21. Maplewood Cottage, Maplewood Hotel, Bethlehem, NH, *photograph, c. 1890, unidentified. Douglas Philbrook, Gorham, NH. This rather awkward looking structure served as a guest annex to the main hotel until it burned in 1943.*

Fig. 4-22. Maplewood Hotel, Maplewood, Bethlehem, NH, *billhead engraving, c. 1877. Author's Collection. The hotel is shown here after Isaac Cruft made a major addition to the Maplewood House in 1875-76.*

line with the former front. This he rebuilt as a modest, three-story, twenty-two-room cottage, retaining the old name. To the remaining half he added a massive three-story, 42-by-110 foot block (later raised to four stories by the addition of a Mansard roof). To the east end he attached a four-story ell, thirty-seven by seventy-five feet (Fig. 4-22). Over the next two years, in 1877-78, guest demand had so increased that Cruft again committed to expansion, adding a thirty-two by forty-foot unit to the east ell. This became the principal facade of the now-immense edifice. With a capacity of over 350 people, the interior contained several new dining rooms and parlors, a large hall with stage, game rooms, an ample lobby (office), and over 130 bedrooms, each lit with gas and connected to the office by ingenious speaking tubes (Fig. 4-23).[48]

A large lithograph, produced by the William H. Brett Engraving Company of Boston around 1878, illustrates why the Maplewood was billed as the "Palace Hotel of the Mountains" in promotional literature (see Plate 7).[49] As a supreme statement of Victorian eclectic cultural taste the building displayed a rich assortment of architectural forms and embellishments, making it virtually impossible to type it stylistically. Two symmetrical elevations facing north and east featured ornate center pavilions flanked by pyramidal-roofed square towers. An open porch (later converted to bedrooms) topped the east elevation and a fifteen-foot-wide piazza at ground level provided an astounding 450 feet of space for unbroken, sheltered promenading and display of the latest clothing fashions. On the exterior were numerous Italian-Revival style decorative elements, among them heavy single eaves brackets, balustraded balconies with canopies, flat and triangular window lintels, and composite piazza support columns. Also evident was the influence of the Second Empire style in the pavilion roof caps and long north-side Mansard roof with linked sections of iron cresting. Even signs of the late Gothic Revival were visible in the tower roofs with their variegated color bands and steep-pitched dormers. Somehow this profusion of adornment managed to come together as a cohesive and powerful whole, perfectly expressing the cultural preferences of the period.

Having created a monument to architectural ostentation Cruft further brought his establishment to the front ranks of American summer resorts. The 28 June 1879 issue of the *White Mountain Echo* reported that he:

... appears now to be intent upon surrounding it with all the accessories of a nobleman's mansion, for he has this year laid out upon its grounds a fine deer park, which he has populated with some handsome specimens of the monarchs of the forest.... He has also constructed ... a tasteful and unique observatory four stories in height, from whose summit most extensive views of the mountain region may be obtained.[50]

In addition Cruft installed extensive gardens and landscaping. He purchased the adjoining 500-acre Maplewood Farm for produce, vegetables and fruit, constructed a reservoir, and tapped springs for a water supply and to provide fire protection. He also erected five Gothic Revival Stick style cottages (eventually there would be fifteen of various styles) on the grounds for families wishing privacy. Another guest facility, Maplewood Hall, was added to the now almost self-contained village in 1882-83 under the proprietorship of Charles B. Goodwin (Fig. 4-24). In 1887-89 it was moved across the main road to a new location a few hundred yards southwest of the hotel, to make room for a new casino. Here it was considerably enlarged, increasing the total guest capacity of the complex to over 500 and thus making it one of the largest resorts in New England. The Cruft family held title to the Maplewood property until 1907, when it was sold to an outside partnership, which owned other hotels on the East Coast.[51]

An outstanding example of Shingle Chateauesque architecture, the Maplewood Casino was conceived by Massachusetts and Littleton architect Edward Thornton Sanderson (1875-1960) in c. 1887 as a place of pleasure for Maplewood guests (see Plate 8). This 120-foot-square, wood and fieldstone structure initially contained a reception area, a large ballroom with stage (capable of seating nearly 1,200 persons), billiard, pool and bowling rooms, a small theater, parlors for the ladies, smoking rooms for gentlemen, an art gallery and studio, protected viewing galleries for golf, tennis and croquet, and a library and reading room in the cylindrical stone corner tower. Some architectural critics perhaps overexaggerated the truth by comparing the new building to McKim, Mead and White's famed Newport (RI) Casino (1880-81). In fact, the visual resemblance is slight and the interior appointments far less lavish.

Fig. 4-23. The Lobby, Maplewood Hotel, Maplewood, Bethlehem, NH, *postcard photograph, c. 1910. Author's Collection. Here the functional simplicity of the furnishings contrasts with the splendor of the architectural detail. Speaking tubes connected the office to each bedroom.*

Fig. 4-24. Maplewood Hall, Maplewood, Bethlehem, NH, *from souvenir album,* Views of Bethlehem and Vicinity *(c. 1890). Author's Collection. Erected in 1882-83, this substantial guest annex was mysteriously demolished in 1898 as it apparently proved unprofitable.*

Nonetheless, the Maplewood Casino was a unique addition to the architecture of the White Mountains and is the only surviving major building from the original Maplewood community.[52] It still stands on the north side of Bethlehem Street and serves as a clubhouse for the golf course once associated with the hotel.

It is well known that fire has been the primary enemy of the White Mountain hotels, but in the case of the Maplewood Hotel and its outbuildings this threat was all too real and recurrent. In August 1942 the main residence and smaller structures at the Maplewood farm were lost to a blazing inferno. The next year fire completely leveled Maplewood Cottage in December. Then on 14 January 1963, after recent sale by the Drier family to Atlantic City hotel entrepreneur Frank T. Moss, the once elegant Maplewood Hotel (operating under the name "Maplewood Club") was burned to the ground by a blaze originating from faulty electrical wiring. In an uncanny sequel event the Lafayette Cottage on the Maplewood tract went up in flames the following June, raising further suspicion that some kind of curse had befallen the former hotel colony.[53] Other Bethlehem hotels have since burned, leaving just four standing today from a peak of over thirty in the 1920s.[54]

The Uplands and the Abbott Family

Though it lacked the grand resort hotel proportions, ambiance, and amenities of the Maplewood, the Uplands' inordinately fine Victorian eclectic architecture places it as one of Bethlehem's most esteemed mid-sized, late nineteenth-century hostelries. Even more significant was its association with the Abbott family; Karl Abbott, after learning the hotel trade as manager of the Uplands for many years, became a hotel impresario of national stature. He owned and operated the New Profile House in Franconia Notch (see Chapter 7) as well as establishments in the South. Karl's unusual and highly successful book, *Open for the Season* (1950), a chronicle of his experience in the hotel field, gave the Uplands a special niche in American hotel history.[55]

Like most of its regional counterparts, the Uplands developed in stages over several years, as customer demand dictated and finances allowed. C. J. Fowler built the first portion as a private residence in 1877 on a terraced hillside site on Main (Bethlehem) Street at the west end of the village. Finally, it was opened to the public in 1880 with C. Henry Abbott, formerly of the White Mountain House, as proprietor.[56] Commanding a superb view north toward the Pilot

Fig. 4-25. "The Uplands, Bethlehem, N. H., White Mountains," business card engraving, c. 1890. Author's Collection. Owned and managed by the well-known Abbott family of hotel keepers, the Uplands received recognition in Karl Abbott's popular book, Open for the Season *(1950).*

Range, the new hotel operated with a forty-guest capacity until it was acquired in 1886 by Frank H. Abbott, Karl's father. Under Frank Abbott's energetic direction, the building received three additions over the next four years with his friend Sylvanus D. Morgan (see Chapter 7) as contractor (Fig. 4-25).[57] Around 1910 Abbott went into business with his son, forming the firm, Frank H. Abbott and Son. They constructed new west and east wings in 1912 and 1914 respectively. These improvements increased the capacity to almost 200, and the hotel remained close to this size until it was badly damaged by fire and subsequently razed in 1990-91 (see Plate 9).[58]

The Uplands was distinguished from other Bethlehem hotels of the period by its nicely balanced composition and its diverse collection of delicate decorative elements, all painstakingly executed in wood. Serving as the dominant central focal point for the complex was a square tower capped by a truncated pyramidal roof with paired support brackets and crested, pitched-roof dormers. The World War I-era west and east wings, the latter offset to the rear of the main structure, both featured octagonal corner towers and were virtually identical in scale and adornment. As they constructed each new section, the Abbotts made a supreme effort to preserve the uniform appearance of their hotel—this was most evident in the Mansard roofs with dormers over each section, some of which considerably post-dated the time of the Second Empire style. A rich selection of details, although dating from different eras, was repeated throughout the building. Most unusual were the molded dormer heads with drop pendants, flat-molded window and door caps with side brackets, and piazza screens with turned support columns and traceried cornice and balustrades. Until the time of its destruction, the Uplands, always well maintained, spoke eloquently for the cultural values and artistic preferences of late Victorian America.

The Second Flume House

Erected in 1871-72 on the foundations of the first Flume House (see Chapter 2), the second Flume House soon became a tourist mecca. At first unsophisticated in appearance, it resembled the smaller boarding houses and inns of the era whose form derived from the vernacular domestic architecture of the region (Fig. 4-26). Protected by a gambrel roof with dormers and displaying rather understated classical entablature, corner, window and door moldings, its only unusual feature was a second-story Stick-

Fig. 4-26. "Flume House, Franconia, N. H.," stereo view, c. 1875, Kilburn #1047. Author's Collection. Successor to the first Flume House on the same site, this building resembled smaller boarding houses and inns from the same period.

style balustraded balcony on the south end, looking down the Pemigewasset River Valley toward North Woodstock. Managed for many years by Seth and Josiah Elliott of Lincoln, it was built and owned by Taft & Greenleaf and run in tandem with their principal hotel, the Profile House, five miles to the north in the heart of Franconia Notch.[59]

Quickly regaining the popularity enjoyed by its predecessor the second Flume House did not maintain its original size for long. In 1882-83, Taft & Greenleaf extended the building to the south, adding several products of advancing American technology.[60] The improvements were proudly announced in a promotional flyer:

The Flume House has recently been enlarged and refitted, and has accommodations for one hundred guests. It is heated by open fireplaces and a furnace, and furnished with electric bells and other modern appliances, including telephone communication with all the towns within a radius of twenty miles, and a quick telegraph connection via the Profile House.[61]

In addition to these benefits, the much altered structure assumed new architectural integrity, in large part the result of a quite striking central pavilion with its steep-pitched, hipped-on-truncated pyramidal roof and two-story front porch (Fig. 4-27). In an enlightened gesture, the owners relocated the Stick style balcony intact from the old house to the new south end.[62] The second Flume House, its mountain views offering "perpetual refreshment" and its service "liberal and pleasing," continued to be operated by Taft & Greenleaf until it was destroyed by fire on 27 June 1918.[63] The economic uncertainties of the World War I epoch precluded its rebuilding.[64]

Sugar Hill Emerges as a Resort Community

Situated just south of Franconia village and forming part of Lisbon Highlands is a bold, largely open ridge known as Sugar Hill, rising impressively some 1,600 feet above sea level. Facing east, with unparalleled views of the Franconia Mountains and the Presidential Range, this beautiful and majestic spot inspired superlative descriptions in the nineteenth-century guidebooks written to attract visitors to the White Mountains. In contrast to Jefferson (see Chapter 3), with which it is often compared, Sugar Hill remained a well-kept secret into the mid-1870s. This was in large part due to its fairly remote and elevated location off the main transportation routes. But with the arrival of the railroad in Lisbon and the establishment of a station stop just seven miles away, Sugar Hill became more accessible to tourists; the village was quickly transformed into a major White Mountain resort community. Over the next decade three new hostelries of consequence would be constructed on the ridge. Each of them—the Goodnow House,

Fig. 4-27. Second Flume House, Franconia Notch, NH, photograph from booklet, Franconia Notch, White Mountains, NH . . . *(c. 1910). Author's Collection. Enlarged in 1882-83, the hotel became a mecca for visitors to the Flume and other natural attractions.*

the Sunset Hill House and Hotel Lookoff (see Chapter 5)—would assume an honored place on the list of White Mountain grand resort hotels.

Positioned on the north end of the ridge just above the village of Franconia was the Goodnow House.[65] This was the earliest of the establishments to open as well as the first to cease operation after being destroyed by fire in 1907. In 1875-76, John Wesley Peckett, a lawyer from Brooklyn, New York, and a frequent summer visitor, joined Eliot H. Goodnow, the proprietor of a local boarding house, to finance and build the initial three-and-a-half-story portion of the new hotel.[66] With room for 40 guests it experienced such immediate success that its owners wasted no time in increasing its capacity to 100 in 1877-78 by adding an ell. In this enlarged form, distinguished by its large front gable, triangular ell dormers and clearly articulated, almost tree-like veranda posts, the hotel appeared in several published engraved and photographic views (Fig. 4-28).[67]

Still the only major hotel on Sugar Hill, the Goodnow continued to attract guests, generating sufficient profits for its owners to expand the structure. In July 1880, the *White Mountain Echo* announced that the hotel had "been considerably enlarged [ell and north end] since last year," enabling it to "double its former number of guests." Faced with competition from the new Sunset Hill House higher up the ridge, Peckett and Goodnow promptly responded in 1881-82, raising the capacity to 250 with a new south

Fig. 4-29. "Franconia Inn, Franconia, N. H.," photograph, c. 1895, C. P. Hibbard, Lisbon, #33. Dartmouth College Library. Renamed in 1893, the Goodnow House was almost perfectly symmetrical in its fully developed form.

extension and ell. In size and appearance, it was an almost mirror image of the north end as it had looked in 1878. In 1888, they extended this new ell, creating a nearly closed courtyard within the complex and expanding the guest capacity to 300. After 1893 Robert Peckett acquired the hotel and changed its name to "Franconia Inn." He also conducted extensive interior refurbishing with minor exterior alterations. During its final years, it presented a symmetrical front elevation (marred only by connected cottages) with balancing gables and a central roof observatory capped by a concave pyramidal roof (Fig. 4-29). With its own farm and rich array of recreational and social opportunities, the Peckett establishment is remembered in the annals of the White Mountains for its near idyllic setting and formidable architectural presence.[68]

In contrast to the Goodnow House, the Sunset Hill House stood for almost a century, until 1973-74, when an outmoded physical plant and declining profits resulted in its demolition following its sale by final owner/manager Warren R. Swift. Destined to become Sugar Hill's largest and best known resort hotel, it originated as an unpretentious, L-shaped, three-story, Mansard-roof structure (Fig. 4-30). Erected in 1879, the hostelry opened the following season under the management of Henry H. Bowles and Seth F. Hoskins of Lisbon. Affording space for 125 patrons the new building contained "capacious entrance halls, drawing, reception, dining and read-

Fig. 4-28. "Goodnow's House, Franconia, N. H.," stereo view, c. 1878, Kilburn, unidentified. Douglas Philbrook, Gorham, NH. Erected in 1875-76, the hotel met with immediate success, in large part because of the phenomenal views of the Franconia Mountains.

Fig. 4-30. Sunset Hill House, Sugar Hill, NH, *engraving from* White & Franconia Mountains: Stork's Grand Ten Day Tour . . . *(1880), p. 5. Author's Collection. This portion of the later grand hotel was built in 1879 by owners Bowles & Hoskins.*

ing rooms, and light, airy, and pleasant sleeping rooms." Bowles and Hoskins must have met with great early success, for within a year of hosting their first guests, they extended their house to the north, creating a modified T-shaped floor plan.[69] A small, architecturally compatible cottage joined the hotel in 1885. Enlarged in 1897 and 1899, it became known as "The Annex" and it survives today as a year-around inn managed under the same name as its progenitor (Fig. 4-31).

Building projects continued in 1887-88 with another north wing, 80 by 40 feet, that increased capacity to nearly 300. This addition contained more sleeping rooms, and a drawing room, billiard hall and several parlors—all with open fireplaces (Fig. 4-32).[70] The next year Sunset Hill's configuration changed again with the appending of a two-story south kitchen ell and the lengthening of its connected verandas to an amazing 500 feet.[71] In the words of a contemporary writer the product of all this rapid construction was "a peculiar style of architecture," the building "domeless, with colors flying from a flag-staff, its appearance . . . suggestive of a fortress, rather than . . . [an] abode of peace and pleasure" (Fig. 4-33).[72] Such an uncomplimentary assessment, however, should not diminish its importance as a representative architectural period piece.

Over the next three decades the Sunset Hill House, still managed by Bowles & Hoskins Company, took on a much more monumental and aesthetically appealing character, and new outbuildings of some design merit joined the complex. In 1892, a casino with a picturesque frontal tower was erected, containing bowling alleys, a reception room, music hall, smoking room, and, of all things, a "Bachelor's Hall," with apartments for "young gentlemen . . . to entice to the Sunset to keep its alarming bevy of young ladies in good order!"[73] Three years later the south ell was furnished with a third story (see Fig. 4-33).

Fig. 4-31. The Annex, Sunset Hill House, Sugar Hill, NH, *photograph, 1991, by the author. Erected in 1884, and later enlarged, the Annex was used for guest overflow and remained open in the fall after the main hotel was closed. It is operated as a small inn today.*

Fig. 4-32. Parlor, Sunset Hill House, Sugar Hill, NH, *photograph, c. 1900, unidentified. Sugar Hill Historical Museum. Furnished with a superb collection of wicker pieces, this informal ladies' parlor was typical of many found in contemporary White Mountain resort hotels.*

Fig. 4-33. Sunset Hill House, Sugar Hill, NH, *photograph, c. 1895, C. P. Hibbard, Lisbon. Douglas Philbrook, Gorham, NH. After several additions to the original, the growing complex, in the eyes of some critics, resembled a fortress rather than a place of leisure and recreation.*

Also in 1895 an "elegant pavilion finished in spruce" and surrounded by an eight-foot piazza appeared on the grounds.[74]

Finally, in 1900-01 the main hotel commenced its metamorphosis to architectural respectability through the addition of a twenty-five-room, hipped-roof south wing. This was framed on the east front by matching octagonal corner towers with sharply pitched spire roof caps.[75] In its 1901 annual summary of hotel improvements, the *White Mountain Echo* published an illuminating interior description of the new wing:

The rooms are all finished with hard wood floors, while the wainscotting and trimming are in natural tints. Brass and iron bedsteads are found in many of the rooms. The dining room has been greatly enlarged, . . . , and with its plate glass scenery windows affords magnificent views to those dining.

The color scheme of the dining room is particularly attractive and harmonizes with the natural ash finish. A new reading and writing room for gentlemen, finished in white and

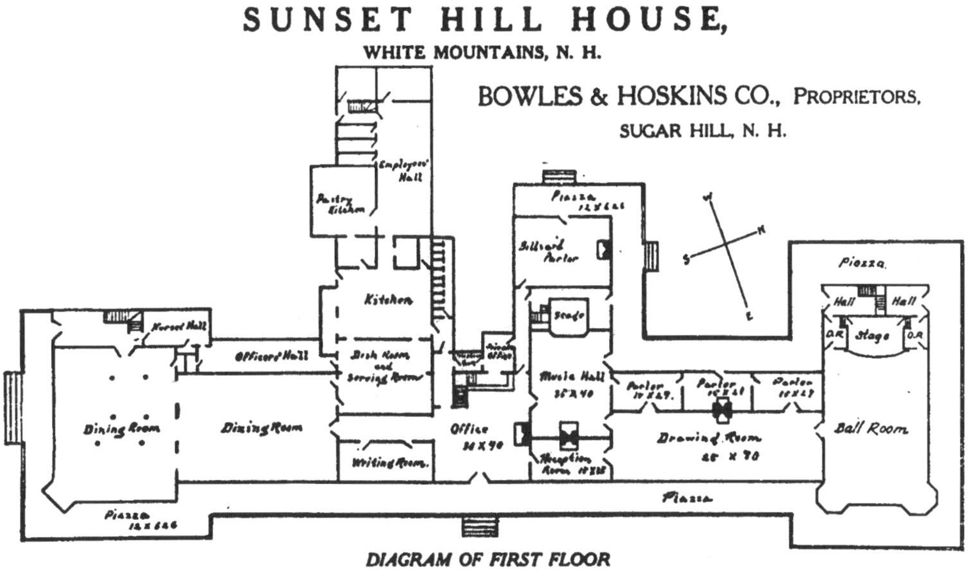

Fig. 4-34. First Floor Plan, Sunset Hill House, Sugar Hill, NH, *from booklet,* Sunset Hill House . . . *(Sugar Hill: n. p., [c. 1910]). Author's Collection. With the post-1900 addition of the new south and north wings the complex boasted over 600 feet of connected piazzas.*

green, opens from the office. Other improvements include a new side hall and capacious closets for dishes, which add to the excellence of the dining room service. Steam heat throughout the house contributes to the pleasure of an autumn sojourn. . . .[76]

Within two years an almost identical north wing was built.[77] This contained a grand ballroom and raised the overnight capacity, including adjoining cottages, to about 325 guests.[78] The complex now assumed an architectural unity and monumentality that it had not formerly possessed—its new wings with their prominent towers counterbalancing each other on opposite ends of the long 375-foot facade (Fig. 4-34). Surmounting the main roof at its center and serving as a visual ordering point for the entire hotel was the cubical observatory dating from the original 1879-80 portion. A photograph taken in fall 1973, just days after its final closing, illustrates the Sunset Hill House devoid of human activity and awaiting demolition. Well manicured and still imposing, its former glory remained palpable, nostalgically displayed in the silent shell (see Plate 10).

George Farr's Oak Hill House

Although it was not a full-service grand resort hotel like the Sunset Hill House, the Oak Hill House possessed many qualities of the grand hotel building type. With a peak capacity of 175 patrons, it was the largest of Littleton's late nineteenth-century hotels.[79] Commencing operation in 1871 with Charles C. Knapp (later manager of the Union House) as its first proprietor, the Oak Hill House, in its earliest phase, was a simple, three-story rectangular block, with ell, front entrance porch and a factory-style, outside stair tower, an unusual feature for hotel architecture of the period (Fig. 4-35). In overall mass, proportions and detail it resembled the first-stage (1879-80) Sunset Hill House, its hipped-on-Mansard roof with dormers and its cube-shaped open cupola its most distinguishing features. Situated on a five-acre hillside tract above the town, with superb views of the Franconia Mountains, the new sixty-guest establishment offered "out-door exercises and amusements," "secluded walks and retreats," "a good billiard and bowling saloon," excellent "tables," and "the purest running water from a never failing spring."[80]

In 1874, George A. Farr, a local businessman and civic official, bought the Oak Hill House. Over the next two decades he would raise the hotel to a position of prominence in the White Mountain region. Under Farr's able direction a series of improvements were undertaken in 1879-80 including interior renovations to the hotel, a new access road and landscaping. In 1881-82, the building received a major addition—doubling its capacity—and practical amenities such as electric bells, gas lighting fixtures and private bathrooms. The interior boasted an expanded office and dining room, a sitting room, a small dance hall and a parlor. New furnishings, oil paintings on the walls, chandeliers, an open fireplace and a steam radiator, conveyed "all the luxury of a city drawing room."[81]

Around 1888-89, the Oak Hill House was further expanded to accommodate 175 guests, nearly achieving fully developed form (Fig. 4-36).[82] Three-and-a-half stories high, the L-shaped building was protected by intersecting pitched roofs, broken by dormers and corniced brick chimneys. Delicately articulated verandas ran the entire length of the principal east and south elevations, their roof rakes trimmed with bargeboard and supported by orna-

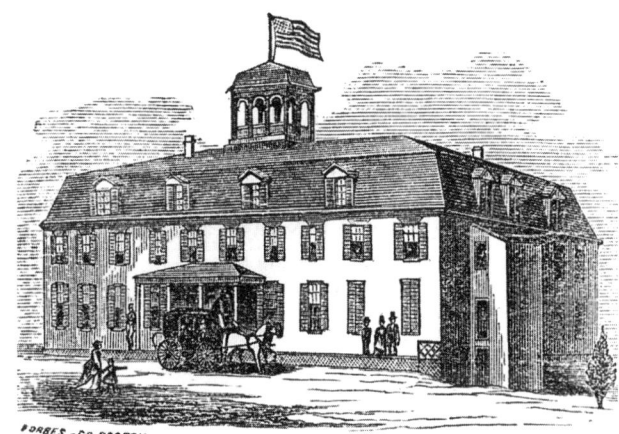

Fig. 4-35. Oak Hill House, Littleton, NH, *engraving from* Keyes' Hand-Book of Northern and Western Pleasure Travel . . . *(1875), p. 72. Author's Collection. The earliest portion of this modest hotel commenced operations in 1871, and featured an unusual outside stair tower.*

Fig. 4-36. "Oak Hill House, Littleton, N. H.," *cabinet photograph, c. 1885, Kilburn, Littleton. New Hampshire Historical Society. Graced by a fine Stick-style tower this spectacularly sited hotel burned in March 1895, just days after its owner, George Farr, unexpectedly passed away.*

mented square posts connected by balustrades. Also present were large open gables on each wall plane, similar to those of the Goodnow House and other area hostelries. Providing the south end of the entire complex with coherence and order was a tall off-center tower with a broken pyramidal roof, open belfry and open balcony stages—reminiscent of bell towers found in contemporary Stick-style ecclesiastical architecture. Other than heavy cornice molding and thin Doric corner pilasters conceived in the classical vein, the tower was the dominant stylistic expression of the building, endowing it with an unmistakable late Victorian flavor.

In an eery and ironical sequence of events, the untimely death of George Farr in 1895 was linked to the destruction of the hotel in which he and the citizens of Littleton had invested such pride. On 19 March, at age sixty, Farr was found deceased in his carriage on the road up Oak Hill from the town center. Within a week of his tragic death, an immense fire totally consumed the Oak Hill House, leaving it a desolate ruin for curious tourists to gaze at the next summer. In the aftermath the *Littleton Courier* theorized that somehow a defective boiler, fired up to provide heat for Farr's funeral service at the hotel, had resulted in its demise. Whatever the cause, it is unprecedented in White Mountain history that a hotelman and his establishment both should pass from the scene so close to one another.[83]

Whether referring to smaller hotels such as the Oak Hill House, the second Flume House and the Uplands, or to larger and more sumptuous grand resort hotels such as the Mount Pleasant House, Fabyan House and the Maplewood, the appearance of these establishments during the 1870s inaugurated an era of hotel construction and enlargement unlike any that the White Mountains had seen before or would see again. Prompted in large part by the full blossoming of the mountain railroad systems, this explosive phenomenon would continue for another two decades. By 1880, just over half the region's grand resort hotels had been constructed. And by

1900, except for a small number of new complexes and additions that would follow, most construction would be completed. The hotel industry in the White Mountains had reached its most competitive level and with further refinements, improvements and promotional activity, it would achieve its apogee and maintain its momentum until the turn of the century.

ಆ Notes ಾ

1. Bulkley, "History," pp. 57-58; Kilbourne, *Chronicles*, pp. 224-25. Erected in 1892 by the B., C. & M., the railroad station at Fabyan's still stands and is used as a restaurant and gift shop.
2. Bulkley, "History," pp. 58-59; Kilbourne, *Chronicles*, pp. 226-28. The year the Portsmouth, Great Falls and Conway Railroad reached North Conway (1872), the new line was leased to the Eastern Railroad. The stations at Glen (c. 1875) and Crawford House (c. 1891) still survive (see Chapter 2, note 46). The P. & O. line through the Notch rose 1,369 feet between North Conway and Crawford's, and the rise per mile was 116 feet for nine miles from Bemis Station to Crawford's. Two notable engineering landmarks along the way were the Frankenstein Trestle (replaced by one of all-steel construction in 1895) and the Willey Brook Bridge. The P. & O. and the Eastern Railroad joined tracks at Intervale, north of North Conway. In 1888 the P. & O. was acquired by the Maine Central Railroad and became its famed Mountain Division. In 1889 the route was laid from Fabyan's to Scott's Mills (via the Twin Mountain House and Whitefield), thereby completing a line that passed entirely through the heart of the White Mountains. Canada was accessed by a farther extension north, which was opened in 1891.
3. Bulkley, "History," pp. 59-60.
4. Bulkley, "History," pp. 61-62; Kilbourne, *Chronicles*, pp. 225-26. The B., C. & M., partial owners of the initial Whitefield and Jefferson Railroad, became sole owners in 1889. The Profile and Franconia Notch Railroad (narrow gauge until 1897) was purchased by the B., C. & M. in 1892, while the Pemigewasset Valley Railroad was leased by the B., C. & M. in 1882.

   The completion of railroad expansion into the center of the White Mountain region put most of the stage lines out of business. However, the route between Gorham, the Glen and North Conway, where there was no rail line, continued to operate.

   The Profile and Franconia Notch Railroad branch to Bethlehem had stations in the middle of town and at the Maplewood Hotel. The town station was moved to a nearby site some years ago and converted to a small residence. Remnants of the latter station (c. 1891) may still be seen in the woods today, not far from the Maplewood Casino and the golf course.
5. Bulkley, "Horace Fabyan," pp. 66-67. Dyer, for all intents and purposes, had held title to at least a portion of the hotel site since 1848 as a result of a controversial decision by the Carroll County Court of Common Pleas. Fabyan, while unwilling to sell to Dyer for over fifteen years, also was unable to rebuild on the foundations of the former Mount Washington House.

   Sylvester Marsh accumulated wealth as an out-of-state provisions dealer, meat packer and grain dealer. A native New Hampshirite he returned to the state in 1864, settling in Littleton. The railway was contemplated as early as 1852, was chartered in 1865, and was built between 1866 and 1869.
6. See the *Coos Republican* (Lancaster), 1 August 1865; *Morris' Tourist Hand Book Illustrated* . . . (Portland, ME: G. W. Morris, [c. 1891]), p. 116; and, *Summer Outings in the Old Granite State* . . . (Boston: Passenger Department, Concord & Montreal Railroad, 1891), p. 109.
7. *Appalachia* 48, No. 4 (15 December 1991), p. 138. In addition to this source there is the mention, "the old Fabian House is being rebuilt," in Charles H. Sweetser, *Book of Summer Resorts* . . . (New York: "Evening Mail" Office, 1868), p. 67. A brief piece entitled "New Hotel" appeared in the 4 September 1868 edition of the *White Mountain Republic* (Littleton).
8. Henry M. Burt, *Burt's Guide of the Connecticut Valley* . . . (Northampton, MA: New England Publishing Co., 1868), p. 253; *Keyes Hand-Book of Northern Pleasure Travel: The White and Franconia Mountains* . . . (Boston: George L. Keyes, Printer, 1873), p. 97; *Snow's Handbook of Northern Pleasure Travel, to the White and Franconia Mountains* . . . (Worcester, MA: Noyes & Snow, 1876), p.123; Gile, *Excursions to the White Mountains*, p. 15. Late editions of the Keyes' and Snow guides repeat the same reference to the fire.
9. Bulkley, "Horace Fabyan," pp. 68-69. These facts refute the popular belief that the hotel was financed and built by the Concord and Montreal Railroad, later absorbed by the Boston and Maine. Appropriately, Albert I. Fabyan, the son of Horace, was employed as the first clerk. See also, the *White Mountain Republic*, 4 April 1872, p.2, 16 May 1872, and 23 May 1872.
10. *New England: A Handbook for Travelers* . . . (Boston: James R. Osgood and Co., 1873), p. 233.
11. Bachelder, *Popular Resorts; and How to Reach Them*, p. 116.
12. *The White Mountains* (1876 ed.), p. 158; Ernest Ingersoll, *Down East Latch Strings* . . . (Boston: Passenger Department of the Boston and Maine Railroad, 1887), p. 178.
13. *ATC* 4, No. 32 (28 August 1880), p. 4.
14. During the 1880s, several basic changes in the complex occurred that did not alter the form of the main building. These included the construction in 1880 of a new 1,500 seat wooden pavilion for the annual conferences of the American Institute of Instruction (*ATC* 3, No. 1 [9 July 1879], p. 8); the installation of a skating rink in the pavilion in 1883 (*ATC* 7, No. 8 [19 July 1883], p. 1); exterior painting, extensive landscaping and the addition of outside shutters in 1885 (*ATC* 9, No. 1 [11 July 1885], p. 1, No. 6 [18 July 1885], p. 1, and No.

29 [29 August 1885], p. 4); and the construction in 1888 of a new railroad station by the Concord and Montreal and Maine Central railroads (*ATC* 16, No. 1 [11 July 1892], p.4). The pavilion was refitted as an automobile garage in 1904 (*ATC* 28, No. 3 [11 July 1904], p.4).

15. *ATC* 20, No. 1 (10 July 1896), p. 4.
16. "Early Days at the Fabyan," *ATC* 19, No. 27 (13 August 1895), p. 4; Bulkley, "History," pp. 63-64; Kilbourne, *Chronicles*, p. 337; "Asa T. Barron," *WME* 10, No. 7 (20 August 1887), p. 7; Bulkley, "Horace Fabyan," p. 74; *Littleton Courier*, 20 September 1951, p. 1. The B. & M. acquired the hotel when it took over the Concord and Montreal Railroad, which had purchased it from the original founding syndicate. Losses from the fire were estimated at $1 million, and the hotel was never rebuilt. Recent owners were J. Alfred and Mary A. Seymour of Twin Mountain from 1938 to 1946, and James Zacher of New York City from 1946 until the hotel's demise.
17. Willey, *Incidents in White Mountain History*, op. p. 89 and p. 89.
18. Burt, *The Story of Mount Washington*, pp. 95-96; Kilbourne, *Chronicles*, p. 246; McAvoy, *And Then There Was One*, p. 56; Bray, *They Said it Couldn't be Done*, pp. 87-88. The hotel was also called the "Mount Washington House" early in its history.
19. *White Mountain Republic*, 13 June 1872, p. 2. For details on Dow, see *Granite Monthly* 17 (1894), p. 218, and 13 (1890), p. 50.
20. *ATC* 3, No. 9 (19 July 1879), p. 4; Frank H. Burt, *Mount Washington: A Handbook for Travelers*, 3rd ed. (Boston: George H. Ellis Co., 1906), pp. 24-25; Kilbourne, *Chronicles*, p. 247; Burt, *The Story of Mount Washington*, p. 96; Jeffrey Leich, "Possession of the Summit: 'A Prolific Subject of Contention,'" *Mount Washington Observatory News Bulletin* 31, No. 1 (Summer 1990), p. 33. The hotel was also supplied with electricity around the turn of the century, and extensive architectural improvements were made in 1887, 1895, 1901 and 1905.
21. Rev. Guy Roberts and Frank H. Burt, *Mt. Washington*, 4th ed. (Whitefield, NH: Guy Roberts, 1927), p. 12; Kilbourne, *Chronicles*, pp. 247-49.
22. "The Fire on Mount Washington," *ATC* magazine number, 1908; Burt, *The Story of Mount Washington*, pp. 119-123; *WME* 30, No. 1 (11 July 1908), pp. 2, 3, 20. After 1894 the Summit House was owned by the Mount Washington Railroad Company. Supplementing the Summit House at the Base Station was the Marshfield House (c. 1871) with space for about fifty persons.
23. *ATC* 19, No. 25 (10 August 1895), p. 4; Kilbourne, *Chronicles*, p. 337; Burt, *The Story of Mount Washington*, pp. 105-106; McAvoy, *And Then There Was One*, p. 53; *The White Mountain Guide Book*, 13th ed. (Concord, NH: Edson C. Eastman, and Boston: Lee & Shepard, 1876), p. 105.
24. *Snow's Handbook of Northern Pleasure Travel* . . . (Worcester, MA: Noyes, Snow & Company, 1879), p. 140.
25. McAvoy, *And Then There Was One*, p. 53; *Chisholm's All Round Route and Panoramic Guide*, 1875 ed., p. 192; *ATC* 1, No. 1 (20 July 1877), p. 1.
26. Burt, *The Story of Mount Washington*, p. 106; *ATC* 5, No. 1 (9 July 1881), p. 1; *ATC* 6, No. 19 (8 August 1882), p. 1; *ATC* 19, No. 25 (10 August 1895), p. 4; *Chisholm's White Mountain Guide-Book* (Portland, ME: Chisholm Brothers, 1881), advertisement. Following this renovation in 1893, a 250-foot-long wooden rusticated observation bridge was constructed behind the Mount Pleasant House by designer and builder Jacob Caler of Providence, RI (*ATC* 6, No. 11 [26 July 1882]). A passenger elevator was installed for the 1883 season (*ATC* 7, No. 6 [17 July 1883]).
27. Burt, *The Story of Mount Washington*, p. 107.
28. *ATC* 8, No. 10 (25 July 1884), p. 1.
29. *ATC* 8, No.33 (27 August 1884), p. 4.
30. Sketchbook, c. 1880-84, John Calvin Stevens Collection, Maine Historical Society, Portland. The Stevens Collection is one of the most comprehensive for a single late nineteenth-century architect in a New England archive.
31. *ATC* 19, No. 4 (13 July 1895), p. 4, and No. 25 (10 August 1895), p. 4.
32. Damie Stillman, et al., *Architecture and Ornament in Late 19th-Century America* (Newark, DE: Department of Art History and the University Gallery, University of Delaware, 1981), p. 20. Other Fassett biographical sketches may be found in the following printed sources: Withey, *Biographical Dictionary of American Architects (Deceased)*, p. 204; Phillip W. McIntyre and William F. Blanding, eds., *Men of Progress: Biographical Sketches and Portraits of Leaders . . . State of Maine* (Boston: New England Magazine, 1897), p. 342; "Pillars of Portland: Francis H. Fassett—Our Oldest Architect," *Portland Transcript*, 22 November 1893; Augustus Moulton, *Memorials of Maine* . . . (New York: American Historical Society, 1916), p. 206; "Oldest Architect in Maine," *Lewiston* (ME) *Journal*, 4-8 January 1908, Illustrated Magazine Section, pp. 1 & 3; *Bath* (ME) *Daily News*, 24 August 1905; Parker M. Reed, *History of Bath and Environs* (Portland: Lakeside Press, 1894), pp. 439-40.
33. Collection of Letters, Francis H. Fassett (FHF) and Edward F. Fassett (EFF), Portland, Maine, to Joseph Stickney (JS), New York City, 1894-95, NHHS, Concord.
34. Payson Tucker, Portland, Maine, to JS, New York City, 30 August 1894, NHHS. Stevens and Tompson were partners with Fassett at separate times.
35. FHF to JS, 6 September 1894, NHHS.
36. FHF to JS, 24 September 1894, NHHS.
37. FHF to JS, 29 September 1894, 5 October 1894, 8 October 1894, 10 October 1894; EFF to JS, 3 November 1894, 15 November 1894, 6 December 1894, 13 December 1894, 19 December 1894, 24 December 1894, 31 December 1894, NHHS.
38. EFF to JS, 2 January 1895; FHF to JS, 11 January 1895, 14 January 1895; EFF to JS, 18 January 1895; FHF to JS, 19 January 1895, 2 February 1895; EFF to JS, 7 February 1895, 19 February 1895; FHF to JS, 7 March 1895; EFF to JS, 9 March 1895; FHF to JS, 14 March 1895, 19 March 1895; EFF to JS, 11 April 1895, 22 April 1895, 26 April 1895, 13 May 1895; FHF to JS, 25 May 1895, 3 June 1895; EFF to JS, 13 June

1895, 21 June 1895, 27 June 1895, 30 June 1895; Robert I. Jenks to JS, 20 June 1895, NHHS.

39. Proposals for Mount Pleasant House (c. 1894); FHF to JS, 2 July 1895; EFF to JS, 4 July 1895, 13 July 1895; EFF to Robert I. Jenks, 16 July 1895, 18 July 1895; FHF to JS, 23 July 1895; EFF to Waldo M. Colby, 24 July 1895; Robert I. Jenks to JS, 2 August 1895; FHF to Robert I. Jenks, 3 August 1895; EFF to JS, 13 August 1895; EFF to Robert I. Jenks, 7 August 1895, 15 August 1895, 16 August 1895; EFF to JS, 5 September 1895; FHF to JS, 12 September 1895, 17 September 1895; Anderson & Price to Robert I. Jenks, 13 September 1895, 16 September 1895; EFF to Robert I. Jenks, __ October 1895, 4 October 1895, 5 October 1895, 8 October 1895, 11 October 1895, 19 October 1895, 28 October 1895; EFF to M. H. Higgins, 12 October 1895, 25 October 1895, 28 October 1895; EFF to JS, 29 October 1895; EFF to Robert I. Jenks, 31 October 1895; FHF to Robert I. Jenks, 16 November 1895, 19 November 1895; EFF to Robert I. Jenks, 21 November 1895, 26 November 1895; FHF to M. H. Higgins, 26 November 1895; EFF to Robert I. Jenks, 3 December 1895, 12 December 1895, 11 January 1896, NHHS.

40. *Gems of the Northland* (Portland, ME: Maine Central Railroad, 1895), op. p. 80.

41. *ATC* 19, No. 4 (13 July 1895), p. 4; *Mount Pleasant House, N. H.* (New York: Mount Pleasant Hotel Co., [c.1895]); *ATC* 20, No. 1 (10 July 1896), p. 4; *WME* 20, No. 12 (18 September 1897), p. 14; *ATC* 19, No. 48 (6 September 1895), p. 4.

42. *Littleton Courier*, 20 July 1939, pp. 1, 4; McAvoy, *And Then There Was One*, p. 257. The site today is occupied by the Lodge at Bretton Woods, formerly the Bretton Woods Motor Inn.

43. Bulkley, "History," pp. 65-66.

44. Marcia Gale Chadbourne to Carolyn K. Tolles, 2 January 1975; *WME* 6, No. 2 (7 July 1883), p. 7; *Eagle Mountain House, Jackson, New Hampshire* (Jackson: n.p., [c.1901]); Merrill, *History of Carroll County*, p. 963; *ATC* 14, No. 22 (5 August 1891), p. 4; typed manuscript by Marcia G. Chadbourne, n.d., Jackson Historical Society; *Littleton Courier*, 20 May 1915, p. 1; *The Reporter* (North Conway), 13 May 1915, p. 1. Surviving the fire were the barn and "The Eaglet," a small cottage just to the south, both of which stand today.

45. Kilbourne, *Chronicles*, pp. 332-34; Wilson, *Bethlehem*, p. 30; Moses, "A Lost Town: A Sketch of Bethlehem," pp. 20-21.

46. Moses, "A Lost Town: A Sketch of Bethlehem," pp. 21-22; Kilbourne, *Chronicles*, p. 334; *WME* 1, No. 8 (31 August 1878), p. 1.

47. Bachelder, *Popular Resorts* (1874 ed.), p. 113.

48. *WME* 1, No. 8 (31 August 1878), p. 1; *WME* 2, No. 1 (28 June 1879), p. 12, and No. 12 (22 July 1878), p. 1; *WME* 3, No. 12 (26 June 1880), p. 12. The first electric lights in the White Mountain region were possibly installed at the Maplewood in 1882.

49. Hugh J. Chisholm, *Chisholm's White Mountain Guide Book* (Portland, ME: Chisholm, 1882), advertisement.

50. *WME* 2, No. 1 (28 June 1879), p. 12.

51. *WME* 1, No. 8 (31 August 1878), p. 1; *WME* 2, No. 2 (5 July 1879), p. 11; *ATC* 10, No. 2 (12 August 1886), p. 4; *ATC* 13, No. 14 (27 July 1889), p. 4; *WME* 13, No. 7 (16 August 1890), p. 1; *Littleton Courier*, 31 October 1907, p. 1; Plan of Maplewood Hotel Company Land at Maplewood, NH, Town of Bethlehem, May 1944, grantor book #719, p. 495, Grafton County Registry of Deeds, Woodsville. W. S. Brooks of Bethlehem was the supervising builder of Maplewood Hall. It was painted a pale yellow with white trim and green shutters, the color combination employed in all other Maplewood estate buildings. For reasons unexplained the new hotel annex proved unsuccessful and it was torn down in 1898 (*ATC* 22, No. 1 [18 July 1898], p. 4). Six years before, however, the ownership had threatened to demolish the building "on account of high taxes imposed upon it by our town fathers." (*Littleton Courier*, 11 May 1892).

52. *WME* 11, No. 1 (11 July 1887), p. 8; Wilson, *Bethlehem*, p. 38; *ATC* 13, No. 2 (13 July 1889), p. 4, and No. 35 (2 September 1889), p. 1; *Magnetic North* 5, No. 4 (Spring 1988), p. 33; Tolles, *New Hampshire Architecture*, pp. 316-17; *WME* 11, No. 2 (30 June 1888), p. 5; *WME* 21, No. 1 (2 July 1898), p. 9. The Casino was completed at a cost of $9,800, with F. L. White as the principal contractor. In 1987-88 it was totally restored to its Gilded Age glory, with a price tag of $1.5 million, by the owning Ristuccia family.

53. *Littleton Courier*, 6 August 1942 and 8 December 1943; *Concord Monitor*, 15 January 1963, p. 1; *Littleton Courier*, 17 January 1963, pp. 1, 4; newspaper scrapbooks, White Mountain Collection, DCL. The Maplewood Motor Inn was constructed adjacent to the hotel in 1962, and, more recently, was demolished. The loss from the 1963 fire was estimated at $500,000 at the time.

54. Each of these hotels accommodated fifty or more guests. Surviving today are the Arlington Hotel, the Highland Hotel, Avenue House (Gramercy; Maplehurst) and Turner House.

55. Karl P. Abbott, *Open for the Season* (Garden City, NY: Doubleday & Company, Inc., 1950).

56. Hattie W. Taylor, *Early History of Bethlehem, N. H.* (Bethlehem: n.p., 1960), p. 46; Tolles, *New Hampshire Architecture*, p. 315; *WME* 3, No. 1 (26 June 1880), p. 8. W. C. Noyes managed the hotel during the mid-1880s.

57. *WME* 12, No. 1 (6 July 1889), pp. 7, 15; *WME* 13, No. 1 (5 July 1890), p. 10; *WME* 14, No. 2 (11 July 1891), p. 11; Williams, "The Saga of 'S. D.' Morgan," p. 13.

58. *WME* 38, No. 1 (17 July 1915), p. 1; *WME* 47, No. 7 (23 August 1924), p. 15; *Resident and Business Directory of the West Side of the White Mountains of New Hampshire* (Littleton, NH, and Beverly, MA: Crowley & Lunt, 1914), p. 343; *Union Leader*, 27 August 1990, p. 5; *Upland Terrace in the White Mountains* (Bethlehem, NH: n.p., [c. 1914]); Plan of the Upland Terrace Company Property, Bethlehem, NH (G. W. Richardson, Surveyor), February 1956, grantor book #881, p. 11, Grafton County Registry of Deeds, Woodsville. In 1924 Frank H. Abbott & Son sold the Upland Terrace Hotel (renamed in 1910) to Elmer Harrington. After World War II, until the time of its destruction, it was owned by Neil Chase

who used it as a dormitory and dining hall for his annual golf and tennis camps.

59. Kilbourne, "A Closed Chapter of White Mountain History," p. 309; *Snow's Handbook of Northern Pleasure Travel* (1879 ed.), p. 130; Child, *Gazetteer of Grafton County, N. H.*, p. 434; *Bicentennial Commemorative Booklet of the Town of Lincoln*, p. 22. According to Child the construction cost was $40,000, and the original occupancy was forty guests.

60. *ATC* 7, No. 6 (17 July 1883), p. 1; *WME* 6, No. 3 (14 July 1883), p. 5.

61. Flyer, "Flume House, Franconia Notch, White Mountains, New Hampshire," Taft & Greenleaf, Proprietors, c. 1883-87.

62. Sometime after 1900 additional bedroom space was created in the attic story and elsewhere, raising the capacity to 150. A new dancing pavilion was added to the complex in 1915 (*ATC*, 13 July 1915, p. 1).

63. Frank W. Rollins, *The Tourists' Guide-Book to the State of New Hampshire*, 2nd ed. (Concord: The Rumford Press, 1902), p. 265; *Littleton Courier*, 4 July 1918, p. 1; Kilbourne, "A Closed Chapter of White Mountain History," p. 309. Daniel Bigelow of Boston was manager at the time of the fire. The loss was about $75,000.

64. After the 1918 fire, and the consequent decision not to rebuild, the new owners erected a tea-room across the road where the stables for the first Flume House formerly had stood. This structure was destroyed with the recent construction of a new visitors' center and parking lots for the Flume.

65. The Town of Sugar Hill was incorporated in 1962 and consists of the former eastern sector of the Town of Lisbon. The site of the Goodnow House is very near the Sugar Hill-Franconia town line.

66. The original Goodnow boarding house, next to the site of the new hotel, was moved across the road in 1893 to become the house of Robert and Katherine Peckett. The couple took in their first guests in 1900, and the house later became the nucleus of the famed resort, Peckett's-on-Sugar-Hill, one of the first guest establishments in the White Mountains to promote the sport of Alpine skiing in the 1930s. For reasons relating to its essentially residential form and modest size, Peckett's is not accorded in-depth treatment in this book. It burned after World War II and was not rebuilt.

67. *Sugar Hill, New Hampshire: A Glimpse Into the Past (1780-1986)*, 2nd ed. (Sugar Hill: Harrison Publishing Company, 1986), p. 25; *The White Mountains*, 1st ed. (1876), p. 255; *Snow's Handbook of Northern Pleasure Travel* (1878 ed.), p. 92, and (1879 ed.), p. 96.

68. "Franconia Inn," *Littleton Courier*, 28 November 1907; *The Idler* 1, No. 1 (23 June 1880), p. 4; *The White Mountains*, 1888 ed., p. 255; *WME* 3, No. 2 (3 July 1880), p. 4; *WME* 4, No. 1 (2 July 1881), p. 12; *WME* 5, No. 2 (8 July 1882), p. 5; Luther L. Holden, ed., *White & Franconia Mountains*, Vol. 5, No. 2 (Boston: Boston, Concord, Montreal & White Mountains R. R., 1882), p. 11 (engraving); *ATC* 4, No. 3 (20 July 1888), p. 4;

WME 16, No. 2 (8 July 1893), p. 2. From 1893 to 1907 the hotel was run by John Wesley Peckett's son Robert and his brother John. The cause of the fire was undetermined. Losses totaled $30,000 to $40,000.

Another Sugar Hill competitor worthy of mention is the Phillips House, erected by W. B. Phillips in 1883-84. Accommodating up to 100 people it was struck by lightning and burned on 22 June 1906. The Breezy Hill House on the road from Lisbon was opened in 1884 by the Jesseman family and was another popular rival hotel in the area. It took in up to 160 guests (see Chapter 5).

69. *The Idler* 1, No. 1 (22 June 1880), p. 4; *ATC* 4, No. 3 (20 July 1880), p. 4, and 20 (12 August 1880), advertisement; *ATC* 5, No. 1 (9 July 1881), p. 1; *WME* 2, No. 2 (28 June 1879), p. 12; *WME* 3, No. 2 (3 July 1880), p. 4; *WME* 5, No. 2 (8 July 1882), p. 5.

70. *WME* 8, No. 2 (4 July 1885), pp. 5, 10, and No. 6 (1 August 1885), p. 8; *WME* 11, No. 1 (10 July 1888), p. 1; *WME* 11, No. 2 (7 July 1888), p. 5. From the year of its construction the Annex was intended to house guests during colder weather after the main hotel had closed each fall

71. *WME* 12, No. 1 (6 July 1889), p. 10; *Sunset Hill House, Sugar Hill, N. H.* (Sugar Hill: n.p., [c. 1888]).

72. Child, *Gazetteer of Grafton County, N. H.*, p. 440; *Sunset Hill House, White Mountains, N. H.* (Sugar Hill: n.p., [c. 1890]).

73. *WME* 16, No. 2 (9 July 1892), p. 2, and No. 11 (22 July 1892), p. 4; *ATC* 16, No. 1 (11 July 1892), p. 4.

74. *WME* 18, No. 2 (13 July 1895), p. 14; *The American Alps; Other Summer Resorts . . .* (Bethlehem, NH: The White Mountain Echo, 1895), p. 31.

75. *WME* 24, No. 2 (13 July 1901), p. 11; *ATC* 25, No. 2 (13 July 1901), p. 4.

76. *WME* 24, No. 2 (13 July 1901), p. 11.

77. *WME* 26, No. 1 (4 July 1903), p. 18. After the construction of the south wing in 1900-1901, advertisements appeared, beginning in 1903, in the *WME* containing the word, "Enlarged." The advertisements continued throughout the decade. It is assumed, therefore, other documentation lacking, that the matching north wing was erected very shortly after the south wing was built.

78. With the construction of the new south and north wings there was much rearrangement of interior spaces, including the sleeping areas. This, however, resulted in only a modest gain in the number of available guest beds.

79. Littleton's other hotels of the period included the Chiswick Inn and Cottages (1884-85; capacity, 100), the Northern Hotel (1898; capacity 100) and The Maples (1888-89; capacity, 50).

80. *Keyes' Hand-Book of Northern Pleasure Travel* (1873 ed.), pp. 50-51; *Keyes' Hand-Book of Northern and Western Pleasure Travel . . .* (Boston: Geo. L. Keyes, 1875), p. 72; *WME* 1, No. 7 (24 August 1878), p. 1; *Snow's Handbook of Northern Pleasure Travel* (1876 ed.), p. 82; *Littleton Courier*, 27 March 1895, p. 1. The hotel was built in the fall of 1870 by a stock company of

which William J. Bellows was president and H. L. Tilton treasurer. It was leased to Charles Knapp.

81. Child, *Gazetteer of Grafton County, N.H.*, pp. 491-92; *The Idler* 1, No. 1 (22 July 1880), p. 4; *WME* 5, No. 2 (8 July 1882), p. 5; *ATC* 6, No. 1 (13 July 1882), advertisement, p. 8, and No. 32 (25 August 1882), p. 1; "Sketch of Littleton," *Granite Monthly* 5, No. 8 (June 1882), p. 302.

82. *Summer Haunts. Hotels and Boarding Houses in the White Mountains and Other Popular Resorts, and at Favorite Winter Retreats* (Bethlehem, NH: The White Mountain Echo, 1889), pp. 22-23. See also, Luther L. Holden, ed., *White & Franconia Mountains*, Vol. 6, No. 1 (Boston: Publication Office, Boston, Concord, Montreal and White Mts. R.R., 1883), p. 35; *Summer Saunterings by the B. & L.* (1885 ed.), p. 137. Fortunately, visual images of the structure are plentiful, and it is through these that the Oak Hill House's architectural attributes may be best examined and analyzed.

83. *WME* 18, No. 1 (6 July 1895), p. 16, and No. 2 (13 July 1895), p. 14; *Littleton Courier*, 27 March 1895, p. 1. On 27 September 1899, the *Littleton Courier* published an article indicating that the former local architect Edward Thornton Sanderson (then of Fitchburg, MA), the designer of the Maplewood Casino, was in town exhibiting plans to interested persons for a new, four-story, 180-room hotel to be built on Oak Hill at the site of the former Oak Hill House. As described the envisioned structure was to be "similar to the old house" having two wings, but with a "large round tower at the corner." The hotel was never constructed, possibly, as the article stated, because an option was not obtained on the land.

Fig 4-37. "Mount Washington Summit House, White Mountains, N.H., John W. Dodge." *Cover for dinner bill of fare and wine list, Wednesday, July 20, 1881. Author's Collection. The cog railway provided the principal means of transportation to and from the mountain top.*

Fig 4-38. "Flume House, Franconia Notch, White Mountains, New Hampshire, Taft & Greenleaf, Proprietors...." *Cover for dinner menu, August 1, 1892. Author's Collection. This attractively designed piece was considered a prized souvenier by hotel guests.*

Fig 5-15. First Gray's Inn, Second Woodbury Hall, *Jackson, NH, construction photography, n.d., photographer unknown. Jackson Historical Society. Owner Charles W. Gray likely designed this building as he did others in the several Gray's Inn complexes erected from the 1880s to the 1920s.*

CHAPTER 5

The Maturation of the Building Type: From the Eighties to World War I

THE ECONOMIC BOOM experienced by the White Mountain hotel industry in the 1870s continued during the 1880s and 1890s until depressing factors prompted a long, slow decline lasting well into this century. Despite clear signs that the industry had peaked and was starting to fade, the grand hotel building type achieved full maturation between the 1880s and World War I, exhibiting new architectural styles and greater size. In many instances ownership passed to wealthy investors and management groups, while an even more affluent and cosmopolitan clientele sought the mountain vacation experience. To satisfy the increasingly sophisticated tastes of their guests, hotels introduced new and more extensive social, recreational and cultural programs. Even as the regional hotels continued to expand and to diversify their offerings, they did so in the face of circumstances that ultimately discouraged their financial health and their potential for future long-term growth and survival.

The conditions that fostered hotel development in the region during the Civil War and Reconstruction eras continued to positively affect the industry until World War I. America's rise to industrial and commercial preeminence between the two wars accelerated the trend toward greater prosperity, producing the money as well as available vacation time to sustain the resort hotels of the nation. The previous pattern of urbanization continued, with cities mushrooming at an almost uncontrollable rate. People continued to try to escape the less than pleasant social and environmental conditions and immerse themselves in leisure and recreation by taking advantage of the rural resort hotel experience. The railroads, other means of transportation, and communications systems advanced to the point that the White Mountains and other vacation areas could be easily reached by those seeking travel and leisure opportunities.

As a consequence of intensifying competition between the hotels and the communities in which they were situated, hotel owners, and local leaders were under constant pressure to initiate improvements. Scientific, programmatic and civic in nature, these changes inevitably increased the demand for more guest space and better facilities. Thus the period 1880 to World War I witnessed the continued construction of new hotel complexes or additions to older ones. Among the technological improvements were elevators, telephones, private toilets, superior water and sanitation systems, and more sophisticated steam heating. Electric lighting first supplemented and eventually replaced gas. Responding to the late-Victorian desire for greater luxury and new recreational alternatives, many hotel owners furnished their properties with billiard rooms, bowling alleys, baseball fields, bicycling paths and tracks, rifle ranges, roller skating rinks, golf courses (after the mid-1890s), casinos, as well as croquet, badminton

[143]

and tennis courts. "Nonparticipant entertainment," as Peter Bulkley has named it, included indoor and outdoor band concerts and plays, community gala days (first introduced in Bethlehem in 1885), and the famed hotel coaching parades (again premiered in Bethlehem in 1887).

The White Mountain resort towns also sought to augment the tourist trade through community improvements. With Bethlehem once more seizing the initiative, these assumed the proportions of a regional reform movement; many competing towns provided better roads and walkways, street lights, signage, improved drainage and waterworks, more effective fire departments, public parks, sanitation services, and boards of trade or civic improvement organizations.[1]

The extensive promotional efforts carried on by the seasonal newspapers, the railroads, the resort towns and the hotels themselves also increased tourism and encouraged hotel expansion. Taking the lead among the newspapers in the North Country were *The White Mountain Echo*, Bethlehem; *Among the Clouds*, Mount Washington summit; and the *Weirs Times and Tourist's Gazette (Calvert's Weirs Times)*, The Weirs in the Lakes Region. Each greatly stimulated tourism through extensive advertising, guest registers, feature articles and special supplements, or editions focused on the hotels and the communities or areas in which they were located. Sometimes they assumed usefully pro-active positions on issues affecting tourism. The railroads went to great ends to enhance their business interests and indirectly those of the hotels by publishing viewbooks, illustrated timetables, and guidebooks—some of which had considerable literary merit. Several resort towns, such as North Conway, Bethlehem and Littleton, sponsored the publication of pictorial booklets and other promotional literature designed to attract tourists. In the 1870s and in a few earlier instances, the hotels (followed by their parent corporations) produced their own business cards, photographic views, circulars with maps, and illustrated promotional/informational booklets and brochures. During the peak years of the hotel industry, from the late 1880s to the late 1890s, the *Echo* supplemented the promotional efforts of the hotels by publishing booklets listing and describing the major White Mountain hotels. These were distributed to the metropolitan areas of the Northeast without charge. Not only did this literary circulation increase regular guest visitation, but it also encouraged the use of the hotels for group meetings (the forerunners of today's conventions) and special excursions. Most of these visits were scheduled for the fall, thereby extending the open summer season from three to over four months.[2]

Countering the forces fostering hotel expansion in the 1880s and 1890s was the blatant economic exploitation of the White Mountain region and its natural resources. The hotels managed to survive, but not without some detrimental effects. The reason for this phenomenon was relatively simple—the state government assumed a laissez-faire posture toward the flourishing White Mountain business interests. Its leaders lacked the foresight or the will to pass laws and regulations protecting these interests, the public, and the natural environment from abuses. The most obvious unsavory activity resulted from careless and uncontrolled lumber operations that temporarily destroyed much of the scenic beauty of the mountains through timber clear-cutting without reforestation or slash removal. Dangerous, polluting forest fires were the all too common result. Lacking inadequate journalistic standards, newspapers promoting other resort areas in the country seized upon the environmental crisis to launch scurrilous and damaging attacks against the White Mountains region and its hotels.

In addition to the environmental problems created by the lumber industry, the hotels themselves created pollution hazards by inefficient and unhealthful sanitary waste disposal. The railroads added to this problem by generating constant noise, steam engine soot, smoke and refuse. Unregulated land speculation also worked against the interests of the hotels. The most highly publicized instance was the legal controversy over the ownership of Mount Washington and contiguous lands, jeopardizing the future and financial stability of the Mount Washington Railway and the large hotel operations nearby. By the beginning of this century, state regulations, such as the inspection and certification of hotels, and state promotion began to rectify the consequences of abuse, but not before

Fig. 5-1. Proposed Electric Scenic Railway and Summit Hotel, Mount Washington, NH, *engraving,* Among the Clouds *34, No. 53 (9 September 1912), p. 4. Author's Collection. The huge donut-shaped hotel—intended to enclose the summit of Mount Washington— and the railway were never built.*

much harm had been done. The hotel industry would never completely recover—decline was slow but inexorable.³

The Notches, the Ammonoosuc Plain and Mount Washington

In the major notches of the White Mountains and on the summit of Mount Washington and in its vicinity, the architectural history of the hotels from 1880 to World War I was marked by some notable new buildings and complexes, as well as significant additions to older establishments. In Crawford Notch the Willey House Hotel was enlarged in the early 1890s, only to burn down in 1899, while the Crawford House underwent minor alterations during the previous decade. On the Ammonoosuc plain at Bretton Woods, the Mount Pleasant House incurred a massive expansion and revitalization between 1881 and 1895, and the grandiose Mount Washington Hotel complex took shape in 1901-03 (see Chapter 8). At Twin Mountain, also on the plain, the more modest Rosebrook Inn was built in 1891-92, followed by the Grand View Hotel in 1916-17.⁴ On the other side of the Presidential Range in Pinkham Notch the fabulous second Glen House was erected in stages from 1885 to 1887, but survived only until 1893 when fire destroyed it (see Chapter 7). To the west in Franconia Notch, the second Flume House was doubled in size in 1882-83. In addition the magnificent New Profile House was constructed in 1905-06 with numerous cottages added to the complex until fire burned the main hotel and all outbuildings in 1923 (see Chapter 7).

On the summit of Mount Washington, after the catastrophic fire in June 1908 leveled the second Summit House, plans for a new hotel were discussed over the next several years. The initial proposal was for a replacement building to be quickly built in time for an August occupancy, but this failed to occur. Subsequently, in July 1910, a cornerstone was laid and work commenced on the foundations of a structure to be built on the old Summit House site; however, this project was discontinued in favor of more elaborate plans. From 1910 to 1913, under the auspices of the Concord and Montreal Railroad, feasibility studies were carried out for a twenty-mile scenic electric railroad that would rise in easy grades and switchbacks from the Base Station up the Castellated Ridge to Mount Jefferson, along the ridge formed by Mount Clay, then around the cone of Mount Washington twice before terminating on the summit. The plan also called for the construction of a voluminous, three-story hotel (Fig. 5-1). Circular in layout and built of concrete, stone, steel and glass, it was to surround the peak of the mountain. On its roof a giant searchlight would be seen at night from hundreds of

Fig. 5-2. "Summit House and Restaurant, Mt. Washington, N.H.," *postcard view, c. 1925. Author's Collection. This third Summit House was erected in 1914-15 under the supervision of Sylvanus D. Morgan, the prolific hotel contractor from Lisbon, NH.*

miles around. With an estimated cost of at least $1.5 million the lines of the building were laid out and the course of the proposed rail route actually surveyed. Fortuitously perhaps, the entire project, including the ambitious hotel, fell victim to a general New England business recession. As a direct result, the Boston and Maine Railroad, parent company of the Concord and Montreal Railroad, was in a precarious financial condition and had failed to consummate a merger with the New York, New Haven and Hartford Railroad. There were also public concerns about over-commercialization of the region. Ultimately the project was abandoned, much to the relief of its many skeptics.[5]

Finally a more practical and affordable scheme was adopted for the third Summit House. In its issue of 10 September 1913, *Among the Clouds* proudly announced that construction of a new building, compatible with the bare, rocky crown of the mountain, would soon begin. Over the next year the sponsoring C. & M. Railroad prepared plans and set aside the requisite funds from the profits of the Mount Washington Railway, which it controlled at the time. During the fall and winter of 1914-15, superintending contractor Sylvanus D. Morgan assembled the frame of the proposed structure in his Lisbon shop. In the spring the framing components were shipped forty miles by rail to the Base Station and then up the cog railway to the construction site. By virtue of this rather remarkable engineering feat, the new Summit House was in fact a largely prefabricated building.[6]

Work commenced at the site in May 1915 only to be hampered by spring snows and other inclement weather, forcing construction crews to suspend their arduous labor for entire days. Still, they made sufficient progress to allow the new hotel to receive guests for a month before the close of the season. Upon completion the new Summit House was set in concrete on the 1910 foundations and firmly anchored to the summit rocks by means of iron bolts (Fig. 5-2). Sheathed with weathered shingles, the building was 168 feet long and 38 feet wide, and one-and-a-half stories tall, one story less than its predecessor (see Chapter 4). Long shed-dormers extended almost the entire length of both planes of its pitched roof, and a large steam locomotive bell sat on the roof of the closed front entrance porch to announce the departure of trains. A slight hint of a Palladian window in each end gable and heavy classical eaves and cornice molding were the only suggestions of any architectural revival styles.

The interior was equally plain and functional; nonetheless, it did contain noteworthy features. Its warm, spacious, dark wood-paneled lobby and dining room took up virtually all the first floor. Exuding an almost country-club-like atmosphere, the lobby possessed large double-sash windows for natural light and a massive brick fireplace in the middle of the floor. Handsomely finished ceiling beams, support columns and braces, impeccably crafted by Morgan and his carpenters, disguised the heavy framework of the building (Fig. 5-3). Also on the first floor were the kitchen, office, a souvenir stand, a bunk-room, rest rooms and store rooms. At the south end of the lobby, a stairway led to the second attic story where there were lavatories and bedrooms (each equipped with twin beds) for guests and employees; their walls and ceilings were paneled in matchwood, and their floors constructed of wide planks. In the basement, under the kitchen, electric lighting and telephone equipment were located, along with a boiler that provided steam heat and hot running water to the rooms above. Including the old Tip-Top House, then called the "Annex," the entire complex accommodated ninety overnight guests. The primary purpose of the third Summit House, however, was to serve as a visitors' center for day

THE MATURATION OF THE BUILDING TYPE: FROM THE EIGHTIES TO WORLD WAR I

Fig. 5-3. Lobby, Third Summit House, Mount Washington, NH, *photo, n.d., by unidentified photographer. Douglas Philbrook, Gorham, NH. This great open space, with its fine ceiling beams, support columns, and braces, featured a large framed photo of the Second Summit House above the fireplace.*

travelers arriving by the cog railroad, the carriage road or by foot on hiking trails.[7]

The history of the third Summit House was marked by auspicious beginnings, but, in stark contrast, an unceremonious farewell. Advertised as equal in appointments and comfort to any mountain-top hotel in the world, it officially opened on 21 August 1915 with a gala series of dedication events. Few other hotels in the White Mountains have had such a baptism. With over 250 people attending—including railroad executives, officials of the Appalachian Mountain Club and local luminaries—the festivities commenced with a noontime flag-raising ceremony. It was followed by a special dinner, dancing, music and an historical address (entitled "The Old Times and the New") by the Reverend Harry P. Nichols of New York City and nearby Intervale. At 9:00 P.M. the celebration attendees watched an unprecedented half-hour fireworks display, which illuminated the summit and neighboring peaks, and, despite hazy weather conditions, was observed from many miles away. Next came a novel three-minute, three-mile slideboard descent of the Mount Washington Rail-way by roadmaster Patrick Camden carrying an ignited railroad flare in each hand! Immediately after his daring exploit a train illuminated by railroad flares went down the mountain. A grand finale dynamite salute came from the Glen House on the opposite side. Sixty-five years later, in April 1980, this last of the Mount Washington hotels, supplanted by the new Sherman Adams Summit Building, was summarily demolished and the remnants burned in a final ritual recalling that happy and unique August evening of so long ago.[8]

The Eastern Towns

The towns of Conway, Tamworth, Bartlett and Jackson in the eastern White Mountain region were sites of several large hotels after 1880, but most new construction consisted of medium and small-size establishments and additions to older buildings. In the Kearsarge Village section of North Conway, the Ridge and Cottages opened in 1885 after evolving from a boarding house into a 100-guest hotel.[9] The more modest Clarendon House was erected a short

Fig. 5-4. Pitman Hall, Lower Bartlett, NH, *embellished photograph from George H. Haynes,* East Side of the White Mountains *(1892). Author's Collection. Initially opened for guests in 1889, this rambling complex became one of the most popular hostelries in the Eastern Slope Region.*

distance away in Intervale in 1890-91. The adjacent Intervale House received two major additions during the 1880s, while the second Hotel Randall replaced the burned first Hotel Randall (Randall House) in 1902-03. This structure in turn burned and was succeeded by the third Hotel Randall (Eastern Slope Inn) in 1926. In Conway, the opening of the Presidential Inn, enlarged from the old Samuel Thom residence in 1916-17, helped ease the loss of Conway House, which fire had destroyed in 1912. In Tamworth Village the Wiggin House (renamed "Tamworth Inn") launched operations in 1888. The Piper House, recalling grand hotel precursors of a half century before, was erected in 1890 at Albany (Pequawket) just east of Mount Chocorua. It enjoyed a close working relationship with the much smaller Chocorua Peak House (1884) situated just under the summit.

North of Conway township, in Bartlett and Jackson, there was also substantial hotel construction. In the center of Upper Bartlett, the Cave Mountain House evolved from a small boarding house about 1888. It burned in 1905 and was replaced by The Howard (Bartlett Hotel) in 1911-12. At Lower Bartlett (Intervale), five new hotels made their appearances—the Langdon House, built as an addition to Pendexter House in 1884; Maple Villa, put up in 1895, doubled in size in 1901-02, and surviving today in modified form; the rambling Pitman Hall, first opened to the public in the season of 1889 (Fig. 5-4); the second Fairview House (The Fairview), con-

structed in 1895-96; and Fosscroft, a striking Colonial Revival edifice erected in 1925-26 on the foundations of the Langdon House after its destruction by fire. In Jackson the Wentworth Hall complex was created around the former Thorn Mountain House and the second Iron Mountain House went up in 1884-85. Arthur P. Gale erected the initial portion of the second Eagle Mountain House in 1915-16, and a series of four hostelries, all known as "Gray's Inn," were built on the same site near the village center between 1884 and 1917.

Of the North Conway guest enterprises built during this period, several were owned by the well-known Randall family. Soon after the loss of the Randall House, work commenced on a successor hotel in late fall 1902. This project was directed by Henry Harrison ("Harry") Randall who had assumed responsibility for the family business interests when his father died in 1898. Readied for the 1903 summer season, this establishment, "The New Hotel Randall," was a pleasant, yet unsophisticated three-story Colonial Revival building. Its most distinctive features were a fifteen-foot-wide, wrap-around piazza and steep, intersecting, flared gambrel roofs. Set back from the main street of the village, the hotel featured a long ell containing a first floor main dining room with superb views of the Saco River intervale and the mountains beyond. The building was enlarged twice on its north end—in 1915-16 and 1921—to create a nicely balanced east front facade and ultimately achieved a guest capacity of 150 (Fig. 5-5). Ironically, during the construction of a third major addition, it went up in flames on 20 November 1925.[10]

Only one month from the day of the fire, a resilient and undaunted Harry Randall initiated construction of the third Hotel Randall—known today as the Eastern Slope Inn in North Conway. Designed by H. E. Mason, an obscure architect from Leominster, Massachusetts, the hotel was built in six months under the direction of local contractor Nelson Thompson.[11] Upon opening in 1926 the new inn immediately won the praise of the regional press (see Plate 11):

And now from the ruins of two disastrous fires has arisen a beautiful and imposing structure which is a monument to the courage and determination of its owner. The house is unusual in its design, well proportioned, and fitting well into the landscape. It is of Southern Colonial style and its broad, red tiled piazzas at once give one the impression of fine old-fashioned Southern hospitality. The [balustraded] roof garden or observatory at the top of the building commands a broad view of mountains on all sides.

Ninety guest rooms, practically all alike, will afford ample accommodations. . . . The equipment is of the latest design.

The grounds are spacious and have been carefully laid out under the supervision of a landscape architect, who has made the most of the space by planting trees, shrubs and flowers.[12]

The characterization of the building as "Southern Colonial," while intended as a compliment, was quite far-fetched if not plain wrong. Its flat Doric pilasters, thick eaves entablature, embellished dormers, and tall front central portico exhibiting a modillioned cornice and closed gable above strongly suggest its Colonial Revival stylistic origins, derived from the New England Adamesque Federal and Greek Revival traditions.

T-shaped in plan, this stately, three-story, hipped-roof, wood-frame structure is 190 feet across its main front elevation, with the ell extending 125 feet to the rear. Not surprisingly, the Randall ownership insisted upon adding the latest in fireproofing technology such as fire breaks and sprinkler systems during the construction.[13] A description of the first floor interior from a local newspaper, *The Reporter*, provides a good sense of the original spatial arrangement, furnishings and general ambiance of the newly opened hotel:

> As one enters the building from any one of three French doors, one steps into a spacious lobby studded with handsome columns. The hardwood floor is broken up with large art squares, grouped with tables, Windsor chairs, and lamps of perfect taste. The white ivory walls are dotted with soft Colonial lamps. Across the lobby, the 21 foot desk greets the eye, and the beautiful Colonial staircase leads invitingly upstairs. Beside the staircase, the latest-design Otis elevator affords another means of ascending. On the north side, a fireplace will furnish warmth and cheer on dull-cold days. On each side of the lobby stretches broad corridors, leading on the left to the billiard and pool room, men's writing room, hairdressing parlor and shops, while on the right to the ladies' writing room, music and ball room, and five chambers.[14]

Fig. 5-5. The New Hotel Randall, North Conway, NH, *photograph from booklet,* The New Hotel Randall, North Conway, New Hampshire *(North Conway: n.p., [c. 1922]), p. 3. North Conway Public Library. Built by the well-known hotelman, Harry Randall, this edifice burned in 1925 while its third major addition was under construction.*

Fig. 5-6. Second Iron Mountain House, Jackson, NH, *photo, n.d., photographer unknown. Jackson Historical Society. A fine example of the Queen Anne style, this modest hotel conducted business from 1885 to about 1948.*

The ell housed the kitchen and a spacious dining room seating 175 persons.

Just over a decade after its debut the third Hotel Randall became a primary focal point in the rise of the new Alpine ski industry in the White Mountain region. In 1937, the complex passed from the Randall family to the New York-based Manufacturers Trust Company of which North Conway native Harvey Dow Gibson was president. Driven by the vision of his home town as a nationally renowned ski center, Gibson spearheaded the development of nearby Mount Cranmore as a ski area and adopted the Randall for winter recreational pursuits. Renaming it "The Eastern Slope Inn," he added new furniture and equipment so that it could function as a state-of-the-art, year-round facility. Gibson also augmented the hotel's regular summer programming with horse shows, tennis and golf tournaments, swimming meets, and civic, social and cultural gatherings, all underscoring its role as the hub of North Conway's booming resort business. A thriving enterprise for the next two decades, the inn was transferred to a succession of owners starting in 1955. It temporarily ceased operation as a hotel in 1976, but was reopened to the public in 1980 by the current owning partnership, Eastern Slope Inn Associates. Under the conscientious supervision of this firm the building has been systematically and sensitively restored to near its original appearance. In 1982, in recognition of its significance in the history of American hotel architecture and outdoor recreation, the Eastern Slope Inn earned a listing on the National Register of Historic Places.[15]

A few miles up the road just south of Jackson village once stood the second Iron Mountain House. With pronounced English Queen Anne form and adornment, it contrasted sharply with the Colonial Revival hotels of H. H. Randall. Situated at the foot of Iron Mountain overlooking the Glen Ellis River, this orderly and refined, pitched-roof building was erected in 1884-85 by James M. and W. A. Meserve (Fig. 5-6). It replaced the first Iron Mountain House, a small inn built on the same site in 1861 and ruined by fire in 1877. With an initial guest capacity of sev-

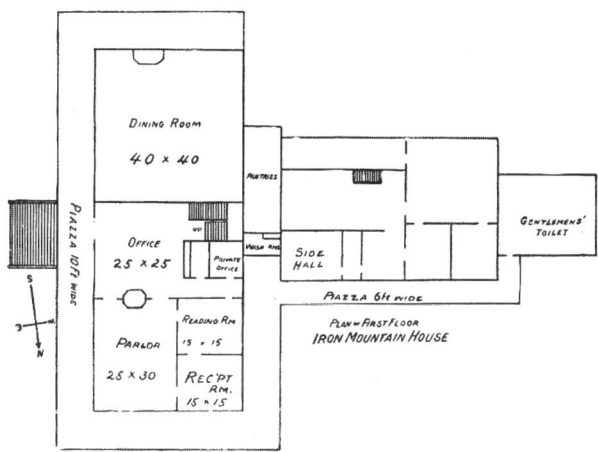

Fig. 5-7. First Floor Plan, Second Iron Mountain House, Jackson, NH, *from booklet*, Iron Mt. House *(Jackson: n.p., [c. 1900]).* Author's Collection. *Twice expanded at its rear, the hotel was able to accommodate 100 guests after 1890. It boasted electricity, modern sanitation, and fresh produce.*

Fig. 5-8. Meserve Hall (Second Iron Mountain House Annex), Jackson, NH, *photograph, 1990, by the author. Built in 1917 this small inn is still operated under the name "Iron Mountain House."*

enty-five, the building was a fine exemplar of its style. Its most distinguishing features were variegated painted shingle siding, truncated main and dormer roofs, a delicate porte cochere, second-story covered balconies, and connected verandas extending around three sides. *Among the Clouds* remarked on the "excellent taste" reflected on the interior, pointing to the "high studded and well lighted" rooms, the stained glass windows of the office and dining room, and the "heavy portieres" dividing the office from the expansive parlor on the first floor level (Fig. 5-7). Enlarged by extension of its rear ell in 1887 and again in 1891, the Iron Mountain House could accommodate up to 100 patrons. The hotel boasted many amenities that included electricity, a system of bells, natural spring water, modern sanitation, produce from an associated farm, open fire places and a first-class livery. Steam heat enabled the Meserves to extend their annual season to the end of October. In 1917 the owners constructed a substantial annex known as "Meserve Hall" to the south, linked to the older building by a roofed walkway. Deemed structurally unsound, the main edifice was demolished about 1948, but the annex has survived, albeit in dilapidated, and less-than-pristine condition (Fig. 5-8). It is now one of only a few pre-World War I hotel structures in the White Mountains still serving its original purpose.[16]

Set high above Jackson village, facing east over a lovely nine-hole golf course, the second Eagle Mountain House has also remained in business—on a basis approaching the sumptuous style and modus operandi of the largest grand resort hotels surviving in the region. Masterminded by Arthur P. Gale (1882-1957), the new hotel was erected in 1915-16 (Fig. 5-9). It was placed on the foundations of the first Eagle Mountain House, owned and managed by Gale's parents and lost to fire in 1915 (see Chapter 3). Gale, who had acquired the property outright, may have prepared the plans with A. Roswell Ward as superintending contractor and Arthur Garland as head carpenter, both from nearby Intervale. Constituting the nucleus of the current complex, the L-shaped building incorporated the latest fireproofing techniques.

Upon entering from the porte cochere on the Carter Notch Road, visitors found a handsome and comfortable lobby with an office counter, telephone switchboard and large fireplace as well as the main stairway (Fig. 5-10). To the right was a small ladies' parlor—also with a fireplace. To the left, flanking the entrance to the dining room, were a writing room and a side hall. The dining room, roughly thirty-six by fifty-four feet, was "one of the finest in the mountains," containing "large plate glass windows offering excellent views of the Wildcat River Valley" (Fig. 5-11). Behind the dining room was the kitchen and

[151]

Fig. 5-9. Second Eagle Mountain House, Jackson, NH, *photo, n.d., photographer unknown. Jackson Historical Society. Designed and built by owner Arthur P. Gale in 1915-16, the hotel remained essentially unchanged until it was doubled in size in 1928-29.*

underneath were music and billiard rooms (now used as meeting spaces). A photographic darkroom, an unusual feature, also existed on this lower level. On the upper three floors were ninety guest rooms, each with ample natural lighting, "an exceptionally large clothes closet," and a telephone; many possessed "private baths *en suite*." After 1926, all rooms were accessible by elevator (by then commonplace), fully electrified, and furnished with steam heat, enabling the hotel to offer year-round service. A ten-foot-wide veranda wrapped around the building on three sides, encouraging guests to promenade and relax in the ever-present rocking chairs. Two small ells attached to the rear accommodated a laundry and workshop, while a large c. 1880 barn to the north, a survivor of the 1915 fire, remained in use.[17]

In 1928-29 Arthur Gale doubled in size the Eagle Mountain House by expanding the older building down the hillside to the south and by appending another large ell to the rear. Gale also likely designed this addition as its materials, proportions, massing and embellishments exactly match the original part of the complex. He also added sixty new guest rooms, most (excluding those on the top floor) with private baths, raising the capacity to 225 persons. Public spaces were also affected when the old dining room was enlarged. A new private dining room was created behind it, and the rooms under the dining room were converted into a modern recreation area. The veranda was extended on two levels across the front of the addition, but not along the south side as had been done before. Other than the work done on Mountain View House in Whitefield, also during the 1920s (see Chapter 7), this was the last major addition built for a White Mountain grand resort hotel after World War I. It certainly attests to the hotel's efficient management, a stable clientele and adaptation to changes in the tourist market brought on by the automobile. With the regional hotel industry declining all around it, this obvious success was no small accomplishment.[18]

Architecturally, the second Eagle Mountain House (see Plate 12) possesses characteristics that recall the Glen House, the first Profile House, the second Crawford House and their smaller forerunners. Three-and-a-half stories tall, with an exposed lower

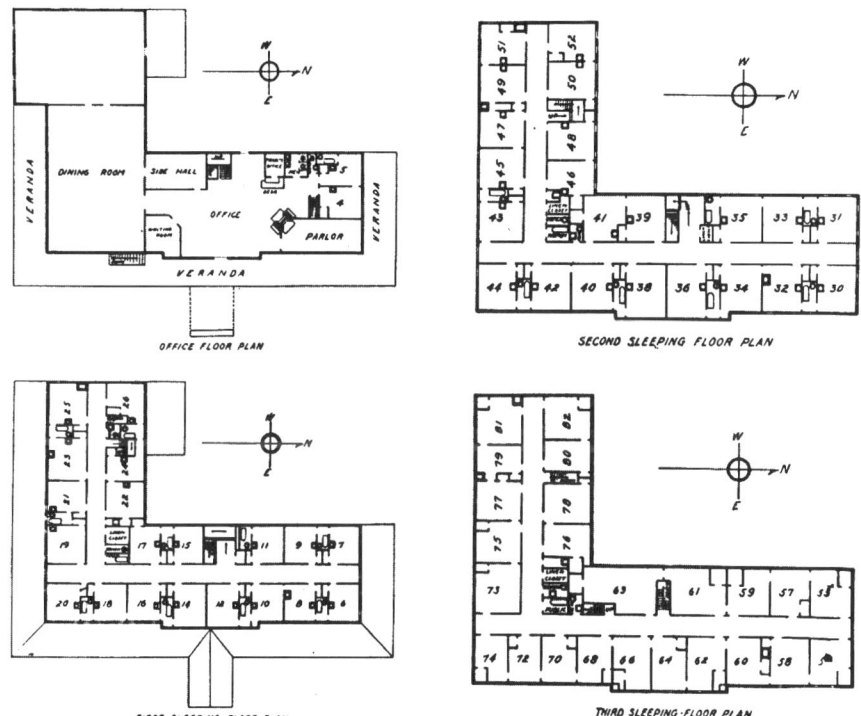

Fig. 5-10. Floor Plans, Second Eagle Mountain House, Jackson, NH, *from booklet,* The Eagle Mountain House . . . *(Jackson: n.p., [c. 1926-27]). Author's Collection. Floor plans such as these are invaluable sources for studying interior layout and hotel operations.*

level at the southern end, this rambling, wooden structure is now U-shaped. It is capped by a moderately pitched roof broken by pedimented gables, shed dormers and five tall brick chimneys. The fenestration is regularly spaced and double-sash with the exception of several rather charming smaller, diamond-pane-sash windows that appear at even intervals in the upper two stories. Traces of the Colonial Revival appear in the corner boarding, diamond-pane windows, the modillioned blocks in the main roof, dormer and gable eaves, and the splayed square posts of the veranda that have square-balustered railings running between them. Like so many of the older nineteenth-century hostelries, it has a vernacular residential quality not present in Jackson's Wentworth Hall and the other surviving grand resort hotels in the mountains (see Chapters 7 and 8).[19]

For more than ninety years, the Gales presided over the two Eagle Mountain Houses. Then in 1973 Arthur Gale's sister Marcia and her husband Orin N. Chadbourne, who had owned and managed it since Arthur's death in 1957, sold the property out of the family. The hotel struggled along under a series of owners until 1985 when Portland developers Barton A. Forbes and Michael Marino purchased it. Under their painstaking direction the aged and deteriorated complex has undergone a model multi-million dollar restoration and refurbishment aimed at returning the hotel to the appearance and standards it enjoyed at the apex of its operational history. Partially self-sustaining (it has its own bakery, water supply, steam

Fig. 5-11. Dining Room, Second Eagle Mountain House, Jackson, NH, *photograph from booklet,* The Eagle Mountain House . . . *(Jackson: n.p., [c. 1926-27]). Author's Collection. This space is used for the same purposes today and offers excellent views of the Wildcat River Valley.*

Fig. 5-12. First Gray's Inn and Cottages, Jackson, NH, *photograph from* Scenic Gems of the White Mountains *(c. 1901). Author's Collection. The core structure of the complex, originally titled "Chesley Cottage," was expanded several times and augmented by other buildings until it took 175 patrons.*

plant, etc.) and offering a full range of recreational and social options, it functions today in a manner reminiscent of the White Mountain hotels before the turn of the century.[20]

The Successive Hotels of Charles W. Gray

The lifetime of Charles W. Gray's four Jackson hotels spanned just under a century, from the opening of the first in 1885 to the destruction of the last in 1983. In a series of events unprecedented in White Mountain history, all fell victim to fire, the unrelenting scourge of the regional hotel industry. On the first three occasions Gray, rebounding from disaster and recouping his resources, rebuilt and commenced new operations. The incredible story of Gray's hotels, all run under the name "Gray's Inn," recalls the Greek myth of the ancient hydra referred to in an 1896 quotation from *Among the Clouds:*

> A mountain hotel is something like the Ancient Hydra. "No sooner is one head lopped off than another springs up to take its place."[21]

After each setback a new Gray's Inn sprouted to supplant its predecessor—the business simply refused to die. When it ultimately did expire and rebuilding proved unfeasible, the cause was as much declining economic prospects as the loss of the physical complex itself.

A versatile and enterprising man (he was also a logger, blacksmith, cabinetmaker and carriage builder), Charles Gray optimistically entered the hotel field in the early 1880s. He first acquired land on the Glen Road at the south end of the village upon which stood a small twelve-guest boarding house known as "Chesley Cottage." Gray had clearly made a sound investment, for the Chesley was the only guest establishment in Jackson from which Mount Washington and neighboring peaks could be seen. Then in 1884-85 he substantially expanded this initial structure into a modest hotel with a capacity of fifty guests. "Sunset Hill House," as it was called, was the third of its name in the mountain district. To eliminate confusion the name of Gray's Inn was adopted in 1886. In 1887, Gray enlarged the complex to shelter over eighty patrons by constructing an annex. About the same time he added two more cottages and a laundry. Three years later, in 1890, he increased the size of the dining room of the main house and added a distinctive tower. In 1892, Gray turned misfortune into success when Woodbury Cottage burned, by replacing it with a larger, more efficient structure, which he entitled "Woodbury Hall." The addition of this building, with its hot and cold running water, electricity (after 1893), and steam heat, raised the guest capacity to 175. Gray's Inn then rivaled Wentworth Hall as Jackson's largest hostelry.[22]

Gray, however, did not rest on his laurels. In response to the ever-increasing guest demand of the 1890s, he continued to expand. Reflecting the emphasis the hotels then placed on recreational and social activities, a new carriage house and casino were put up in 1894-95. The casino contained a great hall for dances, and theatrical and musical performances on its curved-ceiling second story. A billiard room, bowling alley, bazaar and parlors were located on the first floor. Photographic and other evidence (See Fig. 5-15, opening page of this chapter) tells us that somewhat later the original Woodbury Hall burned and was replaced by a larger structure of the same name. In 1899-1900, for a brief time Gray's Inn became the largest hotel south of Bretton Woods, when Merrill Cottage joined the building group, and a new dining room was erected, forty by eighty feet, with sleeping chambers above. It was at this point, fully developed to accommodate between 250 and 275 guests, that the hotel achieved its grand resort hotel status. But this, alas, was only short-lived. In late November 1902, nearly the entire complex, including the main house and several other outbuildings, was quickly reduced to smoldering rubble by a huge fire that could be seen from as far away as Portland, Maine.[23]

The design for the first Gray's Inn (Fig. 5-12) in many respects resembled that of Wentworth Hall (see Chapter 3). Over the years, hearsay suggests that Charles Gray, working with local builders, may have served as his own architect, but this has yet to be solidly documented. Whether or not this is true, there seems little doubt that the planner of Gray's Inn was strongly influenced by the plan devised by architect William A. Bates for the Wentworth some years earlier. The Inn incorporated many of the same principles of the Wentworth's cottage system, in which a central service facility was surrounded by smaller residential units and outbuildings devoted to specialized service, or recreational and social functions. In terms of style, however, Gray's Inn was less a pure example of the English Queen Anne than an amalgam of this and the newer, increasingly fashionable Shingle Chateauesque. The major buildings comprising the complex featured the steep-pitched intersecting roofs, varied painted shingle wall sur-

Fig. 5-13. First Gray's Inn and Cottages, Jackson, NH, *photograph, c. 1895, by C. P. Hibbard, Lisbon, NH, #234. Douglas Philbrook, Gorham, NH. Complementing the main building (left center) were Woodbury Hall (1892), and behind it, the Casino (1894-95).*

Fig. 5-14. Second Gray's Inn, Jackson, NH, *postcard photograph, 1903. Richard N. Johnson, Jackson. This rare image depicts a hotel of some architectural distinction which was destroyed by fire during the summer of 1903 before opening to the public.*

faces and stacked bay windows usually found in the Queen Anne style. These were combined with the fragilely constructed piazzas, and tall conical and octagonal corner towers of the Shingle Chateauesque (Fig. 5-13). Like the Wentworth, the Inn possessed a homey, intimate atmosphere for guests that was less intimidating and more relaxed than that of the larger, predominantly single-building grand resort hotels.

For his second hotel, however, Charles Gray decided in favor of just this type of plan (Fig. 5-14). Undeterred by the sudden loss of his first venture, he immediately initiated the building of a successor hotel on the same site with the intention that it be ready for occupancy during the 1903 summer season.[24] Gray envisioned it as a single four-story building, "somewhat similar in architecture" to its predecessor, with three octagonal front corner towers topped by steep-pitched conical roofs, recalling the north facade of bygone Woodbury Hall (Fig. 5-15, see chapter opening). There were also to be stacked bay windows comparable to those in the former main building. Said to contain 100 rooms, "with plenty of ground for enlargement," it was conceived for year-round use "to meet the growing demand for accommodations for parties of winter guests." In scale, detail and proportions Gray's second inn closely resembled the buildings of the first complex, as well as the two hotels that would follow. Thus, it is safe to conjecture that Gray served as his own architect for this project. Unfortunately, we have only limited knowledge of the final exterior appearance and interior layout of the building itself—in an unfinished and unopened state, delayed by the late arrival of lumber, the building was ravaged by another immense fire in mid summer. Scarcely a trace remained, leaving Gray to start all over again.[25]

Undoubtedly discouraged, yet determined to continue in business, the indomitable Charles Gray promptly rebuilt again on the same site. His third inn officially opened on 15 August 1904. As he may have previously, Gray definitely served as "his own architect and builder" on this occasion. While the new building did bear some resemblance to his earlier hotels, Gray designed it on a much larger scale in a more pronounced Shingle Chateauesque style (Fig. 5-16). With 116 bedrooms, 86 of them in suites with private baths, the new edifice was able to take up to 250 guests. The plan was a modified dog-leg L with two major elevations, one facing north towards the road and the other northwest, both with spectacular mountain vistas. Three-and-a-half stories in height the principal north facade was a perfectly balanced symmetrical composition. It contained a central gambrel-roofed pavilion with porte cochere flanked by stacked bay windows rising above the main gambrel roof line. Framing the facade at the corners were octagonal towers with pyramidal spire roofs that provided strong vertical accents, effectively countering the essentially horizontal lines of the complex. The northwest elevation was also symmetrical but lacked a central pavilion. Across the length of the two elevations an open veranda extended for 420 feet. Adjacent to the main building were a powerhouse and maintenance facility, utility plants, a casino and bowling alleys modeled after those lost in 1902, and several cottages—a couple of which were hardy survivors of the previous fires.[26]

Among the Clouds provides a nearly definitive description of the hotel's inside:

The finish of the interior is of cypress and redwood, with birch and maple floors, all on natural wood . . . through the folding doors [of the main entrance] one enters the reception hall,

THE MATURATION OF THE BUILDING TYPE: FROM THE EIGHTIES TO WORLD WAR I

Fig. 5-16. Third Gray's Inn, Jackson, NH, *photograph from booklet,* Gray's Inn, Jackson, NH *(Jackson: n.p., [c.1910]). Author's Collection. Raised in 1903-04, this Shingle Chateauesque building was conceived on a much larger scale than its predecessors on the same site.*

opposite the office, and finds himself facing an artistic brick fireplace, with rubble ornamentation, extending to the ceiling. To the right are the parlor [Fig. 5-17] and reception rooms, the former with a similar large fireplace, and to the left the large and beautiful dining room [Fig. 5-18]. The hall is 50 x 45 feet, and the dining room (on the northeast corner) lighted by numerous windows and electric lights, is 70 x 50 feet. The ceilings all are of handsomely patterned steel sheathing made to order. The dining room will seat 250.

As to the guests' rooms, none are smaller than 12 x 16 feet, and some are larger. Only three have at least two windows and some as many as six [located in the towers and considered highly desirable]. The carpets in the halls and rooms are wilton and velvet, and the furniture was made by the Beecher Falls Company, being the best in their line.

The house has its own electric plant, with a capacity of 2,000 lights. . . . Electric bell appliances are in guests' rooms throughout the house. There is also a plant for furnishing gas in

Fig. 5-17. Parlor, Looking Toward the Office, Third Gray's Inn, Jackson, NH, *photograph from booklet,* Gray's Inn, Jackson, NH *(Jackson: n.p., [c. 1910]). Author's Collection. The furnishings of the parlor consisted of a curious collection of wooden, upholstered and wicker pieces from the Victorian era.*

Fig. 5-18. Dining Room, Third Gray's Inn, Jackson, NH, *photograph from booklet,* Gray's Inn, Jackson, NH *(Jackson: n.p., [c. 1910]). Author's Collection. This large, open space featured mass-produced wooden "institutional" furnishings and a ceiling of patterned steel sections.*

[157]

Fig. 5-19. Fourth Gray's Inn, Jackson, NH, *photo c. 1925, photographer unknown. Littleton Area Historical Society. Charles Gray's final hotel, which stood from 1917 to 1983, was almost identical in appearance to its immediate predecessor.*

case the electrics fail.... The first three floors... are steam heated—halls and rooms—which assures plenty of warmth in the upper sleeping rooms in cold weather.

. . . The open plumbing is of the best approved pattern, and the sanitary arrangements are as perfect as now known. The bath tubs are of white porcelain and of ample size, and all the appliances of the toilet rooms are ... most modern—for many advances have been made in that line of late years.[27]

An "abundant supply of pure water" flowed to the hotel through six and eight-inch iron pipes from Israel's Brook under Giant Stairs Mountain, two-and-one-half miles away. An elevator ran to all floors. In its design, furnishings and technology, the third Gray's Inn was modern and was able to maintain a quite competitive position with its White Mountain rivals. These obvious virtues were aggressively promoted in the hotel's marketing literature and paid advertising.

On 21 February 1916, the third Gray's Inn burned to the ground. Although the hotel was partially filled with winter recreation enthusiasts, mercifully there was no loss of life. Once more Charles Gray pledged to rebuild quickly, and by the middle of the following summer work was well underway. When he completed his fourth and final inn later that year, people were amazed by the close resemblance to its immediate predecessor. Using plans employed in the construction of the 1903-04 building, Gray fabricated a three-and-a-half-story, wood-frame complex along nearly identical lines (Fig. 5-19). Variations included the presence of a round, spire-capped observatory atop the front central pavilion, slight differences in wall fenestration, double dormer windows in the upper gambrel roof planes and subtle refinements in decorative detail. The photographs and text contained in hotel informational booklets and flyers indicate that the interior floor plan was also altered very little. In fact, despite the addition of an annex in the 1920s, the guest capacity was actually reduced to 225; private baths were added to many rooms, decreasing the amount of available bed spaces. Owner Gray did all he could to preserve the welcoming atmosphere he had fostered in his earlier hotels; as one promotional piece noted, he consistently strove for the ideal, thinking "not only of building a hotel, but of having that hotel so homelike and cheerful that each guest may feel that he or she is one of a happy family."[28]

Plate 11. Third Hotel Randall (Eastern Slope Inn), North Conway, NH, *photograph, 1990, by the author. Erected in 1925-26, this elegant Colonial Revival structure became a major focal point for the burgeoning Alpine ski industry in the White Mountains.*

Plate 12. Second Eagle Mountain House, Jackson, NH, *photograph, 1991, by the author. Still in operation today, the Eagle Mountain House was built in 1915-16, and successfully catered to the automobile tourist business. After a considerable enlargement in 1928-29, the guest capacity of the hotel increased to 225.*

Plate 13. Deer Park Hotel, North Woodstock, NH, *colored cover lithograph from booklet,* Deer Park, North Woodstock, N. H. *(North Woodstock: n.p., [c. 1889]). Author's Collection. Combining several late Victorian eclectic styles, the Deer Park was distinguished by the matching observatory towers on its front elevation.*

Plate 14. Center Tower Section, Mountain View House, Whitefield, NH, *photograph, c. 1976, by the author. In 1911-12, with the creation of an enlarged central portion featuring a monumental observation tower, the building assumed the appearance of a grand resort hotel.*

Plate 15. West Elevation, Mount Washington Hotel, Bretton Woods (Carroll), NH, *photograph, 1992, by the author. This 465-foot frontage reveals the Spanish Renaissance character of the hotel, combined with the Colonial Revival detailing of the long, double-tiered piazza.*

Plate 16. East Elevation, Mount Washington Hotel, Bretton Woods (Carroll), NH, *photograph, c. 1976, by the author. In this view the hotel is perfectly positioned in the natural surroundings. The main longitudinal axis is oriented toward Crawford Notch, while the east elevation affords a spectacular view of the Presidential Range.*

Plate 17. Dining Hall, Mount Washington Hotel, Bretton Woods (Carroll), NH, *photograph, c. 1985, by William C. Roy, Lebanon, NH. Mount Washington Hotel. This grand octagonal-shaped space provides an unusually fine dining environment. In the past, the dining room staff would form a singing group that performed at dinner time.*

Plate 18. Front Perspective Elevation, Design for a New Hotel, The Balsams, Dixville Notch, NH, *photograph of original drawing. The Balsams Grand Resort Hotel. Henry S. Hale commissioned a thus far unidentified architect to prepare this design for a new hotel in the Notch. It is signed by artist W.H. Campbell and dated 1909. The complex was never built, probably due to the economic effects of World War I.*

Plate 19. Hampshire House, The Balsams, Dixville Notch, NH, *photograph, 1991, by the author. Designed by Manchester, NH, architect Chase R. Whitcher in 1916, this intriguing Rhenish eclectic structure rivals the Mount Washington Hotel in architectural splendor.*

Plate 20. Northwest View of The Balsams, Dixville Notch, NH, *photograph, 1990, by the author.* From this vantage point the exterior of the hotel appears little changed since 1918 when the finishing touches to Hampshire House (right) were applied.

As was typical of so many of the White Mountain hotels that lasted until after World War I, the final years of Gray's Inn were marked by economic and physical decline and changes in ownership. In 1935 the inn was taken over by local banks. In turn it was sold to E. M. Loew who also had a financial interest in Wentworth Hall (see Chapter 3). After operating as a hotel for several more years it assumed a new identity as a summer youth camp under the name "Hampshire House," before closing completely in the late 1960s. For over a decade the hotel set vacant and deteriorating, conveying an impression of abandoned helplessness—a gigantic, gaunt reminder of a once glorious era of White Mountain history, yearning for a future that would be sympathetic to its fine architecture. Despite last-minute efforts to resurrect it for other uses, a fire of suspicious origins leveled the building on a hot summer afternoon, 14 July 1983. On this occasion Charles Gray was no longer there to rebuild—his symbolic ancient hydra had finally died.[29]

Bethlehem: The Town of Thirty Hotels

Among those towns situated west of the Presidential Range and on the northern edge of the White Mountains, Bethlehem experienced the greatest rate of hotel growth after 1880. The initial momentum generated by John Sinclair, Henry Howard and Isaac Cruft continued apace until after World War I. While no new grand hotels were constructed, additions were made to existing establishments, several new small and medium-sized hotels erected, and numerous cottages built. Of Bethlehem's existing grand hotels the Sinclair House received ell additions in 1891 and 1900-01, and the Maplewood Hotel added several cottages and two major associated structures—Maplewood Hall in 1882-83 and the Maplewood Casino in c. 1887. Sustained by the on-going tourist boom, the more modest older hostelries also were enlarged, some two and three times. New hotels of comparable scale appeared, some finding their origins in residential structures. Generally bland, architecturally undistinguished and accommodating between fifty and ninety patrons, these buildings included (see Appendices): Idlewild Hotel (West Hotel; Hotel Roosevelt) (1884); The Woodlawn (Bethmer Inn, Colby Inn, The Stage Depot) (1887-88); Echo Hill House (1891-92); Central Cottage (The Columbus; Columbia Hotel) (1892); the second Prospect House (c. 1896); Eastview (Lyndhurst; Park View) (c. 1890); and the Reynolds Hotel (c. 1895). By the 1920s, before the local hotel industry underwent an abrupt decline, there were thirty hotels in the town, each with space for at least fifty guests. The Bethlehem Board of Trade widely publicized this in a series of regular illustrated publications. At their peak of success, the Bethlehem hotels were able to house over 2,000 people at one time, substantially more than any other mountain community. While this housing figure is impressive and certainly had a favorable influence on the regional economy, the architectural legacy of the Bethlehem hotels, with the notable exceptions of the Sinclair, the Maplewood, and the Uplands, is not outstanding.[30]

The Western Towns

West of Bethlehem, in the towns of Franconia, Littleton and Lisbon (including Sugar Hill), there was comparable development from 1880 onward. On Pine Hill, above the village of Franconia, the Forest Hills Hotel was built in 1882-83. This establishment was enlarged and remodeled to eventually become a major resort complex. On the main street of Franconia, the first Franconia House made its debut in c. 1878. The accomplished hotel contractor Sylvanus D. Morgan (see Chapter 7) opened his own inn under the name "Elmwood House" in 1885, and the House of Seven Gables (appropriately retitled "The Hawthorne" in 1890) went into business about the same time. A few miles down the Gale River Valley in Littleton three new hotels joined the Oak Hill House during the 1880s and 1890s—the Chiswick Inn and Cottages (1884-85), consisting of several contiguous units; The Maples (1888-89), a fifty-guest inn with corner tower situated on the hillside overlooking the town; and the Northern Hotel (1898), with its imposing south-facing Colonial Revival facade fronting on Main Street.

Fig. 5-20. Breezy Hill House, Lisbon, NH, *photograph, c. 1885, by Rev. Samuel Nickerson, Sugar Hill. Sugar Hill Historical Museum. Displaying classical molding and corner pilasters this medium-size hostelry commanded superlative vistas westward to Vermont.*

Lisbon, the next town south of Littleton, experienced the majority of its hotel growth between 1880 and 1905. In the town center, Brigham's Hotel was opened to the public in 1883-84. The Lisbon Hotel (Hotel Moulton; The Warren) was built in 1901-02, damaged by fire, and rebuilt in 1923-25 (it is still in existence). On the road east of the Sugar Hill section of the town, the Breezy Hill House, a hostelry of broad reputation, was erected in two box-like portions in 1883-84 and 1887-88 (Fig. 5-20). High on Sugar Hill ridge the Goodnow House (Franconia Inn) was expanded three times during the 1880s. Its principal competitor, the Sunset Hill House, received several wings, ells and new outbuildings over a period of a quarter century. Joining these large establishments were the Hotel Lookoff, of similar size, in 1886-87; and four smaller hotels—Phillips House, 1883-84; The Mount View House, 1888; the Miramonte Inn, 1893; and The Echoes, 1895. In just two decades, with these new buildings, additions and other small boarding houses, Sugar Hill could claim a hotel capacity of 750.

The Forest Hills Hotel, opened for the 1883 season, was one of the most beautifully sited and architecturally fetching hostelries built in the western sector of the mountains after 1880. Conceived by its first proprietors Harry W. Priest and James W. Dudley, it immediately caught on with the summer resort clientele. This was in large part due to its magnificent hilltop panorama overlooking the Gale River Valley with the Franconia Mountains and the Presidential Range in the background. It also benefited

Fig. 5-21. Forest Hills Hotel, Pine Hill, Franconia, NH, *engraving from* Summer Saunterings by the B. & L. *(1885), p. 87. Author's Collection. This handsome view, with its insert detail of the hotel, demonstrates the importance of good siting for optimum guest enjoyment.*

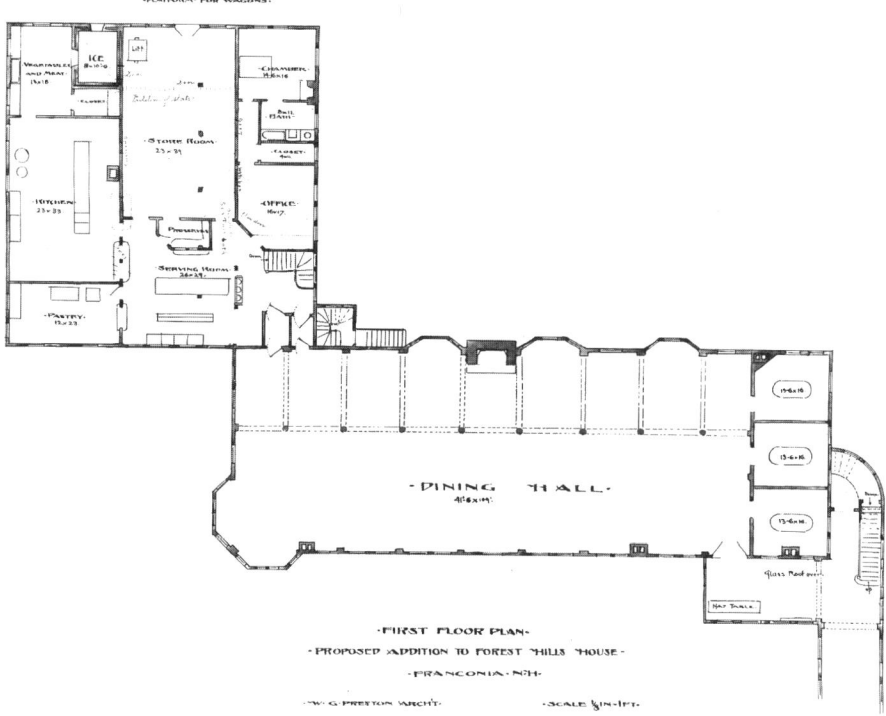

Fig. 5-22. "First Floor Plan, Proposed Addition to Forest Hills House—Franconia, N.H.," *by William G. Preston, architect, Boston, c. 1891. Boston Public Library. Referred to as "The Hall," this English Tudor annex to the main hotel contained seventy-five sleeping rooms, a new main dining hall, private dining rooms, a kitchen, and a sun parlor.*

from an initial five-year tax exemption voted on by the townspeople. The new hotel was able to board up to 150 guests and boasted all the latest technological advances—gas, steam heat, hot and cold running water, spring beds, electric bells, a telegraph and "model plumbing." An added attraction for patrons were over fifty acres of carefully maintained grounds, consisting of open lawns and groves of trees accessed by an extensive system of drives and walking paths. Immediately upon its opening, the Forest Hills responded to the physical fitness craze of the era by offering a livery, bowling alleys, a roller skating rink, a baseball field, a quarter-mile bicycle track, fishing and hiking.[31]

Contemporary tourist guidebooks, normally devoid of references to hotel architecture, remarked about the unusually fine design qualities of the new four-story complex (Fig. 5-21). Specific references were made to its 500 feet of double-tiered verandas, balconies with geometric stickwork balustrades, and a tall front central observation tower, protected by a square, truncated pyramidal roof. Stylistically, the building was a hodgepodge of late Victorian eclectic elements, with evidence of the Italian Revival in its paired cornice brackets, the Stick style in its veranda support posts and balustrades, and the Second Empire in its Mansard roof and false side tower caps. Later additions incorporated other compatible decorative features.

Associated with the Forest Hills Hotel were several outbuildings; each of these had a specialized function and its own distinctive name. In 1887, a bachelor's apartment house was constructed, followed by a large Colonial Revival stable in 1889. In 1889-90, "The Lodge" was erected behind the main hotel. It was primarily for winter use, with furnace heat provided in every room. Two new cottages made their appearance in 1891, one of which, "The Log Cabin," was built of six-inch spruce logs in an attempt to simulate early-American wilderness domestic structures. At the same time, a farm joined the hotel real estate, and a two-acre artificial lake was formed on the grounds. The next year, in 1891-92, the capacity of the hotel complex doubled with the

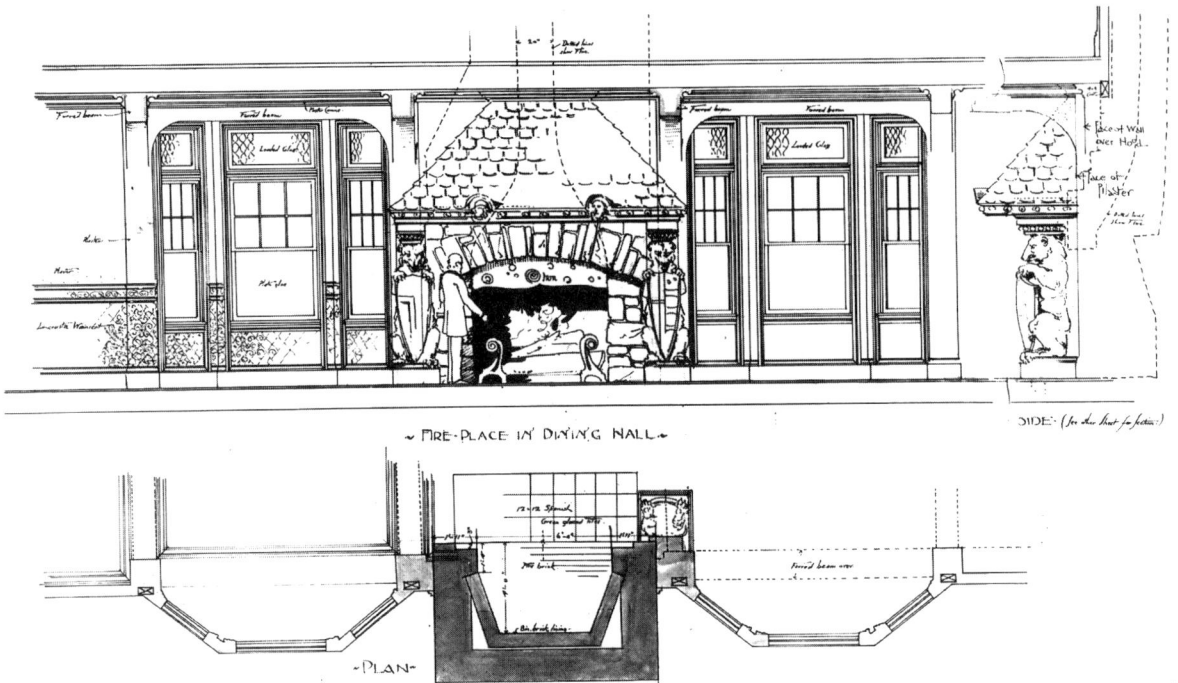

Fig. 5-23. "Mssrs. Priest & Dudley, Franconia, N.H.," *detail drawing by William G. Preston, architect, Boston, c. 1891. Boston Public Library. This unusual rendering depicts the proposed main fireplace and identical flanking alcoves in the main dining hall. The English Tudor spirit is in evidence.*

building of "The Hall." This was an English Tudor annex containing seventy-five sleeping rooms, a main dining room, several private dining rooms, a kitchen and an extensive sun parlor. Floor and detail plans at the Boston Public Library indicate that architect William G. Preston (1844-1910) prepared the plans (see Figs. 5-22 and 5-23). Then, in 1895, came a new casino, "tastefully furnished in hemlock bark," containing a bowling alley, billiard room, and "gentleman's smoking room." Elm Cottage was secured by the management for those desiring rates lower than those charged at the hotel.

The property remained unchanged until 1902 when new owner Herbert Hunt initiated extensive remodeling, built a new cottage, laid out new croquet grounds and changed the name to "Hunt's Forest Hills Hotel." Mr. Hunt made further improvements prior to the 1908 season. He erected a new building to house servants' quarters and a kitchen, remodeled an older residence into the "Farm-House" cottage, established a new golf course, and expanded other sports facilities. Supposedly the hotel was to receive a major addition in 1908-09, doubling the number of available sleeping spaces; for some reason this expansion failed to occur for another decade. Before the 1920 season the main dining room was tripled in size, more bedrooms were added in extended wings, and the capacity of the complex reached its peak of about 250 persons. When a complete $200,000 remodeling was implemented in 1922-23, a new Colonial Revival porte cochere was placed before the main front entrance. The management of the Forest Hills, striving to remain competitive with its rival hotels, never relaxed its efforts to stay modern and to appeal to a broad spectrum of guests.[32]

The final decades of the Forest Hill House also carry an interesting history. In 1918, Karl Abbott, of the Bethlehem hotel family, formed a syndicate and purchased the property, making it the first of what would eventually become a large chain of Eastern hotels, including the Profile House (see Chapter 7). It was under Abbott that the complex had its final growth spurt and experienced its last period of prosperity. Surviving the Depression and World War II years, the hotel remained open for guests until 1962. At this time George W. Collier, the owner after 1954,

Fig. 5-24. "Hotel Lookoff, Sugar Hill, N. H., Hiram Noyes & Sons, Proprietors," *photograph of original artwork*, Town and City Atlas of the State of New Hampshire *(1892)*. *Author's Collection. Constructed in 1886-87, the Lookoff was set at a higher elevation (1,900 feet) than any other White Mountain hotel with the exception of those on Mount Washington.*

donated it to the University of New Hampshire with the hope that it would be used in conjunction with the University's hotel management program. When this scheme proved unsuccessful, the entire property was sold to Franconia College, a two-year, coeducational, liberal arts institution that held title until it closed in 1978. In May of that year the contents of the complex were sold at auction, and the main building sat vacant and derelict until the remaining shell was demolished for salvage in 1984.[33] By virtue of the Franconia College phase of its history, it departed with the rather surprising distinction of being the only White Mountain grand resort hotel ever to undergo rehabilitation in order to serve another purpose.

Across the valley on the shoulder of Mount Lookoff, south of Franconia village, stood the Hotel Lookoff. Built in 1886-87, it was the third and last of Sugar Hill's grand resort hotels. The new house was situated just one-half mile from the Sunset Hill House, but at a higher elevation (1,900 feet), with even more spectacular views of the Franconia Mountains, the Presidential Range and the Pilot Range and neighboring peaks to the north. Financed and developed by the firm of Hiram Noyes & Sons, which operated it for the first fifteen years, the hotel accommodated 200 guests. This was another of the many White Mountain hotel contracting projects of Sylvanus D. Morgan. Morgan, then based in nearby Lisbon, is also thought to have built additions to the Sinclair House and the Uplands in Bethlehem and the Forest Hills Hotel in Franconia Notch. He would later erect the New Profile House in Franconia Notch (see Chapter 7). As the Lookoff possessed many features present in Morgan's other commissions, some of which he unquestionably designed, it is quite conceivable that he also served as architect of this hotel.[34]

Facing east over twenty acres of lawns, maple and poplar groves, and recreational venues the new establishment was a large ark-like wood-frame and clapboard building (Fig. 5-24). Except for its unusual raised, pitched-roof center section, it was a rather conventional example of regional hotel architecture. Modeled on a T-shaped floor plan it was perfectly symmetrical, with matching four-story wings and a rear ell to which were attached a one-story kitchen and storage shed. Each was protected by a flat Mansard roof with single dormers, quite reminiscent of the additions to the Sunset Hill House as they looked in the early 1880s. A typically long (324 feet) veranda of fragile construction extended across the main facade, along part of the south side, and across the entire north side of the complex, allowing ample space for enjoyment of the mountain vistas in relaxed circumstances. Small, similarly delicate balconies, more decorative than functional, were present at the center windows of the raised section and end walls above the first story level. Consistent with its late Victorian eclectic character, certain classical features, albeit very understated, were evident in the cornice molding, Doric corner pilasters, and main center doorway surround with its plain entablature.

Following the standard pattern of its counterparts, the Hotel Lookoff both expanded and changed its appearance and offerings over the course of its existence. In 1887-88, Hiram Noyes introduced steam heat to the hotel. He also had a new adjacent employee cottage built—thirty by fifty feet, two stories high and covered by a Mansard roof, providing him twenty-five more rooms for his clientele where the employees had formerly been housed. A 140-acre farm joined the hotel's holdings in 1891, allowing the Lookoff to operate on a more self-sufficient basis. Several years later, in August 1895, a grand celebration was held on the hotel grounds to mark the completion of a stunning series of important technological improvements—a new electrical lighting plant, claimed to be "the most extensive of any in use at the mountain hotels"; indoor and outdoor arc and incandescent lights; a new steam-powered passenger elevator with "open work above the cage"; an enlarged reservoir and system of waterworks, including stand pipes and firehouses throughout the hotel; and, an expanded mineral springhouse with soda fountain counter. Like other selected hotel owners, the Noyeses carbonated and bottled spring water and manufactured soda to augment revenue, using the hotel name to marketing advantage. All of these upgraded amenities, coupled with gas lights, "scientific plumbing," electric bells, telephones, a telegraph, iron fire escapes, toilet rooms, spring beds and hair mattresses, placed the Lookoff at the front rank of the mountain hotels in the intense competition for the tourist dollar towards the end of the nineteenth century.[35]

After 1900, when the hotel passed to a succession of owners, it continued to maintain the highest standards and retained much of its traditional patronage. In 1910-11, the new proprietorship of Merrill & Sanborn equipped the sleeping rooms with hot and cold running water, private baths and steam heat. They also renovated some of the public areas with new hardwood floors and fashionable tile-like "art squares." To reduce crowding, increase guest pleasure and enjoyment, and promote a "home-like atmosphere," they reduced the total capacity to 150 guests, a move virtually unheard of in the regional hotel industry. Escaping fire, but not eventual decline in patronage, the hotel was demolished in 1964 and was replaced by several attractive year-round residences.[36] It left behind a legacy of excellent management, where a premium was placed less on the architectural beauty of the physical plant and more on providing the latest technology, high quality cuisine, and superb and varied recreational and social facilities.

The Northern Towns

With the creation of grand hotel complexes such as the Mountain View House at Whitefield and The Balsams at Dixville Notch, and the construction of other more modest hostelries, hotel expansion after 1880 in the towns north of Bethlehem and the principal White Mountains massif was extensive but more dispersed than in other areas. At Gorham, where the railroad first penetrated the mountains, the Mount Madison House doubled in size in 1907. Just to the east, in Shelburne, the Shelburne Spring House went up around 1890, and the Philbrook Farm and Cottages was transformed from a small country inn into a seventy-five-guest hostelry through additions in 1905 and 1934. A few miles to the west of Gorham the town of Randolph saw the construction of the famed Ravine House (Fig. 5-25), an elongated domestic structure opened in 1877 with four additions by 1915, and the Mount Crescent House (initially known as the Randolph Hill House) in 1883-84. The Waumbek Hotel in Jefferson underwent dra-

Fig. 5-25. The Ravine House, Randolph, NH, photograph originally published in Historical New Hampshire *23, Nos. 2 & 3 (Fall 1981), p. 249. New Hampshire Historical Society. Opened in 1877, and with four additions before 1915, the hotel was long a favorite place of accommodation for hikers climbing on the Presidential Range.*

matic physical growth, absorbed other hotels in the town, and added cottages to the extent that its capacity reached 600 persons by the first decade of this century (See Chapter 3).

Farther to the west and north the story was much the same. At Whitefield the Carlton House opened for sixty guests in c. 1880, followed by Levi Bowles' Overlook House (The Outlook) in 1891-92—a slightly larger facility situated high on Kimball Hill south of the village center. Northward in Lancaster the second Lancaster House, a 150-capacity Queen Anne-style hotel, was built in 1881-82 (Fig. 5-26). The following year William H. Smith erected the much smaller Mount Prospect House on the top of Mount Prospect (2,090 feet) south of town, later the site on the Weeks family estate. Up the Connecticut River Valley at Colebrook, T. J. Rowen & Company erected the second Monadnock House in 1895-96 (it was doubled in size to take 100 guests in 1924). The Hampshire Inn (Parson's Farm) opened in a renovated farmhouse in 1897, and the Colebrook House —the successor to the old Mohawk House—was constructed in 1903-04 and still survives. Buoyed by persistent optimism about business potential, this quite impressive phase of hotel development occurred in the upper North Country despite its great distance from major Eastern urban centers and the signs of incipient decline in the regional hotel industry.

Fig. 5-26. Second Lancaster House, Lancaster, NH, engraving from, Mountain, Lake & Valley, *by the B. & L. (1887), op. p. 134. Author's Collection. This fine Queen Anne-style hotel was built in 1881-82 and accommodated 150 guests.*

Hotels South of Franconia Notch

During the years between 1880 and World War I, the growth of the hotel industry south of Franconia Notch was restricted largely to one key community, North Woodstock. Strategically situated in the northern Pemigewasset River Valley, twenty miles above Plymouth, North Woodstock literally became a "village of hotels" during the 1880s and 1890s.[37] This phenomenon may be partially attributed to the beautiful panoramic vista of the Notch and the Franconia Mountains enjoyed from the town, and also to the scenic advantages afforded by the Pemigewasset, its smaller tributaries and other natural attractions close at hand. The major reason, however, for the town's economic take-off was its position as the northern terminus of the Pemigewasset Valley Railroad after 1882. The establishment of this vital transportation link led to the building in North Woodstock of two grand resort hotels, the Deer Park and The Alpine, as well as several smaller hostelries including the Fairview House (1881-84), Russell House (c. 1875), French's Hotel (1896-97), and in nearby Lincoln, the Lincoln Hotel (c. 1890).

Described in *Among the Clouds* as "the most thoroughly constructed house in the mountains," the Deer Park Hotel was erected in 1886-87 at the instigation of John Bell, a member of the well-known family that furnished New Hampshire with two United States senators and one governor. Drawing its name from a park on the grounds where tamed deer were kept until 1905, the new hotel opened with accommodations for 150 guests. Operated by John's nephew Samuel, in concert with the firm of Buchanan (Collins M.) and Willis (Freeman C.), it experienced smashing success during its first season in part because of its convenient location and excellent view, but also due to "the tact and personal popularity of its managers," an important consideration for vacationers when selecting a hotel.[38] A response to the guest demand was quickly forthcoming.

In 1887-88 the proprietors greatly enlarged the Deer Park to create a picturesque, three-story, L-shaped complex of pleasant proportions and eye-catching detail (see Plate 13 and Fig. 5-27).[39] Buchanan

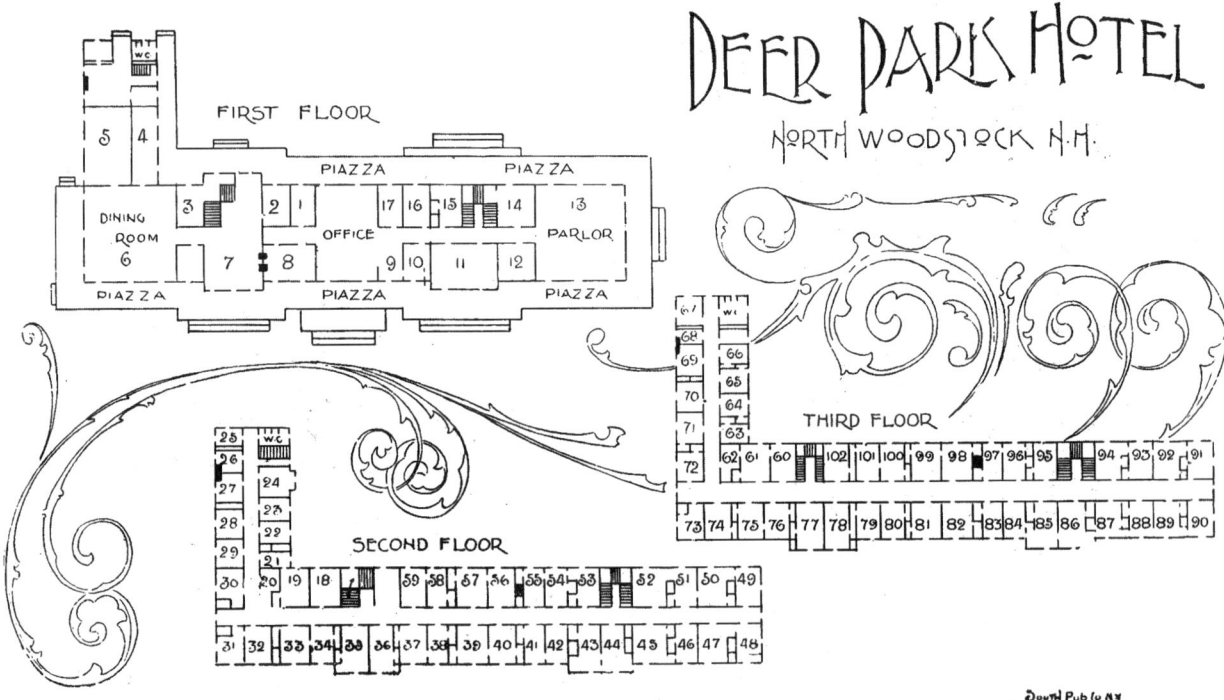

Fig. 5-27. Floor Plans, Deer Park Hotel, North Woodstock, NH, *from booklet,* Deer Park, North Woodstock, N. H. *(North Woodstock: n.p., [c. 1889]). Author's Collection. The vista from the L-shaped complex offered spectacular views of Franconia Notch and the Franconia Mountains to the north.*

Fig. 5-28. Private Dining Room, Deer Park Hotel, North Woodstock, NH, *from booklet*, Deer Park, North Woodstock, N. H. *(North Woodstock: n.p., [c. 1889]). Author's Collection. The 1887 addition to the hotel provided forty-two new bedrooms, a parlor, and this sparsely decorated but serviceable space.*

Fig. 5-29. Looking From the Parlor Into the Main Dining Room, Deer Park Hotel, North Woodstock, NH, *from booklet*, Deer Park, North Woodstock, N. H. *(North Woodstock: n.p., [c. 1889]). Author's Collection. The interior contained wide, double-loaded corridors with high ceilings and simple furnishings.*

and Willis recounted the circumstances of the expansion and provided a useful interior description in the hotel's first substantial promotional booklet:

> In 1887 the accommodations were not sufficient and we enlarged the house by an addition of one hundred feet [totalling approximately 250 feet across the front], giving us an extra parlor and forty-two additional sleeping rooms; also a private dining room [Fig. 5-28]. The house is furnished throughout without regard to expense. The office, halls [87 by 40 feet] [Fig. 5-29] and dining room are finished in oak, the parlors in white wood. There are large fireplaces in the side parlor and office. Steam heat on the first and second floors, gas throughout the house. Electric bells, barber shop, bath rooms, a good laundry, billiard and pool tables, bowling alleys, and a good stable, well equipped for mountain travel. The stable is one hundred rods from the house.
>
> The water supply comes from Loon Mountain, through a three-inch pipe, with hydrants on either side of the house, for sprinkling lawns and to use in case of fires. . . . The piazzas are twelve feet wide and extend entirely around the house. The halls are nine feet wide, with doors at each end opening out on to the balconies. The house will accommodate two hundred guests.[40]

Blending French Second Empire, late Gothic Revival and English Queen Anne-style features, the southeast oriented facade was perfectly balanced, with matching gambrel-roofed pavilions, above which were cubical open observatory towers capped by broken pyramidal roofs with steep-pitched dormers. Serving both functional and aesthetic purposes, these towers acted as strong vertical accents, contrasting effectively with the horizontality of the building mass so forcefully emphasized by the long hipped-on-Mansard roof and the expansive wrap-around piazzas. With typical late Victorian flair, the building was adorned with various colorful paint combinations over the years, which, when combined with its architecture, gave it a festive and inviting look. While the names of the architect and builder are unknown, they certainly met the objectives of quality hotel design with good taste and keen imagination.

As the complex aged and passed to successive proprietors and owners, every effort was made to stay competitive with the rest of the White Mountain hotel industry. Under the management of Josiah R. Elliott, who formerly ran the Flume House, the Deer Park, like the Hotel Lookoff at Sugar Hill and other rivals, made numerous technical improvements. These included upgraded steam heating, new water supply and sanitation systems, and bathrooms and bedroom closets.[41] While Hermann W. Sanborn was the owner between 1915 and 1946, the physical plant

Fig. 5-30. The Alpine House, North Woodstock, NH, *photograph, c. 1891, photographer unknown. Dartmouth College Library. A Batchelder family enterprise for some seventy years, The Alpine originated with this building in 1891.*

remained the same size but was routinely upgraded as required and maintained in excellent condition. Under Sanborn's stewardship, the Deer Park gained favor as a haven for musicians, attracting many famous personalities from the music field—including the world-renowned Polish pianist and statesman Ignace Jan Paderewski. Its final owners, Norman Grimm and Joseph Durocher both of Newton, Massachusetts, operated the establishment for just six years until it was destroyed by a spectacular fire on 23 June 1952, only a few days before it was to open for the summer season.[42]

The Alpine (Hotel Alpine), North Woodstock's other grand resort hotel also was initiated as a family operation, but physically developed at a slower pace. James H. Batchelder, a successful periodicals and newspaper store owner from Exeter, New Hampshire, built the first portion of what was to become a large and spacious complex, in 1890-91. Situated on an elevated thirty-acre tract just north of the town center on the Franconia Notch road, Bacheldor operated the new hotel (Fig. 5-30) in tandem with the Alpine Cottage, an older building on the property. Together they took in about 100 guests, boasting interiors that were "lighted with gas and well ventilated," "drained," and "elegantly furnished." For the next twenty-five years the hotel continued to operate on a modest scale. The only obvious exterior changes were the addition of a kitchen wing on the west in 1892—to "remove the odor of cooking"—and the construction of a long piazza along the south side in 1895. The three-and-a-half-story, hipped-roof structure was extremely plain and functional, resembling many other White Mountain hostelries of comparable size where business motives outweighed aesthetic concerns.[43]

In 1915-16, James Batchelder, assisted by his son Charles, undertook an ambitious building program that moved The Alpine into the august company of the White Mountain grand resort hotels. Encouraged by years of profitable operation and undeterred by the sobering effects of World War I, the Batchelders more than doubled the size of their establishment, adding public space and increasing total guest capacity to 200. With its dog-leg floor

Fig. 5-31. Hotel Alpine (The Alpine), North Woodstock, NH, *postcard, c. 1950. Author's Collection. The Alpine was one of the few regional grand resort hotels not to succumb to fire. It was demolished during the 1960s.*

plan, the transformed complex (Fig. 5-31) displayed the same roof lines, fenestration and unadorned quality of the original section. Two matching square towers with low pyramidal roofs, possibly inspired by the twin pavilion towers of the Deer Park, anchored the building to the ground and provided it with logical scale. *Among the Clouds* described the interior:

> The house is well planned. Every guest room is a front room, with two large windows, running water, telephone, twin beds, hardwood floors, beautiful rugs and furnishings. The corridors are all very wide. The office or lobby is large with a massive stone fireplace, around which are drawn a number of comfortable chairs. Adjoining it are the ladies writing room, small parlors, dance hall, men's smoking room and a barber shop. All the new public rooms are handsomely furnished and decorated, with large art squares covering the floors. The dining room is one of the many attractions, with its large plate glass windows and seating capacity for 300 people. There is also a large side hall.... A perfectly sanitary kitchen with white tile floor, is opened to the daily inspection of ... guests....[44]

Like its business rivals, The Alpine was also equipped with the latest technological advances—but in addition to now quite conventional private baths, electric lighting and steam heating were an electric vacuum cleaning system and a mail chute ("novel ... in the mountains") whereby letters could be dropped from an upper floor to the office. Fully developed and modernized later than most other post-1880 hotels, The Alpine maintained a competitive edge over most of its area rivals well into this century. Passing to the management of James H. Batchelder, Jr. after 1918, the family sold it in the 1960s; no longer a viable financial enterprise, the Hotel Alpine was demolished.[45]

Though not of grand hotel pretensions, the Fairview House, a mile outside North Woodstock center, possessed architectural and local historical interest (Fig. 5-32). Erected by Albert W. Sawyer between 1881 and 1884, the family owned and operated it for over fifty years until sagging business fortunes forced its closure and sale after World War II.

Fig. 5-32. Fairview House, North Woodstock, NH, *engraving after sketch from booklet,* Fairview House *(North Woodstock: n.p., [c. 1906]), supplement. Author's Collection. Built over a three-year period by Albert W. Sawyer, the building was actually smaller than its appearance suggests.*

Located on a raised grassy site to the east of the Pemigewasset River, the hotel, in its initial incarnation, was a three-and-a-half-story, gambrel-roof edifice. Among its most striking characteristics were piazzas on three sides, a two-story open front porch, and a long, L-shaped, two-and-a-half-story ell extending to the rear. With space for 60 to 100 people, the Fairview attracted its clientele mostly by word-of-mouth, doing virtually no advertising in the summer newspapers and other frequently consulted tourist publications. Apparently this marketing approach worked to positive advantage for in 1906-07 the Sawyers added a twenty-room extension to the west end. Its most pronounced feature was a four-story octagonal corner tower popular with guests at many of the larger hotels. Highly deceiving in appearance, the complex gave the impression of being much larger and more lavish than it actually was, no doubt the intention of its owner/financiers as well as its builders.[46]

From its opening in 1886 to its destruction by fire in 1953, the Moosilauke Inn (Breezy Point House) stood as one of the most stylistically interesting hotels in the White Mountains (Fig. 5-33). It lacked the "mammoth proportions" of the great resort complexes, but it benefited from its position east of the North Woodstock-Warren road, on the 1,700-foot high spur of Mount Moosilauke. This provocative T-shaped, three-and-one-half-story, wood-frame structure, though uncharacteristically symmetrical on its east-facing facade, displayed a rich collection of

[169]

Fig. 5-33. Moosilauke Inn, Warren, NH, *cabinet view, n.d., photographer unknown. New Hampshire Historical Society. Designed by the architectural firm of Merrill & Cutler, this hotel was one of the most interesting stylistically in the White Mountains.*

architectural elements that otherwise typed it as English Queen Anne in style. Designed by the relatively unknown firm of Merrill & Cutler from Lowell, Massachusetts, it was erected in just fifteen weeks under the supervision of Charles F. Varnum. The building imaginatively combined various brightly painted shingle and clapboard wall treatments, closed-end gables, steep-pitched front dormers, classical cornice moldings with heavy brackets, and ground-level wooden arches—many with enclosing lattice-work screens. A long wrap-around veranda with front porch (supporting stacked balconies above) incorporated delicate balustrades, turned posts and curved angle brackets. Merrill & Cutler also designed a smaller recreational facility known as "The Racket" in 1889. This connected to the main house on the north side by a covered walkway and conveyed much the same Queen Anne message, blending stylistically with the main house. The added space provided by four cottages to the rear allowed roughly 100 guests to board at the complex. Offering a full range of recreational and social options the Moosilauke functioned in much the same manner as the grand resort hotels, benefiting from a physical plant aesthetically superior to many of them.[47]

Twenty miles to the east over two mountain ranges in Waterville Valley, the Waterville Inn compiled an admirable record of service to several generations of regular summer clients. However, it lacked the size, luxury and magnificence of the grand resort hotels and the architectural quality of the more modest hostelries like the Moosilauke. In its simplicity and its vernacular form the Inn reflected the design of some of the earliest White Mountain guest establishments. Surrounded by 4,000-foot peaks—Mount Tecumseh, the Osceolas, the Tripyramids and Sandwich Dome—the hotel had its origins in Nathaniel Greeley's 1840s farmhouse, known locally as "the little red cottage," to which he had attached a large east wing and took in sixty guests in 1868. Operated for several years as "Greeley's Summer Boarding House" and "Greeley's Mountain House," Greeley transferred it to his son Merrill, who subsequently sold it in the fall of 1885 to Silas B. Elliott who then retitled it "Elliott's Hotel." The next year Elliott added a new east wing, containing a large parlor, to the hotel (Fig. 5-34). He next attached a nearly matching west wing with rear kitchen ell in 1895. It was in this form, with its capacity peaked at 175, that the hotel passed to the modern era. Its large open wing and end wall gables, intersecting roofs, and dormer windows recall the first Glen House, the first and second Crawford houses and the first Profile House—the earliest of the grand resort hotels. A new barn was built in 1891, followed by a guest annex called "Tecumseh Lodge" in 1901-02, a power house and reservoir in 1901, and a bowling alley in 1904.[48] Augmented by several cottages, built over a thirty-year period, the complex was long the centerpiece of the tiny village—its economic base almost solely dependent on summer vacationers and tourism.

Frederick W. Stickney and the Second Senter House

The second Senter House (New Senter House), as one railroad guidebook author observed, "must be numbered amongst the great hostelries of the White Mountain region . . . [for it is] far more ornate and modern in construction and appointments than most of them."[49] With an exotic, picturesque quality rivaling that of The Metallak, built in Colebrook five years later, the second Senter House was the White Mountain's finest example of Shingle-style hotel architecture. One would have to go to the New England coast to find a building of equal quality.

Financed by a joint stock company and erected in 1887-88 under the direction of the proprietors James L. Huntress & Son, the second Senter House occupied a gradually sloping site in Center Harbor overlooking Lake Winnipesaukee. This advantageous waterfront location was directly across Main Street from the spot where the first Senter House had stood before it burned the year before. The new site, no doubt, had great appeal to the hotel's clientele, for it made "every room a front room, either commanding a view of the lake on the south, or the village and the mountains upon the north." Like its predecessor the second Senter House was Lake Winnipesaukee's

Fig. 5-34. Greeley's Hotel (Waterville Inn), Waterville Valley, NH, *cabinet view, c. 1880, photographer unknown. Author's Collection. The only hotel in Waterville Valley for a century, the building was surrounded by imposing 4,000-foot mountains.*

Fig. 5-35. "The Senter House: Centre . Harbor. N. H., F. W. Stickney . Archt. . Lowell . Mass.," *front elevation perspective engraving from* American Architect and Building News *23, #634 (18 February 1888), op. p. 79. Morris Library, University of Delaware, Newark, DE. This double-page architect's rendering shows the hotel almost exactly as it was built.*

finest destination resort hotel and also served as a vital stop-over point for people traveling to and from the White Mountains.[50]

Fortunately, the name of the architect may be readily identified. In its 18 February 1888 issue, the *American Architect and Building News* published a superb

[172]

two-page perspective rendering (Fig. 5-35) of the west or inland facade of the hotel, along with small first and second floor plan inserts. The main title included the inscription, "F. W. Stickney. Arct. . Lowell . Mass." Frederick Stickney (1853-1918) was an architecture graduate of the Massachusetts Institute of Technology and had worked as a draftsman in the office of Merrill & Cutler, the planners of the Moosilauke Inn. Regarded as a specialist in the design of school buildings, Stickney was also the architect of commercial structures, residences, public buildings and suburban hotels in or near Lowell. It is not known how or

Fig. 5-36. "Senter House, Center Harbor, N. H.," *cabinet view, c. 1890, by Kimball, Concord, NH. New Hampshire Historical Society. The lakeside elevation contained an extra ground-level story due to the sloping hillside site.*

under what conditions he received the commission for the Senter House—he did, however, have hotel design experience and may have had connections with Boston-based directors of the stock company.[51]

The second Senter House (later called "The Colonial," c. 1913) had attributes that took into account aesthetic, engineering and recreational considerations. Typical of the Shingle style the three-and-a-half-story edifice possessed asymmetrical principal elevations with low-sweeping gambrel-roofed pavilions, broad, balustraded verandas, and heavy bracketing.[52] On each elevation octagonal towers, topped by steep-pitched spire cappings, punctuated the main gambrel roof. At the main entrance on the west facade was an arched port cochere under which carriages and automobiles could deliver or pick up guests. The east or lake facade displayed a greater number of bay windows and a two-tiered veranda (necessitated by the slope of the land) from which paired central stairways descended in stages towards the shoreline (Fig. 5-36).

Fig. 5-37. Dining Hall, Senter House, Center Harbor, NH, *photograph from booklet,* Senter House *(Center Harbor, NH: n.d., [c. 1902]). Author's Collection. The stark interior dining space and furnishings contrasted sharply with the elaborate exterior Shingle Style details.*

The first floor contained the office, main dining (Fig. 5-37) and serving rooms, the kitchen, parlors and music room, while above were 91 sleeping rooms for 150 to 200 patrons. The entire building was initially painted a vivid "Pompeian red"! Amongst the building's practical or technological features were a steam-heating system for public areas, open fireplaces in bedrooms, electricity, natural spring water, telephones and telegraph, and "the most expensive and perfect system of drainage [sanitation] ever put into a summer hotel."[53] While the range of its recreational facilities and offerings was somewhat limited by its less mountainous location and other factors, the hotel did offer boating, fishing, horseback riding, tennis, croquet, swimming, bowling, billiards, and "countless walks and drives."[54] Morning concerts and evening promenades and hops were comfortably accommodated in its ample public spaces. When the Senter House was lost to fire on 20 June 1919, the regional hotel industry experienced a serious blow, and an unusually outstanding specimen of hotel architecture disappeared.[55]

In addition to this group of grand and near-grand hotels, six major complexes from the same period representing the highest architectural accomplishment of the regional industry will be treated in the final three chapters of this book. One hotel, The Metallak, which was prevented by an untimely natural disaster from ever opening to the public, will be the topic of Chapter 6. In Chapter 7, three substantial and unusually outstanding resort establishments—the second Glen House, the second or New Profile House, and the Mountain View House will be discussed. Lastly, in Chapter 8, the two splendid surviving nonpareils of White Mountain grand resort history, the Mount Washington Hotel and The Balsams, will undergo intensive and admiring examination. Both of these immense complexes are operational today, and continue to defy the forces and conditions that have all but eliminated the grand scale hotel industry from the White Mountains during the twentieth century.

✥ Notes ✥

1. Bulkley, "History," pp. 76-89; Wallace, "A Social History of the White Mountains," in Campbell, et al., *The White Mountains*, pp. 29-30.
2. Bulkley, "History," pp. 107-115.
3. *Ibid.*, pp. 90-101.
4. The first Rosebrook Inn burned in 1922 and was immediately replaced. Both the second or New Rosebrook Inn, and the Grand View Hotel still stand in Twin Mountain village.
5. Kilbourne, *Chronicles*, pp. 365-66; *ATC* 32, No. 3 (7 July 1910), p. 3; *ATC* 34, No. 1 (8 July 1912), p. 4; Walter J. Mitchell, Jr., "The Mount Washington Summit House," *Mount Washington Observatory News Bulletin* 6, No. 4 (December 1965), pp. 5-6; Glen M. Kidder, *Railway to the Moon* (Littleton, NH: Courier Printing Company, 1969), pp. 98-100; Bray, *They Said it Couldn't be Done*, p. 118; "Concord & Montreal Railroad Extension to the Summit of Mount Washington, Plan, July 1912," Author's Collection. It was also intended that the B. & M. extension, seven miles from Fabyan Station to the Base Station, would be electrified and used as the lower portion of the new system.
6. *ATC* 35, No. 50 (10 September 1913), p. 1; *ATC* 37, No. 1 (12 July 1915), pp. 1, 8; *Lisbon Courier*, 7 November 1940, p. 1; Williams, "The Saga of 'S. D.' Morgan," p. 13; Kilbourne, *Chronicles*, pp. 367-68. Supposedly the building was designed by a man named Fletcher (no first name given) from the Boston and Maine Railroad architectural department, but Morgan himself likely drafted the plans.
7. Kilbourne, *Chronicles*, p. 368; *ATC* 37, No. 1 (12 July 1915), pp. 1, 8, No. 9 (23 July 1915), p. 1, No. 19 (6 August 1915), p. 1, No. 20 (7 August 1915), p. 1; Bray, *They Said it Couldn't be Done*, p. 118; Mitchell, "The Mount Washington Summit House," p. 6. Spring water from the Lakes of the Clouds was pumped to a large holding tank on the summit and supplied the new hotel.
8. Kilbourne, *Chronicles*, p. 369; Mitchell, "The Mount Washington Summit House," p. 6; *ATC* 37, No. 29 (21 August 1915), p. 1, No. 30 (23 August 1915), p. 1; *WME* 38, No. 6 (28 August 1915), p. 9 and No. 8 (11 September 1915), p. 1; Fred B. Maynard, "Skyline Fireworks," *Appalachia* 28, No. 1 (June 1950): 40-47; Greg Gordon, "Au Revoir, Summit House (1915-1980)," *Mount Washington Observatory News Bulletin* 21, No. 2 (June 1980), p. 39; Bray, *They Said it Couldn't be Done*, pp. 156-57. Ironically, the new Summit House was open only a week when on August 29 the famous Tip-Top House next door lost its roof and wooden interior to a fire. Due to the direction of the wind the Summit House was spared. The State of New Hampshire acquired title to the structure when it purchased the summit of Mount Washington in 1964, thereby opening the way for the erection of the current facility fifteen years later.
9. The Ridge and Cottages burned in October 1899 and was replaced on the same site by the New Ridge and Cottages in 1899-1900. This group of buildings in turn burned in 1905 and was not rebuilt.
10. Janet M. Hounsell, "Eastern Slope Inn's Roots Deep in North Conway," *The Valley Visitor*, 9 June 1988, p. 3; Harry H. Randall, "The Randall Hotels," typescript of address delivered at the annual meeting of the Conway Historical Association, 17 January 1958, p. 1, Conway Public Library; *ATC* 27, No. 5 (17 July 1903), advertisement, p. 2; *WME* 27, No. 1 (9 July 1904), p. 13; *New Hotel Randall, White Mountains, North Conway, N. H.* (North Conway: n. p., [c.1918]); *The Reporter* (North Conway), 26 November 1925, p. 1. The loss from the

fire amounted to approximately $175,000 and was only partially covered by insurance. In 1917 Harry Randall bought the Sunset Pavilion next door and managed it as an adjunct to his hotel until it burned in 1940 (see Chapter 3).

11. Hounsell, "Eastern Slope Inn's Roots . . . ," p. 3; Robert B. Kantack, National Register of Historic Places Inventory—Nomination Form for Hotel Randall, New Hampshire State Historic Preservation Office, 1982.
12. *WME* 49, No. 1 (10 July 1926), p. 10.
13. "North Conway's Hotel Randall," *The Mountaineer*, 5 July 1985, p. 3.
14. *Ibid.*, p. 3.
15. Kantack, National Register . . . Inventory—Nomination Form; Robert B. Kantack, "The Eastern Slope Inn," *Outlook* 9 (Fall 1983): 36-38; "National recognition for the historic Eastern Slope Inn," *White Mountain Reporter*, 8 September 1982, p. 4; Michael L. Trainor, "The lovely inns of yesterday," *The Irregular & The Mount Washington Valley News* (North Conway), 27 January 1981, p. 25; site plan, Eastern Slope Development Corporation, North Conway, N.H. (Thaddeus Thorne, Surveyors, Inc., Center Conway), 23 July 1985, plan book #85, p. 57, CCRD.
16. Garland, *Yesterdays*, p. 33; *ATC* 9, No. 1 (11 July 1885), p. 1, and advertisement, p. 3; *WME* 8, No. 2 (4 July 1885), pp. 5, 7; *ATC* 11, No. 1 (11 July 1887), p. 4, and No. 2 (12 July 1887), p. 1; *WME* 10, No. 1 (2 July 1887), p. 7; *WME* 14, No. 2 (11 July 1891), p. 11; *WME* 15, No. 1 (2 July 1892), p. 19; *Iron Mountain House, Jackson, N. H.* (Jackson: n. p. [c. 1918]). With the addition of Meserve Hall to the complex the guest capacity was increased by 50% to over 150.
17. Garland, *Yesterdays*, p. 21; *ATC* 38, No. 13 (26 July 1916), p. 1; *The Eagle Mountain House, Jackson, N. H.* (Jackson: n. p. [c. 1916]); Marcia Gale Chadbourne to Carolyn K. Tolles, 2 January 1975; Elizabeth Durfee Hengen, National Register of Historic Places Registration Form for the Eagle Mountain House, State of New Hampshire, Department of Resources and Economic Development, Concord. Despite the change in ownership the hotel's corporate title was "C. E. Gale & Son." This initial portion of the current hotel accommodated 125 people, while 175 could be seated in the dining room. In nearly all large White Mountain hotels dining room capacity exceeded bedroom capacity to provide for non-overnight diners and increase food service profitability.
18. Hengen, National Register . . . Registration Form; typed manuscript by Marcia G. Chadbourne, n. d., Jackson Historical Society; Janet M. Hounsell, "Eagle Mountain House Firmly Rooted in Jackson's Past," *The Valley Visitor*, 6 October 1988, p. 4. According to Marcia G. Chadbourne, Arthur Garland once again was hired as head carpenter.
19. Hengen, National Register . . . Registration Form.
20. Marcia Gale Chadbourne to Carolyn K. Tolles, 2 January 1975; Hengen, National Register . . . Registration Form; Hounsell, "Eagle Mountain House," p. 4; Karen Cummings, "Jackson Landmark is Transformed," *Mountain Ear* (North Conway), 18 July 1986; condominium site plan, Eagle Mountain House Association, Jackson, N. H. (H. Edmund Bergeron, Civil Engineers, North Conway), 16 May 1986, plan book #92, p. 13, CCRD. The Eagle Mountain House today operates under the name "Eagle Mountain Resort" and is managed by Colony Hotels & Resorts.
21. *ATC* 2, No. 47 (2 September 1896), p. 4.
22. Garland, *Yesterdays*, p. 27; *The Reporter*, 20 July 1983, p. 1; *WME* 8, No. 2 (4 July 1885), p. 5; *WME* 9, No. 1 (3 July 1886), pp. 7, 14; *ATC* 9, No. 1 (11 July 1885), p. 1; *WME* 10, No. 2 (9 July 1887), p. 5; *ATC* 11, No. 1 (11 July 1887), p. 4; *ATC* 14, No. 2 (12 July 1890), p. 8, and No. 49 (5 September 1890), p. 4; *ATC* 16, No. 1 (11 July 1892), p. 4; *WME* 15, No. 1 (2 July 1892), p. 19; *ATC* 17, No. 1 (17 July 1893), p. 4. When he introduced electricity in 1893, Charles Gray claimed that his hotel was the only one in the mountains with electric lights in every room. A stable was also constructed on the property the same year. Associated with the hotel were three large area farms that provided a fresh daily supply of vegetables, berries and produce.
23. *WME* 18, No. 1 (6 July 1895), p. 15, and No. 2 (13 July 1895), p. 14; *ATC* 24, No. 4 (17 July 1900), p. 4; *WME* 23, No. 1 (7 July 1900), p. 10; *White Mountain Reporter* (North Conway), 4 December 1902, p. 1. Supposedly the fire was caused by an uncovered live wire running through an unfinished room. Mr. Gray was reportedly on the phone when the blaze broke out. Immediately all electricity in the complex was shut off as a result of the fire. Insurance coverage was $65,000. Two of the cottages survived the blaze.
24. Newspaper references and one rare postcard photograph (Fig. 5-14) reveal Gray's vision for his second hotel.
25. *ATC* 27, No. 2 (14 July 1903), p. 8; Garland, *Yesterdays*, p. 27. For many years afterwards, rumor circulated that arson was the cause of the fire.
26. "The New Gray's Inn," *ATC* 28, No. 41 (24 August 1904), pp. 1, 4; Garland, *Yesterdays*, pp. 27-28; *WME* 29, No. 1 (7 July 1906), p. 19; booklet, *Gray's Inn, Jackson, N. H.* (Jackson: n.p., [c. 1905]). The paint colors of the main hotel were cream-white with light yellow window trimmings, and olive and ruddy brown roofing.
27. "The New Gray's Inn," pp. 1, 4.
28. *The Reporter*, 24 February 1916, p. 1; *Littleton Courier*, 24 February 1916, p. 1; *ATC* 38, No. 4 (14 July 1916), p. 1; Kilbourne, *Chronicles*, p. 173; *Gray's Inn, Jackson, N. H.* (Jackson: n. p., [c. 1925]). Most of the 150 guests staying at the hotel lost all their belongings when the 1916 fire occurred. It broke out about 4:00 p.m. in zero degree temperatures. The fire originated in the attic and was caused either by spontaneous combustion or a defective chimney. The building cost $100,000 to rebuild and was partially covered by insurance.
29. Garland, *Yesterdays*, p. 28; *The Reporter*, 15 October 1982, pp. 1, 12; *The Reporter*, 20 July 1983, pp. 1, 10; *The Irregular*, 20 July 1983, pp. 1, 2, 14; *Union Leader*, 15 July 1983; *Northern Light*, 19 September 1988, pp. 1, 5; Plan of Land in Jackson, N.

H., Property of Elias M. Loew, Boston, MA, known as Gray's Inn (Burnell Land Surveying, Conway), 17 October 1970, plan book #43, p. 36, CCRD. At the time of the fire, Mark Pinardi, a businessman from Jamaica Plains, Massachusetts, had an option on the property, and had revealed his plans to make the hotel into time-sharing condominiums for middle-income people. The exterior was to be restored to its original appearance. The refurbished resort would also have featured a swimming pool, health club, restaurant and pub. With a financing goal of $4 million Pinardi was attempting to attract investors at the time of the fire. The cause of the fire was believed to have been incendiary, although this was never substantiated. The thirty-three-acre plot on which four Gray's Inns stood was sold to the town of Jackson in 1988.

30. Kilbourne, *Chronicles*, p. 333; Bulkley, "History," p. 104; *Bethlehem, New Hampshire in the Heart of the White Mountains* (Bethlehem, NH: Board of Trade, [1922]).

31. Child, *Gazetteer of Grafton County*, pp. 268-69; *ATC* 8, No. 15 (27 July 1883), p. 1; *The White Mountains* (1884 ed.), p. 259; *WME* 6, No. 3 (14 July 1883), p. 5, and No. 8 (18 August 1883), p. 14; Holden, *White and Franconia Mountains* (1883 ed.), p. 36. The hotel was centrally situated four miles from Bethlehem village as well as the Profile House in Franconia Notch.

32. *ATC* 13, No. 17 (31 July 1889), p. 4; *WME* 13, No. 1 (5 July 1890), p. 11, and No. 2 (12 July 1890), p. 19; *WME* 14, No.2 (11 July 1891), p. 11; *ATC* 16, No. 1 (11 July 1892), p. 4, and No. 19 (1 August 1892), p. 1; *WME* 15, No. 1 (2 July 1892), pp. 15, 20, and No. 2 (9 July 1882), p. 2; *The Great Resorts of America (Illustrated)* . . . (Portland, ME: Wilbur Hayes, 1894), advertisement; *The White Mountain Clarion*, 5 August 1896; *WME* 18, No. 1 (6 July 1895), p. 17, and No. 2 (13 July 1895), p. 14; *ATC* 26, No. 1 (12 July 1902), p. 1, and No. 10 (23 July 1902), p. 4; *WME* 25, No. 3 (19 July 1902), p. 3; *Littleton Courier*, 27 December 1907, p. 1; *WME* 30, No 1 (11 July 1908); *WME* 43, No. 1 (10 July 1920), p. 7; *WME* 46, No. 2 (21 July 1923), p. 10. According to his obituary in the *Lisbon Courier* (7 November 1940, p. 1), Sylvanus D. Morgan did contracting work on the hotel and/or its outbuildings. It is unknown when this occurred and what Morgan's actual responsibilities were. "The Lodge," the only building in the complex that has survived, was totally remodeled as an English Tudor cottage under Karl Abbott's ownership in the early 1920s.

33. Jim McIntosh, "Notes Toward a History of the Forest Hills Hotel and Franconia College," *Magnetic North* 7, No. 1 (Summer 1989): 56-59, 62; Abbott, *Open for the Season*, p. 158; *Littleton Courier*, 8 September 1960, p. 1; *Hanover Gazette*, 31 January 1963; Plan of the Franconia College Land, Franconia, N. H. (G. H. Richardson, Surveyor), January 1963, grantor book # 985, p. 43, Grafton County Registry of Deeds, Woodsville. Other owner/managers between Abbott and Collier were Norman Pancoast, John Cola and Ross W. Thompson. Franconia College became a four-year accredited school in 1967. In 1989, a consortium (Forest Hills Associates) advanced plans to reconstruct the hotel as the centerpiece of a large condominium community, but this has yet to occur due primarily to the depressed state of the national economy in the 1990s.

34. *WME* 9, No. 12 (18 September 1886), p. 8; *ATC* 11, No. 1 (11 July 1887), p. 4, and No. 50 (6 September 1887), p. 5; *Lisbon Courier*, 7 November 1940, pp. 1, 12; *WME* 10, No. 1 (2 July 1887), p. 10, and No. 2 (9 July 1887), p. 5. The Lookoff (also spelled "Look-Off") was situated at a higher altitude than any other hotel in the mountains, with the exception of the Mount Washington Summit House. The recreational facilities included croquet and baseball grounds, a lawn tennis court, a lawn for bowling, a livery stable and a nearby golf course.

35. *ATC* 12, No. 1 (10 July 1888), p. 1; *WME* 11, No. 2 (7 July 1888), p. 5; *WME* 14, No. 2 (11 July 1891), p. 1; *WME* 18, No. 5 (1 August 1895), p. 2; *ATC* 19, No. 2 (15 July 1895), p. 1; *ATC* 22, No. 2 (19 July 1892), advertisement, p. 6; *White Mountain Clarion* 2 (1897), advertisement; *WME* 22, No. 1 (8 July 1899), p. 14. The springhouse still exists, transformed in recent years into an unusual summer residence.

36. Newspaper scrapbooks, Sugar Hill Historical Museum; booklet, *Hotel Lookoff* (Sugar Hill, NH: n.p., [1911]); Hazel A. Pickwick, Mable S. Jesseman, and Barbara Jesseman, *Lisbon's Ten Score Years, 1763-1963, Plus One Score More, 1963-83* (Lisbon, NH: Friends-in-Council Civics Committee, 1983), p. 83; Plan of the Hotel Lookoff Property, Sugar Hill, N. H. (G. H. Richardson, Surveyor), June 1955, grantor book #880, p. 414, Grafton County Registry of Deeds, Woodsville. Other owners before 1911 included H. M. Crohurst, A. E. Safford, and the Eagle Rock Company (which changed the name temporarily to "Mount Lookoff"). After Mrs. Sanborn died in 1926, Mr. Merrill and his sister ran the business. In 1946, it was sold to the Arthur Roberts hotel chain of Rochester, Minnesota, before being acquired by the Ronald Fentons in 1954. The final owner, Arthur Lemire, purchased the property in 1963 with plans for a motel or cottage colony.

A sizeable garage, one of the former outbuildings, was later converted to a year-round residence. It sits prominently on the west side of the ridge. Slightly to the east is the former employees' dormitory, also renovated as a four-season dwelling.

37. Bulkley, "History," pp. 106-107.

38. *WME* 10, No. 1 (2 July 1887), p. 10 and No. 2 (9 July 1887), p. 5; *ATC* 11, No. 1 (11 July 1887), p. 4, and No. 4 (14 July 1887), p. 1; *The Plymouth Record*, 26 June 1952, pp. 1, 12; "Deer Park Hotel," *ATC* 12, No. 6 (16 July 1888), p. 1. The firm of Buchanan (Collins M.) and Willis (Freeman C.) was formerly the proprietor of the Black Mountain House in Campton that had burned down a few years before.

The Deer Park Hotel was located on a plateau on the road to Lincoln near the former North Woodstock railroad station. It was four miles from the Flume House and ten miles from the Profile House. The site is now occupied by condominiums. The proprietor's cottage, however, still stands.

39. *ATC* 12, No. 1 (10 July 1888), pp. 1, 3, advertisement; *WME* 11, No. 1 (30 June 1888), p. 10, and No. 2 (7 July 1888), p. 5.

40. *Deer Park, North Woodstock, N. H.* (New York: South Publishing Co., 1888), n.p.

41. *WME* 18, No. 2 (13 July 1895), p. 14.

42. *The New Deer Park Hotel, North Woodstock, N. H.* (North Woodstock: n.p., [1915]); *Plymouth Record*, 26 June 1952, pp. 1, 12; *Manchester Union Leader*, 25 June 1952, p. 1; *Littleton Courier*, 26 June 1952, p. 1.

43. *WME* 14, No. 1 (4 July 1891), p. 7, No. 2 (11 July 1891), p. 11, and No. 4 (25 July 1891), p. 16; *WME* 15, No. 1 (2 July 1892), p. 11, and No. 2 (9 July 1892), p. 2; *ATC* 39, No. 1 (13 July 1895), p. 4; *The Batchelder Family News-Journal* 6, No. 4 (Machias, ME) (July 1974). In addition to The Alpine, James Batchelder operated a hotel in Florida in the late 1890s. Many White Mountain hotel owners also had guest establishments in the south. These complementary business ventures allowed them to shift their activities back and forth with the change in seasons. Oftentimes hotel employees would accompany the owners as they made the moves from north to south, and back north again, each year.

44. *ATC* 38, No. 17 (1 August 1916), p. 1. The resort was replete with a golf course and putting green, clay tennis courts, an outdoor swimming pool, a badminton court and shuffleboard facilities. There were also opportunities for horseback riding, mountain climbing, trail hiking, hunting and fishing. The site today is occupied by condominium units.

45. *ATC* 38, No. 17 (1 August 1916), p. 1.

46. *WME* 15, No. 12 (17 September 1892), p. 4; newspaper clipping file, North Woodstock (NH) Public Library; *ATC* 31, No. 5 (13 July 1907), p. 5, and No. 12 (26 July 1907), pp. 1, advertisement, and 4; *ATC* 32, No. 3 (7 July 1910), advertisement, p. 5; Carpenter, *Guide Book to Franconia Notch...* (1898 ed.), pp. 53-54; booklet, *Fairview House* (North Woodstock, NH: n.p., [c. 1907]). The Fairview was situated near the railroad, with a special flag station 400 feet from the hotel complex. Thomas and Raymond Sawyer ran the hotel after their father's death in 1923. It was torn down in the early 1960s, literally piece by piece over a three-year period, by its last owners, Mr. and Mrs. L. Fitzgerald.

47. "The Moosilauke," *ATC* 10, No. 19 (31 July 1886), p. 4; *WME* 9, No. 1 (3 July 1886), p. 10, and No. 3 (17 July 1886), p. 5; *WME* 12, No. 2 (6 July 1889), p. 7, and No. 5 (3 August 1889), p. 14; "A Visit to Moosilauke," *Concord* (NH) *Monitor* [1886]; *Plymouth Record*, 10 September 1953, p. 1. The inn was situated at the head of the Mount Moosilauke Carriage Road by which one could gain access to the Tip-Top House (see Chapter 2) on the summit. An older, smaller hotel known as the Breezy Point House had stood by the same spot from 1877 until it burned in 1884. Guests at the hotel enjoyed magnificent views of mounts Cushman, Kineo and Waternomee to the east, the summit of Mount Moosilauke to the north, and Mount Carr and the Baker River Valley to the south.

The inn was financed by the Breezy Point Hotel Company, formed by A. B. and E. B. Woodward and Willis D. Thompson of Concord, Charles S. Keene of Boston, John F. Thayer of Nashua (the first proprietor), and E. F. Mann and Chester Abbott of Woodsville, NH. The Moosilauke Inn should not be confused with the Moosilauke House, a more modest hostelry (sixty guests) formerly situated at the village center of Warren.

48. A. L. Goodrich, *The Waterville Valley: A History, Description, and Guide* (Waterville, NH: n.p., 1904), pp. 13-16; Nathaniel L. Goodrich, *The Waterville Valley: A Story of a Resort in the New Hampshire Mountains* (Lunenburg, VT: The North Country Press, 1952), pp. 8-23; Grace H. Bean, *The Town at the End of the Road: A History of Waterville Valley* (Canaan, NH: Phoenix Publishing, 1983), pp. 10-11, 13-15, 21, 23-27, 106-107; *Concord Monitor*, 24 February 1967, pp. 1, 8; *Manchester Union Leader*, 24 February 1967, p. 1. The site of the Waterville Inn was just east of the junction of the Valley Road and the West Branch Road where tennis courts can be found today. It replaced an earlier, smaller hotel that occupied a nearby site briefly in 1860-61 until it was lost to fire. The Waterville Inn was burned to the ground on 23 February 1967 while it was under the ownership of Ralph Bean.

49. *Summer Outings in the Old Granite State...* (Boston: Passenger Department of the Concord & Montreal R.R., 1890), p. 44.

50. *WME* 10, No. 5 (30 July 1887), p. 14; *ATC* 11, No. 2 (7 July 1888), p. 5; *WME* 11, No. 1 (30 June 1888), p. 11, and No. 4 (21 July 1888), p. 12; *The White Mountains* (1888 ed.), p. 370; *Center Harbor, New Hampshire* (Center Harbor: Center Harbor Historical Society, 1986), p. 52. The company directors were George L. Huntress of Winchester, Massachusetts, Henry L. Huntress, and George H. Pearl and William Sheafe, both of Boston. The site of the first Senter House was transformed into a park and tennis court for the new hotel.

51. "The Senter House, Centre Harbor, N.H.," *American Architect and Building News* 23, No. 634 (18 February 1888), op. p. 79; Withey, *Biographical Dictionary of American Architects (Deceased)*, pp. 574-75.

52. *WME* 11, No. 2 (7 July 1888), p. 5. Typical of the Shingle style, the second Senter House was misleadingly referred to as "Dutch Colonial."

53. Booklet, *Lake Winnipesaukee...the Senter House* (Center Harbor, NH: n.p., [c. 1895]).

54. Rollins, *The Tourists' Guide-Book to the State of New Hampshire* (1902 ed.), p. 84.

55. *Manchester Union*, 21 June 1919, p. 1; *The News and Critic* (Laconia), 25 June 1919, p. 1; *Laconia Democrat*, 21 June 1919, p. 3. The final owner was William A. McLean of Center Harbor. The cause of the fire was "undetermined." The hotel had been scheduled to open just ten days after the blaze occurred.

Fig. 5-38. West front elevation, second Senter House, Center Harbor, NH. *Photo from booklet,* Senter House *(1902).
Author's Collection.*

Fig. 5-39. East front elevation, Second Eagle Mountain House, Jackson, NH. *Photo, n.d., photographer unknown.
Jackson Historical Society.*

Fig. 6-1. "The Metallak" on Lombard's Hill, Colebrook, NH, *front elevation perspective drawing by John Calvin Stevens, Architect, Portland, Maine. Avery Architectural and Fine Arts Library, Columbia University, New York, NY. This well-executed presentation drawing was used as an illustration in the* Annual Architectural Review *(London, 1892) and possibly other architectural periodicals. It was also employed for advertising purposes by the hotel's financiers.*

CHAPTER 6

The Hotel That Blew Down: The Metallak, the Surviving Record, and the Symbol

THE STORY OF "The Metallak," or "The Nirvana" as it was also called, constitutes one of the most important and fascinating pieces of grand resort hotel history in the White Mountains (Fig. 6-1). Planned in the early 1890s for a spectacular site in Colebrook overlooking the upper Connecticut River Valley and northeastern Vermont, this large, rambling complex fell victim to the unpredictable forces of nature before it ever opened, only to be partially resurrected in another location in Maine several years later. Although this curious history alone is sufficient reason to grant it special attention, The Metallak is further compelling in that, unlike most hotels in the region, it was designed by an architect. Conceived in a "high-style" version of the popular Shingle style, enhanced by Colonial Revival elements, it was the only nineteenth-century hotel in the White Mountain area for which a near complete visual documentary record survives. Ironically, although the building existed but a few months in incomplete form, we know more about it today than any other hotel structure of its era in the region.

The task of financing and constructing The Metallak was approached with considerable diligence and optimism. For most residents of Colebrook and nearby towns the successful realization of the hotel project held an economic promise clearly no longer possible through the traditional pursuits of agriculture, lumbering, or small manufacturing. Funds to erect the building, however, came from a group of Portland investors headed by treasurer and general manager E. G. S. Ricker, who formed the sponsoring Mt. Monadnock Mineral Springs and Land Company in October 1891. This new business consortium promptly purchased 250 acres of land on Lombard's Hill at an elevation of 1,500 feet, some 400 feet above Colebrook village. They then contracted the accomplished Portland architect John Calvin Stevens (1855-1940) to prepare plans for the new 250-foot-long complex (Fig. 6-2). Estimated at $50,000, The Metallak was to be of the latest architectural style, outfitted with the most modern conveniences, and equipped to accommodate over 200 guests, making it the largest hotel in the northern White Mountains.[1]

It is not surprising that his Portland associates selected Stevens to be the architect for the new hotel, for by 1891 his reputation had become well established in Maine and elsewhere. Following his graduation from high school in 1873 he was hired as office boy by Portland's Francis H. Fassett (see Chapter 4), then considered to be Maine's leading architect. Stevens quickly made his mark in Fassett's firm, becoming a junior partner in 1880, and moving to Boston to head a new branch office for the next eighteen months. Returning to Maine with an expanded knowledge of the current Queen Anne and Shingle styles, Stevens left Fassett and opened his own office in 1884, completing an impressive group of imagina-

[181]

Fig. 6-2. Portrait of John Calvin Stevens (1855-1940), *photograph, c. 1900, Maine Historic Preservation Commission, Augusta. John Calvin Stevens was the architect of The Metallak, Colebrook, NH, and the Bay of Naples Inn, Naples, ME.*

tive and aesthetically pleasing domestic commissions in Portland and on the Maine coast. In 1888, Stevens entered into partnership with Albert Winslow Cobb (1858-1941), formerly a draftsman in the office of the distinguished Boston architect William Ralph Emerson (1833-1917), whose influence converted Stevens to embrace the concepts, both practical and philosophical, behind the new styles. Many of Stevens' best Shingle style designs dating from 1884 to 1889 were published in a collaborative work with Cobb entitled *Examples of American Domestic Architecture* (New York: W. T. Comstock, 1889).[2] Stevens, though, is still best admired for the innovative, picturesque cottages and other surviving buildings he actually created. He returned to independent practice in 1891 (in which he remained until 1906) just about the time that the Mt. Monadnock Company secured his services. It was then that Stevens began to move away from the Shingle style to the later Georgian and Colonial Revival vernaculars, a shift toward a more formalistic design orientation that is strikingly evident in The Metallak and his subsequent work.[3]

Newspaper articles and other printed sources provide a fragmentary, but interesting picture of the initial 1892 construction phase and the amenities that the new hotel would offer. With Stevens committed as the architect, and his plans largely completed by spring, the financing consortium then hired the well-known Portland contractor J. W. Burrowes to carry out the construction.[4] Originally the specifications supplied by Stevens called for a July 1 completion date, but this soon proved unrealistic and it was advanced into the following year.[5] Still, as late as July 15, the *Industrial Journal* of Bangor announced an anticipated opening date of August 10 for the hotel while extolling the virtues of its 102 guest rooms and other spaces.[6] The 1892 edition of the *United States Hotel* provides an enticing description of the envisioned interior:

> Every room is large, airy, handsomely furnished and so arranged that any number can be connected in suites; many have private baths attached. Each room has a large closet of such size as will take the largest trunk and yet have ample room for other purposes.
> At the southern end facing Mount Monadnock [in Vermont], is the fine dining hall, 43 x 85 feet, with pilasters and heavy beams of cypress, and with broad and generous windows.
> At the extreme . . . [northern] end is the large parlor or amusement hall, 43 x 42 feet, and opening from it are numerous cardrooms, private parlors, etc.
> Open fire-places are among the attractive features to temper the evening air.
> The table will be supplied with all the luxuries and delicasies [sic] the market affords, and the service will be prompt and efficient.
> All views from the piazzas which extend along the front and ends are grand and impressive.
> . . . . No expense has been spared in the construction or furnishings to render the house worthy of immense patronage.[7]

July issues of the *White Mountain Echo* contained box advertisements announcing the expected August opening. These described the "new and elegant" interior, highlighting such appointments as elevators, and gas and electric lights, and proclaimed the scenic and recreational advantages of hotel "summer comfort" (Fig. 6-3).[8]

Unfortunately, this wonderful vision of a first-class luxury hotel in the north woods of New Hampshire was never to be realized. Possibly because of financial shortfalls or construction delays, completion of The Metallak was deferred until spring 1893, leaving its unfinished framework skeleton vulnerable to the natural elements. On April 21, one of the company partners, D. W. Yoemans of Portland, received a telegram informing him that the framework had been blown down by a gale the previous night and that it was a complete loss.[9] Newspapers describe a great storm, likely a hurricane, that over several days swept across the eastern United States leaving extensive destruction in its path. The April 22 issue of the *Manchester Union* reported a "terrific wind storm" accompanied by snow and hail and that a "partially constructed hotel at Colebrook [had been] razed to the ground."[10] The *Berlin Independent*, also reported the sad fate of The Metallak: "not a timber was left standing and the hotel is a total wreck."[11] *The White Mountain Republic Journal* in Littleton presented the grim financial facts that apparently ruled out the possibility of its reconstruction—the estimated loss was in the vicinity of $16,000, with the contractor carrying a lien on the property.[12] The Mt. Monadnock Company promptly terminated the project; all hope for a major hotel in the Colebrook region was lost to this day.[13] Plans to develop a related mineral spring, commercial bottling plant, and park with hiking trail system on the east side of Mt. Monadnock were also abandoned.[14]

The Documentary Record

While the history of The Metallak is unfortunately brief, the existence of superb documentation is a happy consolation. Preserved at the Maine Historical Society is a presumably complete set of preliminary drawings, detail sketches and final working plans with typewritten contractor's specifications.[15] Included in this outstanding collection are front and

Fig. 6-3. Advertisement for the Metallak (Nirvana), White Mountain Echo 15, No. 1 (2 July 1892), p. 13. Author's Collection. It was ironical that ads were published proclaiming the opening of a new hotel that never occurred.

rear elevations, end elevations, floor plans for each of the five stories, floor and elevation frame plans, and interior details such as fireplaces, mantels, doorways and wall elevations (see Figs. 6-4 to 6-10). Each of these—some possessing the architect's pencil revisions—reflect Stevens' unusual skill as a draftsman, as well as his conscientious attention to proportion, detail and the interrelationship of architectural elements. While the building itself may be gone, these drawings and plans all but bring it back to life. Regrettably drawings and plans like these for other nineteenth-century White Mountain hotels have yet to surface. So it is indeed fortunate The Metallak collection exists to better inform us about the hotel building type at a time when tourism in the White Mountains was achieving its high point.

A close examination of the Stevens drawings and plans for the hotel provides an opportunity to ana-

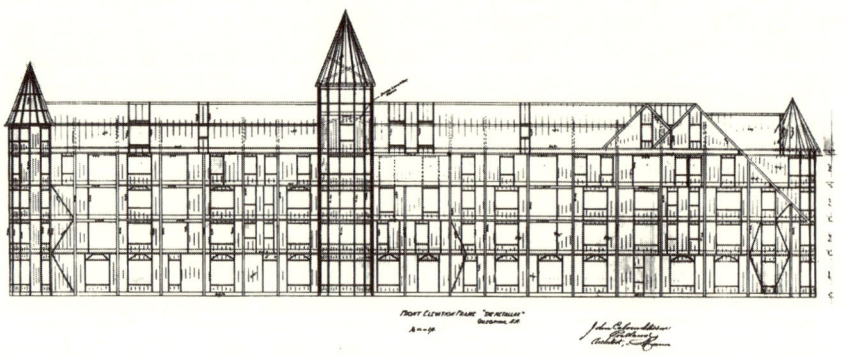

Fig. 6-4. Front elevation frame drawing, "The Metallak," Colebrook, NH, *by John Calvin Stevens. Stevens Collection, Maine Historical Society, Portland. Contractor J.W. Burrowes of Portland and his colleagues used copies of this and other working drawings on site for the construction of The Metallak.*

Fig. 6-5. Rear side elevation drawing, "The Metallak," Colebrook, NH, *by John Calvin Stevens. Stevens Collection, Maine Historical Society, Portland. The architect's pencil alterations in the fenestration are visible in this drawing.*

Fig. 6-6. End elevation, "The Metallak," Colebrook, NH, *by John Calvin Stevens. Stevens Collection, Maine Historical Society, Portland. This drawing illustrates how the architect combined features of the Shingle style with the more "modern" Colonial Revival. A fine Palladian window is contained in the end gable.*

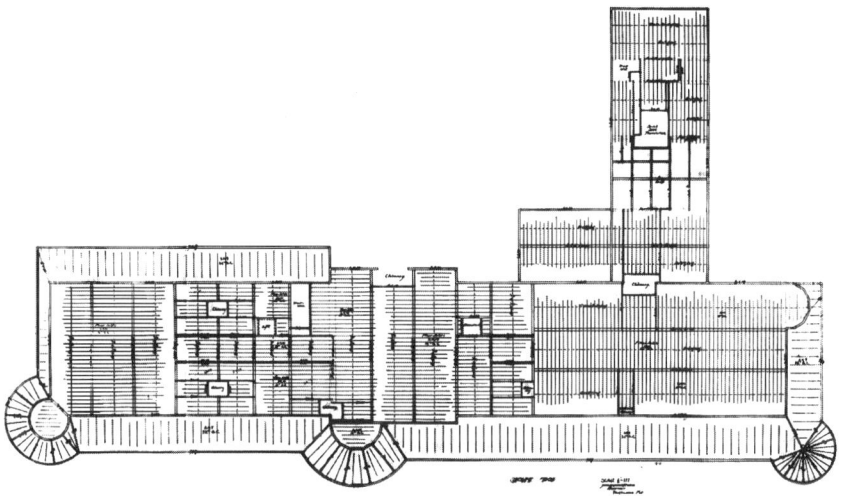

Fig. 6-7. Ground floor and piazza joist and bridging drawing, "The Metallak," Colebrook, NH, *by John Calvin Stevens. Stevens Collection, Maine Historical Society, Portland. The complexities of framing a large wooden building are evident in this exhaustively detailed drawing.*

lyze The Metallak's style and functional layout. Seemingly rooted in and yet rising from the ledgerock of its elevated site, like many of the architect's Maine coast cottages, the wood-frame and shingle complex makes a strong visual statement, combining imposing presence with crisp, fine detail. The powerful sweeping horizontal lines of the roof and piazzas are effectively countered by the vertical accents of the brick chimneys and cylindrical towers that serve to stabilize the building on its mortared stone foundation walls and piers. Other features common to the Shingle style may be observed in the asymmetry of the elevations, the interesting juxtaposition of building materials, and such details as conical tower roofs, bay windows and high-pitched roof dormers. However, the new Colonial Revival style is evident in the piazza, porch, porte cochere and loggia columns, flanking tower window pilasters, balustrades and north-end gable Palladian window. Though not unusual for its time, the L-shaped floor plan efficiently concentrates all service, administrative and recreational facilities on the ground level. The guest

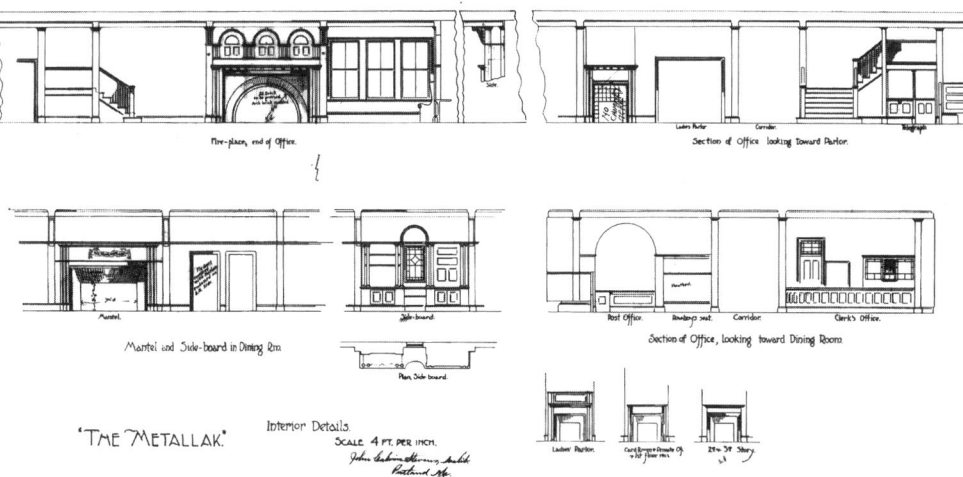

Fig. 6-8. Interior details, "The Metallak," Colebrook, NH, *by John Calvin Stevens. Stevens Collection, Maine Historical Society, Portland. Old photographs reveal that these details, originally conceived for the ill-fated Metallak, were subsequently executed in various hard-woods, brick and tile, in the ground floor public rooms of the Bay of Naples Inn. See Fig. 6-12.*

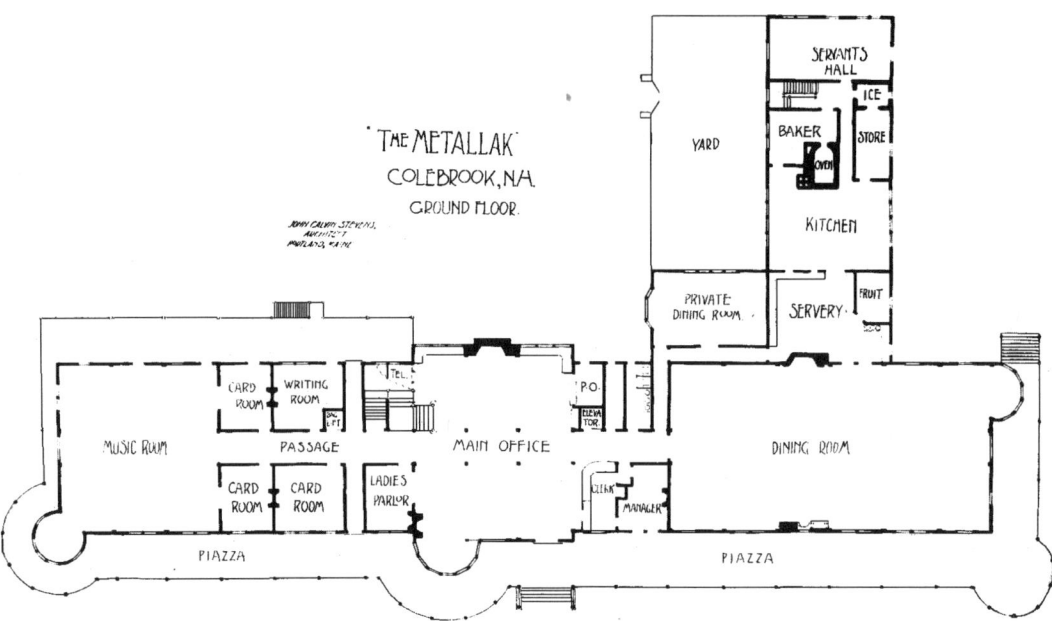

Fig. 6-9. Ground floor plan, "The Metallak," Colebrook, NH, *by John Calvin Stevens. Stevens Collection, Maine Historical Society, Portland. The ground floor plan, opening up on a series of piazzas, possesses a free-flowing quality associated with Shingle style architecture of the 1890s.*

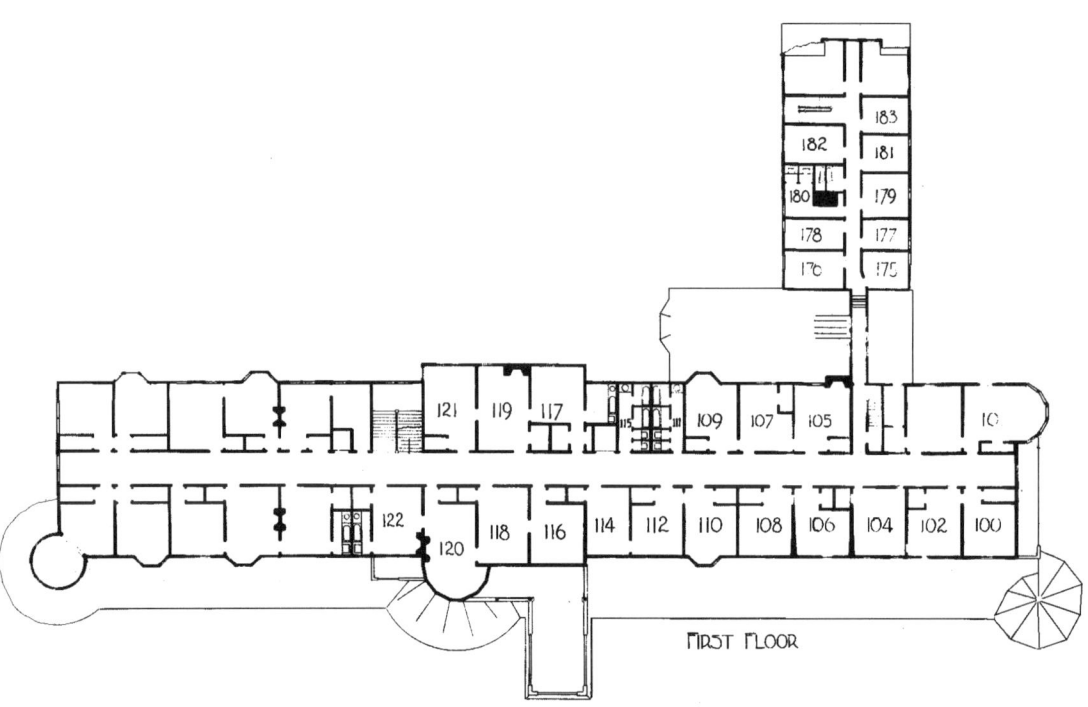

Fig. 6-10. First floor plan, "The Metallak," Colebrook, NH, *by John Calvin Stevens. Stevens Collection, Maine Historical Society, Portland. In this plan, similar to those for the floors above, private baths and closets were intended for most of the guest rooms. The plan was quite flexible, allowing certain rooms to be combined to form suites. Furthermore, only the rooms on the southern end and in the ell were numbered. This suggests that the plan was ultimately adapted for the Bay of Naples Inn, but that the full Metallak design was never completely developed.*

Fig. 6-11. Bay of Naples Inn, Naples, ME, *after designs by John Calvin Stevens. Postcard view, c. 1910. Maine Historic Preservation Commission, Augusta. The hotel was a near reproduction of the southern three-fifths of The Metallak and was built from the architect's plans for the Colebrook complex after it was blown down by a hurricane in 1893.*

rooms with baths are arranged on either side of long end-to-end corridors on the floors above. Had it ever been completed and opened to the public, The Metallak would have quite nicely combined the aesthetic with the practical.

The Successor: The Bay of Naples Inn

John Calvin Stevens' design for The Metallak, or at least a slightly modified major portion of it, was to have a second chance; it would endure for sixty-five years in the form of another hotel complex. In its 21 July 1900 edition, *Among the Clouds* announced:

> Another splendid summer resort, with strong and varied attractions, has been added to the number in the White Mountain region by the opening of the Bay of Naples Inn. The building is an architectural gem,... and all appointments are of first-class order, with the best of modern appliances and improvements to add to the comfort and enjoyment of guests.[16]

Situated on a knoll at the southern end of Long Lake in Naples, Maine, the new hotel faced directly on Mount Washington and the east side of the White Mountains. A comparison of photographs (Fig. 6-11) with the drawings and plans for The Metallak suggests the Bay of Naples Inn was inspired by Stevens' Metallak conception; it was a nearly identical reproduction of the southern three-fifths of the destroyed hotel. The architect's efficient and economical use of the design for The Metallak at another location would prove fortuitous for students of late nineteenth-century architecture.

The Bay of Naples Inn, or the resurrected Metallak, had its origins in the mind of Naples native Charles L. Goodridge. He was the manager of the Sebago Lake, Songo River and Bay of Naples Steamboat Company and needed a large hostelry to accommodate his passengers. A stock company was formed to finance and direct the project, and construction commenced in November 1898 with Stevens as architect. Not only were the designs for The Metallak reused for the new hotel, but it is believed that Goodridge acquired some of the unused wooden trusses from the Colebrook building and used them to create "one of the finest and most commodious dining rooms in the country" with an unobstructed floor area. The Bay of Naples opened on 26 July 1899 with

Fig. 6-12. Main office and lobby, Bay of Naples Inn, Naples, ME. *Photo from promotional booklet,* Bay of Naples Inn, Naples, Maine *(1908). Maine Historic Preservation Commission, Augusta. A comparison of this view with architect John Calvin Stevens' interior details plans for The Metallak (Fig. 6-8) indicates that Stevens used the same interior details for the Bay of Naples rooms. These included the fireplace surround and overmantel, and the stairway rails and balusters.*

80 bedrooms affording space for 160 guests. Supposedly the original plan called for a northern wing beyond the central tower, suggesting that the initial intent had been to duplicate The Metallak. The $50,000 price tag for the completed portion, the same figure as the estimate for the entire Metallak several years earlier, probably precluded completion of the entire project at once—an addition was never seriously contemplated after that time.[17]

Promotional booklets for the hotel spanning the years 1899 to 1922 contain valuable descriptive information, exterior perspective views and interior photographs. Not only did the Bay of Naples apparently closely resemble The Metallak's design on the outside, but also on the inside where the same central office space (Fig. 6-12), kitchen, cavernous dining room, ladies parlor, card rooms, writing room, and single and *en suite* bedrooms with private baths were present. An elevator, electric power, a laundry and local spring water rounded out other available amenities.[18] Curiously, the author(s) of these booklets expressed no particular reverence for Stevens' design for the new hotel remarking that "no attempt was made in its erection toward great architectural beauty." It was further granted, though, that the Bay of Naples was "sufficiently imposing for its surroundings" and "in full accord with them!"[19] Over time the building proved its worth, remaining open through the 1951 season. In 1964, when deemed no longer profitable, it was demolished.[20] Thus the physical legacy of The Metallak, its premature demise now a part of New Hampshire local legend, was ended.

The Symbol

Although its history was brief and not widely known, The Metallak is in the same class as the second Glen House, the enlarged Mount Pleasant House, and the expanded Waumbek, each possessing a distinctive architectural style, being designed by a recognized architect, and dating from the decade 1885-95. These complexes, and the business operations based within them, represented the best of the now quite mature grand resort hotel tradition in the White Mountains. Only in physical size, and in the extent and sophistication of their guest services, were these hostelries equalled or surpassed by the last and most ambitious group of hotels soon to be fully developed in the region—the second or New Profile House, the Mountain View House, the Mount Washington Hotel and The Balsams (see Chapters 7 and 8). But The Metallak and its contemporaries were no less imaginatively conceived, impressive in scale and appointments, or sumptuously fitted out for their era. By fine example they laid the basis for the final burst of grand hotel growth that would occur in the mountains during the first quarter of this century. Of this group of hotels, The Metallak, with the expectations of its backers quickly raised and then crushed by untimely disaster, provided a most apt symbol of the volatility of the regional hotel industry, and presaged its general decline after 1900.

ൊNotes൦

1. *Industrial Journal* (Bangor, ME), 29 April and 15 July 1892; William H. Gifford, *Colebrook: "A Place Up Back of New Hampshire"* (Colebrook, N.H.: The News and Sentinel, Inc., 1970), p. 276; *Coos County Democrat* (Lancaster), 12 March 1890, p. 2, and 28 October 1891, p. 8; *Portland* (ME) *Transcript*, 27 April 1892. The Balsams, ten miles east of Colebrook in Dixville Notch, was a modest fifty-guest inn known as "Dix House" in 1892 and did not receive its current name until it was acquired by Henry S. Hale in 1895. It was greatly enlarged under his direction over the next two decades.

2. A facsimile edition entitled *American Domestic Architecture: A Late Victorian Stylebook by John Calvin Stevens and Albert Winslow Cobb* was published in 1978 (Watkins Glen, NY: American Life Foundation) under the editorship of Earle G. Shettleworth, Jr. and William David Barry.

3. John Calvin Stevens maintained an architectural practice, in partnership with his son John Howard Stevens, from 1906 to 1940. Records at the Maine Historical Society suggest that he may have done work on the Hotel Wentworth (New Castle, NH) in 1909 and for Henry Hale at The Balsams about the same time, although this fact has not been substantiated. It is known, however, that he planned remodelings of two noted Maine hotels—the Poland Springs and the Samoset at Rockland. For information on Stevens see Adolf K. Placzek, ed., *Macmillan Encyclopedia of American Architects*, Vol. 4 (New York: The Free Press, 1982), p. 130; Withey, *Biographical Dictionary of American Architects (Deceased)*, pp. 572-73; Stillman, et al., *Architecture and Ornament in Late 19th-Century America*, p. 66; Jane Gregory, "The Shingle Style," *Down East* 32, No. 7 (February 1986): 49-51, 69, 71, 110; *Architectural Forum* 72 (April 1940), p. 112 (obituary); John Calvin Stevens, II, and Earle G. Shettleworth, Jr., *John Calvin Stevens, Domestic Architecture, 1890-1930* (Scarborough, ME: Harp Publications, 1990).

4. *Portland Transcript*, 27 April 1892; *Industrial Journal* (Bangor), 29 April 1892.

5. Specifications for The Metallak, Colebrook, N.H., n.d., John Calvin Stevens Collection, Maine Historical Society, Portland.

6. *Industrial Journal* (Bangor), 15 July 1892.

7. Richard F. Leavitt, *Colebrook Yesterday: A Picture Visit Through the Old Home Town* (Colebrook, NH: Colebrook Public Library, 1970), p. 43; excerpt from *United States Hotel* (1892).

8. *WME* 15, No. 1 (2 July 1892), p. 13.

9. *Lancaster Gazette*, 26 October 1892, p. 3, and 29 March 1893, p. 3; *Industrial Journal* (Bangor), 28 April 1893; *Portland* (ME) *Daily Press*, 22 April 1893, p. 5.

10. *Manchester Union*, 22 April 1893, p. 2.

11. *Berlin Independent*, 26 April 1893, p. 5.

12. *White Mountain Republic Journal* (Littleton), 29 April 1893, p. 1.

13. In his 1970 book, *Colebrook Yesterday* (p. 42), Richard Leavitt notes that part of the old cellar hole was still visible, though hidden by bushes and trees on the abandoned site.

14. Gifford, *Colebrook*, p. 333; supplement to *The Sunday Telegram* (Portland, ME), 6 March 1892.

15. These are part of a larger collection of Stevens drawings and other papers owned by the Society. In addition, a substantial collection of Stevens drawings and plans was donated by his son John Howard Stevens to the Avery Architectural and Fine Arts Library at Columbia University in 1944. There is only one drawing of The Metallak (see Fig. 6-1), however, at the Avery.

16. *ATC* 24, No. 8 (21 July 1900), p. 4.

17. *Portland* (ME) *Sunday Telegram*, 22 November 1964, p. 2C; Robert J. Dingley, *Now I Will Tell You... The Story of Naples, Maine, Its History and Legends* (Naples, ME: Naples Historical Society, 1979), pp. 28-29. In anticipation of the complex's completion, the first known promotional booklet for the hotel (see note 18, below), published in 1899, displayed an altered version of Stevens' front-elevation perspective of The Metallak (see Fig. 6-1).

18. *The Bay of Naples Inn, Naples, Maine* (Naples, ME: Bay of Naples Inn, 1899); *The Bay of Naples Inn, Naples, Maine* (Naples, ME: Bay of Naples Inn, 1900); *From Maine* (Naples, ME: Bay of Naples Inn, 1906); *The Bay of Naples Inn, Naples, Maine* (Naples, ME: Bay of Naples Inn, 1908); and *Bay of Naples Hotel* (Naples, ME: Bay of Naples Inn, 1922). Floor diagrams, used for guests to select rooms, are contained in the 1906 and 1908 booklets.

19. *Bay of Naples Inn, Naples, Maine* (Naples, ME: Bay of Naples Inn, 1910).

20. *Portland* (ME) *Sunday Telegram*, 22 November 1964, p. 2C.

Fig. 7-1. The Second Glen House, Pinkham Notch, NH, *etching after a front elevation perspective sketch by Francis H. Fassett, by the Robinson Engraving Company, Boston, 1881. Dartmouth College Library. This rendition of the hotel is very likely derived from an earlier presentation drawing by the architect.*

CHAPTER 7

The Full Evolution of the Building Type: The Second Glen House, the New Profile House, and the Mountain View House

THE SECOND GLEN HOUSE, the second or New Profile House, and the Mountain View House are outstanding late nineteenth-century examples of the White Mountain grand resort hotel tradition and merit careful attention. Along with The Metallak, they form a small and exclusive group of tourist complexes whose architectural histories are among the most compelling of the regional hostelries of their era. Unlike The Metallak, however, these three significant guest establishments lack substantial documentary records. As a result their stories, like so many of the White Mountain hotels, are based solely on visual, oral and secondhand printed sources. Nonetheless, critical narratives of each may be compiled with sufficient depth to confirm their legacies in the annals of White Mountain hotel history. In many respects, they were as important, architecturally and historically, as the region's two largest surviving operational hotels, the Mount Washington and The Balsams. Sadly, only the Mountain View House remains standing today, currently closed and awaiting an uncertain future.

From Ashes to Ashes: The Second Glen House

I just come up through Pinkham Notch
    And to the Glen House I did stop.
They have built a new house and call it Glen,
    And it is kept by C. R. Milliken.
The top of the house is painted green
    And is the most wonderful house that
      ever was seen;
And Soloman's Temple did not begin
    With the finish of the Glen.
              FRANKLIN LEAVITT (1885)[1]

This stilted but illuminating verse by the renowned Lancaster guide and map maker appropriately introduces a treatment of the second Glen House, one of the true masterpieces of White Mountain hotel architecture. From Leavitt's few lines it is evident that this expansive, flamboyant, and splendid edifice must have been very special. Conceived on a more ambitious scale than The Metallak at Colebrook , it serves as a suitable bridge to a discussion of the larger complexes that were soon to be built.

The destruction of the first Glen House at Green's

[191]

Fig. 7-2. "Glen House, White Mountains, N. H.," *advertising engraving from Lucy Crawford,* The History of the White Mountains . . . *(1886 ed.), p. 179. Author's Collection. The first or south portion of the hotel, erected in 1884-85, is shown here.*

Grant in the fall of 1884 (see Chapter 2) was a severe blow to the proprietors, the traveling public and the economy of the district east of Mount Washington and the rest of the Presidential Range. In *Chronicles of the White Mountains*, Frederick Kilbourne refers to this loss as a "public misfortune," further noting that "without a hotel the region was at once thrown back into its primitive solitude."[2] Of particular economic significance was the loss of a vital link in the chain of White Mountain grand resort hotels; a twenty-mile gap was left between the hostelries of Jackson and Gorham. Owner Charles Milliken was not one to allow his great property resource to lie fallow, however, and, responding to pressures for a new hotel on the same terrace site, he took prompt steps to rebuild.[3]

The opportunity to build anew was in many respects a blessing for Milliken and his devoted guest clientele. Although the former house had gained wide fame throughout the Northeast over three decades, it had grown in a haphazard fashion and had become inefficient and outmoded. So a strange quirk of fate provided Milliken the chance to construct a modern hotel that he hoped would fare better in the fiercely competitive White Mountain tourist marketplace. In his promotional publication, *The Glen House Book*, the owner recounted his scheme for the new building as it took shape:

> It was now determined to erect a structure homogenous in all its parts, adapted throughout to the requirements of the day, attractive in its architecture and elegant in its appointments,—in short, a house in which simple elegance, solid comfort, and studied attention to every possible want, however minute, from an electric bell to an elevator, should announce to the most fastidious guest a first-class hotel conducted on first-class principles.[4]

Selected as designer to enact this scheme was Francis H. Fassett, the accomplished Portland architect, whose firm would plan and execute extensive

Fig. 7-3. Second Glen House, Pinkham Notch, NH, *photograph from glass plate negative, c. 1887. Douglas Philbrook, Gorham, NH. This lavish, Queen Anne-style hotel was erected in two major stages between 1884 and 1887, and accommodated up to 500 guests.*

renovations to the Mount Pleasant House at Bretton Woods in 1894-95 (see Chapter 4).[5] The only visual evidence of Fassett's work on the second Glen House is a superb 1887 etching (Fig. 7-1) of the hotel, probably derived from an earlier front-elevation perspective presentation drawing made by the architect before construction commenced in 1884. In some ways this lovely view is conjectural, for later photographs of the completed building (see Fig. 7-3) reveal a somewhat less grandiose structure, lacking some of the envisioned embellishment and the proposed north wing with ell.[6]

In addition to studying this etching, and photographs and advertising illustrations, one must turn entirely to printed sources to narrate the origins and development of the second Glen House. These publications reveal that Fassett's plan for the new house was consummated in two stages over a three-year period; the magnificent and palatial complex rose Phoenix-like from the ashes of its predecessor between the fall of 1884 and the summer of 1887. The first phase, involving the southern half of the building, was completed (along with two new stables and service buildings) in time to take in guests during the 1885 social season (Fig. 7-2). Officially opened on August 1, it had an advertised maximum capacity of 250 people and was intended to be the "parlor wing" of the still-to-be-finished hotel. *Among the Clouds* relates that work on the second, L-shaped phase of the complex began in October 1885 and, although scheduled for completion the following summer, it was substantially and inexplicably delayed.

In July 1887, the hotel finally achieved its full growth, with double the number of bedroom spaces (Fig. 7-3). Joining Charles Milliken in the management of the greatly enlarged operation were two new partners, Captain E. A. Gillett, who had hotel experience in the Catskills and the South, and Louis P. Roberts of the Parker House in Boston.[7] Fitted "with every appliance for comfort in accordance with

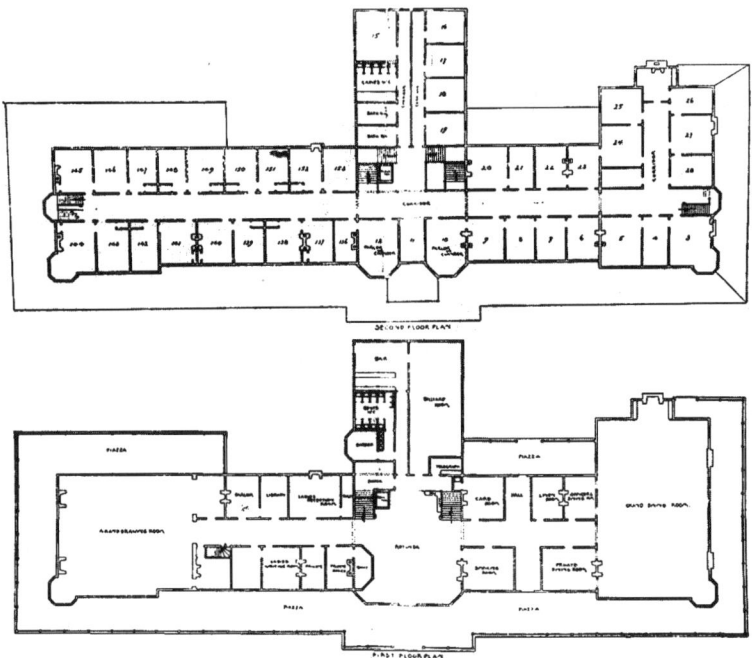

Fig. 7-4. First and Second Floor Plans, Second Glen House, Pinkham Notch, NH. *Dartmouth College Library. Architect Francis Fassett's plan concentrated all public space onthe first floor and the sleeping rooms on the three floors above.*

refined taste," the rebuilt structure was now fully operational. Its piazzas offered guests magnificent "views of Carter Dome and Wildcat to the south, the valley of the Peabody to the north and the noble peaks of the Presidential Range to the west."[8]

Milliken's 1889 *Glen House Book* describes the new hotel with pride. Appearing at the end of the passage is the inscription of "F. H. Fassett, Architect" suggesting that perhaps he, and not Milliken, was the author:

Architecturally the Glen House is one of the finest of the kind in New England. It is of the English Cottage [Queen Anne] style; the roof-line is well broken by gables, which are well ornamented by showing timber construction. At each angle of the front are octagonal pavilions which are carried above the roof-line and terminate in curved roofs. The roof, with its gables, dormers, and turrets, has a very picturesque effect, and harmonizes perfectly with the surrounding scenery.

The building has a frontage of nearly three hundred feet, is three stories in height above the basement, and covers an area of seventeen thousand feet, exclusive of the verandas and bays.

The veranda is sixteen feet wide and has a length of about four hundred and fifty feet, making one of the finest promenades under cover to be found among the White Mountains.

Many rooms in the front have large bay-windows which, with the projections of the pavilions and chimneys, break the front with a pleasing variety.

The interior of the building is one of the most pleasing of its kind in this country [Fig. 7-4]. Many of the rooms are in suites of two to five; all are large, and nearly every sleeping-room is provided with a roomy clothes-closet. Open wood fireplaces are in every suite and many single rooms. The main feature of the first floor is the grand rotunda, which is forty-two by forty-eight feet [Fig. 7-5]. At the right, as you enter, is a very spacious and ornate fireplace. At the left is the office, and in the rear are two broad flights of stairs, in the wells of which is located the [Pullman] elevator. The ceiling is finished in wood, the walls are wainscoted to a

[194]

height of six feet above the floors, and the rest tinted in pleasing colors. Stairways are plentiful throughout the house, providing ample means of escape in case of fire.

The parlors and dining-rooms are designed on a magnificent scale, well-lighted and well-ventilated, and having open fireplaces. Besides the parlors and dining-rooms on the first floor, there are reception, conversation, card, smoking, and billiard rooms.

The corridors throughout the house are broad and well-lighted; there are no dark passage-ways in the building.

The sanitary arrangements are of the very best,—the plumbing having been done in the most scientific manner, every closet being well ventilated.

The water supply is sufficient to flush the whole cistern in the most ample manner.

The whole exterior is painted in the most pleasing colors [various shades of green and other subdued tints] and has a very artistic effect.[9]

Supplementing this descriptive account is an 1887 excerpt from the *White Mountain Echo* that describes the other major public rooms of the hotel:

The grand parlor occupies the entire end of the southeast wing. Here are three large fireplaces, elaborately finished in terra cotta and pressed brick; the ceiling is paneled in wood; the polished floor, covered in the centre with a magnificent rug which is of more than ordinary interest. Made in India for Queen Victoria, to be used in Windsor Castle, it eventually came into possession of a wealthy Philadelphian, a Mr. Sturgis, and was recently, through a Boston firm, purchased for the Glen House. The dining-hall, enlarged this season to a seating capacity of 300, with its huge fire-places, handsome draperies and portieres, and frescoed ceilings, is one of the prettiest in the country. Here the [college] student waiters attend to the wants of the guests and richly deserve the praise lavished on their efforts. In the new addi-

Fig. 7-5. "The Rotunda and Office," Second Glen House, Pinkham Notch, NH, *photograph from Charles R. Milliken,* The Glen House Book *(1891 ed.), p. 28. Author's Collection. The primary focus of the first floor, this generous space featured a finished wooden ceiling and wooden wall wainscoting.*

tion also is the club-room, an apartment of unique design, which proves attractive to ladies as to gentlemen.[10]

Sumptuously appointed, no expense was spared to provide the height of luxury and convenience. These interior benefits, combined with a picturesque asymmetrical facade that openly invited patronage, made the second Glen House a model of aesthetic and functional distinction.

While the new hotel gained immediate favor with an affluent clientele and seemingly possessed every feature and amenity that mountain sojourners could desire, its business success was short-lived; the prosperity of the pre-1885 years did not return. In large part this was because of the hotel's distance from the railroad as well as mounting competition from new and expanding grand resort hotels to the west of the Presidential Range. In a curiously ironic way it was perhaps merciful that the magnificent structure caught fire on the evening of 16 July 1893, soon after its official opening for another summer season. In just over an hour it was reduced to smoldering ruins and ashes. Once again the site, known to this day as "the Glen," was desolate but for a few remaining outbuildings. Operational for only a brief period, the hotel, despite its supreme architectural quality, failed to acquire much in the way of tradition, and its social history has remained largely shrouded in obscurity.[11]

Fig. 7-6. Help's Quarters, Second Glen House, Pinkham Notch, NH, *photograph, c. 1890, photographer unknown. Douglas Philbrook, Gorham, NH. In 1901, the former hotel property was acquired by E. Libby & Sons Company of Gorham, and the help's quarters were opened as the third Glen House.*

Fig. 7-7. "Sketch of New Glen House for E. Libby and Sons Co., Gorham, N. H.," *by Marland A. Perkins, Architect, Boston, MA. Douglas Philbrook, Gorham, NH. The Libby Company commissioned a plan for a new Glen House around 1910, but the hostelry was never built.*

The embers from the fire had barely cooled before speculation about rebuilding began; it would continue for many years. At first Charles Milliken declined to commit to such a momentous project, preferring to limit his business interests at the site to the stage line, the wagon transit on the Mount Washington Carriage Road and the hotel farm. Still the regional tourist newspapers persisted in presenting a strong case for another guest establishment there. Only a month after the fire the *White Mountain Echo* observed, "The Glen is a natural location for a hotel, and . . . this is a location which will not long remain vacant." In August 1899, *Among the Clouds* proclaimed that an electric railroad was to be constructed linking Berlin, Gorham and the Glen, and that Milliken had plans to build a new 250-room hotel on the spot occupied by the first two hostelries. Surely "the spirit of enterprise and progress" was in the air, but for unexplained reasons, neither project materialized.[12]

In the spring of 1901, the Glen secured a new lease on life when Milliken sold the former hotel property and related business holdings to the Gorham firm of E. Libby & Sons Company. The Libbys remodeled the modest building that had served as the help's quarters for the second Glen House into a small forty-guest inn also named "Glen House" (Fig. 7-6). The firm also reactivated the old stables as the headquarters for renewed wagon service up and down Mount Washington. In 1906, the Libby Company purchased the Pingree stock in the carriage road, firmly consolidating its entrepreneurial interests on the east side of Mount Washington.

During the decade prior to World War I, demand for increased sleeping space prompted the company around 1910 to commission Boston architect Marland A. Perkins to prepare a plan for a new medium-sized hotel building. A surviving front elevation sketch shows the influence of the then popular Bungalow and Prairie styles (Fig. 7-7). Although construction of this building was never successfully realized, this did not stop the occasional rumor of the possibility of a new hotel at the Glen.[13] While this may yet come to pass it appears that with the burning of the second Glen House the era of gracious living at the Glen has come to an end. The mammoth grand resort hotel, and "the hundreds of fashionably dressed guests, the immense dining room with its exquisite table appointments, the fine orchestra and the glamorous balls, the gay coaching parties, and the other trappings of society"[14] belong to another age and in all likelihood will never return.

Sylvanus D. Morgan and the New Profile House

In 1905 Colonel Charles H. Greenleaf, his sponsoring Profile and Flume Hotels Company and the cottage owners, after long deliberation, made the

Fig. 7-8. New Profile House, Franconia Notch, NH, *photograph, c. 1925, taken for* The Automobile Blue Books *(New York, Chicago and San Francisco). Douglas Philbrook, Gorham, NH. Erected by Lisbon, NH, contractor Sylvanus D. Morgan, this magnificent resort hotel mimicked the form of the first Profile House but introduced new stylistic elements and building materials.*

decision to replace the deteriorating first Profile House with a new modern edifice (see Chapter 2). At the same time they decided to retain all existing cottages and other outbuildings, preserving the appealing self-contained community character of the still relatively isolated Franconia Notch resort establishment. For promotional purposes, they called the second Profile House the "New Profile House." It was to perpetuate the grand hotel design tradition established by its predecessor and the first Glen House, while adopting the best features of the major hostelries constructed after 1885. For ideas and inspiration, Greenleaf and the other company stockholders undoubtedly turned to three White Mountain examples of suitable size and splendor—the second Glen House, as well as the rebuilt Mount Pleasant House (see Chapter 4) and the Mount Washington Hotel (see Chapter 8), both at Bretton Woods.

Like so many other regional owner/proprietors preceding him, Colonel Greenleaf conceived the over-all plan for the new building and personally supervised its construction phases. The major share of credit for successful completion of the project, however, must go to Sylvanus D. Morgan (1857-1940) of Lisbon, renowned to this day as the White Mountain's most prolific hotel builder. Based on his previous work, there is every reason to believe that Morgan, translating Greenleaf's ideas into formal designs, performed the role of architect, also serving as materials procurer and chief contractor. As a young man in Bethlehem, Morgan learned the hotel business as an employee at the palatial Maplewood. He further developed his skills under the tutelage of Frank Abbott, owner of the Uplands (see Chapter 4), who took him south where he participated in building two of the Abbott family hotels. Returning north he again settled in Bethlehem, relocating to Franconia where he built and managed the Elmwood House, a small inn, for five years until it burned. During this period he built additions to the Uplands for his old friend Abbott, as well as to the Forest Hills Hotel in Franconia (see Chapter 5), and erected the entire Hotel Lookoff at Sugar Hill (see Chapter 5). After moving to Lisbon where he established a con-

Fig. 7-9. Lobby, New Profile House, Franconia Notch, NH, *photograph from* Franconia Notch, White Mountains, N. H. *(c. 1910). Author's Collection. This, the grand foyer, with its rich Colonial Revival decor, contained red rugs that contrasted with the green tiles of the fireplaces.*

tracting firm, Morgan is believed to have followed the New Profile House commission with contracts for the construction of an addition to the Mount Washington Hotel, the third Mount Washington Summit House, and enlargements to The Balsams. While he was primarily known for his hotel work, Morgan was simultaneously designing and building numerous houses, schools, commercial blocks and other structures. His legacy in New Hampshire's North Country has been widespread and enduring, with the New Profile House perhaps his proudest accomplishment.[15]

On 1 October 1905 the first Profile House was systematically demolished to make way for the new hotel. Only a small portion was saved for incorporation into the building. Under Morgan's experienced direction, the shell of the new hotel was raised and closed in before December 1 by a crew of 300 men who took up temporary residence in the Notch. With the aid of steam heat and large stoves, work continued all winter, which, quite fortunately, proved to be one of the mildest on record. Throughout the spring, Colonel and Mrs. Greenleaf, with the assistance of house staff, carefully selected the furnishings, reusing some of the pieces from the former hotel. Finally, without the ceremony that so often accompanied the christening of new hotels in the mountains, the New Profile House opened its doors and registered its first guests on 1 July 1906.[16]

The overall design of the New Profile House, while borrowed to a large extent from the previous hotel, introduced more fashionable stylistic details and up-to-date technology. Generous in scale and four stories in height, it was taller than the first Profile House and yet displayed a markedly similar balanced main facade, its central pavilion flanked by nearly identical east and west wings (Fig. 7-8). The floor plan was also T-shaped, but here the resemblance to the old structure ended. Embracing Greenleaf's vision of "a Colonial-style palace in a vast wilderness,"[17] Morgan erected a building with crisper lines and plainer embellishments.

Protected by low intersecting hipped roofs drawn from Federal-era New England, the New Profile House possessed distinctive classical cornice brackets, as well as veranda columns and balustrades. Reflecting the influence of seventeenth-century New England houses and their impact on the late nineteenth-century Shingle style, expansive planar wall surfaces were sheathed with unstained shingles. The

Fig. 7-10. Dining Room, New Profile House, Franconia Notch, NH, *photograph from Franconia Notch, White Mountains, N. H. (c. 1910). Author's Collection. Octagonal in form this spectacular space measured ninety feet across. It was illuminated by plate glass windows and a dome roof with side lights.*

fenestration was correspondingly simple and traditional, with six-over-six double-sash windows, both single and paired, set between green shutters on all story levels. The veranda extended from the west wing across the south front of the structure, and partly around the east side where it ended at an auto entrance (later supplied with a porte cochere). Another porte cochere, intended solely for the use of horse-drawn carriages and stagecoaches, was attached to the central pavilion. Although it would be remiss to call the building anything other than Colonial Revival stylistically, it did show evidences of mid-western Prairie influence in its horizontality and general massing, its main roof and veranda lines. In certain respects, it was reminiscent of the coastal hotel architecture of its era more than its peers in the mountain resorts of the Northeast. However, it fit comfortably into its environment and drew positive assessments from contemporary architectural critics.[18]

The July 1906 issue of *Among the Clouds* comprehensively described the interior of the New Profile House:

> Entering the vestibule it needs only a glance to see that you are in a ... far more magnificent house than the old. A grand foyer [160 by 50 feet] [Fig. 7-9] with walls richly decorated in red and handsome white columns makes beautiful vistas to right, to left and straight ahead. The effect is heightened by the rugs and the great fireplaces lined with green tiles.
>
> Opposite the door the middle wing leads to the magnificent new [two-story] dining hall [seating 400 guests] [Fig. 7-10], which is octagonal in form, measuring 90 feet across and having a floor area of 8300 square feet.... Large landscape windows look out on Eagle Cliff and Bald and Cannon Mountains, and it is overtopped by a cupola 35 feet high.
>
> The prevailing tone in the decoration is green and the same wild grape vine is used for decorating about the lower portion of the cupola which appears on the dainty china. The dining room connects at the left with the spacious and airy kitchen, which with its accessory rooms was built last year.
>
> Off the corridor in the central wing are the porter's room, with freight elevator, the post office and souvenir stand. Opposite the post office is a well lighted recess fitted up for a writing room, with handsome octagonal tables.

The fine staircase is on the right [of the front entrance] where the central wing joins the main house, with two flights meeting in a common landing. On the left is the office, spacious and convenient, and beyond it the stenographer's room and Colonel Greenleaf's private office. Across the corridor are small reception rooms for ladies, with lavatories.

In the west wing is the only part of the old house which remains, a part of the old dining room, which is remodeled into an elegant ball room. Between it and the front of the house are the cafe, men's toilet rooms and billiard room.

In the east wing, on the ground floor, are several reception rooms and card parlors and a number of sleeping room suites, and at the extreme end a cozy sun parlor.

Up stairs are two hundred sleeping rooms, arranged in suites and with an outside bathroom between every two rooms. It is needless to say that the plumbing and furnishings are of the very finest. Every room has a large closet, electric lights and steam heat. In every wing on each of the upper floors are baths and toilet rooms for men and women, in addition to the great number of private baths.[19]

Other features included a special breakfast room off the main dining room and a palm garden between the west and middle wings.[20] The indoor arrangement of the hotel remained unaltered until 1922, when the Abbott family rearranged certain public rooms (lobby, office, ball room, etc.) and redecorated the entire interior.[21]

The new main hotel continued to serve as the core of Colonel Greenleaf's self-proclaimed Alpine village (Fig. 7-11). By 1921, the number of privately owned guest cottages, positioned in rows on the side of Cannon Mountain, had grown to twenty, embodying a variety of styles from the Stick to the Colonial Revival. These separate wooden buildings, each containing from eight to seventeen bedrooms, were arranged on terraces and connected to the hotel by covered walkways with red carpeting. The extensive property also featured a guest annex, employees' dormitories (including the remodelled "Lafayette Cottage") capable of housing 300 people, a laundry, a powerhouse, a large stable building (see Chapter 2), various railroad structures, a 200-car garage and several other buildings all designed to meet specialized functions. Souvenir shops and gazebos were scattered about the property, and a boat house and bath house were situated at Echo Lake. At its peak capaci-

Fig. 7-11. New Profile House and Cottages, Franconia Notch, NH, *photograph, c. 1910, photographer unknown. Douglas Philbrook, Gorham, NH. The hotel was the centerpiece of Colonel Charles H. Greenleaf's "Alpine village."*

ty the immense complex accommodated up to 600 guests and encompassed 11,000 acres spread over valley and mountain property.[22]

In 1921, at the age of eighty, Colonel Greenleaf decided to retire from the hotel business and to sell the New Profile House and the marvelous lands and natural attractions that surrounded it. He immediately extended a purchase option to the firm of Frank O. Abbott and Son (Karl L.), at the time the owner of the Uplands in Bethlehem (see Chapter 4) and the Forest Hills Hotel in Franconia (see Chapter 5). In his 1950 book *Open for the Season*, Karl Abbott recalled being summoned by Greenleaf to the Profile House, asked if he "planned growing up to be a big hotel man," and being offered the property. Karl formed a syndicate to finance the acquisition and at age thirty-two, assumed the proprietorship of the hotel. He always regarded this opportunity as the high point of his career—the Profile "was strictly 'big time,' comparing favorably with such famed resorts as the Poland Spring House, the Mount Washington at Bretton Woods, the Homestead at Hot Springs, and the Greenbriar at White Sulpher."[23]

The Abbott ownership, however, was to be all too brief. On Thursday, 2 August 1923, while Karl Abbott was returning from a business trip to South Carolina, the entire main hostelry, adjacent cottages and major outbuildings were destroyed by perhaps the most complete, tragic and celebrated fire in White Mountain hotel history (Fig. 7-12). For a brief time firefighters expressed confidence that the complex could be saved, but inadequate water pressure made this impossible and some twenty-six buildings were leveled in just over four hours. Ironically, this catastrophic episode shared nationwide headlines with news of the unexpected death the same day of President Warren G. Harding in San Francisco. Although theories abounded, the real cause of the conflagration was never concretely determined.

In *Open for the Season* Abbott recounted a poignant scene described by one staff member as the fire spread rapidly to the dining room wing of the hotel:

> . . . it was an awe-inspiring sight to look through the great plate-glass windows and watch the splendid dining room with all its snowy Irish linen and gleaming glass and silver set up for the noonday meal, with the bright flames playing through the dome.[24]

The day of this great holocaust saw many acts of generosity and heroism, without a single loss of life, but also unethical if not illegal conduct, as sightseers arrived in the Notch from miles around, a few looting furnishings and other articles that had been removed from the buildings "like vultures to the kill." Before dark over 200 guests, some without belongings, had been moved to other area hotels, and 275 staff members had been paid a full summer's wages and many relocated to new jobs elsewhere in the mountains.[25]

Karl Abbott told of returning to "our beautiful little mountain community" at mid-day on August 3. Met by "an area of smoldering ashes" and desolate, charred brick chimneys, he naturally wondered what the future would hold for the site and Franconia Notch. Upon inspecting the ruins late in the afternoon, his father reportedly counseled him to "always look at the rising sun, never the setting sun." Karl's first thought was that a new Profile House should rise on the site of the old. That evening he telephoned an old friend, Boston architect Harold Field Kellogg, and asked him to prepare rough drawings for a new grand resort hotel in the form of a large Swiss chalet to be situated south of the old site overlooking Profile Lake. Kellogg worked incessantly for the next twenty-four hours and soon arrived at the Notch with the plans to begin discussions with the Abbotts.[26]

Fig. 7-12. The Burning of the New Profile House, Franconia Notch, NH, 2 August 1923, *photograph by unidentified amateur photographer. Sugar Hill Historical Museum. The fire was considered by many the most disastrous in White Mountain hotel history, leveling the main house, the cottages and all major outbuildings.*

At this meeting a critical decision was made that would forever affect the future of the Franconia Notch region. After two or three days of discussions between Kellogg and the Abbotts, they reached a consensus not to proceed with the building project; for all intents and purposes this decision ended the era of luxurious summer residency in the Notch. Although newspapers continued to report that a new hotel was imminent, Karl, persuaded by the vision of his father, ultimately committed the family company to the sale of the property with the intent that it would become a state-owned and administered public park. Finally, after some negotiations, the lands were sold for $400,000, one half provided by the State of New Hampshire and the other half by the Society for the Protection of New Hampshire Forests. James J. Storrow of Boston generously donated $100,000 to the Society, and the Society raised the remainder of its share with the assistance of the New Hampshire Federation of Women's Clubs. On 16 September 1928, with Governor Huntley N. Spaulding and other state officials in attendance, the Franconia Notch Forest Reservation and Memorial Park was dedicated in an impressive and history-making ceremony at the Notch. The sudden demise of the New Profile House complex, although a serious setback to the White Mountain hotel industry, created unprecedented opportunities for environmental preservation and broad public benefit. The now-titled "Franconia Notch State Park," containing the Old Man of the Mountain, the Flume and other spectacular sights, has indeed been "a fit successor to the vanished greatness of the old hotel." Sylvanus Morgan had built well, but the natural assets of the Notch had quite properly outlasted his human handiwork.[27]

The Dodge Family's Mountain View House

Better than any other examples in the region, the Mountain View House at Whitefield and The Balsams at Dixville Notch illustrate the architectural evolution from a small-scale precursor to full-blown grand resort hotel complex on a single site. Fortunately both hostelries still stand—The Balsams alive with activity and completely operational; the Moun-

Fig. 7-13. The Dodge Farmhouse and Mountain View House, Whitefield, NH, *photograph, c. 1870, photographer unknown. Whitefield Historical Society. Erected in 1866, the initial Dodge hotel was a small country inn, accommodating about twenty patrons.*

tain View, in stark contrast, closed down, silent and empty, awaiting a resolution of its fate under new ownership. While most of the regional hotels have come under the control of large corporations in the twentieth century, both The Balsams and the Mountain View have continued to be owned and managed by private parties or small partnerships. But in one instance worth noting, the ownership and management history of the Mountain View is unique—remarkably, this White Mountain hotel remained in the hands of a single family, the Dodges, for over a century, from its inception in the 1860s until its sale in 1979. Benefiting from the continuity and stability provided by the Dodges over this extended period, the venerable resort establishment evolved logically in response to the demands of the tourist market, embodying principles of conservative, functional design and sound construction.

Legend has it that the Mountain View House began quite by accident. Supposedly, on a rainy summer night in 1865, a stagecoach carrying two well-to-do passengers was passing through Whitefield on its way north from Boston to Montreal. On the hills two miles outside of the village the stage encountered impossibly muddy roads, was disabled, and could proceed no farther that night without repairs. To seek refuge the passengers were directed to the small farmhouse of Mr. and Mrs. William F. Dodge, situated one-half mile to the east along a narrow dirt road. Reaching their hilltop objective, the wet and weary travelers were warmly welcomed by the

THE FULL EVOLUTION OF THE BUILDING TYPE

Fig. 7-14. Mountain View House, Whitefield, NH, *photograph, c. 1880, by W. C. Rideou, Landscape Photographer, Portland, ME. Author's Collection. The growing hotel was doubled in size in 1880 with the addition of a compatible Second Empire-style wing to the older building core.*

farmer and his wife who provided them with fine overnight accommodations and delicious food. The next morning after the weather had cleared the guests were awestruck by the magnificent, nearly 360-degree panoramic view—the Franconia Mountains to the south; the hills of Dalton and the Green Mountains of Vermont to the west; Mount Washington and the Presidential Range to the east; and the Kilkenny mountains to the north, vistas that would ultimately endow the Mountain View House with its name (it became fondly known as "The View") and contribute to its broad reputation. Impressed by the hospitality of the Dodges and the beautiful, inviting natural surroundings, the guests prevailed upon their hosts to permit them to stay a few days longer. The following summer they returned for a sojourn of several weeks, inspiring the Dodges to enlarge their farmhouse to take in vacationers. In a sequence comparable to several other great White Mountain hostelries, this episode launched the development of the Mountain View House toward grand resort hotel status. Ultimately, it would eclipse all but a few rivals in the regional hotel business.[28]

The physical growth of the Mountain View House began in 1866 when the Dodges opened what was initially a modest country inn and then attached an addition to the east end of the original one-and-a-half-story, Cape-Cod-type farmhouse. That first

Fig. 7-15. "Mountain View House, Whitefield, N. H.," *photograph of sketch from* Town and City Atlas of the State of New Hampshire *(1892), p. 296. Author's Collection. This view depicts the hotel after the 1884 and 1891-92 extensions. The original art work was sold at the 1989 auction.*

[203]

addition was a plain two-and-a-half-story, pitched-roof guest annex recalling the earliest highway inns in the mountains (Fig. 7-13). Displaying understated Greek Revival details, the most striking feature of this new wing was the two-story piazza set under the front roof overhang and supported by square Doric columns. As soon as the mortgage on the first addition had been paid, the Dodges built in 1872 a new three-story building that took the place of the old farmhouse on the west side. Raising the capacity to fifty guests, this second enlargement was totally "modern" in its Second Empire-style architectural trappings. The most pronounced was its hipped-on-Mansard roof, topped at its center by a cubical cupola or observatory with a pyramidal roof and finial. Other noteworthy details were the wide entablatures with regularly spaced cornice brackets, the flat hood-molds over the windows and doorways, the corner quoining, and the delicately fabricated front piazza with fragile, stylized square posts. The structure's overall form and embellishment were maintained when the Dodges doubled it in size by another addition to the west side in 1880 (Fig. 7-14).[29]

Operating from the first by the corporate name, W. F. Dodge & Son, in 1884 the Mountain View House came under the proprietorship of Van Herbert Dodge, one of Frank's two sons, assisted by his wife Alice. His tenure, which lasted until 1919, saw the development of the hotel from a medium-sized country inn to a substantial resort complex. Simultaneous with the change in management, the main building was again expanded to the west, opening for the 1884 summer season with space for 100 patrons. In 1891-92, they built yet another addition on the west end, but set it back farther from the road (Fig. 7-15). Like the older section it was three stories tall and protected by a low-hipped roof. Exhibiting a Colonial Revival-inspired central pavilion with closed gable, the front elevation of this wing was symmetrical, with the exception of a left-side octagonal corner tower capped by a concave spire roof. This tower, while providing coveted sleeping rooms in the upper stories, also served as an effective visual counterbalance to the cupola atop the older portion of the complex. Allowing the Dodges to entertain up to 140 guests, the expansion encompassed enlargements to the office, dining room and main parlor, as well as twenty-nine new guest suites above. Eugene Gale, an accomplished contractor from Jefferson, may have built this addition as well as a corresponding east wing, a near reverse image reproduction of the 1891-92 construction, in 1904-05 (Fig. 7-16). It also possessed an octagonal corner tower, which, with the west wing tower, framed the entire long south facade and provided matching vertical accents on what was otherwise a quite monotonous, essentially horizontal building mass.[30]

A descriptive passage from Robert Greive's *Guide Book to the Mountains of New Hampshire . . .* offers an illuminating picture of the hotel's best features and amenities, as it gradually made its transition to the status of grand resort hotel at the end of the nineteenth century:

> The Mountain View House . . . is so arranged that all the sleeping rooms (which are large, each containing a closet), command a fine view; and the house being fitted with electric bells,

Fig. 7-16. Mountain View House, Whitefield, NH, *photograph, c. 1906, photographer unknown. Whitefield Historical Society.* Illustrated here are the 1891-92 addition, and its near reverse mirror image east wing, erected in 1904-05.

Fig. 7-17. Center Tower Section and East Wings, Mountain View House, Whitefield, NH, *photograph, c. 1976, by the author. In 1927-28, the 1904-05 east wing was furnished with a new fourth story and roof, and extension, raising the hotel's capacity to approximately 300 guests.*

Fig. 7-18. Lobby, Mountain View House, Whitefield, NH, *photograph, c. 1970, from Barbara D. Dodge,* The Dodge Family and Their Hotel *(Whitefield, NH: Mountain View House, 1973). Author's Collection. This modern view of the lobby illustrates the influence of the Colonial Revival style on architectural detailing and furnishings.*

telegraph, local and long-distance telephone, billiard hall, parlor for dancing and theatricals, fire-places in public rooms, with a bowling alley and laundry connected, the guests do not experience the loss of any of the comforts of their city homes. The table is given special attention. Competent cooks are employed and fresh milk, cream, and vegetables from the Mountain View Farm, together with choice products of the markets, render this important feature most excellent. The water is from the purest of mountain springs and the drainage is perfect. Near the house are delightful pine and maple groves. The extensive lawns are provided with tennis courts, croquet, base ball and golf [only after the hay was cut for the horses!] grounds, which give ample opportunity for out-door recreation, and in-doors music is furnished for dancing. An excellent livery is connected, where good teams and experienced drivers can be secured at reasonable rates.[31]

Of further interest, steam heat was installed in the complex in 1901, and complete electric lighting was introduced in 1905, in both instances considerably later than at other comparable hotels in the region.[32]

During the months between the 1911 and 1912 seasons, the physical evolution of the Mountain View House continued. Guests arriving for summer vacations in 1912 were welcomed by a brand new central front facade, four stories in height with a low-hipped roof and a dominant front square observation tower (see Plate 14). Conceived in the late Italian Revival style to simulate a campanile, the tower provided the visual focal point that the now vast, rambling complex had lacked. At the same time it conveyed the strong message that the Mountain View, with its growing accommodations and diverse offerings, had become an undisputed major player in the region, joining the ranks of those elite White Mountain hostelries with space for over 200 guests.[33]

As its reputation spread, so did the demand for rooms at the Mountain View House. The Dodges met the challenge. Under the leadership of Frank Schuyler Dodge, the manager from 1919 until his death in 1948, significant additions were made to the complex, particularly during the decade of the 1920s. In 1921-22 an L-shaped extension devoted solely to sleeping rooms was built on the 1891-92 west wing, with compatible Colonial Revival architectural elements. Among these were tapered round Doric piazza columns, a heavy cornice and thick entablature, and Doric end-wall pilasters. At the same time, a large, domed octagonal dining hall, similar to that of the New Profile House, was added to the rear of the complex. Arthur Simonds of Lancaster (with the likely involvement of Eugene Gale) served as chief contractor for these projects and also remodeled the main section of the hotel, with James Purdon of Boston as architect. Following this, in 1927-28, the 1904-05 east wing was furnished with a new fourth story and roof, and expanded by the addition of a hipped-roof wing (Fig. 7-17). The end of this wing featured bay windows, a porte cochere for automobiles, and a balustraded sunporch above. According to the Dodge family this addition was designed by architect George Glover and built by Whitefield contractor Allison H. Nevers. This final major construction project completed the Mountain View House as it can be seen today; its capacity at the time peaked at 300 guests.[34]

At the larger resort hotels the public rooms were critical to guest satisfaction and business success and the Mountain View was no exception:

The public rooms, although larger, have much the charm and atmosphere of the living rooms of a big country house. The lobby [Fig. 7-18] is spacious and well lighted and here everyone comes together for visits around the fires, or a game of bridge. Here many friendships are renewed and the events of the day retold. A large music room, a dignified and attractive drawing room, card rooms and two smaller reading rooms furnished with fireplace and book cases, all provide additional space and comfort. The [450-seat] dining room [Fig. 7-19], oval in shape with windows on all sides [and an octagonal dome with side windows], ivory and green in its colorings, it provides a cool and restful setting . . . [and] a cuisine and service of the highest standard.[35]

Of these rooms, the two largest, the lobby and the dining room, illustrate particularly well the powerful impact of the Colonial Revival in their round and square Doric columns, thick cornice moldings, and, in the lobby, exposed molded ceiling beams

Fig. 7-19. New Dining Room, Mountain View House, Whitefield, NH, *photograph, c. 1965. Richard Hamilton, Littleton, NH, from the* Littleton Courier. *This immense space, oval in shape with an octagonal dome roof, could seat up to 450 people.*

and joists, and finely articulated fireplace surrounds.

The years since World War II have seen few alterations or additions to the hotel's physical plant, but have witnessed several changes in management and ownership. In 1939, toward the end of Frank Schuyler Dodge's long proprietorship, a new sports clubhouse was erected across the road to the east of the main building. This was joined in 1946 by a swimming pool. Following Frank Dodge's untimely death two years later, his wife Mary Bowden Dodge ran the Mountain View House for five years until her two sons, John B. and Frank Schuyler, Jr., came of age and became co-managers. During their tenure in 1965, Century Hall, a modern and highly functional entertainment and conference center, was constructed to the east of the hotel. In 1967, when John shifted to the field of real estate development, Frank Schuyler took over complete management of the enterprise.

Finally, in 1979, faced with a changing tourist market, automobile fuel shortages and financial instability, the descendants of William F. Dodge wisely sold the complex and its over 3,000 acres to a group named "Mountain View Associates," headed by Robert and Ann Diltz.[36] Thus ended the association of the Dodge family with the Mountain View House, an affiliation whose claim as "the oldest resort in the United States to be owned and operated continuously by the same family living on the same property" was singular.[37]

The last functioning years of the Mountain View House were fraught with stress and uncertainty. In 1986, after several summers producing marginal financial returns, the hotel closed its doors at the conclusion of its 122nd season, possibly for the last time. In 1987, when the ownership was unable to meet mortgage payments, its primary creditor, Empire

Fig. 7-20. Mountain View House, Whitefield, NH, *aerial photograph, c. 1965. Richard Hamilton, Littleton, NH, from the* Littleton Courier. *Viewed from the east the complex is configured in the form of a giant question mark, presaging the uncertain future of the Mountain View and the entire White Mountain hotel industry.*

America Federal Savings Bank of Buffalo, New York, announced a foreclosure and auction; however, this was temporarily averted when new financing was secured. But obstacles to reopening the business remained, and in late 1987 the bank purchased the Mountain View for $3 million. The entire property and contents were put up for auction in July 1989. Although the contents were dispersed, no acceptable bids were received for the hotel and surrounding lands. Several months later, however, in March 1990, the establishment was again sold, on this occasion to a partnership headed by a New Jersey man, Charles Carroll. Additional years have passed, but time has yet to clarify its fate.[38]

An aerial photograph of the Mountain View House, taken before the 1965 construction of Century Hall, reveals a massive, monumental, sprawling complex, surrounded by various specialized outbuildings and expansive lawns, gardens, meadows and woodlands (Fig. 7-20). Here, captured in one spectacular view, is the entire architectural development of the hotel from the mid-nineteenth-century farmhouse of William F. Dodge, to the great multifaceted resort facility of his descendants.[39] In one significant respect the photograph suggests a dichotomy—while it appears that the main edifice seemingly grew without order and foresight, history reveals the contrary. Driven by business concerns, as well as a desire for aesthetically appealing architecture, the Dodge family meticulously and prudently planned the hotel's growth, year after year, phase after phase. For those sympathetic to the grand resort hotel experience, it is hoped that the care, affection and sound management lavished upon this complex will not go unrewarded. A turn of the book to show the Mountain View House from the right, or east end, illustrates the complex configured in the shape of a giant question mark—this, it seems, is what the future holds for this magnificent hotel, and the last remnants of the White Mountain hotel industry.

ಉNotesಲ

1. Tatham, "Franklin Leavitt's White Mountain Views," pp. 227-28.
2. Kilbourne, *Chronicles*, p. 339.
3. Charles R. Milliken, *The Glen House Book, White Mountains* (Cambridge, MA: John Wilson and Son, 1889), p. 24.
4. *Ibid.*, pp. 24, 27.
5. *Ibid.*, p. 30.
6. Campbell, *The White Mountains*, p. 20. Unfortunately for students of nineteenth-century hotel architecture, Fassett correspondence apparently has not survived, in sad contrast to that existing for the Mount Pleasant House project. Nor have plans comparable to those drafted by John Calvin Stevens for The Metallak (see Chapter 6) yet surfaced.
7. Charles R. Milliken, *The Glen, White Mountains, N.H.* (Boston: Robinson Engraving Co., 1891), p. 41; *The White Mountains* (1888 ed.), p. 106; *WME* 8, No. 2 (4 July 1885), pp. 5, 6; *WME* 9, No. 1 (3 July 1886), p. 6, and No. 3 (17 July 1886), p. 5; *ATC* 9, No. 7 (21 July 1885), p. 1, and No. 33 (27 August 1885), p. 14; *WME* 8, No. 6 (1 August 1885), p. 14; *WME* 10, No. 1 (2 July 1887), pp. 6, 8, and No. 2 (9 July 1887), p. 5. The corporate title of the hotel company was "C. R. Milliken & Co."
8. *WME* 10, No. 1 (2 July 1887), p. 6.
9. Milliken, *The Glen House Book* (1889 ed.), pp. 28-30.
10. "The New Glen House," *WME* 10, No. 6 (6 August 1887), p. 6. Adjacent to the main house, the Glen Farm maintained a large herd of Swiss and Jersey cows for daily produce, and raised vegetables and fruits for the hotel table. In the stable nearby a hundred horses were boarded to assist the hotel, stagecoach and livery business. In addition the hotel housed a Western Union office and was in direct telegraph communication with all points, including the summit of Mount Washington, for the convenience of those guests who wished to arrange for rooms, carriages and meals at the Summit House. The Millikens were among the first White Mountain hotel proprietors to hire college students and African Americans as waiters.
11. Burt, *The Story of Mount Washington*, p. 104; Kilbourne, *Chronicles*, p. 340; "The Glen House Burned," *ATC* 17, No. 1 (17 July 1893), p. 1; "Embers from the Glen Fire," *ATC* 17, No. 2 (18 July 1893), p. 4; *WME* 16, No. 4 (22 July 1893), p. 14. The second Glen House cost well over $100,000 to build, and the amount of insurance carried was about $130,000. Much hotel and personal property was saved from destruction. At the time of the fire the hotel was under the management of O. L. Frisbie and Charles T. Wilson, working for C. R. Milliken & Co. The fire was said to have originated in the upper part of the building over the office, possibly the result of sparks from the boiler-room chimney falling on the roof.
12. Burt, *The Story of Mount Washington*, p. 104; Kilbourne, *Chronicles*, p. 340; *WME* 16, No. 4 (22 July 1893), p. 7; *WME* 16, No. 6 (15 August 1893), p. 5; "Ruin and Decay at the Glen," *ATC* 19, No. 4 (3 August 1895), p. 4; "A New Glen House," *ATC* 23, No. 26 (12 August 1899), p. 1.
13. "Stage Line From Glen," *ATC* 25, No. 3 (15 July 1901), p. 4; Mary Ahearn, "Fire at the Glen House," *Mount Washington*

Observatory News Bulletin 8, No. 1 (March 1967), p. 3; "The Curse of the Glen," *Berlin Register*, 22 March 1967; "The Glen," *ATC* 26, No. 22 (6 August 1902), p. 4; *ATC* 27, No. 45 (2 September 1903), p. 4; *WME* 48, No. 10 (12 September 1925), p. 6. The so-called third Glen House burned in 1924. The Libby Company, however, promptly rebuilt on the old foundations. This new structure, the fourth Glen House, was a modified Swiss chalet accommodating about twenty-five guests. It burned on 19 March 1967 while under the proprietorship of Mr. and Mrs. Douglas A. Philbrook.

14. Burt, *The Story of Mount Washington*, p. 104.
15. "The New Profile House," *ATC* 30, No. 7 (19 July 1906), p. 8; *Lisbon Courier*, 7 November 1940, pp. 1, 12; Williams, "The Saga of 'S. D.' Morgan . . . ," pp. 10-13. Morgan was known to his closest friends and working colleagues as "S. D."
16. "The New Profile House," *ATC* 30, No. 7 (19 July 1906), pp. 1, 8; *WME* 28, No.1 (8 July 1905), p. 11; *WME* 28, No. 12 (28 September 1905), p. 6.
17. *WME* 29, No. 9 (1 September 1906), p. 1.
18. *Ibid.*; *WME* 29, No. 1 (7 July 1906), p. 2; *ATC* 29, No. 53 (12 September 1905), p. 1. The new building was 275 feet across, with a central ell extending 300 feet to the rear.
19. "The New Profile House," *ATC* 30, No. 7 (19 July 1906), p. 1.
20. *ATC* 29, No. 53 (12 September 1905), p. 1.
21. *Profile Events* 2, No. 1 (22 July 1922), pp. 1, 2. This was the news bulletin for New Profile House guests, published after the Abbotts assumed ownership.
22. Abbott, *Open for the Season*, pp. 162-63; *WME* 29, No. 5 (4 August 1906), p. 16, and No. 9 (1 September 1906), pp. 1, 20. The garage was of the same general form as the hotel, with shingle siding.
23. Abbott, *Open for the Season*, pp. 161-63. For a biographical sketch of Abbott, see George H. Clark, "Karl P. Abbott," *Granite Monthly* 58, No. 6 (June 1926): 175-76.
24. Abbott, *Open for the Season*, pp. 161-63.
25. *Ibid.*, pp. 175-77; *Littleton Courier*, 9 August 1923, pp. 1, 12; *WME* 46, No. 4 (4 August 1923), p. 7; Hancock, *Saving the Great Stone Face*, pp. 65-69; J. Holland Beal, *White Mountain Yesteryears* (North Conway, NH: The Reporter Press, 1966), pp. 39-40. The fire is believed to have started on the fourth (attic) floor in the bell boys' quarters. Spontaneous combustion, prompted by the intense heat of the main hotel fire, caused buildings up to a quarter of a mile away to ignite. The value of the destroyed property, with its contents, was estimated at $1 million.
26. *Ibid.*, pp. 175-77; "Profile House to be Rebuilt," *WME* 46, No. 6 (18 August 1923), p. 8. A golf course was planned for the site of the burned hotel and outbuildings, and, had it been built, would have extended north to Echo Lake.
27. Abbott, *Open for the Season*, pp. 177-78; Kostechke, ed., *Franconia Notch: An In-Depth Guide*, p. 17; scrapbook articles, White Mountain Collection, DCL. During the period between the fire and the sale, the Abbott family maintained concessions in Franconia Notch and received revenue from admissions to the Flume. In addition, it collected fees for permitting lumber concerns to cut and sell large quantities of timber. The latter circumstance inspired a fundraising appeal to save the Notch from further exploitation and to establish a state reservation and park.
28. Barbara Derrington Dodge, *The Dodge Family . . . and Their Hotel* (Whitefield, NH: Mountain View House, 1973), pp. 2-3; Kevin R. Nilsen, *A History of Whitefield, New Hampshire, 1774-1974* (Whitefield: Published by the Town, 1974), p. 30; J. J. Kramer, *The Last of the Grand Resort Hotels* (New York: Van Nostrand Reinhold Co., 1978), p. 31; Gordon B. McKinney, "The Land No One Wanted: An Economic History of Whitefield, New Hampshire," *Historical New Hampshire* 28, No. 4 (Winter 1972), p. 201; Andrew Hepburn, *The Great Resorts of North America* (New York: Doubleday & Co., Inc., 1965), pp. 31-32; John B. and F. Schuyler Dodge, *One Hundred Years of Gracious Hospitality: The Story of the Dodge Family of the Mountain View House of Whitefield, New Hampshire* (Whitefield: Mountain View House, 1965).
29. Dodge, *The Dodge Family*, p. 3; *The White Mountains* (1876 ed.), p. 168; Nilsen, *A History of Whitefield*, pp. 57-58. The 1865-66 addition was moved to the rear of the hotel in 1904-05 when the first of two large east wings was constructed. For many years it was used as a dormitory for female employees. At this writing the building is still standing.

The capacity of the hotel after the 1880 addition was sixty guests (*WME* 6, No. 2 [7 July 1883], p. 7). It is conceivable that the old farmhouse was absorbed as part of the 1872 addition, and was, therefore, not torn down.

30. Kramer, *The Last of the Grand Resort Hotels*, p. 31; *The White Mountains* (1890 ed.), p. 168; *WME* 7, No. 2 (5 July 1884), pp. 5, 10; *WME* 8, No. 2 (4 July 1885), p. 10; [Merrill], *History of Coos County*, p. 419; C. Douglas McIntyre, "The History of Whitefield" (M.A. thesis, University of New Hampshire, 1942), p. 20; *WME* 15, No. 2 (9 July 1982), p. 2; *ATC* 16, No. 1 (11 July 1892), p. 4; *WME* 16, No. 1 (1 July 1893), p. 19; *ATC* 29, No. 2 (14 July 1905), p. 4; *WME* 28, No. 4 (29 July 1905), p. 16; "Mountain View House," *ATC* 30, No. 17 (31 July 1906), p. 4. The 1884 addition had dimensions of 41 by 90 feet, while the 1891-92 addition measured 40 by 100 feet. The 1904-05 wing included a new writing room, additions to the music room and office, and thirty sleeping rooms. It could be isolated from the rest of the hotel and opened separately during the cold weather months. The large 200-foot-long barn, formerly to the northeast of the hotel, was built in 1891-92.
31. Robert Grieve, ed., *Guide Book to the Mountains of New Hampshire and the Shores of Southern New England* (Providence, RI: Journal of Commerce Company, 1899), pp. 105-106. Golf was added to the recreational options at the hotel in 1899.
32. *WME* 24, No. 1 (6 July 1901), p. 1; *WME* 28, No.4 (29 July 1905), p. 16.

33. Placard photographs of the Mountain View House with captions, Whitefield Historical Society; Dodge, *The Dodge Family*, pp. 14-18; advertisement, *White Mountain Directory, 1917-1919*, p. 408.

34. Placard photographs of the Mountain View House; Dodge, *The Dodge Family*, pp. 16-18; Frank Schuyler Dodge, Jr., to Carolyn K. Tolles, 23 January 1974; *WME* 44, No. 12 (24 September 1921), p. 14. To this day the hotel has retained its color scheme of the pre-World War II era—pastel yellow clapboard walls with white trim, green shutters and a green asphalt shingle roof.

   Eugene Gale (1871-after 1953) was born in Whitefield and had an outstanding career as a contractor in New Hampshire. Builder or remodeler of houses, barns, garages, tenements, commercial blocks, theaters, libraries, warehouses, public buildings, churches and hospitals, he claimed to have "repaired fifteen hotels and built six new ones." It is known that he did work at the Waumbek Hotel (see Chapter 3), the Twin Mountain House, the Stratford Hotel (Stratford), and the Spaulding Inn (Whitefield), in addition to the Mountain View House. For a time he lived in Rochester, NH, and ran the Glendon Hotel there (see *New Hampshire Profiles* 2, Nos. 3, 4 and 5 [March, April and May 1953]).

35. *Mountain View House in the White Mountains, Whitefield, N. H.* (Whitefield: F. W. Dodge and Son, [c. 1925]).

36. McIntyre, "The History of Whitefield," p. 20; Dodge, *The Dodge Family*, pp. 9-11; Charles J. Jordon, "The Mountain View and How it Grew," *Coos Magazine* 1, No. 2 (July 1989), p. 25; warranty deed, W. F. Dodge & Son, Inc. to Diltz Ford Sales, Inc. (Salem, NH), 20 June 1979, grantor volume 620, p. 257, Coos County Registry of Deeds, Lancaster.

37. Dodge, *The Dodge Family*, p. 13.

38. *Appalachia* 46, No. 4 (15 December 1987), p. 145; Jordon, "The Mountain View and How it Grew," pp. 25-26; *Appalachia* 48, No. 1 (15 June 1990), p. 140.

39. The Mountain View House developed from farmhouse to grand resort hotel, so far as it is known, without the demolition of any major portion of the complex.

Fig. 7-21. "Glen House, White Mountains, NH." *Dinner menu cover, Sunday, September 15, 1889, Robinson Engraving Co., Boston. Author's Collection.*

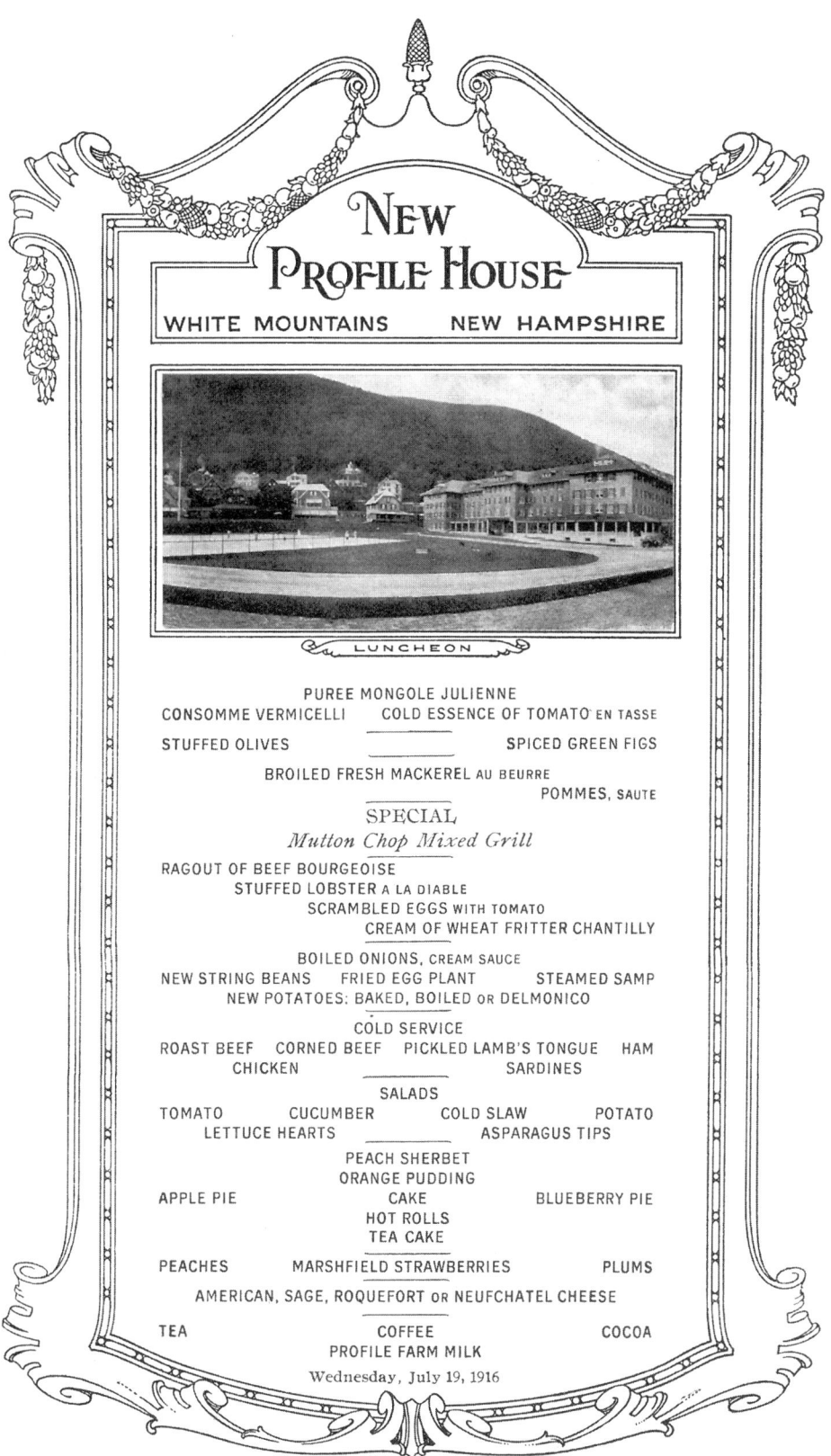

Fig. 7-22. "New Profile House, White Mountains, New Hampshire." *Luncheon menu, Wednesday, July 19, 1916. C. B. Webster & Co., Boston. Author's Collection.*

Fig. 8-1. Mount Washington Hotel, Bretton Woods (Carroll), NH, *aerial photograph, c. 1965. Richard Hamilton, Littleton, NH. This sprawling complex is widely regarded as the most ambitious and elaborate of the White Mountain grand resort hotels.*

Chapter 8

Paragons of Style and Elegance:
The Mount Washington Hotel at Bretton Woods
and The Balsams at Dixville Notch

THE MOUNT WASHINGTON HOTEL at Bretton Woods and The Balsams at Dixville Notch have endured the test of time and nature despite the overall decline of the White Mountain hotel industry during the twentieth century. Still open to the public on a regular schedule, they are survivors of a prolonged and agonizing attrition that has all but eliminated their competition. They are the last material evidence of the flourishing entrepreneurial activity that once dominated the mountain region and established leisure-time standards for the rest of the United States. Both hotels are real paragons of style and elegance, providing atmospheres and amenities that reflect the best of the past, while at the same time catering to the demands of our fast-paced, mobile, modern society. They accomplish this, however, in contrasting architectural and natural settings—the Mount Washington, a single, great edifice largely erected at one time, positioned in an open, grandiose, panoramic landscape; The Balsams, planned and constructed in contiguous stages over four decades, nestled in a quaint, but spectacular bowl, the surrounding hills and mountains pressing in on all sides. While their physical circumstances differ, and their histories reflect varying patterns of development, both rank at the top of the list of White Mountain grand resort hotels. Each has long enjoyed a reputation for quality and excellence—across the country and around the world.

Joseph Stickney and His Mount Washington Hotel

Of the thirty grand resort hotels erected in the White Mountains between 1850 and 1930, the Mount Washington Hotel at Bretton Woods is, in the eyes of most critics, the most ambitiously conceived, elaborately appointed and conspicuously palatial (Fig. 8-1). Moreover, unlike most of its counterparts, it did not evolve piecemeal over time on a previously occupied site, nor did it grow from humble origins as a private residence, or a small inn or hotel. On the contrary, it was planned and built as a single homogeneous complex on virgin land, unquestionably the greatest hotel construction project undertaken in the region to the present day. This monumental, 600-guest establishment was executed in the Spanish Renaissance Revival, one of the most lavish and yet among the more orderly of the late-Victorian eclectic styles. It quickly became the centerpiece of the entire White Mountain hotel industry and a major contributor to the area's economy, a position it still holds in our day. Added to the National Register of Historic Places in 1978 and designated a National

Historic Landmark in 1986, the Mount Washington has gained distinction for its architecture as well as its rich and eventful history. Rivaling America's most magnificent and sumptuous grand resort hotels, its past reveals a fascinating story.[1]

The idea underlying the Mount Washington Hotel is believed to have originated as early as the mid-1880s in the minds of Joseph Stickney, the affluent New York-based owner of the Mount Pleasant House, and his closest business associates. The key figure in the conceptualization process was John Anderson, the co-proprietor of the Mount Pleasant, whose father, Samuel J. Anderson, the first president of the Portland & Ogdensburg Railroad Company, had opened the rail route through Crawford Notch in 1875. Familiar with the White Mountains since his childhood in northern New England, the younger Anderson participated in the creation of the landscaping, roads and walkways, and other outdoor recreational attractions of the Mount Pleasant complex. While pursuing his interest in the natural world and contemplating future hotel development, he discovered a site potentially more impressive than that occupied by the Mount Pleasant. It was situated just three quarters of a mile to the east of the hotel in the center of the Ammonoosuc plain at an elevation of 1,600 feet and was part of the large tract Joseph Stickney and his former partner Oscar V. Pitman had purchased along with the Mount Pleasant in 1881 (see Chapter 4).[2]

Despite its close proximity to the Mount Pleasant House, the undeveloped site possessed advantages that were far superior, perhaps unparalleled to others in the region. Nowhere else in the White Mountains is it possible to enjoy such impressive vistas across flat lands in every direction. A 1901 account from the *White Mountain Echo* confirms Anderson's understandable enthusiasm for the site:

[the] location is grand beyond description. It is upon a [long and lofty glacial] ridge [similar to ancient Giant's Grave at Fabyan's] jutting out from the mountain range on the north into the center of a beautiful green plateau traversed by the crystal stream of the Ammonoosuc fresh from its mountain source, and completely surrounded by the great peaks of the White Mountains; the Presidential Range on the east with Mount Washington in the center, apparently not a rifle shot distant; the fine group of Mounts Willard, Willey, Field and Tom in the south, three miles distant; the Rosebrook Range in the west but three-quarters of a mile away, and the Deception and Dartmouth Range on the north, the dense balsam fir growth upon its slopes coming down to the edge of the . . . [site] . . . [which] looks directly into Crawford Notch. . . .[3]

Such an expansive and extraordinary setting merited a hotel complex of monumental scale and unusually fine architectural quality. The enterprising and determined Joseph Stickney and his colleagues were to prove equal to the challenge.

Planning for the envisioned hotel commenced in the late 1890s with the selection of an architect. It is logical to suppose that Stickney might well have bestowed this honor on the Fassett firm in Portland, responsible for the 1894-95 transformation of the Mount Pleasant House (see Chapter 4), or some other nationally known architect. Instead, following the advice of his friend, the Florida hotel entrepreneur Henry M. Flagler (see Chapter 3), Stickney chose Charles Alling Gifford (1861-1937), a relative-

Fig. 8-2. Construction of the Mount Washington Hotel, Bretton Woods (Carroll), NH, *photograph, c. 1901. Mount Washington Hotel. After ground-breaking in late 1900, the granite masonry foundations were readied the following spring by a large force of skilled laborers from Italy.*

ly unknown New York City designer. Although Flagler had commissioned the renowned New York partnership of Carrere and Hastings (see Introduction) to design his major Florida hotels, he may have hired Gifford to perform other design work, thereby gaining an appreciation of his talents. Stickney's confidence in Flagler's recommendation was well founded, for it was Flagler who had been instrumental in securing for him the services of John Anderson and John D. Price (see Chapter 4) to run the Mount Pleasant, beginning in 1895. Furthermore, to Gifford's credit as a professional, he had established his own solid reputation, having planned the New Jersey State buildings at the World's Columbian Exposition in Chicago in 1893. In addition, Gifford was experienced in working with Mediterranean eclectic styles, represented by Flagler's great Ponce de Leon and Alcazar hotels in St. Augustine and at other Florida resort establishments before the turn of the century. Later in his career, Gifford would design the well-known Hotel Clifton at Niagara Falls, Canada. Stickney clearly wanted an architect who would produce a hotel design to equal if not eclipse others of its time in the country. He would not be disappointed.[4]

Unfortunately, while documentation exists for the latter portion of this period and several years beyond, hotel records and correspondence for the planning and construction phases have either been destroyed, are unlocated at the Mount Washington Hotel, or are in private hands. To trace the physical creation of the complex, therefore, one must rely almost exclusively on printed and visual materials, some of which provide erroneous or misleading data that must be discounted. The immense task of preparing the site, building the new hotel, and completing the grounds and recreational facilities began in 1901. It extended over two years into 1903, although the official opening occurred in the summer of 1902. William G. Phillips represented Gifford at the contracting site as superintendent of construction. Anderson, nominated by Stickney to manage the completed hotel, served as general overseer and principal correspondent with Stickney's Mount Pleasant Hotel Company, based in New York City. Contracts for the stone foundation work, the superstructure, and finishing of the hotel were let, respectively, to E. O. Getchell of Plymouth, New Hampshire and C.M. Russell & Company of Newark, New Jersey, with B. F. Robinson as the on-site company representative. This critical information about the builders of the hotel dispels unsubstantiated assertions that Sylvanus D. Morgan, contractor of other White Mountain hotels, also played a major role in the construction of the Mount Washington. Morgan, however, may have been involved with later expansion in 1905-06 (see below).[5]

After ground-breaking ceremonies in late 1900, work on the massive edifice commenced in early 1901. Attention was first devoted to leveling the ground along the ridge and raising the rough granite stone masonry foundations (Fig. 8-2). *Among the Clouds*, in describing this initial phase, likened the embryonic structure to "some huge fortification . . . under construction."[6] Some 250 Italian laborers, specialists in carpentry, masonry and stained glass, made up the work force and were housed in special dormitory quarters adjacent to the building site. Over the summer and fall of 1901, the main body of the wood-frame, supposedly "fireproof" building, partially supported by steel posts and girders, took form (Fig. 8-3). From late 1901 to the summer of 1902, the wood plank siding and roof underlay were added, towers and brick chimneys erected, the stucco (Portland cement)-on-wire wall covering applied, metal roof sheathing (imitating of Spanish tile) installed, and interior wood and plaster finish substantially completed. During its construction the hotel gained

Fig. 8-3. Construction of the Mount Washington Hotel, Bretton Woods (Carroll), NH, *photograph, c. 1901. Mount Washington Hotel. During the summer and fall of 1901, the steel-supported, wood-frame corpus of the building gradually assumed form.*

Fig. 8-4. Mount Washington Hotel, Bretton Woods (Carroll), NH, *photograph, c. 1906, unidentified. Douglas Philbrook, Gorham, NH. Predominantly Spanish Renaissance Revival in style, the new hotel resembled a self-contained, landlocked ocean liner in appearance and function.*

the distinction of being the largest, almost exclusively wooden, structure ever to be built in New Hampshire. It still enjoys this unique status today.[7]

With work still in progress the new hotel was opened to the public on 28 July 1902, coincidentally fifty years to the day after the christening of the first Summit House on Mount Washington (Fig. 8-4). This momentous occasion was met with a thirteen-gun salute and the raising of banners and flags, one of them red with a green "M. W." monogram, from various points above the building's roofs and piazzas. The doors of the hotel were then swung open to eagerly awaiting guests. Throughout the afternoon the front porte cochere accommodated hundreds of horse-drawn carriages and coaches from points near and far, their occupants satisfying their curiosity about the latest of the White Mountains' great hostelries. At a special dinner on August 1, over 250 people were seated in one large space, while owner Stickney hosted visiting dignitaries in an adjoining banquet hall. Among those present were Governor Chester B. Jordon, John Wingate Weeks (a member of Congress from 1905 to 1913), architect Gifford, representatives of the construction and hotel staffs, employees of the Mount Pleasant Hotel Company, and owners and managers of hotels across the country. After dinner an informal "hop" was held in the ballroom, highlighted by a brief concert and dancing, and culminating with a Virginia reel of sixteen couples led by Stickney himself. Few other hotels in White Mountain history have been launched in such an auspicious and ambitious style.[8]

The new Mount Washington presented a spectacular sight from the west with the Presidential Range as a moving backdrop or an over-sized stage setting. Its floor plan is in the shape of a huge capital Y and the main body of the structure runs north and south

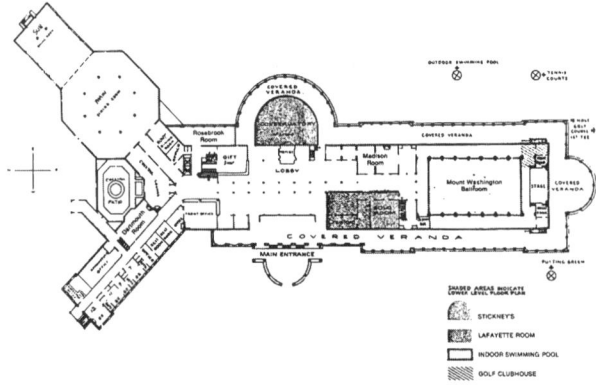

Fig. 8-5. Main Floor Plan, Mount Washington Hotel, Bretton Woods (Carroll), NH. *Mount Washington Hotel. Modeled on the original plan by architect Charles Alling Gifford, this scheme displays the major public rooms of the hotel.*

Fig. 8-6. South End, Mount Washington Hotel, Bretton Woods (Carroll), NH, *photograph, 1992, by the author. Strong evidence of a Colonial Revival influence is apparent in the fluted Doric columns, connecting balustrades, and heavy entablatures of the semi-circular end and flanking side piazzas.*

(Fig. 8-5). Two wings diverge from the northern octagonal tower at forty-five degree angles to the principal longitudinal axis. Extending farther north from the intersection point in a straight line are the kitchen building and a large male employees' dormitory (the staff-guest ratio was roughly 3:1). Originally detached, these were eventually joined to the main complex. Most impressive of the hotel's many physical statistics are its west frontage (see Plate 15) of 465 feet, its wide, wrap-around (and in some places two-tiered) piazza some 900 feet in length, and its vertical dimensions of 70 feet from foundations to roof peak and roof garden, and 114 feet to the tops of the five-story octagonal towers. A virtually self-contained service unit, much in the tradition of its White Mountain forerunners, it resembles a huge luxury ocean liner set upon the land—a small, unified village offering elegance, pleasures, and diversions to an appreciative clientele.[9]

This analogy of the Mount Washington Hotel to a liner was no doubt in the mind of the architect when he designed the complex and determined its relationship to the surrounding landscape. It is not far-fetched to presume that Gifford may have been influenced by mid-Westerner Frank Lloyd Wright whose inventive Prairie style was gaining national

[217]

Fig. 8-7. Porte Cochere, Main Entrance. Mount Washington Hotel, Bretton Woods (Carroll), NH, *photograph, 1992, by the author. Located at the west front entrance to the hotel, this fine protective canopy possesses tapered, fluted Doric columns and other neo-classical elements.*

recognition when the Mount Washington was being constructed. Like Wright's domestic buildings (albeit of much smaller scale), the hotel effectively melds horizontal and vertical visual lines—the horizontal expressed in the long, low building mass (accentuated by the piazzas), and the vertical annunciated in the major octagonal and corner square towers with their low-pitched roofs. Typical of Wright's Prairie style commissions, the hotel (see Plate 16), with its longitudinal axis focused perfectly on Crawford Notch to the south, appears rooted in the ledge-rock and soil while simultaneously it strives to move across the land as a passenger ship would on an open sea. This interpretation of Gifford's vision of the Mount Washington suggests that he brought a degree of intellectualism to the design task atypical of nearly all other planners of the White Mountain grand resort hotels.

In addition to the form and building materials appropriate to the Spanish Revival style, numerous decorative features enhance the complex. Among these are the many balconies with their heavy balustrades and console support brackets, semicircular and segmental arch window lintels, thick cornice moldings, wall pilasters, triangular window pediments with brackets, and emblems with garlands in relief on the upper square tower stages. Strong suggestions of the Colonial Revival style also may be observed in the long piazzas and semicircular south and east porches with their fluted Doric columns, connecting balustrades, and heavy entablatures (Fig. 8-6). These same details are repeated in the front (west) porte cochere, with the addition of small cornice brackets, and paired columns with paneled bases forming an inside screen for the main entrance (Fig. 8-7). These powerful classical elements indelibly condition the guest's aesthetic appreciation of the hotel.[10]

While one may visit the interior today and savor its finest qualities, it remains an interesting comparative exercise to examine descriptions published when the hotel was being built. A lengthy, but vivid

Fig. 8-8. Main Lobby, Mount Washington Hotel, Bretton Woods (Carroll), NH, *photograph, c. 1905, unidentified photographer, Mount Washington Hotel. Also referred to as the "lounge" or "assembly hall," this cavernous room is one of the largest ever built at the White Mountain hotels.*

portrayal, written with an eye to the future opening, appeared in the hotel's first publicity booklet in 1901:

> Beginning with the main or office floor, the visitor will come in at the main entrance on the west front, finding himself in the large [French Renaissance] assembly hall [also referred to as the "lounge" or lobby] [Fig. 8-8]. Directly facing him is [a large fieldstone fireplace, and] what is known as the "hemicycle," a half-moon shaped [sun parlor] projection, the front [east side] almost entirely of plate glass, which will afford a magnificent mountain prospect. Turning to the left toward the business office, he will pass an alcove where hot and cold spring water will always be ready and another alcove reserved for bell boys. Pausing at the office to await assignment to his room, he will notice the northwestern wing, where are the manager's private office, resident physician's room and other business rooms, as well as the dining-room for children and nurses and the ladies' cafe and billiard room. The banquet hall, to be elegantly furnished for private parties, is in the apex between the two wings, and near it is the elevator by which the guest will be taken speedily to his apartments.
>
> Once located in his room the visitor will return to the office floor for a further examination of its attractions. To the south of the assembly hall he will see on the west front the ladies' parlor, with open fire and upholstered wicker furniture, writing-room and several small card rooms, and on the east a series of card rooms of various sizes. All of these connect by sliding doors, so that the whole can be united for large parties. A beautiful foyer leads the way to the [Italian Renaissance] ballroom [Fig. 8-9], 115.6 x 73 feet, which occupies the south end of the house. At the extreme south of the ballroom is the stage, fully fitted up for theatricals, with dressing-rooms provided with

Fig. 8-9. Ballroom, Mount Washington Hotel, Bretton Woods (Carroll), NH, *photograph, c. 1985, by William C. Roy, Lebanon, NH. Mount Washington Hotel. This spacious Italian Renaissance room possesses a large plate-glass window behind the stage. The window looks directly on Crawford Notch.*

running water. At the back of the stage a plate-glass window twelve feet wide looks toward Crawford Notch, while one may promenade the colonnade [Fig. 8-6] outside at night and witness the gay scenes in the ballroom and general hall beyond.

The ground floor will next attract the visitor. Under the hemicycle will be found the billiard room [later converted to a restaurant], a beautiful room looking out over the plain and toward the mountains. Under the assembly room are bowling alleys with deadened walls, beneath the grand entrance are the squash courts [subsequently replaced by the Cave Grill], and at the southern end of the house is what no mountain hotel possesses, an indoor swimming-pool, which will be fed by water from the Ammonoosuc, tempered by jets of steam. Adjoining this is the room for the masseur and Turkish baths. Near the pool are [spaces for commercial shops,] ample locker rooms for golfers, with bath room attached, besides a large bicycle room. Under the dining-hall a large area is given up for the children's playroom, with toilet and washroom attached, and a portion for an amusement hall and assembly room for help....

Being ready for dinner the guest will readily find his way to the northeast wing, where the novel arrangements of the [high-vaulted] dining hall [see Plate 17] will engage his interest. It is octagonal, 84.8 x 84.8 feet, with immense plate windows looking out on the grand landscapes before referred to. The kitchen ... is separated from the main house by a beautiful fern garden. The communication with the dining-room is at the middle of its northwest side, and there is a small waiting-room for the waitresses.... The kitchen is in every particular one of the most complete ever built ... there will be a cold-storage system of refrigeration by cold pipes. The kitchen will be but one story high, with monitor roof to secure perfect ventilation, and will form no obstruction to the view from any rooms above the office story. On the ground floor beneath the main kitchen are extensive storerooms and the help's kitchen and dining-hall.[11]

Similarly, laudatory comments about the guests' quarters appeared in a 1902 summer issue of *Among the Clouds*:

> In the bedrooms [350 in number] the finish and furnishings are of the most beautiful and modern style. The bedsteads are about equally divided between brass and wood. The promise of the architect that there should not be an undesirable room in the house is amply fulfilled. Nearly every room has a mountain view. The doors are of mahogany, and the woodwork throughout is painted with white fireproof paint. There is a bath connected with nearly every room. The suites in the central tower compare in size and elegance with the finest in any hotel in the world.[12]

From these descriptions, it is strikingly evident that Joseph Stickney had satisfied his desire to create a resort establishment of optimal luxury and comfort—a mecca in the mountains for those of wealth, fashion, social prominence and professional stature.[13]

It took another four years after the 1902 opening before the Mount Washington Hotel complex had all its outbuildings in place. From the outset, an eighty-foot-long, three-story female employee dormitory supplemented the main house. Located at its northwest corner this building matched the men's quarters adjacent to the kitchen, but was torn down after World War II. Other structures on the nearly 10,000-acre property included a boiler and power plant, a gas house, a site manager's cottage, a large horse barn, a livery stable, a water-powered print shop and maintenance buildings. A nearby 1896 farmhouse captured the attention of the developers

Fig. 8-10. The Bretton Arms, Mount Washington Hotel, Bretton Woods (Carroll), NH, *photograph, 1990, by the author. Designated a National Historic Landmark in 1986, this low, rambling building became a chauffeur's hotel in 1907.*

in 1907 when a new automobile garage was in the planning stages. The house was promptly renovated to serve as a 100-room hotel for the chauffeurs of guests who brought their own vehicles with them while on vacation (Fig. 8-10). Designated a National Historic Landmark in 1986, this plain wood-frame and clapboard building was restored during the next year, and, under the name "Bretton Arms," is now open for guests on a year-round schedule. A new caretaker's cottage, mimicking the form and features of the adjacent hotel, appeared on the grounds in the fall of 1903.

In responding to instantaneous business success, the hotel edifice itself was enlarged in 1905-06 by a four-story extension to the northeast wing. This added seventy feet to the dining hall (creating the "Sun Dining Room"), sixty-five new bedrooms and connected the kitchen unit to the rest of the complex. Another of the outbuildings is an impressive T-shaped Colonial Revival stable (c. 1902) located a short distance north of the chauffeur's hotel (Fig. 8-11). Still serving its original purposes in summer and doubling as a ski touring center during the winter months, this structure boasts a symmetrical main facade with a central pavilion. This unit is composed of two sets of paired Doric columns supporting a gambrel-roofed pediment. Underneath, a wide doorway with a semi-elliptical pediment embellished with an urn and festoons echoes the larger form above.[14]

On 21 December 1903, well before the completion

Fig. 8-11. Stable, Mount Washington Hotel, Bretton Woods (Carroll), NH, *photograph, 1992, by the author. This symmetrical Colonial Revival structure was built about 1902 and still serves its original function during summer seasons.*

of the complex, Joseph Stickney unexpectedly died, leaving the responsibilities of ownership in the hands of his much younger wife, Carolyn Foster Stickney. Although he had the pleasure of seeing the Mount Washington in operation for only a year, he had quickly brought it to the forefront of great American resorts. It was without question, as he had hoped, a worthy competitor of Newport, Bar Harbor and other swank New England vacation centers. In doing so, Stickney had shrewdly adapted his hotel enterprise to the new era of the gasoline-powered automobile, charting the way other hotel magnates would follow in this century. In 1906 Carolyn Stickney graciously paid homage to Joseph's memory by constructing the small stone Neo-Gothic Stickney Memorial Chapel that still stands on the main highway just south of the entrance to the hotel tract.

Carrying on the tradition of flexible and excellent service that her husband had established, she added a certain Old World luster to the hotel, perhaps as a result of her marriage to a French nobleman, Prince Clarigny de Lucinge, in 1908. After the prince was killed in World War I at the Battle of Verdun, she carried on alone until her death in 1936. The Mount Washington's ties with European royalty are commemorated today by the cocktail lounge known as the "Princess Room," formerly a private dining area for the owner and her select circle of friends.[15]

Since the death of Princess Carolyn, the hotel has had a series of owners, particularly in recent years when it has endured swings in the national economic cycle, changing tourist preferences and inconsistent profitability. The vast property, together with all buildings (under the corporate title of the "Bretton Woods Company"), first passed to the Princess' nephew, F. Foster Reynolds of Providence, Rhode Island. Despite setbacks, he ran the hotel through the Depression and well into World War II. Reynolds suspended operations in 1943 and sold out to a Boston syndicate the following year.

As the new owners prepared to open for the 1944 summer season, they fell heir to good fortune when the United States government requested the use of the facilities for the World Monetary Fund Conference (known more commonly as the "Bretton Woods Conference"). Organized by the newly formed United Nations to deal with post-war global economic problems, this historically significant gathering, attended by representatives of forty-four nations, laid plans for currency stability through the establishment of the World Bank and the International Monetary Fund, and the linking of the gold standard to the U.S. dollar. A star-studded group, including economist John Maynard Keynes and Secretary of the Treasury Henry Morgenthau, occupied the entire hotel during the first three weeks of July while conducting their deliberations. This occasion was subsequently marked by a bronze plaque in the principal meeting room (The Gold Room) and name plates on the doors of the participants' bedrooms. The Mount Washington benefited not only from the income generated by the conference, but also from the refurbishing required to ready the hotel for the participants, and the accompanying publicity. After 1944, the name Bretton Woods was well implanted in the popular mind, and the hotel gained added stature from perhaps the most important chapter in its history.[16]

There have been no major alterations to the hotel complex since World War II, other than cosmetic improvements and the removal of a few outbuildings. It has, however, continued to experience ownership changes and increasingly varied uses. In 1955, the Boston syndicate sold the property to Mr. and Mrs. Morris Fleisher of Philadelphia, who operated the establishment primarily as a convention center for fifteen years. In 1969, they transferred title to the Mount Washington Development Company, a

Philadelphia partnership led by Donald Cohan. This group developed the neighboring Bretton Woods Ski Area, began to redecorate the hotel, promoted tennis and golf, and built condominiums, all in an effort to create a self-reliant four season resort community under the name "Bretton Woods Village." When this ambitious venture encountered financial difficulties, the Bretton Woods Corporation, a subsidiary of the Massachusetts and New York-based Institutional Investors Trust, acquired the property in 1975. During its tenure the ski touring center became one of the largest in the country, condominium construction was accelerated and the social guest business was revived. In a popular as well as financially logical gesture, 6,500 acres of the original Stickney lands were sold to the federal government for inclusion in the White Mountain National Forest. The resort next passed to a twenty-investor partnership, Bretton Woods Associates, in 1980. Then in 1988 the hotel was purchased by First Commonwealth Development, Inc. of Boston; at the same time the remaining 2,500 acres (called "Bretton Woods Resort") along with the ski area were acquired by Satter Companies of New England, a Lincoln, New Hampshire-based real estate development firm. Plans to winterize and restore the hotel, however, failed and again the grande old dame of the mountains, its financial underpinnings unstable, fell on hard times.[17]

The year 1991 was full of uncertainty. In that spring, the hotel reached the nadir of its recent history when the Federal Deposit Insurance Corporation, after taking over the interests of a failed bank creditor, was unable to sell the property and decided to foreclose. At a special auction on June 26, the hotel, adjacent buildings and ninety-seven acres of land were sold for $3.15 million to Mountain Properties Preservation Corporation, a Littleton partnership. News of the acquisition met with a generally positive reaction, particularly within New Hampshire. It is reassuring that the members of the purchasing group are all from the Littleton area, with investments in other White Mountain tourist attractions.[18] A feeling of optimism, therefore, exists that the present era of stewardship will perpetuate the tradition of superlative service established by their predecessors. The future of the Mount Washington Hotel looks bright, and there is every reason to believe that its rich architectural heritage is in caring and respectful hands.

In the early part of this century, guests arriving at the Mount Washington by train would ride by carriage nearly a mile from Bretton Woods Station, contemplating the exquisite mountain panorama incorporating the hotel—the magnificent man-made incursion into the landscape. Today, although the automobile has supplanted this older form of transportation, the unusual and moving experience of first viewing the hotel is still possible.

Henry S. Hale and The Balsams

Like the Mount Washington Hotel, The Balsams has outlived most of its nineteenth-century counterparts, not only in the White Mountains but elsewhere in the United States (Fig. 8-12). It continues to thrive today as a result of innovative management, effective marketing, sound maintenance practices, and the persistent appeal of its location, physical plant and its offerings to a devoted clientele. Situated east of Colebrook in the beautiful, almost idyllic, landscape of Dixville Notch, this venerable establishment is the northernmost of the White Mountain's grand resort hotels, attracting American, Canadian and international patrons. In the large, sprawling complex, its various components dating from the post-Civil War era to World War I, the entire architectural history of the region's grand resort hotels can be seen. An added benefit for us today is that the complex itself, the tangible record of this history, remains for us to examine, speculate about and enjoy.

Part of the charm, fascination and historical interest of The Balsams derives from its remote, if not virtually isolated, location, its pleasant climate, and its unusually lovely and enthralling natural surroundings. The buildings sit on a natural plateau at an elevation of 2,000 feet. The most compelling features of the landscape are described in the thorough and typically florid vocabulary of a 1901 hotel promotional booklet:

> The Dixville Mountains are a group of picturesque, cathedral-like peaks, rising in the

Fig. 8-12. Bird's Eye View of The Balsams, Dixville Notch, NH, *photograph, c. 1990. The Balsams Grand Resort Hotel. A comprehensive view of the century-old Balsams complex set in the surrounding mountains is seen from nearby Table Rock.*

tapering northern end of . . . New Hampshire. Geographically they may be regarded as an outlying spur of the White Mountains, though the latter, strictly so-called, lie forty miles to the south. Set between the headwaters of the Connecticut and the Androscoggin, these mountains form the water-shed for the two great river systems, and their lofty ridge affords a cycloramic view of the mountains and lakes of Maine, New Hampshire, Vermont and Canada. Geologists assume that . . . the erosive force of a mighty glacier wore through this peaceful range, and left agape the precipitous [rough-hewn and rugged] palisades of the now famous Dixville Notch. . . . [the Notch] is remarkable for its "Gothic architecture," the cathedral-like peaks and spires that line its sides, together with the tumbled-down boulders at their feet, giving the illusion of the ruins of a vast basilica.[19]

The origins of The Balsams date from 1805 when Colonel Timothy Dix, the father of Major General John Adams Dix, governor and U.S. Senator from New York, was granted the unorganized township of Dixville in return for service in the Revolutionary War. In 1812, Ezekial and the later renowned statesman Daniel Webster—attorneys and agents for Colonel Dix—hired John Whittemore of Salisbury, New Hampshire, to come to Dixville and care for the interests of the Dix family there. Whittemore and his wife Betsey lived there for many years, establishing a large farmstead. On the east side of the Notch they built a house that doubled as a rustic wayside inn and well-known stopping place for travelers through the Notch.[20] But it took another three decades before the potential of this location for hotel development was formally recognized. This occurred in 1844 when Charles T. Jackson, in his *Final Report on the Geology and Mineralogy of the State of New Hampshire*, prophetically stated, "as the tide of travel sets to the northward, [Dixville Notch] will become a place of resort for lovers of picturesque scenery."[21]

Upon the death of Whittemore in 1846, the Notch reverted to wilderness, settled sporadically and briefly for the next twenty-five years. During this

Fig. 8-13. Dix House, Dixville Notch, NH, *photograph, c. 1875, unidentified. The Balsams Grand Resort Hotel. This earliest portion of the present Balsams complex was opened by George Parsons in 1874 as a small inn.*

period, however, the key to its future as a resort spot was unlocked. In the mid-1850s the Atlantic and St. Lawrence Railroad (later the Grand Trunk Railroad) was completed as far as North Stratford in the Connecticut River Valley, allowing for easy stagecoach or wagon access to the Notch via Colebrook. The first to take advantage of the improved transportation links was Frank P. Walker, who in 1870 constructed a small hostelry, supposedly near the western entrance. A stereo view exists of an unfinished two-story wooden structure and barn, situated just west of the present hotel complex, but it is uncertain if this actually shows Walker's venture. Walker was in business only for a brief time, because his buildings were destroyed by fire in spring 1872.[22]

The next individual to attempt a hotel enterprise either in or near the Notch was Colebrook native George Parsons. In the summer of 1874, he erected a two-and-one-half-story inn with an attached barn (Fig. 8-13). Accommodating fifty guests, it is sited exactly on the spot where the oldest portion of The Balsams now stands. This simple, vernacular pair of buildings, while extensively modified both inside and out, were (contrary to some assertions) never torn down and form part of the current complex. Named "Dix House" in honor of General Dix, the new hostelry was dedicated on 4 July 1875 at a reunion of his descendants and opened to the public for the summer season. Given its obvious natural advantages, as the *White Mountain Echo* noted, it quickly became known for its "beautiful walks, lovely rides, tumbling

Fig. 8-14. The Balsams, Dixville Notch, NH, *blue-print photograph from viewbook*, The Balsams, Dixville Notch, N. H. *(Dixville Notch: n.p., [c. 1902]). The Balsams Grand Resort Hotel. In 1895 Henry S. Hale of Philadelphia acquired Dix House and substantially enlarged it under its new name, "The Balsams."*

cascades, and easy Alpine climbs." It could also boast fine spring water, pure and bracing air, primeval forest, sublime peaks and palisades, and superb fishing and hunting. Discovering the special qualities of the Notch, visitors from the towns and cities to the south came in increasing numbers. After Parsons died in winter 1890, his wife carried on the business and responded to the growing demand by enlarging and remodeling the inn in spring 1892, thereby increasing its capacity to seventy people.[23]

Regular summer guests at the Dix House during the 1880s were Mr. and Mrs. Henry S. Hale of Philadelphia, both of whom suffered from severe hay fever. Like others similarly afflicted, they sought relief in the rarified atmosphere of the North Country and over the years their health improved. As a consequence, Mr. Hale, the successful inventor and manufacturer of the Pullman car reversible seat, decided to invest his wealth in a hotel for victims of the hay fever scourge. In 1895, under the aegis of the new Dixville Improvement Company, he acquired the Dix House from George Parsons' widow. Under the new name of "The Balsams"—after the abundant local fir tree—he launched an ambitious development scheme. Over the next year the edifice was transformed into a substantial hotel capable of sleeping up to 150 guests (Fig. 8-14). Marked by its distinctive late-Victorian cylindrical and octagonal corner towers, Hale's new resort also advertised an informal, comfortable and home-like interior, with "well arranged and commodious" public rooms.[24] An account in *White Mountain Life* offers an excellent overview of The Balsams' inside spaces soon after its acquisition by Mr. Hale and the subsequent expansion:

> The architectural style of The Balsams provides good out-looks from all rooms. Its piazzas extend along both sides and in front and are

[226]

Fig. 8-15. Office, The Balsams, Dixville Notch, NH, *blue-print photograph from viewbook*, The Balsams, Dixville Notch, N. H. *(Dixville Notch: n.p., [c. 1902])*. The Balsams Grand Resort Hotel. *This inviting and informal space doubled as an entrance parlor and business venue for guests.*

Fig. 8-16. Dining Hall, The Balsams, Dixville Notch, NH, *blue-print photograph from viewbook*, The Balsams, Dixville Notch, N. H. *(Dixville Notch: n.p., [c. 1902])*. The Balsams Grand Resort Hotel. *Bright and cheery, the dining room featured typical hotel period furnishings including oil lamps on each table, and late Victorian oakwood Windsor chairs.*

well shaded. The office [Fig. 8-15] has a comfortable air of good fellowship in its roomy freedom, and is accessible from the reception room, which fills the lower corner of the floor; from the bright and cheery dining hall [Fig. 8-16] which fills the recess between the towers in front, or from the billiard and reading rooms in the rear. A broad stairway also leads from this office to the chamber floor above, beside which there are a few ground floor sleeping rooms.

. . .the [sleeping] rooms [are] . . . of good size and most happily planned with regard to outlook. One of the most delightful chambers . . . occupies the full tower corner of the second floor, describing a perfect circle, with an outlook charmingly varied by its many windows. Other rooms are equally large, and all are splendidly furnished in quartered oak, among the furnishings being such blessed comforts as first-rate [spring] beds, Morris chairs, heavy bevel plate mirrors, and the like.

Throughout the house the finish is uniformly of handsome hard pine in its natural effect. Many of the floors are of hard wood spread with soft rugs, and others are covered with the richest and softest of carpets. There are several bath room suites, all baths being fitted with the most approved appliances for ventilation and beauty.

To these rooms is connected the same pure, cold spring water, inexhaustible in its supply, which is used for all purposes throughout the premises. In these finest rooms, also, broad fireplaces are ready for use, while the entire house may be steam heated in the coldest of winter weather. In fact, no detail which makes for the most complete comfort and luxury of the guest seems to have been ignored.[25]

Other additions to the complex between 1895 and 1897 included quarters for male and female employees, a laundry building, stable, carriage barn, storage structure, and several log cabins and arbors. At the same time the grounds were greatly improved by the creation of a nine-hole golf course, new walking paths, and new roads to and from the main house. Even a dam was constructed in front, to form an artificial impoundment, Lake Gloriette, for boating, fishing, swimming and aesthetic pleasure. Gradually local farms were acquired to provide food for the hotel table. Hale was clearly on his way to realizing his master plan for the hotel and its 2,000-acre tract in the Notch to become the "Switzerland of America."[26]

Over the first fifteen years of this century, Hale vigorously and attentively pursued his objective, committing several million dollars to the enterprise. Around 1900 engineers constructed a reservoir east

Fig. 8-17. Architect's Sketch, "Old" Complex, The Balsams, Dixville Notch, NH, *illustration from booklet,* The Balsams, Dixville Notch, N. H. *(Philadelphia: The Dixville Notch Corporation, [1912]). The Balsams Grand Resort Hotel. This idealized view depicts the original central portion (Dix House), and the new west (1910) and east (1911-12) wings, the work of a hitherto unidentified architect.*

of and above the hotel from which water made its way by large pipe to drive an electric generating plant and to supply a fish hatchery. A men's employee dormitory and servants' dining room were built in 1902. The Dixville farmstead, situated about one mile from The Balsams, was opened as a thirty-guest annex in 1904. In 1906 Hale completed a new summer cottage adjacent to the hotel for himself and his family and later added other cottages for guests. He also created a second and then a third artificial lake (Abenaki and Coashaukee) for recreation and water power below Lake Gloriette. The hotel plant was further augmented by the erection of a new building behind the old east center ell. Connected by an enclosed passageway, it contained small dining rooms, a barber shop and a bazaar. A 125 by 30-foot structure was also built to accommodate blacksmith and woodworking shops, a garage, employees rooms and storage space. In 1910 the hotel received a major addition when the west wing (Fig. 8-17), with its skylighted, octagonal end section, was expanded, according to oral tradition, by Sylvanus D. Morgan. It provided seventy-five new bedrooms and increased the size of the common rooms on the ground floor. From fall 1911 to summer 1912 the capacity rose to 150 persons, when a new northeast ell with four-and-a-half-story end section was built. It contained more bedrooms, a new music room and more dining space. That year a new eighteen-hole golf course, conceived by Donald J. Ross, was laid out on the side of Keyser Mountain above the complex.[27] What is today regarded as the "old" portion of the complex was essentially completed (Fig. 8-18).

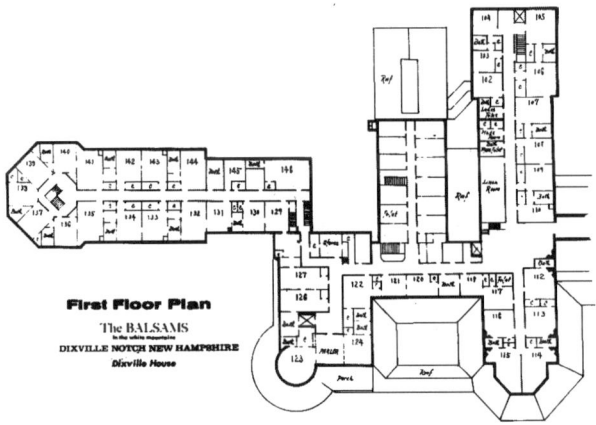

Fig. 8-18. First Floor Plan, The Balsams, Dixville Notch, NH. *The Balsams Grand Resort Hotel. This c. 1990 plan illustrates the current arrangement of the rooms on one guest floor in the "old" portion of the complex.*

But Hale's master plan for his progressive program of expansion did not come easily. For a time, he had flirted with the idea of constructing a major new hotel similar to Henry Flagler's massive Florida complexes on the shores of the two lower lakes. Sometime between 1912 and 1914, he had commissioned a hitherto unidentified architect to prepare a preliminary perspective design, a fine, restored colored rendering of which hangs today in the parlor adjacent to the main dining room (see Plate 18). Such a grandiose scheme, had it been implemented, would have necessitated the relocation and reorientation of the old complex, completely altering the ambiance of the Notch. Perhaps due to the outbreak of World War I in Europe in 1914 and related economic concerns, Hale changed his mind about a possible new hotel; nevertheless, he committed his company to the most ambitious expansion during The Balsams' existence.[28] The new outbuildings and massive guest wing, in terms of scale, proportion, style and interior layout, would comprise a distinct and highly eclectic specimen of World War I-era hotel architecture.

Fortunately, thanks to the conscientious archival policy of the H. P. Cummings Construction Company of Ware, Massachusetts, complete documentation of this important period in the building history of The Balsams has survived. From 1914 to 1918 Cummings secured a series of contracts with the Dixville Notch Corporation, the records, construction photographs, correspondence, specifications and certain blueprint drawings for which are preserved at the company's administrative headquarters. This incredible treasure of original source material is unique; there is no other twentieth-century White Mountain hotel for which a similar collection is believed to exist. Based on this documentation we know that Cummings built a stone golf house in 1914 (Fig. 8-25) and a two-story lobby and dining room addition in 1916 (Fig. 8-19). Also during 1916, a remarkable year of construction activity at the hotel, the firm erected the so-called "New Dormitory" (Fig. 8-20), the connected "Garage-Dormitory" and the forty-guest "Winter Inn," all great, barn-like Colonial Revival structures

Fig. 8-19. Dining Room, The Balsams, Dixville Notch, NH, *photograph, c. 1990. The Balsams Grand Resort Hotel. A lobby and dining room addition to the "old" complex was erected in 1916 by H. P. Cummings Construction Company of Ware, Massachusetts.*

Fig. 8-20. "New Dormitory," The Balsams, Dixville Notch, NH, *photograph, 1991, by the author. This was one of several buildings that comprised Henry S. Hale's ambitious expansion scheme of 1914-18.*

topped by gambrel roofs punctuated by dormers.[29] These effectively complemented each other as well as the main hotel, the sheer massiveness of the building group being its most overwhelming architectural characteristic.

The efforts of Cummings Construction Company for Henry Hale and his Dixville Notch Corporation culminated in 1916-18 with the construction of Hampshire House (see Plate 19). This semi-detached, six-and-a-half-story guest wing was appended to the new 1916 connector on the south side of the complex. The first steel-frame, tile and concrete masonry structure to be erected in New Hampshire, it represented a major engineering step for the hotel industry, offering its occupants state-of-the-art fire protection (Fig. 8-21). Conceived in the Rhenish

Fig. 8-21. Hampshire House Under Construction, The Balsams, Dixville Notch, NH, *photograph, c. 1917. The Balsams Grand Resort Hotel. This new guest annex was the first steel-frame, tile, and concrete masonry building in New Hampshire.*

eclectic vein to fit Hale's Alpine village image of The Balsams, this imposing, almost pretentious building brought national attention to the hotel, permanently assuring it grand resort hotel status. Particularly striking were eight tall square towers with low, pyramidal tile roofs, like those of the Mount Washington Hotel, inspired by the campaniles of Renaissance Italy (Fig. 8-22). The round-arched apertures of these towers recall Romanesque architecture, while certain of the gables and window embellishments are reminiscent of nineteenth-century domestic buildings of the German Rhine Valley. Arranged along traditional double-loaded corridors (Fig. 8-23), the interior bedrooms, individually and in suites, increased the advertised capacity of the full complex to 800 guests, although the figure of 400 is more accurate and is the official guest capacity today. The construction of Hampshire House was accomplished for approximately $200,000, just under half the total amount Hale expended on his four-year improvement program.[30]

For the architect of Hampshire House, Hale selected Chase R. Whitcher (1876-1940), a Massachusetts Institute of Technology-trained native of Lisbon, New Hampshire, whose offices were in Manchester for most of his practicing years (Fig. 8-24). He was known as "one of the leading and most successful architects of Northern New England," having "designed and furnished plans for some of the most important public buildings in the state." During his career Whitcher is credited with the design of over 300 buildings in New Hampshire and elsewhere in the United States, including town halls, municipal buildings, schools, commercial blocks, health care facilities, "fine homes and country places" and hotels. Among his commissions in the state were the Millville School, Statehouse Annex, and additions to the New Hampshire State Hospital in Concord, the Merchants Bank and Masonic Temple in Manchester, the Normal School and State Sanitarium in Keene, the State School and Masonic Temple in Laconia, the Bald Peak Colony Club on Lake Winnipesaukee (Melvin Village), and the Shepard Block in Franklin. Outside of New Hampshire he had commissions as far afield as Bermuda where he planned the Princess Hotel.[31] It is not known exactly how he forged a working relationship with the Dixville Notch Corporation, but he was socially and politically well connected, and undoubtedly referred by many for the project at The Balsams. Since the entire record (ten blueprint plan sheets, specifications, correspondence, construction photographs) of his work on Hampshire House has been preserved by the Cummings Construction Company, we can intensively study the processes of design and contracting, as well as the final architectural product. Hale and his colleagues were clearly proud of Whitcher's creation and made available a postcard reproducing a presentation perspective sketch for the use and enjoyment of hotel guests (Fig. 8-25).

The construction of Hampshire House all but completed The Balsams complex (see Plate 20). Since 1920, there have been only smaller additions and periodic refurbishings, as is typical of the surviving American grand resort hotels. The ownership, while recently more stable than that of the Mount Washington Hotel, has changed several times over the years. The first transfer of title took place in 1922 when Henry Hale, his resources depleted by losses from unsound pre-World War I German investments, regretfully auctioned off the property. J. J. Lannin, a New York businessman, acquired the hotel for the modest sum of $150,000, along with a $1,500,000 mortgage. Perhaps best known as the owner of the Boston Red Sox baseball team, Lannin ran the operation through 1927, maintaining the Hale connection by retaining Warren Hale, Henry's son, as the resident manager.[32]

The next owner of The Balsams was Frank Doudera, a successful New York interior decorator to whom Lannin supposedly granted the property, sight unseen, in exchange for the Hotel Grenada, which Doudera owned in Brooklyn. His rise to wealth was an American success story. As a young member of the New York Police Department, about 1904 Doudera miraculously saved the baby daughter of a wealthy socialite from a fire. This courageous act received national media attention, in large part because the child was named Evelyn Nesbit Shaw Walker for Evelyn, the wife of Harry K. Thaw, the notorious murderer of the celebrated architect Stanford White. The episode resulted in Doudera's receiving wide-

Fig. 8-22. Tower Detail, Hampshire House, The Balsams, Dixville Notch, NH, *photograph of blueprint drawing. H. P. Cummings Construction Company, Ware, MA. This is one of eight square towers depicted in a complete set of plans owned by the contractor.*

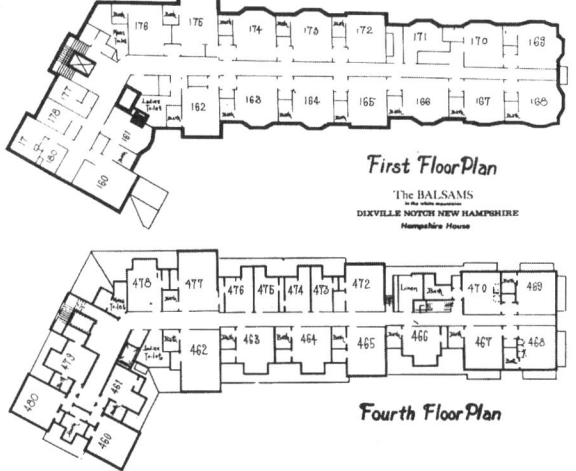

Fig. 8-23. First and Fourth Floor Plans, Hampshire House, The Balsams, Dixville Notch, NH, *photograph of c. 1990 originals. The Balsams Grand Resort Hotel. Guest rooms are arranged along traditional double-loaded corridors, individually as well as in suites.*

Fig. 8-24. Chase R. Whitcher (1876-1940), Architect of Hampshire House, The Balsams, Dixville Notch, NH, *photograph from Hobart Pillsbury,* New Hampshire: Resources, Attractions, and People, *(1927), Vol. 6, op., p. 68. Author's Collection. Whitcher spent most of his career designing New Hampshire buildings.*

spread positive publicity, a promotion to mounted policeman with the rank of honorary Captain, and a handsome monetary reward from little Evelyn's family. After serving in World War I, he rejoined the department, resigning soon thereafter. He then invested his money in real estate and formed the Doudera Decorating Company, which realized substantial profits during the booming 1920s. Upon acquiring The Balsams, Doudera developed and promoted additional recreational options, among them riding trails, skeet and trap shooting ranges, tennis courts, a polo field and a special wooden swimming pool in Lake Gloriette. Despite and throughout the Great Depression, the hotel prospered, attracting an affluent clientele, many of whom were listed in the *Social Registers* of East Coast cities. For Captain Doudera this was a dream fulfilled—as one writer put it, "now the ex-policeman golfs with millionaires, rides with gentleman jockeys, and dances with debutantes."[33]

During the World War II era, the hotel passed through uncertain and financially perilous times, as did so many of its resort counterparts across the country. Like the Mount Washington Hotel it had a brief fling with European royalty. In 1941 Frank Doudera sold it for $700,000 to Baron Gerald de Nieuwenhove, the cousin of King Leopold of Belgium and the owner of several tracts of prime Florida real estate. Doudera leased back the establishment for operation in 1943, at which time it was again placed on the market and sold to Alvin and Zara Kallman of New York City. Facing the reality of people's changing leisure-time patterns, Kallman placed prime emphasis on the summer social season hoping that the time-proven magic of the hotel and its environs would continue to attract the well-to-do and socially prominent. Unfortunately, Kallman's well-intentioned efforts failed, and in 1954 The Balsams went into bankruptcy and was again put on the auction block. Failing to attract the required $200,000 bid, it was purchased by a federal agency, the Reconstruction Finance Corporation, which commenced a search for a proper buyer. What had once been a prize symbol of America's moneyed aristocracy had apparently become a victim of a total and irreversible revolution in national life styles.[34]

Neil Tillotson, however, did not share the view that history had passed by The Balsams. Acquiring the property from the R. F. C. in a negotiated sale, Tillotson—the founding owner of a Massachusetts manufacturer of latex rubber balloons and medical gloves—launched plans to develop the hotel and surrounding lands into a four-season resort with social and convention periods, and early spring and late fall close-down times. Tillotson invited Captain Doudera out of retirement to serve as managing partner, which he did for two years until age and physical infirmities forced him to sell his interest. Through innovative and enlightened management the hotel has been returned to successful operation and is more self-sufficient than ever before. Around 1962 the headquarters of the Tillotson Rubber Company (now Tillotson Corporation) were moved from Needham, Massachusetts, to rear buildings in the complex

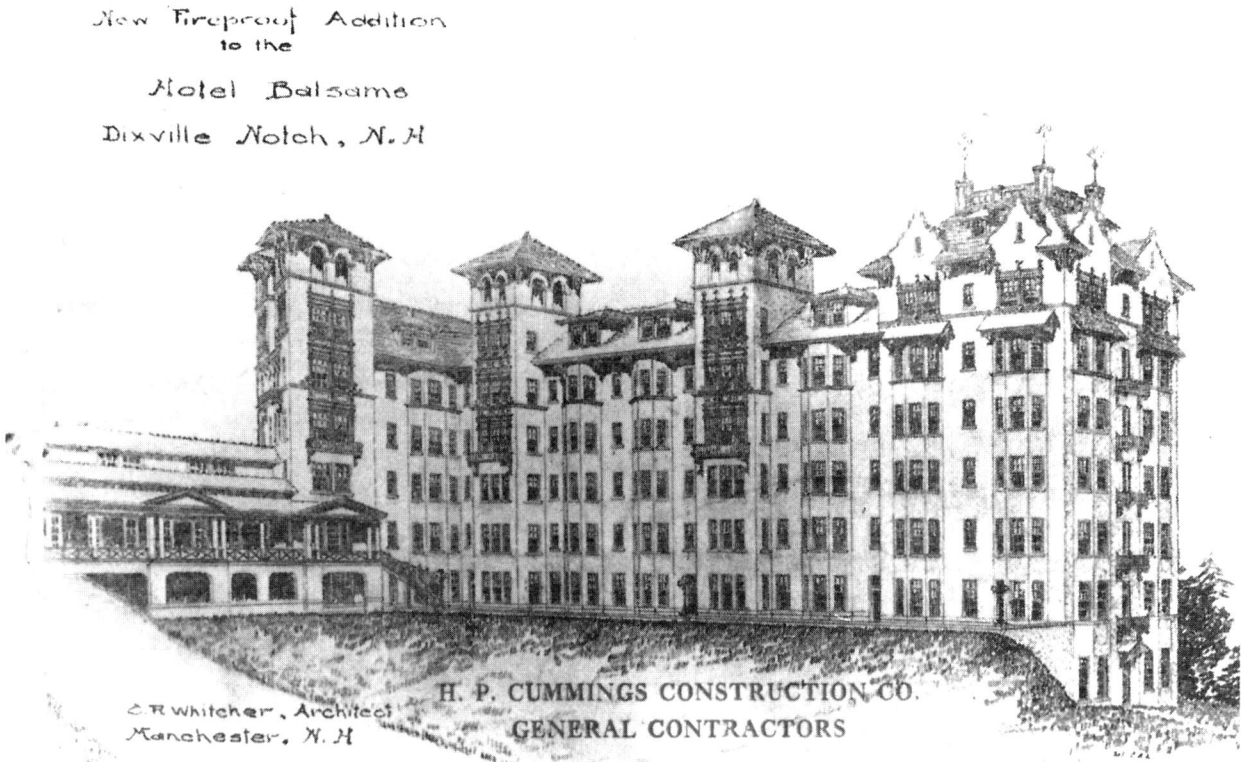

Fig. 8-25. "New Fireproof Addition to the Hotel Balsams, Dixville Notch, N. H.," *postcard view, c. 1917. The Balsams Grand Resort Hotel. This west elevation perspective sketch of Hampshire House was prepared by Chase R. Whitcher, architect for the building project.*

where the company continues to thrive today, providing rental income for the hotel corporation and welcome employment for area residents. The Balsams' lumber needs as well as additional operating funds are provided by a sawmill on the property and by tree harvesting from 15,000 acres of carefully managed forests. All heat and most electricity are co-generated in a custom-designed wood-waste energy facility realizing substantial operational savings.

A winter season was added to the hotel's schedule when the Balsams/Wilderness Alpine and Cross-Country Ski Area opened in 1966. The complete "winterizing" of the physical plant, and the inclusion of other sporting opportunities such as ice-skating, toboganning, sledding, snowshoeing and snowmobiling also attract visitors to the now multi-seasonal resort. Formed as a partnership in 1971, the current management team—consisting of Stephen P. Barba, Warren E. Pearson, Phil Learned and Raoul Jolin—leases the property from Tillotson. It has overseen and paid for the carefully staged renovation of the entire complex, providing vital daily hands-on direction for a new, modified American-plan enterprise. Today, under the marketing title "The Balsams Grand Resort Hotel," it thrives, its amalgam of architectural forms and styles under responsible care, still serving its original purposes.[35]

A c. 1928 promotional booklet, published by J. J. Lannin Company, Inc., contains an introductory passage that captures the essence of the hotel and its milieu, both then and now:

> At Dixville Notch, two great New Hampshire highways, east and west, join to form a natural playground for lovers of the great out-of-doors.
>
> And here in the midst of an enchanting panorama of wooded mountains, peaceful valleys, shimmering lakes and roaring waterfalls, stands a rendezvous of peculiar excellence— The Balsams. Seemingly in the very heart of remoteness, yet with the world at its threshold, The Balsams has combined a happy out-of-

doors' spirit with the comfort and luxury of the most exclusive of metropolitan hotels....

Those who come to rest will find here every accommodation; luxurious appointments, cuisine and service that will satisfy the most critical and exacting, all combine to produce a home-like charm so conducive to quiet comfort.[36]

In the nearly seventy years that have lapsed since this pronouncement, the hotel, the natural setting, and the visitor experience have changed very little.

WHILE THE Mount Washington Hotel and The Balsams have continued to operate, most of their counterparts and a far greater number of smaller hostelries have not enjoyed this good fortune. Since the nineteenth century the entire regional hotel industry has experienced gradual but agonizing decline until today there are only a half dozen guest establishments pre-dating World War II still in business. Fortunately, there are several more examples of the building type available for study, but even this architecture is disappearing at a rapid rate. This trend has been encouraged by the lack of alternative uses for structures aged and substantial in size, built to serve a single purpose and often removed from even modest population centers. As a consequence the efforts needed to preserve them has not been forthcoming, and even when attempted, the results have been sporadic and generally unsuccessful.

The historic factors resulting in the near elimination of the White Mountain hotels are complex, interrelated and largely economic. Dramatic changes in transportation systems, technology and uses have to be considered primary causes. By 1900, the traditional symbiotic relationship between the hotels and the railroads had begun to break down. This led to major reductions and ultimately the complete elimination of railroad passenger service to the region after World War II. The downward spiral and then ascendency was hastened at the turn of the century by the advent of the automobile, which had an immediate and negative impact on both the railroads and the hotels. Providing greater freedom, mobility and flexibility, the automobile gradually supplanted the railroads as the primary means of transportation in the mountains. At the same time it detracted from the business of the hotels, as travelers and vacationers opted for shorter, less expensive and more loosely structured visits—often preferring to spend their leisure time touring the region point to point, driving considerable distances. In response to this changing tourist market, roads were greatly improved, and smaller hotels and inns, cabins, camping sites and, more recently, motor courts and motels with lower operating costs took the place of the older and much larger hostelries. Reinforcing these developments were the periodic downward plunges in the economic cycle, exacerbated by the dampening effects of World War I, the Great Depression and World War II.

Changing American life styles have also worked to the detriment of the White Mountain hotel industry. Toward the end of the nineteenth century many more affluent individuals and families, some former hotel guests, chose to build their own cottages in the region, seeking the privacy, independence, and appreciation of their own real estate. The condominium movement of the past four decades is a modern manifestation of this same desire for a permanent commitment to a particular location and has further set back the hotels that have not adapted. The inauguration of the federal income tax early in this century combined with other economic factors, reduced people's disposable income; as a direct outgrowth, fewer patrons of means have been able to spend entire or major portions of summers at resort hotels pursuing leisure-time activities. In addition, as the century progressed, more and more individuals, particularly women, have taken on full-time careers, again allowing for less inclination as well as free time to spend extended periods of time away from home and a job.

Additional reasons for the near demise of the White Mountain hotels may be found in the buildings themselves, their locations and the realities of their operation. Virtually all were built of wood and were highly susceptible to fire, the scourge that has destroyed the vast majority of them. Furthermore, local firefighting forces did not, and probably could not, possess the proper equipment, expertise, or sufficiently trained personnel to save them, as most were large in size and many remotely situated. Because financiers and owners often emphasized profit over quality materials and building practices, some hotel structures (if they escaped fire) simply wore out from prolonged and heavy use and were summarily torn down. Some facilities that lasted until after World War II became outmoded, losing their appeal to patrons, and also were demolished. For the remaining owners attempting to maintain solvent hotel enterprises, modernization or replacement was not always financially feasible.

The increasingly high expense of operations, particularly at the grand resort hotels, has further diminished the prospects of the regional industry in the twentieth century. Over recent decades the costs of labor, utilities, heating fuel, maintenance and supplies have dramatically increased, requiring higher occupancy rates and steady increases in lodging, food and service charges to assure "bottom line" financial success. As a consequence some hotels have literally priced themselves out of existence or have become financially unfeasible vacation options for all but the most affluent. The competition for customers between the few establishments that have survived, therefore, has intensified as the potential guest market has shrunk.

Despite forces that have all but eliminated the White Mountain hotel industry, those few grand resort hotels that exist, as well as their smaller counterparts, have managed to adapt successfully to our changing national economic and social fabric. Much of their appeal continues to rest with their historic traditions, aesthetics, amenities, and their overall ambiance. While the future of the Mount Washington Hotel, The Balsams and the few other survivors will probably always be unsure, these magnificent complexes are the last giants of a once flourishing hotel community, the final compelling reminders of a vanishing architectural legacy.

Notes

1. Kilbourne, *Chronicles*, p. 343; brochure, "The Life and Times of Bretton Woods" (Bretton Woods, NH: The Mount Washington Hotel & Resort, [c. 1988]).
2. Kilbourne, *Chronicles*, p. 343; Burt, *The Story of Mount Washington*, pp. 107-108.
3. *WME* 24, No. 7 (17 August 1901), p. 24.
4. McAvoy, *And Then There Was One*, p. 145; Withey, *Biographical Dictionary of American Architects (Deceased)*, p. 233; *ATC* 25, No. 28 (13 August 1901), p. 4; *WME* 24, No. 7 (17 August 1901), p. 24.
5. *The Bugle of Bretton Woods*, No. 50 (1 October 1902), p. 7; *ATC* 25, No. 28 (13 August 1901), p. 4; Williams, "The Saga of 'S. D.' Morgan," p. 13. The Mount Washington Hotel possesses records for post-1920 operations, although these are incomplete.
6. *ATC* 25, No. 28 (13 August 1901), p. 1.
7. *Ibid.*, pp. 1-4; "The Life and Times of Bretton Woods." The wooden building used to house a portion of the Italian labor force, although in run-down condition, still stands to the northeast of the hotel. It is currently used for storage.
8. *ATC* 26, No. 13 (26 July 1902), p. 1, and No. 15 (29 July 1902), p. 1; Burt, *The Story of Mount Washington*, p. 108; *WME* 25, No. 5 (2 August 1902), p. 8; McAvoy, *And Then There Was One*, p. 137.
9. Kilbourne, *Chronicles*, p. 344; booklet, *In the Heart of the White Mountains* (Bretton Woods, NH: Mount Pleasant Hotel Company, [1901]); Carolyn Pitts, National Historic Landmark Nomination Form, Interagency Resources Division, National Park Service, Washington, DC. For those interested in statistics, the structure has over 2,000 doors, 1,200 windows, and is roughly 1,100 feet long including the wings. In addition the hotel upon opening boasted its own ingenious water, sewage treatment, heating, telephone and electric generation systems, the latter water-power driven.

    In 1992, the descendants of Charles Alling Gifford commemorated the fiftieth anniversary of the official opening with a visit to the Mount Washington Hotel. On that occasion they presented the new owners with materials pertaining to the architect and the hotel, including photocopies of the original floor plans.
10. The building at first possessed gray-green walls, intended to imitate stone masonry, as well as white trim and dark green shutters. Today the exterior is entirely white, with the exception of red-painted metal roofs. The shutters were removed some years ago, due to the expense of maintenance.
11. *In the Heart of the White Mountains*, pp. 3, 5, 7.
12. "The Mount Washington," *ATC* 26, No. 13 (26 July 1902), p. 8.
13. Obituary, "Joseph Stickney," *ATC* 28, No. 20 (30 July 1904), pp. 1, 4. Stickney's initial investment in the hotel and grounds was approximately $2 million.
14. *WME* 25, No. 28 (13 August 1901), p. 1; McAvoy, *And Then There Was One*, pp. 146, 150, 328; Bretton Arms National Historic Landmark Plaque, Mount Washington Hotel, Bretton

Woods; John Anderson to Robert I. Jenks, 25 April 1903, Edward Betts to Robert I. Jenks, 26 June 1903, Charles A. Gifford to Robert I. Jenks, 7 August 1903 and 9 October 1903, New Hampshire Historical Society; *ATC* 30, No. 1 (12 July 1906), p. 1; property insurance description, Mount Pleasant Hotel Company, "The Mount Washington," Carroll, N. H., John C. Paige & Co., Insurance, Boston, New Hampshire Historical Society; *The Bugle of Bretton Woods*, No. 50 (10 October 1902), p. 9. The refurbished Brettons Arms contains thirty-two guest rooms, two guest suites, a fifty-seat dining room, a bar, and a parlor and meeting room for small conference groups.

15. Burt, *The Story of Mount Washington*, pp. 109-110; McAvoy, *And Then there Was One*, pp. 140, 141, 144-47; National Historic Landmark Nomination Form; Rod Lemson, *America's Grand Resort Hotels* (Charlotte, NC: The East Woods Press, 1985), p. 125. According to the *Yearbook of Bretton Woods* (New York: Charles Francis Press, [1910]), by Arthur William Emerson, the management of the hotel embraced the automobile early on and became an active promoter of auto touring in the White Mountain region. Recommended auto routes were published in special flyers, or were included in annual guest manuals. Both the Mount Washington and the Mount Pleasant became official hotels of the larger and better established automobile clubs. As a result Joseph Stickney and his associates deserve credit for attracting to the mountains a patronage that ultimately revolutionized the hotel industry there and in certain ways hastened its decline.

16. National Historic Landmark Form; "The Life and Times of Bretton Woods;" McAvoy, *And Then There Was One*, pp. 267-69; James E. Westhall, "The Renaissance of Bretton Woods," *New Hampshire Echoes* 3 (August 1972), p. 27; Lehr, *Carroll, New Hampshire*, p. 29.

17. "The Life and Times of Bretton Woods;" McAvoy, *And Then There Was One*, pp. 318-32; Westhall, "The Renaissance of Bretton Woods," pp. 27-28, 30-31; Daniel Ford, "The Life and Hard Times of the Sports Village at Bretton Woods," *Country Journal* (May 1977), pp. 33, 34, 36, 37; Daniel B. Hoik, "The Protected Village of Bretton Woods Resort," *Outlook* 4, No. 1 (Spring 1978), pp. 24-27; Arnold Zeitlin, "Grand Old Resort Hotel Fights for Survival," *Laconia* (NH) *Evening Citizen*, 31 August 1982, p.5.; Kevin Early, "The grand old hotel enjoys a renaissance," *Northern Light* 6, No. 32 (6 August 1985), pp. 1, 4; Tom Eastman, "Mount Washington Hotel: Landmark's restoration key to development plan," *Real Estate & Business News* (North Conway), 7 July 1988, pp. 1, 2, 13; *Appalachia* 47, No. 2 (15 December 1988), p. 132. The capacity of the hotel is currently about 450, a decrease from a previous peak figure of 600. This is a result of interior alterations and the conversion of double to single rooms.

Bretton Woods Associates, headed by Jack Sylvester, Jr., a former Boston investment banker, acquired the property for $6 million. In the 1988 sale the president of the Satter Companies was Robert Satter, while Michael, Paul and Roger Dowd were the principals of FDC, Inc.

18. "Mount Washington Hotel going on auction block," *The North Conway Daily Sun* 3, No. 95 (13 May 1991), pp. 1, 8; "Mount Washington Hotel goes on block today," *The North Conway Daily Sun* 3, No. 133 (26 June 1991), pp. 1,6; "Mount Washington Hotel up for bids today," *Boston Globe*, 26 June 1991, p. 69; "Saving a New England 'Grande Dame'," *New York Times*, 26 June 1991, pp. D1, D6; "Sold! Mount Washington Hotel properties go for $3.15 million," *The North Conway Daily Sun* 3, No. 134 (27 June 1991), pp. 1, 8; Daina Chiacu, "New Hampshire corporation buys hotel for $3.15 million," *Portland* (ME) *Press Herald*, 27 June 1991; "New Owners take over at Mount Washington Hotel," *The Northern Beacon* (Coos County Democrat), 26 July 1991, pp. 1, 2; *Appalachia* 48, No. 4 (15 December 1991), p. 139. Among other buildings acquired at the 1991 auction were the Bretton Arms hotel, the Lodge at Bretton Woods motel, and the restaurant at Fabyan's railroad station. The Mountain Properties Corporation includes Joel and Cathy Bedor, brothers Jere and John Eames of Littleton, Wayne and William Presby of Lisbon, and Robert Clement of Bethlehem.

19. Booklet, *Dixville Notch and The Balsams* (Dixville Notch, NH: Dixville Notch Corporation, 1901).

20. "History of The Balsams and Environs," *The Balsams Guest Directory* (Dixville Notch, NH: The Balsams Corporation, 1991), p. 5; [Merrill], *History of Coos County*, pp. 649.

21. Charles T. Jackson, *Final Report on the Geology and Mineralogy of the State of New Hampshire*... (Concord, NH: Carroll & Baker, State Printers, 1844), p. 106.

22. Balsams Time Line, The Balsams Grand Resort Hotel, Dixville Notch, NH; Eastman, *The White Mountain Guide Book* (1858 ed.), pp. 101-102; [Merrill], *History of Coos County*, pp. 649-50; *The Northern Sentinel* (Colebrook), 25 May 1871, p. 3; *White Mountain Republic*, 19 September 1872, p. 1. It has been conjectured that Walker may have started construction as early as 1864, but supporting evidence has yet to surface. Walker's inn and other buildings were insured by the Etna Insurance Company for $2,000, curiously just five days before they burned. The insurance award was for $1,775.

The railroad line from North Stratford to Colebrook opened in November 1887.

23. "History of The Balsams and Environs," p.5; [Merrill], *History of Coos County*, p. 650; brochure, "The Dix House," c. 1876; Farrar, *Farrar's Illustrated Guide Book to the Androscoggin Lakes* (1884 ed.), p. 194; *WME*, 5 July 1884, p. 10; *ATC* 14, No. 5 (16 July 1890), p. 4; *WME* 15, No. 1 (2 July 1892), p. 20. Farrar's *Guide* refers to a "main house," yet to be constructed, but planned to be "36 x 160 on the ground, and three stories high, the establishment containing when finished about one hundred and fifty rooms" (p. 194). Apparently the 1892 expansion represented the fulfillment of this plan, but on a less ambitious scale than originally envisioned.

24. "History of The Balsams and Environs," p. 5; *The News and Sentinel*, 16 January 1896, p. 3, and 26 March 1896, p. 3; Eleanor Early, *Behold the White Mountains* (Boston: Little, Brown and Co., 1935), pp. 148-49; *WME* 18, No. 2 (11 July 1896), p. 13; warranty deed, Clara L. Parsons of Columbia, NH, to Henry S. Hale of Philadelphia, 27 September 1895, grantor book #77, p. 313, Coos County Registry of Deeds, Lancaster. The first manager under Hale's ownership bore the marvelous name of Orville C. Bumford. After one year he was succeeded by James C. Trickey of the family associated with the Jackson Falls House in Jackson (see Chapter 2). Hale's business operated under the name of the Hale & Kilburn Car Seat Company and employed 500 workers at its peak.

25. "Travels of a Tourist," *White Mountain Life* 1, No. 4 (22 July 1897).

26. Ibid.; *White Mountain Life* 1, No. 1 (1 July 1897), and No. 2 (8 July 1897); *WME* 20, No. 1 (3 July 1897), p. 5, No. 2 (10 July 1897), p. 9, No. 5 (31 July 1897), p. 8, and No. 7 (14 August 1897), p. 20; "Dixville Notch—The New Hotel," *ATC* 21, No. 1 (19 July 1897), p. 4; *WME* 22, No. 1 (8 July 1899), p. 8. The description of the White Mountains as "The Switzerland of America" may have been popularized by painter Thomas Cole in his widely known "Essay on American Scenery" of 1836.

27. "History of The Balsams and Environs," p. 5; *WME* 23, No. 1 (7 July 1900), p. 14; *WME* 25, No. 1 (5 July 1902), p. 20; *WME* 27, No. 1 (9 July 1904), p.4; *WME* 28, No. 1 (18 July 1905), p. 8; *WME* 29, No. 3 (21 July 1906), p. 14; *WME* 30, No. 1 (13 July 1907), p. 14; *WME* 39, No. 2 (22 July 1916), p. 2; booklet, *The Balsams, Dixville Notch, N. H.* (Philadelphia: The Balsams Corporation, 1912), p. 6; *The News and Sentinel*, 16 May 1907, p. 3; *Littleton Courier*, 7 June 1907, p. 1; *The Colebrook Sentinel*, 26 March 1914, p. 5. In 1929 the dam retaining the water in Lakes Abenaki and Coashaukee was washed out in a storm, and seventy homes were destroyed along the Mohawk River flowing west to Colebrook. Altering the site, polo grounds were created in place of Lake Coashaukee. In turn these were replaced by a new nine-hole "executive" golf course in the late 1960s on the land formerly occupied by both lakes.

28. *WME* 37, No. 11 (7 November 1914), p. 4; "History of The Balsams and Environs," pp. 5-6.

29. Benjamin P. Harrington (H. P. Cummings Construction Company) to Warren Pearson and Stephen Barba (The Balsams), 23 May 1990, The Balsams, Dixville Notch, NH; construction photographs, 1916-17, for The Balsams, H. P. Cummings Construction Company, Ware, MA; booklet, *The Balsams, Dixville Notch, N. H.* (Philadelphia and New York: Dixville Notch Corporation, [1917]), pp. 4, 5, 27.

30. Construction photographs, Hampshire House, The Balsams, H. P. Cummings Construction Company, Ware, MA; Specifications, Additions to Hotel Balsams, Dixville Notch Corporation, 15 November 1916, H. P. Cummings Construction Company; Estimate, Fireproof Addition to Hotel, Dixville Notch Corporation, 4 October 1916, H. P. Cummings Construction Company; *The Balsams*, [1917], p. 4; *The Colebrook Sentinel*, 27 December 1916, p. 1; "History of the Balsams and Environs," p. 6; booklet, *The Balsams, Dixville Notch, N. H.* (Dixville Notch: Frank Doudera Company, Inc., [c. 1931]).

31. Chase R. Whitcher obituary, *Manchester Union Leader*, 26 August 1940; William F. Whitcher, *Descendants of Chase Whitcher of Warren, N. H.* (Woodsville, NH: News Book and Job Print, 1907), p. 53; Hobart Pillsbury, *New Hampshire: Resources, Attractions and People* (New York: Lewis Historical Publishing Company, 1927), Vol. 6, p. 68; Millville School, Concord, NH, National Register of Historic Places Nomination Form, New Hampshire Division of Historical Resources, Department of Cultural Affairs, Concord.

32. "History of The Balsams and Environs," p. 6; interviews with Stephen P. Barba, president of The Balsams Grand Resort Hotel, Dixville Notch, NH, 5 and 6 November 1990; warranty deed, Dixville Notch Corporation to J. J. Lannin Co., Inc., 20 May 1922, grantor book #214, p. 32, Coos County Registry of Deeds, Lancaster.

33. Historic scrapbooks, *The Balsams Grand Resort Hotel*; Early, *Behold the White Mountains*, pp. 149-50; Ernest Poole, *The Great White Hills of New Hampshire* (Garden City, NY: Doubleday and Co., 1946), p. 335; "History of The Balsams and Environs," pp. 6-7; interviews with Stephen P. Barba, 5 and 6 November 1990; *New Hampshire Sunday Times*, 4 April 1954, p. 1; deed, J. J. Lannin Company, Inc., to Doudera Construction Company, Inc., 2 April 1928, grantor book #245, p. 189, Coos County Registry of Deeds, Lancaster.

34. Historic scrapbooks, The Balsams Grand Resort Hotel; "History of The Balsams and Environs," p. 6; *New Hampshire Sunday News*, 4 April 1954, p. 1; warranty deed, Frank Doudera Co., Inc. to The Balsams, Inc., 29 April 1941, grantor book #315, p. 45, Coos County Registry of Deeds, Lancaster.

35. "History of The Balsams and Environs," pp. 7, 32; historic scrapbooks, The Balsams Grand Resort Hotel; interviews with Stephen P. Barba, 5 and 6 November 1990; Limerick, et. al, *America's Grand Resort Hotels*, p. 65; Lynn Harnett, "The Grand Hotel," *New Hampshire Profiles* 35, No. 12 (December 1986): 37-40; "The Wizard of Dixville Notch," *New England Business* (January 1989); Charles Kenney, "Grand Hotel in the Wilds," *The Boston Globe Magazine* (31 August 1980): 14-18; Linda C. McGoldrick, "Dixville Notch: Up-Country Success Story," *New Hampshire Profiles* 33, No. 11 (November 1984): 50-53. The current management team functions under the aegis of The Balsams Corporation, formed to operate The Balsams. The modified American plan (MAP) includes under one guest rate the costs of room, meals, and recreational/social facilities.

36. Booklet, *The Balsams, Dixville Notch, N. H.* (Dixville Notch: J. J. Lannin Company, Inc., [c. 1928]).

Fig. 8-26. "Golf Club House, The Balsams, NH", *photograph from promotional booklet,* The Balsams, Dixville Notch, N.H. *(Philadelphia and New York: The Dixville Notch Corporation, 1917), p. 14. Author's Collection. Erected in 1914, this stone edifice, with half-timbered gable ends and dormers, serviced a new eighteen-hole golf course designed by Donald J. Ross.*

Fig. 8-27. "Southwest View of The Balsams, Dixville Notch, NH," *photograph, 1992, by the author. With Mount Abenaki as a backdrop, this recent winter scene of the "old" complex (see Fig. 8-17) looks much the same as it did around 1912.*

Appendix A

A List of Pre-1930 White Mountain Hotels Accommodating Fifty or More Guests
(This is arranged according to town, village or locale. Alternative hotel names are included.)

Earliest Building Date(s)	Hotel	Destruction Date	Estimated Guest Capacity
Albany (Pequawket)			
1890	Piper House (Clement Inn; Wing's Tavern)	1940	60-70
Bartlett (Lower) (Intervale)			
1854	Pequawket House (Inn) (Smith's Tavern)	c. 1960	50-75
c. 1874	Pendexter Mansion and Cottages (Region House)	After 1963	50-70
c. 1870	East Branch House	1898	125
1884	Langdon House (The Langdon)	1913	50-60
1888-89	Pitman Hall	c. 1935	100-125
1895	Maple Villa (Hampshire House)	Extant	50
1895-96	Second Fairview House (The Fairview)	1919	65
1925-26	Fosscroft Inn (Fosscroft)	197?	50-70
Bartlett (Upper)			
c. 1872	Bartlett House	Partially extant	50
c. 1888	Cave Mountain House	1905	50-75
1893	Pleasant Valley Hall (Bernerhof; Glenwood by the Saco)	Extant	50-60
1911-12	Bartlett Hotel (The Howard)	1989	100
Berlin			
18??	Berlin House	Unknown	85-100
18??	New Revere House	Unknown	100-150
Bethlehem			
1805	Turner House and Cottage (Turner's Tavern)	Extant	75
1857	Sinclair House (Hotel)	1978	350
1870	Mt. Agassiz House (The Agassiz)	19??	150
c. 1870	First Howard House	1874	80
1874	Strawberry Hill House	198?	100-125

1874	Hillside House (Inn) and Central House (Blandin House)	c. 1930	85-100
1874	Bethlehem House (Sunset House)	1910	75
1875	Bellevue House	1900	90
1876	Ranlet's Hotel (Park House; Altamonte House)	19??	75-100
1876	Centennial House (Arlington Hotel)	Extant	75-100
1876	Avenue House (The Gramercy; Maplehurst)	Extant	75-100
1876-77	Alpine Hotel (House)	1991	100
1877	Upland Terrace (The Uplands)	1990-91	150-200
1877	Mt. Washington House (Hotel) (Perry House)	1958	125
1878	Second Howard House (The New Howard)	1958	250+
1879-80	Sunset Hill House	Unknown	125
1879-80	Highland Hotel (House)	Extant	85-100
1884	Idlewild Hotel (West End Hotel; Hotel Roosevelt)	1952	50+
1887-88	The Woodlawn (Bethmer Inn; Colby Inn; The Stage Depot)	19??	50+
c. 1890	Park View Hotel (Eastview; Lyndhurst)	After 1974	125
1891-92	Echo Hill House	Unknown	70
1892	Central Cottage (The Columbus; Columbia Hotel)	After 1974	60-90
c. 1895	Reynolds Hotel	1958	80
c. 1896	Second Prospect House	1923	85

Bethlehem (Maplewood)

1816	Maplewood Cottage (Inn)	1943	150
1876	Maplewood Hotel (The Maplewood; Maplewood Club)	1963	500+
1882-83	Maplewood Hall	1898	150

Campton

18??	Black Mountain House	c. 1883	100
18??	Hillside Inn (House) and Annex (Albamont)	Unknown	100
c. 1840	Sunset Hill House	Unknown	60-80

Carroll (Fabyan's and Bretton Woods)

c. 1818	Mount Washington House (Crawford's Old Moosehorn Tavern)	1853	150±
c. 1831	White Mountain House	1929	150-200
1867-68	First Fabyan House	1868	Unknown

APPENDIX A

1872-73	Second Fabyan House (White Mountain House)	1951	400+
1875-76	Mount Pleasant House	1939	250-300
1901-1903	Mount Washington Hotel	Extant	550-600

Carroll (Twin Mountain)

1868-69	Twin Mountain House (Hotel)	1960	250-300
1891-92	First Rosebrook Inn	c. 1920	50
1916-17	Grand View Hotel	Extant	50+
c. 1922	New Rosebrook Inn	Extant	65

Center Harbor

1825	First Senter House	1887	150-200
c. 1834	Moulton House (Hotel)	c. 1950	75
c. 1880	Garnet Inn	1994	100±
1887-88	Second Senter House (Colonial Hotel)	1919	150-200

Colebrook

1862	Parsons House	1890	125
c. 1867	First Monadnock House	1895	150
1892-93	The Metallak (The Nirvana)	1893	225
1895-96	Second Monadnock House	c. 1977	100
1897	Hampshire Inn (Parson's Farm)	19??	100
1903-1904	Second Colebrook House (Hotel) (New Colebrook House)	Extant	60-70

Conway (Center)

1850-51	Conway House	1912	75-125
1916-17	Presidential Inn	c. 1970	100

Crawford Notch

c. 1793	Willey House and Hotel	1899	60±
Before 1820	Mount Crawford House	c. 1900	60+
1827-28	Notch House	1854	75
1850-52	First Crawford House	1859	250+
1859	Second Crawford House	1977	350-400

Dalton

c. 1860	Sumner House	c. 1900	75

Dixville Notch

1874-75	The Balsams (Dix House)	Extant	400+

Franconia

c. 1870	Spooner Farm House (Franconia Inn)	Extant	50-65
c. 1878	Edson House (Franconia House)	1913	50
1882	Mount Lafayette House	1911	75

1882-83	Forest Hills Hotel	1984	250+
1884-85	Elmwood House	c. 1889	50

Franconia Notch

c. 1835	Lafayette House	1923	50±
1852-53	First Profile House	1905	550-600
1905-1906	Second Profile House (New Profile House)	1923	600

Gorham

c. 1837	Lary House (Mountain View Hotel)	1907	75±
1850-51	White Mountain Station House (First Alpine House)	1872	250
1853	Gorham House	Extant	50+
c. 1870	Eagle Hotel (House) (Mount Madison House)	c. 1967	50+
1875-76	Second Alpine House (Mount Madison House)	c. 1967	75-100

Holderness

1873	Asquam House	1946	130
1888-90	Mt. Livermore Hotel (Estates; House)	1923	250
1895-96	Holderness Inn (Central House)	Extant	60

Jackson

c. 1850	Hawthorne Inn	1973	50
1857-58	Jackson Falls House (Falls Hotel)	1978	100
1869	Wentworth Hall and Cottages (Thorn Mountain House)	Partially Extant	250
1875-76	Glen Ellis House	1982	80-125
1879	First Eagle Mountain House	1915	125
1884-85	Second Iron Mountain House	c. 1948	150+
1884-85	First Gray's Inn (Sunset Hill House)	1902	250-275
1902-1903	Second Gray's Inn	1903	200
1903-1904	Third Gray's Inn	1916	250
1915-16	Second Eagle Mountain House	Extant	225
1916-17	Fourth Gray's Inn	1983	225

Jefferson

1860	Waumbek Hotel (The Waumbek)	1928	500-600
1872	Jefferson Hill House (The Jefferson)	1993	100
c. 1872	Plaisted House (Waumbek Hall)	1980	125
Before 1876	Maple House	Unknown	50

APPENDIX A

	1879	Grand View House	Extant	50
	c. 1879	Starr King House	c. 1965	80

Jefferson Highlands

	c. 1864	Mount Adams House	1913	50-75
	c. 1870	E. A. Crawford House	1905	75
	c. 1875	Highland House	1971	50-60
	c. 1875	Pliny Range House	c. 1965	75

Lancaster

	1857-58	First Lancaster House	1878	150
	1881-82	Second Lancaster House (Lancaster Inn)	1954	150

Lincoln

	c. 1847-48	First Flume House	1871	200±
	1871-72	Second Flume House	1918	100-150
	c. 1890	Lincoln Hotel	1975	150

Lisbon

	1883-84	Breezy Hill House	1922	125-160
	1883-84	Brigham's Hotel	Unknown	50+
	1901-1902	Lisbon Inn (The Warren; Hotel Moulton)	Extant	75±

Littleton

	c. 1850	Thayers Hotel (Inn) (White Mountain House)	Extant	100
	1870	Oak Hill House	1895	175
	1884-85	Chiswick Inn and Cottages	1955	100
	1888-89	The Maples	After 1919	50
	1898	The Northern Hotel (Hotel Northern)	c. 1924	100

Mount Moosilauke

	1853	Tip-Top House (Prospect House; Summit House)	1942	60

Mount Washington

	1853	Tip-Top House	Partially Extant	80+
	c. 1871	Marshfield House (at Base Station)	1896	50
	1872-73	Second Summit House	1908	150-200
	1914-15	Third Summit House	1980	90

North Conway

	c. 1780	McMillan House	1899	80+
	1789	Moat Mountain House	Extant	50
	c. 1812	Washington House (The Cliff)	After 1963	50+

THE GRAND RESORT HOTELS OF THE WHITE MOUNTAINS

c. 1840	Centre Villa	Extant	50+
1858	North Conway House	Partially Extant	80-100
1861	Kearsarge House	1917	250-300
1864	First Hotel Randall (Randall House)	1902	80
1867	Sunset Pavilion (House) (Sunset Inn; The Sunset)	1940	150-175
1871	Mason's Hotel	1882	75+
c. 1872	Eastman House (Hotel Eastman)	1917	160
Before 1874	Artist's Falls House (Forest Glen Hotel) (Inn)	19??	75
1902-1903	Second Hotel Randall (New Hotel Randall)	1925	150
1925-26	Third Hotel Randall (Eastern Slope Inn)	Extant	150±

North Conway (Kearsarge Village)

1815	Orient House	1907	50
c. 1863	Russell Cottages	Extant	150-170
1885	The Ridge and Cottages	1899	100
1899-1900	The New Ridge and Cottages	1905	100

North Conway (Intervale)

1785	The Idlewild (The 1785 Inn)	Extant	50
1868	Intervale House	1923	250-300
1871-72	Bellevue House (The Bellevue)	1938	100-125
1890-91	Clarendon House	1962	100

North Woodstock

c. 1875	Russell House	c. 1942	60-75
c. 1875	Three Rivers House (Mt. Adams Inn)	Extant	100-125
1881-84	Fairview House	c. 1962	100
1886-87	Deer Park Hotel	1952	200-250
1890-91	Alpine House (Hotel Alpine; Dearborn House)	1966	200+
1896-97	French's Hotel	Unknown	50-75

Pinkham Notch (The Glen)

1850-52	First Glen House	1884	500-600
1884-87	Second Glen House	1893	500

Plymouth

c. 1800	First Pemigewasset House	1862	150
1862-63	Second Pemigewasset House	1909	250-300
1912-13	Third Pemigewasset House	1958	125-150

APPENDIX A

Randolph

1877	Ravine House and Durand Hall	1963	125
1883-84	Mount Crescent House (Randolph Hill House)	c. 1972	60-75

Sandwich

c. 1880	Sandwich House	1916	50

Shelburne

c. 1834	Philbrook Farm and Cottages	Extant	50-75
c. 1890	Shelburne Spring House	19??	75

Stratford

1858	Willard House	1895	50

Sugar Hill

1875-76	Goodnow House (Franconia Inn)	1907	300
1879-80	Sunset Hill House	1973-74	300-325
1883-84	Phillips House	1906	75-100
1886-87	Hotel Lookoff (The Mount Lookoff; Tree Top Lodge)	1964	200+
1888	Mount View House	19??	50
1893	Miramonte Inn	19??	75
1895	The Echoes (Echo Farm)	Partially Extant	50
c. 1906-1907	Peckett's-on-Sugar Hill	1967	100+

Tamworth

1863	Chocorua Inn (House; Hotel)	1945	150
1888	Tamworth Inn (Wiggin House; Hotel Tamworth)	Extant	75

Warren

c. 1843	Moosilauke House (Langdon House)	1911	60
1877	Breezy Point House (Hotel)	1884	50+
1885-86	Moosilauke Inn and Cottage Annex (Breezy Point Hotel)	1953	100

Waterville Valley

1867-68	Waterville Inn (Greeley's Mountain House; Elliot House)	1967	175-200

West Campton

1820	Sanborn's Inn (Stag and Hounds)	19??	125
c. 1840	Blair's (Blair Hotel)	Unknown	60

West Ossipee

c. 1803	Bearcamp River House (Bank's Hotel)	1880	75

Whitefield

1866	Mountain View House	Extant	300-350
c. 1870	Hotel Spruces	After 1932	60
c. 1880	Carlton House	c. 1890	60
1891-92	Overlook House (The Outlook)	1918	75
1925-26	Spalding Inn	Extant	60-80

Wolfeboro

1795	Lake House (Jewell's; Rust's Tavern; Sheridan House)	c. 1938	100
1849-50	Pavilion Hotel (Kingswood Inn)	1899	250-300
1873-74	Glendon House (Hobbs-Is-Inn; Hotel Elmwood)	1933	150-200

Woodstock

18??	Mountain View Hotel	1955	75

Connecticut Lake House, Pittsburg, NH. Engraving from "Topographical Map of Coos County, New Hampshire" *by H. F. Walling (New York: Smith, Mason & Co., 1861). Dartmouth College Library. Accommodating about thirty guests, this quaint, Gothic Revival-ornamented hostelry was located farther north than any other White Mountain region hotel.*

Appendix B

Lists of Known Pre-1900 Paintings, Printed Views, and Illustrated Maps Depicting White Mountain Hotels (measurements of paper items are of the image and do not include margins.)

Paintings

1. "Echo Lake and Profile House," by Edward Hill (1843-1923). Oil on canvas (1887), 96.5 x 157.5 cms. New Hampshire Historical Society.

2. "Echo Lake, Sunset (or Flume House White Mountains, Sunset, 1862)," George Loring Brown (1814-89). Oil on canvas (?) (1862), 41.9 x 57.2 cms. Current location unknown (on sale, Old Print Shop, New York City, 1947).

3. "Franconia Notch, The White Mountains, Echo Lake and Profile House," by Edward Hill (1843-1923). Oil on canvas (1887), 90.8 x 151.8 cms. Current location unknown (on sale, Richard Bourne, Inc., 1976; New Hampshire Historical Society exhibition, 1965). Other Hill paintings illustrating the Profile House very likely exist.

4. "Interior at the Mountains," by Otto Grundmann (1844-90). Oil on canvas (1879), 45.7 x 68.9 cms. Private collection (Hood Museum, Dartmouth College, exhibition, 1988). Depicts interior of a guest suite, Mountain View House, Whitefield, with view of Franconia Mountains to the south through the window.

5. "Lafayette and Profile House," by Edward Hill. Oil on canvas (?), dimensions unknown. Current location unknown (Crawford House auction, 1976; New Hampshire Historical Society exhibitions).

6. "The Notch in the White Mountains," by Thomas Cole (1801-48). Oil on canvas (1839), 101.6 x 156.0 cms. National Gallery of Art, Smithsonian Institution, Washington, DC. Shows the Notch House to the left of the Gateway.

7. "The Notch House, Crawford Notch," by Frank H. Shapleigh (1842-1906). Oil on canvas (1879). 48.5 x 76.0 cms. Private collection (New Hampshire Historical Society exhibition, 1982).

8. "Rigour of the Game, Kearsarge Hall, N.H. (or Croquet Game, Conway, N.H.)," by George Inness (1825-94). Oil on canvas (c. 1875), 50.8 x 76.2 cms. Private collection (University of Texas Art Museum Catalogue, 1965.)

9. "View of the Presidential Range and Crawford House, White Mts., N.H., From Mount Avalon," by Jean Paul Selinger (1850-1909). Oil on canvas (c. 189?), @ 75.2 x 127.0 cms. Formerly hung in the Crawford House lobby, Crawford Notch (either removed before or sold at the 1976 Crawford House auction; current location unknown).

10. "View to the Glen House," by William L. Sonntag (1822-1900). Oil on canvas (n.d.), 25.4 x 30.5 cms. Private collection.

Printed Views (This list contains the major published engravings, lithographs and etchings of White Mountain hotels. Numerous printed views of these buildings also appeared in guidebooks, periodicals, newspapers, viewbooks, promotional booklets and brochures, flyers, and railroad and other paper ephemera between 1850 and 1930.)

1. Two engravings from N. P. Willis (Nathaniel Parker), *American Scenery; or land, lake, and river illustrations of transatlantic nature*. 2 vols. (London: George Virtue, 1837-38, and later editions).

    a. "The Notch House, White Mountains. (New Hampshire)," signed W. H. Bartlett (L), and R. Wallis (R). 12.0 x 18.0 cms.

    b. "The Willey House.," signed W.H. Bartlett (L), and E. Benjamin (R). 11.9 x 17.9 cms.

2. Four lithographs from William Oakes, *Scenery of the White Mountains* (Boston: Little & Brown, and Cambridge: George Nichols, 1848). Each signed J. H. Bufford's Lith., Boston, or Bufford's Lith., Boston (R), and I. Sprague (L).

    a. "Mt. Crawford, near the White Mountains, with the Mt. Crawford House." 21.5 x 28.9 cms.

    b. "The Notch of the White Mountains, with the Willey House." 23.0 x 33.0 cms.

    c. "The Gate of the Notch of the White Mountains, with the Notch House." 22.0 x 30.2 cms.

    d. "The Franconia Notch, with the Lafayette House." 21.2 x 28.4 cms.

3. "White Mountains!!: Summit House, Mt. Washington, N.H." Engraved broadside view by Staples and Lunt, Printers, Portland, ME (c. 1854). 24.9 x 30.2 cms.

4. "Top of Mount Washington: 6285 Feet Above the Level of the Sea." Engraving by John Andrew, published by Evans & Plumer, Printers and Engravers, Boston (c. 1854-56). 15.3 x 20.4 cms. With Tip-Top House and the first Summit House.

5. "Top of Mount Washington: 6285 Feet Above the Level of the Sea." Orange-toned lithograph after John H. Spaulding scene by Bufford's Lith. (1855). 9.2 x 15.3 cms. With tower and United States flag (same view exists without tower and flag), and Tip-Top House and the first Summit House.

6. "Pemigewasset House, Plymouth, N.H., On the line of the Boston, Concord and Montreal Rail-Road, the Most Direct Route to the Franconia and White Mountains." Lithograph by John H. Bufford, Boston (c. 1855). 41.0 x 56.7 cms. Train in front of hotel.

7. "Pemigewasset House, Plymouth, N.H." Lithograph by John H. Bufford, Boston (c. 1855). 34.0 x 48.9 cms. Train to the right of the hotel.

8. "Pemigewasset House, Plymouth, N.H." Lithograph by John H. Bufford, Lith., Boston (1857). 34.4 x 50.3 cms. Side view from the southwest.

9. "The Notch House, White Mountains." Colored lithograph by Currier and Ives, New York City (after 1857). 19.0 x 31.1 cms.

10. "Summit of Mount Washington: 6390 Feet Above the Level of the Sea." Lithograph after Benjamin B. G. Stone by Sabatier. Published by M. Knoedler, successor to Goupil & Co., New York City (1858). Also published by Goupil in London and Paris. 32.4 x 42.5 cms. Includes Tip-Top House and the first Summit House.

11. "Lakes and Mountain Views in New Hampshire" series, lithographs after John Badger Bachelder by Endicott & Co., Lith., New York City (1858). Each 12.0 x 20.0 cms.

    a. "Valley of the Pemigewasset, Franconia Mts., N.H." Includes the first Flume House.

    b. "Senter House, Center Harbor, N.H."

    c. "Summit of Mt. Washington." Includes the Tip-Top House.

12. "White Mountain Station House, by J. R. Hitchcock & Co., Gorham, N.H." Lithograph by J. H Bufford, Boston (c. 1860). 38.7 x 65.0 cms.

13. "The Notch House, White Mountains, New Hampshire." Colored lithograph by Kellogg & Buckeley, Hartford, CT (186?). 20.0 x 30.8 cms. Mirror image (reversed) of the Currier and Ives lithograph of the same title.

14. "The Maplewood, White Mountains, Bethlehem, N.H." Lithograph by D. Drummond, published by the William H. Brett Engraving Co., Boston (c. 1875). 48.3 x 65.4 cms.

15. "Kiarsarge House, Thompson, Son & Andrews, Proprietors, N. Conway, N.H." Lithograph by Armstrong & Co., Lith., Boston (c. 187?). 45.4 x 27.3 cms. Trade poster.

16. "White Mountain Series" etchings by Robinson Engraving Company, Boston (1887). Each 10.5 x 16.5 cms.

    a. "The Crawford House"

    b. "Fabyan House"

    c. "Glen House"

Note: Hotels and boarding houses are also depicted in bird's-eye views published for the towns of Jefferson (1883), Whitefield (1883), Plymouth (1883), Littleton (1883), Lancaster (1883), Bethlehem (1883), Lisbon (1883), Colebrook (1887), Gorham (1888), Bartlett (1896), and Conway (1896).

Illustrated Maps (These maps contain small insert views or vignettes of White Mountain hotels.)

1. "A Map of the White Mountains," drawn by Franklin Leavitt, guide (Boston: John G. Bufford, Lith., 1852). 48.5 x 89.4 cms. Cuts of the first Crawford House and the White Mountain Station House, Gorham.

2. "Leavitt's Map with Views of the White Mountains, New Hampshire," by Franklin Leavitt (Lancaster, NH: Franklin Leavitt, 1854). 63.0 x 64.2 cms. Small cuts of ten inns and hotels.

3. "The Notch, White Mountains," from "Smith's Railroad, Steam Boat & Stage Route Map of New England, New-York and Canada." (New York: J. Calvin Smith, 1858). 58.3 x 68.5 cms. Insert view showing the Notch House.

4. "Leavitt's Map with Views of the White Mountains, New Hampshire," drawn by Franklin Leavitt (Lancaster, N.H.: Franklin Leavitt, 1859). Engraved by S. E. Brown, Boston. 52.7 x 67.8 cms. Small cuts of twenty-two inns and hotels.

5. "Map of the White Mountains, New Hampshire, From Original Surveys," contained in Harvey Boardman, *A Complete and*

Accurate Guide to and Around the White Mountains (Boston: Crosby, Nichols & Co., 1859). Engraved by Smith, Knight & Tappan, Boston. 51.0 x 56.5 cms. Small cuts of the White Mountain House, Littleton; Crawford House, Crawford Notch; White Mountain House, Carroll; Tip-Top and Summit houses, Mount Washington; Alpine House, Gorham; Willey House, Crawford Notch; Profile House, Franconia Notch; Flume House, Lincoln; and Glen House, Pinkham Notch. Also 1864 edition (same cuts), and 1871 edition, revised by H. S. Fifield, New Hampton, NH (Boston: John H. Bufford) (same cuts with altered titles).

6. "Topographical Map of Carroll County, New Hampshire, from actual surveys under the direction of H. F. Walling" (New York: Smith and Peavey, 1860). Roll map, 136.0 x 138.0 cms. Small views of Falls Hotel, Jackson, and Conway House, Conway.

7. "Topographical Map of Grafton County, New Hampshire, from actual surveys by H. F. Walling" (New York: Smith, Mason & Co., 1860). Roll map, 152.0 x 152.0 cms. Small views of Profile House, Franconia Notch; Flume House, Lincoln; Pemigewasset House, Plymouth.

8. "Topographical Map of Coos County, New Hampshire, from actual surveys by H. F. Walling" (New York: Smith, Mason & Co., 1861). Roll map, 162.0 x 106.5 cms. Small views of Summit of Mount Washington (Tip-Top and first Summit houses); second Crawford House, Crawford Notch; Alpine House, Gorham; Waumbek House, Jefferson; Sumner House, Dalton; Lancaster House, Lancaster; Connecticut Lake House, Pittsburg.

9. "Leavitt's Map with Views of the White Mountains, New Hampshire," drawn by Franklin Leavitt, Lancaster, N.H. (Boston: A. Williams & Co., 1871). 58.7 x 90.1 cms. Small cuts of thirty-eight inns and hotels.

10. "Leavitt's Map of the White Mountains, New Hampshire" (Lancaster, NH: Franklin Leavitt, 1878). Engraved by G. E. Johnson, Boston. 30.6 x 46.0 cms. Small cuts of over sixty hotels and boarding houses.

11. "Leavitt's Map of the White Mountains, New Hampshire" (Lancaster, NH: Victor Leavitt, 1882). 51.3 x 77.0 cms. Small cuts of over eighty hotels and boarding houses. An 1888 edition is identical except for the imprint date.

"Valley of the Pemigewassett, Franconia Mts., N.H. (Downward View)," *colored lithography after John Badger Bachelder by Endicott & Co., Lith., New York City, 1858. Douglas Philbrook, Gorham, NH. From the Bachelder series, "Lake and Mountain Views in New Hampshire."*

"White Mountains!!: Summit House, Mt. Washington, N.H.," *engraved broadside by Staples & Lunt, Printers, Portland, ME, c. 1854. Dartmouth College Library.*

Bibliography

This bibliography lists printed works consulted in the preparation of this book. Included are book, pamphlet, newspaper, magazine and journal titles. Paintings, printed views, and illustrated maps are listed in Appendix B. Due to the lack of surviving manuscript materials pertaining to the White Mountain hotels, the book is based almost exclusively on these sources.

I. *Books and Pamphlets*

A. General Works

Abbott, Karl P. *Open for the Season*. Garden City, NY: Doubleday & Company, Inc., 1950.

Andrews, Wayne. *Architecture in New England: A Photographic History*. Brattleboro, VT: Stephen Greene Press, 1973.

The Architecture of the American Summer: The Flowering of the Shingle Style. Introduction by Vincent Scully. New York: Rizzoli International Publications, 1989.

Blockman, B., E. Cromley and N. Harris. *Resorts of the Catskills*. New York: St. Martin Press, Inc., for The Architectural League of New York and the Gallery Association of New York, 1979.

Brown, Dona L. *Inventing New England: Regional Tourism in the Nineteenth Century*. Washington, D.C.: Smithsonian Institution Press, 1995.

Buckell, Betty Ahern. *Old Lake George Hotels: A Pictorial Review*. Lake George, NY: The Buckle Press, 1986.

Burchard, John, and Albert Bush-Brown. *The Architecture of America: A Social and Cultural History*. Boston: Little, Brown and Co., 1961.

Coke, E. T. *A Subaltern's Furlough: Descriptive Scenes in Various Parts of the United States . . . During the Summer and Autumn of 1832*. 2 vols. New York: J. & J. Harper, 1833.

Dingley, Robert J. *Now I Will Tell You . . . The Story of Naples, Maine, Its History and Legends*. Naples: Naples Historical Society, 1979.

Dorsey, Leslie, and Janice Devine. *Fare Thee Well: A Backward Look at Two Centuries of Historic American Hostelries, Fashionable Spas & Seaside Resorts*. New York: Crown Publishers, Inc., 1964.

Donzel, Catherine, Alexis Gregory and Marc Walter. *Grand American Hotels*. New York: The Vendome Press, [c.1990].

[Dwight, Theodore Jr.]. *Sketches of Scenery and Manners in the United States*. New York: A. T. Goodrich, 1829.

Farrar, Capt. Charles A. J. *Through the Wilds: A Record of Sport and Adventure in the Forests of New Hampshire and Maine*. Boston: Estes & Lauriat, 1892.

Gillon, Edmund V., Jr. *Early Illustrations and Views of American Architecture*. New York: Dover Publications, 1971.

Hamlin, Talbot F. *Greek Revival Architecture in America: Being an Account of Important Trends in American Architecture and American Life prior to the War Between the States*. New York: Oxford University Press, 1944. Reprinted, New York: Dover Publications, Inc., 1964.

Harnett, Lynn. "The Grand Hotel," *New Hampshire Profiles* 35, No. 12 (December 1986): 37-40.

Haynes, George H. *Souvenir of New England's Great Resorts*. New York: Moss Engraving Co., 1891.

Hepburn, Andrew. *The Grand Resorts of North America*. New York: Doubleday & Co., Inc., 1965.

Holt, Jeff. *The Grand Trunk in New England*. Toronto: Railfare Enterprises, Ltd., 1986.

Johnson, Ron, ed. *Maine Central R.R., Mountain Division*. So. Portland, ME: 470 Railroad Club, 1985.

Kramer, J. J. *The Last of the Grand Hotels*. New York: Van Nostrand Reinhold Co., 1978.

Lawliss, Chuck. *Great Resorts of America*. New York: Holt, Rinehart and Winston, 1983.

Lemson, Rod. *America's Grand Resort Hotels*. Charlotte, NC: The East Woods Press, 1985.

Limerick, Jeffrey W. "The Grand Resort Hotels of America," *Perspecta 15: The Yale Architectural Journal* (1975): 87-109.

Limerick, Jeffrey, Nancy Ferguson and Richard Oliver. *America's Grand Resort Hotels*. New York: Pantheon Books, 1979.

Maddox, Diane, ed. *Built in U.S.A.: American Buildings from Airports to Zoos*. Washington, DC: The Preservation Press of the National Trust for Historic Preservation, 1985.

Platt, Frederick. *America's Gilded Age: Its Architecture and Decoration*. So. Brunswick, NJ, and New York: A. S. Barnes and Co., 1976.

Roth, Leland M. *A Concise History of American Architecture*. New York: Harper & Row, 1980.

Sculley, Vincent J., Jr. *The Shingle Style: Architectural Theory and Design from Richardson to the Origins of Wright*. New Haven and London: Yale University Press, 1955. Revised ed., 1971.

Thompson, Deborah, ed. *Maine Forms of American Architecture*. Camden, ME: Downeast Magazine for the Colby Museum of Art, 1976.

Van Zandt, Roland. *The Catskill Mountain House*. New Brunswick, NJ: Rutgers University Press, 1966.

Whiffen, Marcus, and Frederick Koeper. *American Architecture, 1607-1976*. Cambridge, MA: MIT Press, 1981.

Willis, Nathaniel P., with views by William H. Bartlett. *American Scenery*. 2 vols. London: George Virtue, 1838-40.

Wilson, Richard Guy, ed. *Victorian Resorts and Hotels: Essays from a Victorian Society Autumn Symposium*. Philadelphia: Victorian Society of America, 1982.

Withey, Henry F., and Elsie R. Withey. *Biographical Dictionary of American Architects (Deceased)*. Los Angeles: Hennessey & Ingalls, Inc., 1970.

B. New Hampshire and the White Mountain Region

Anderson, John, and Stearns Morse. *The Book of the White Mountains*. New York: Minton, Balch & Co., 1930.

Bacon, George F. *Central New Hampshire and Its Leading Business Men. . . .* Boston: Mercantile Publishing Co., 1890.

Bardwell, John D., and Ronald D. Bergeron. *The White Mountains, New Hampshire: A Visual History*. Norfolk, VA: The Donning Co., 1989.

Barker, Shirley F. "The Heydey of the Grand Hotel," *New Hampshire Profiles* 5, No. 8 (August 1956): 18-21, 43; No. 9 (September 1956): 26-28, 47-48.

Bartelink, Susan, comp. "Summer in New Hampshire: A Catalogue of an Exhibition," *Historical New Hampshire* 20, No. 2 (Summer 1965): 42-49.

Beal, J. Holland. *White Mountain Yesteryears*. North Conway, NH: The Reporter Press, 1966.

Bennett, Randolph, comp. *The White Mountains*. Bath and Augusta, ME: Alan Sutton, 1994. "The Old Photographs Series."

Boardman, Harvey. *A Complete and Accurate Guide To and Around the White Mountains*. Boston: Crosby, Nichols, & Co., 1859. Revised ed., 1871.

Bulkley, Peter B. "A History of the White Mountain Tourist Industry, 1818-1899." M. A. thesis, University of New Hampshire, 1958.

———. "Horace Fabyan, Founder of the White Mountain Grand Hotel," *Historical New Hampshire* 30, No. 2 (Summer 1975): 53-77.

———. "Identifying the White Mountain Tourist, 1853-54: Origin, Occupation and Wealth as a Definition of the Early Hotel Trade," *Historical New Hampshire* 35, No. 2 (Summer 1980): 106-62.

Campbell, Catherine H. *New Hampshire Scenery: a dictionary of nineteenth-century artists of New Hampshire mountain landscapes*. Canaan, NH: Published for the New Hamsphire Historical Society by Phoenix Publishing, 1985.

Campbell, Catherine H., Donald D. Keyes, et. al. *The White Mountains: Place and Perceptions*. Hanover, NH: Published for the University Art Galleries, University of New Hampshire, by the University Press of New England, 1980.

Charlton, Edwin H. *New Hampshire As It Is*. Claremont, NH: Tracy and Sanford, 1855.

Clark, George H. "Karl P. Abbott," *Granite Monthly* 58, No. 6 (June 1926): 175-176.

Colby, Fred Myron. "The White and Franconia Mountains," *Granite Monthly* 8, Nos. 5 & 6 (May and June 1885): 138-158.

Coolidge, A. J., and J. B. Mansfield. *A History and Description of New England. New Hampshire*. Boston: Austin J. Coolidge, 1860.

Crawford, Lucy. *The History of the White Mountains, From the First Settlement of Upper Coos and Pequawket*. White Hills, 1846.

———. *The History of the White Mountains, From the First Settlement of Upper Coos and Pequawket*. 2nd ed. Portland, ME: Hoyt, Fogg & Donham, 1883. Preface by Henry Wheelock Ripley.

———. *The History of the White Mountains, From the First Settlement of Upper Coos and Pequawket*. 3rd ed. Portland, ME: B. Thurston & Co., 1886.

Drake, Samuel Adams. *The Heart of the White Mountains: Their Legend and their Scenery*. London: Chatto & Windus, 1882.

Early, Eleanor. *Behold the White Mountains*. Boston: Little, Brown and Co., 1935.

The Enterprise of the North Country of New Hampshire. Lancaster, NH: White Mountains Region Association, 1982. Contains essay, "The Grand Hotels: The Glory and the Conflagration," by Randall Spalding.

Fogg, Alonzo J., comp. *The Statistics and Gazetteer of New Hampshire*. Concord, NH: D. L. Guernsey, 1874.

Gale, Eugene. "Memoirs of a Master Builder." *New Hampshire Profiles* 2, No. 3 (March 1953): 64-66; No. 4 (April 1953): 45-46; No. 5 (May 1953): 62.

Garvin, James L. and Donna-Belle. *On the Road North of Boston: New Hampshire Taverns and Turnpikes, 1700-1900*. Concord, NH: New Hampshire Historical Society, 1988.

Gems of the Granite State. Concord: Edward N. Pearson, Public Printer, for the Agricultural Department, State of New Hampshire, [1893].

Giffen, Daniel H. "Museum Notes: In the Notches: wash drawings by James Elliot Cabot, 1821-1902," *Historical New Hampshire* 23, No. 2 (Summer 1968): 32-36.

———. "Summer in the White Mountains," *Historical New Hampshire* 20, No. 2 (Summer 1965): 32-41.

———. "Summer in the White Mountains," *The Magazine Antiques* (August 1965): 195-199.

Gile, Rev. George W. *Excursions to the White Mountains with Dr. Ordway's Parties of '75 and '76*. Lawrence, MA: George S. Merrill & Crocker, 1877.

Hamilton, Richard. "The Golden Era of Grand Hotels," *New Hampshire Profiles* 21, No. 7 (July 1972): 32-39.

Hanrahan, E. J., ed. *Bent's Bibliography of the White Mountains*. Somersworth, NH: New Hampshire Publishing Co., 1971. A new edition of Allen Bent's *Bibliography of the White Mountains*, first published by the Appalachian Mountain Club, Boston, 1911. Supplements by Bent, 1918, and Walter W. Wright, 1947, Appalachian Mountain Club.

———. *Hammond's Check List of New Hampshire History*. Somersworth, NH: New Hampshire Publishing Co., 1971. First published by the New Hampshire Historical Society, Concord, 1925. By Otis G. Hammond.

Haskell, John D., and T. D. Seymour Bassett. *New Hampshire: A Bibliography of Its History*. Boston: G. K. Hall & Co., 1979. Vol. III of Bibliographies of New England History.

Hixon, Robert, and Mary Hixon. *The Place Names of the White Mountains: History and Origins*. Camden, ME: Down East Books, 1980.

"Hotels of New Hampshire," *Granite Monthly* 4, No. 11 (August 1881): 467- 474.

Jackson, Charles T. *Final Report of the Geology and Mineralogy of the State of New Hampshire. . . .* Concord, NH: Carroll & Baker, State Printers, 1844.

Julyan, Robert and Mary. *Place Names of the White Mountains*. Rev. ed. Hanover and London: University Press of New England, 1993.

Kilbourne, Frederick W. *Chronicles of the White Mountains*. Boston and New York: Houghton, Mifflin, Co., 1916.

———. "The White Mountains in 1909," *Appalachia* 29, No. 4 (December 15, 1953): 470-478.

King, Thomas Starr. *The White Hills: Their Legends, Landscape, and Poetry*. Boston: Crosby, Nichols, Lee and Company, 1860. 1887 ed., Boston: Estes and Lauriat.

Lakes and Summer Resorts in New Hampshire. Manchester: John B. Clarke, 1891. Published for the Commissioner of Agriculture and Immigration, State of New Hampshire.

Lakes and Summer Resorts in New Hampshire. Concord: Ira C. Evans, 1892. Published for the Office of the Board of Agriculture, State of New Hampshire.

Lane, Charles S., comp. *New Hampshire's First Tourists in the Lakes and Mountains*. Meredith, NH: The Old Print Barn, 1992.

Lapham, Donald A. *Former White Mountain Hotels: A Pictorial Collection with Brief Historical Data.* New York: Carlton Press, 1975.

Leavitt, Richard F. *Yesterday's New Hampshire.* Miami, FL: E. A. Seemann Publishing, [1974].

"Leisure and Elegance," *New Hampshire Profiles* 14, No. 6 (June 1965): 28-30.

McClintock, J. N. "The White Mountains," *Granite Monthly* 3, No. 11 (August 1880): 491-501.

Morse, Stearns, ed. *Lucy Crawford's History of the White Mountains.* Boston: Appalachian Mountain Club, 1978. 5th ed. 4th ed., Hanover, NH: Dartmouth Publications, 1966.

Mudge, John T.B. *The White Mountains: Names, Places & Legends.* Etna, NH: The Durand Press, 1992.

Oakes, William. *Scenery of the White Mountains with Sixteen Plates from the Drawings of Isaac Sprague.* Boston: William Crosby and H. P. Nichols, 1848. 1970 reprint ed., Somersworth, NH: New Hampshire Publishing Co. Foreword and Commentary by Sherman Adams.

Parks, Roger. *Bibliographies of New England History: Further Additions to 1994.* Pp. 155-174. Hanover, NH and London: University Press of New England, 1995. Vol. IX of Bibliographies of New England History.

Parks, Roger. *New England: Additions to the Six State Bibliographies.* Pp. 419-500. Hanover, NH and London: University Press of New England, 1989. Vol. VIII of Bibliographies of New England History.

Pillsbury, Herbert. *New Hampshire: Resources, Attractions and Its Peoples.* 5 vols. New York: Lewis Historical Publishing Company, 1927.

Poole, Ernest. *The Great White Hills of New Hampshire.* Garden City, NY: Doubleday & Co., 1946.

Prime, Samuel, I. *Under the Trees.* New York: Harper & Brothers, 1874.

Resident and Business Directory of the West Side of the White Mountains of New Hampshire. Littleton, NH and Beverly, MA, etc.: Crowley & Lunt, etc., 1914-59.

Smith, Steve. "A Grand Way of Life," *White Mountains Traveler's Almanac* 2, No. 2 (Fall, 1990): 22-23.

Spaulding, John H. *Historical Relics of the White Mountains.* Boston: Nathaniel Noyes, 1855. 3rd ed., Mt. Washington: J. R. Hitchcock, 1858. 4th ed., Mt. Washington: J. R. Hitchcock, 1862.

Tatham, David. "Franklin Leavitt's White Mountain Verse," *Historical New Hampshire* 33, No. 3 (Fall 1978): 208-231.

_____. "Moses Foster Sweetser's Views in the White Mountains," *Historical New Hampshire* 36, Nos. 2 & 3 (Summer/Fall 1981): 119-148.

Taylor, William L. "Getting There," in Richard Ober, ed., *Shaping the Land We Call New Hamsphire: A Land Use History.* Concord, NH: New Hampshire Historical Society and the Society for the Preservation of New Hampshire Forests, 1992. Pp. 24-35.

_____. "The Gilded Age of Tourism in the White Mountains," in Naomi R. Kline, et. al., *Edward Hill: A Man of His Time (1843-1923).* Pp. 13-16. Plymouth, NH: Plymouth State College, 1985.

Tetreault, Barbara. "The Last Grand Hotels: Relics of Days Gone By," *New Hampshire Sunday News* (Manchester, NH), 17 October 1982.

Tolles, Bryant F., Jr. *The Grand Resort Hotels and Tourism in the White Mountains. Historical New Hampshire* 50, Nos. 1 and 2 (Spring/ Summer, 1995). Proceedings of the third Mount Washington Symposium, Bretton Woods, NH, June 24-25, 1994. Nine essays.

_____, with Carolyn K. Tolles. *New Hampshire Architecture: An Illustrated Guide.* Hanover, NH: Published for the New Hampshire Historical Society by the University Press of New England, 1979.

Town and City Atlas of the State of New Hampshire. Boston: D. H. Hurd & Co., 1892.

Tuckerman, Frederick. "The White Mountains in the Early Seventies," *Appalachia* 15, No. 4 (April 1924): 431-439.

Wight, D. B. *The Androscoggin River Valley, Gateway to the White Mountains.* Rutland, VT: Charles Tuttle Company, 1967.

Willey, Benjamin D. *Incidents in White Mountain History. . . .* Boston: Nathaniel Noyes, 1856.

Williams, Paul A. "The Saga of 'S. D.' Morgan, Master Hotel Builder of the North Country," *New Hampshire Echoes* 1, No. 4 (Winter 1970): 10-13.

C. Guidebooks

The American Alps, Other Summer Resorts. Bethlehem, NH: The White Mountain Echo, 1892. Also 1893, 1894, 1895, 1896, 1897 and 1898 eds.

Androscoggin Lakes, Illustrated. . . . Boston: Rockwell and Churchhill, Printers, for the Androscoggin Lakes Transportation Co., 1888. Also 1886 ed.

Appleton's General Guide to the United States and Canada: Part I, New England and Middle States and Canada. New York: D. Appleton and Co., 1886.

Appleton's Illustrated Hand-Book of American Summer Resorts. New York: D. Appleton and Company, 1876. Also 1883 ed.

Bachelder, John B. *Popular Resorts, Routes to Reach Them. . . .* 1st ed. Boston: John B. Bachelder, 1872. 2nd ed., *Popular Resorts; and How to Reach Them,* 1874.

Beckett, Samuel B. *Guide Book of the Atlantic and St. Lawrence, and St. Lawrence and Atlantic Rail Roads including . . . the White Mountains.* Portland, ME: Sanborn & Carter, and H. J. Little & Co., 1853.

Bradlee's Pocket Guide for the Use of Travellers to the White Mountains and Lake Winnipiseogee. Boston: John E. Bradlee, 1860. Also 1861 ed.

Bradlee's Pocket Guide to the White Mountains, Lake Winnipiseogee and Lake Memphremagog. Boston: John E. Bradlee, 1862.

Burt, Frank H. *Mount Washington: A Handbook for Travelers.* Boston: George H. Ellis Co., 1904. Also 3rd ed., 1906.

_____. *A Tour Among the Mountains—Mount Washington and Its Surroundings.* Mount Washington, NH: Among the Clouds, 1879. Also 5th ed., 1886.

Burt, Henry M. *Burt's Illustrated Guide of the Connecticut Valley. . . .* Northampton: New England Publishing Co., 1868.

_____. *Burt's Guide Through the Connecticut Valley to the White Mountains and the River Saguenay.* Springfield, MA: New England Publishing Co.,1874.

Carpenter, Frank O. *Guide Book to the Franconia Notch and the Pemigewasset Valley.* Boston: Alexander Moore, 1898. 2nd ed.

Chisholm, Hugh H. *Chisholm's White Mountain Guide Book.* Portland, ME: Chisholm Brothers, 1880-1917. All editions after 1885 written by Moses F. Sweetser.

Chisholm's All Round Route and Panoramic Guide of the St. Lawrence...; The White Mountains; Portland; Boston; New York. Montreal: C. R. Chisholm & Bros., 1873. Also 1874 and 1875 eds.

Connecticut River Route: A Guide Book of the Most Direct Route from New York to the White Mountains.... New York: Taintor Brothers, Merrill & Co., 1876.

The Eastern Tourist: Being a Guide.... New York: J. Disturnell, 1848.

Eaton, John S. *Guide to the Boston & Maine Rail Road, The White Mountains, and all Principal Points in the New England States.* Boston: John S. Eaton, 1870.

Farrar, Capt. Charles A. J. *Farrar's Illustrated Guide Book to The Androscoggin Lakes....* 9th ed. Boston: Lee and Shepard, 1884. Also 11th ed., 1887.

Faxon's Illustrated Handbook of Travel.... Boston: C. A. Faxon, 1874. Rev. ed.

Field, George F. *Hand-Book of Travel over the Eastern and Maine Central Railroad Line to the Shore Watering Places, White Mountains, and the Lower Provinces....* Boston: Passenger Department of the Eastern & Maine Central Railroad Line, 1873.

Gage, William C. *"The Switzerland of America": A Popular Guide Book to the Scenery of New Hampshire....* Manchester, NH: C. F. Livingston, 1875. Also 1878 ed., Manchester, NH: Thomas W. Love.

Gems of the Northland.... Portland, ME: Maine Central Railroad, 1896.

Glimpses of the Great Pleasure Resorts of New England.... Portland, ME: G. W. Morris, [c. 1888].

The Great Resorts of America (Illustrated) Together with Places of Interest in Colorado, New York, Maine, New Hampshire and Canada. Portland, ME: Wilbur Hayes, 1894.

The Great Vacation Route—Chicago, Niagara Falls, White Mountains and Portland Line.... Portland, ME: H. Wilbur Hayes, Publisher, 1891.

Greive, Robert, ed. *Guide Book to the Mountains of New Hampshire and the Shores of Southern New England.* Providence, RI: Journal of Commerce Company, 1899.

Guide to the Lakes and Mountains of New Hampshire via ... the Boston, Concord & Montreal Railroad.... Concord: Tripp & Osgood, 1852.

Guide to the White Mountains and Lakes of New Hampshire.... 1st ed. Concord, NH: Tripp & Morril, Printers, 1850.

Guide to the White Mountains and Lakes of New Hampshire.... 2nd ed. Concord, NH: Tripp & Osgood, 1851. Also 3rd ed., 1851.

Guide to the White Mountains and Lakes of New Hampshire.... 4th ed. Boston: Redding & Company, 1852. Also 5th ed.

Guild, William. *New York and the White Mountains....* Boston: Bradbury & Guild, 1852.

Hand-Book of the Portland & Ogdensburg Railroad. Portland, ME: G. W. Morris for the P. & O. Railroad, [1888].

Hand-Book of Travel Over the Eastern & Maine Central R. R. Line to the Shore Watering Places, White Mountains, and the Lower Provinces.... Boston: Passenger Department of the Eastern and Maine Central Railroad Line, 1874.

Hawkes, W. S., ed. *Mountain, Lake and Valley, by the B. and L....* Boston: Passenger Department, Boston & Lowell Railroad, 1887.

_____. *Winnipesaukee and About There....* Boston: Passenger Department, Boston & Lowell Railroad, 1887.

Holden, Luther L., ed. *White & Franconia Mountains.* Boston: Boston, Concord, Montreal & White Mountains Railroad, 1882.

_____. *White & Franconia Mountains.* Boston: Publication Office, Boston, Concord, Montreal & White Mountains Railroad, 1883.

Ingersoll, Ernest. *Down East Latch Strings: or Seashore, Lakes and Mountains by the Boston & Maine Railroad.* Boston: Passenger Department of the Boston & Maine Railroad, 1887.

Keyes' Hand-Book of Northern Pleasure Travel: The White and Franconia Mountains.... Boston: Geo. L. Keyes, Printer, 1873. Also 1874 ed.

Keyes' Hand-Book of Northern and Western Pleasure Travel to the White and Franconia Mountains.... Boston: Geo. L. Keyes, Printer, 1875.

Kostechke, Diane M., ed. *Franconia Notch: An In-Depth Guide.* Concord: Society for the Protection of New Hampshire Forests, 1975.

McQuill, Thursty [Wallace Bruce]. *From New York to the Summer Resorts of New England....* New York: New York News Company, 1880.

_____. *The Connecticut by Daylight....* New York: American News Company, 1874.

_____. *The White and Green Mountains....* New York: n.p., 1872. Also 1873 ed.

Morris' Scenic Guide, Embracing the Famous Hunting and Fishing Territory, and all the Great Summer Resorts at the Mountains, Lakes, Woods, Springs and Sea Shore. Portland, ME: G. W. Morris, Publisher, [1901-1902].

Morris' Tourist Hand Book, Illustrated, With Descriptive Matter of Interest. Portland, ME: G. W. Morris, [c. 1891].

New England: A Handbook for Travellers.... Boston: James R. Osgood and Co., 1873.

Northern New England and Canada Resorts: A Handbook for Tourists and Travelers.... New York: Taintor Brothers, Merrill & Co., 1877. Also 1884 ed.

Official Hand-Book of the Boston and Maine Railroad, to the Sea-Shore, Lakes, and the White Mountains. Boston: Batchelder, Amidon & Co., 1877.

A Railway Manual Containing Railroad Maps of the Entire Route from Boston North, ... to which is added a Complete Guide to Lake Winnipiseogee and the White Mountains. Boston: George W. Briggs, 1849.

Randall, Peter E. *Mount Washington: A Guide and Short History.* Hanover, NH: University Press of New England, 1974. 2nd ed., Camden, ME: Down East Books, 1983. 3rd ed., 1992.

Richards, T. Addison. *Appleton's Illustrated Hand-Book of American Travel....* New York: D. Appleton & Co., 1857.

Rollins, Frank West. *The Tourists' Guide-Book to the State of New Hampshire.* 2nd ed. Concord, NH: The Rumford Press, 1902.

Routes to the White Mountains and Lake Winnipiseogee.... Boston: Pathfinder Publishing Co., 1851.

Sears, Edward S. *Faxon's Illustrated Hand-Book of Summer Travel to the Lakes, Springs and Mountains of New England and New York.* Boston: Charles F. Faxon, 1875. New and rev. ed.

Snow's Handbook of Northern Pleasure Travel to the White and Franconia Mountains.... Worcester, MA: Noyes & Snow, 1876. Also 1878, 1879 and 1880 eds.

The Summer Excursionist of the Central Vermont Railroad Company.... Boston: Central Vermont Railroad Co., 1874. Also 1875 and 1878 eds.

Summer Haunts. Hotels and Boarding-Houses in the White Mountains and Other Popular Resorts, and at Favorite Winter Retreats. Bethlehem, NH: White Mountain Echo, 1889. Also c. 1891 ed.

Summer Haunts and Winter Retreats. Bethlehem, NH: White Mountain Echo, 1890.

Summer Outings in the Old Granite State . . . via the Merrimack Valley Route. Boston: Passenger Department, Concord & Montreal Railroad, 1890. Also 1891 ed.

Summer Saunterings by the B. & L. 1st ed. Boston: Passenger Department, Boston & Lowell Railroad, 1885.

Sweetser, Charles H. *Book of Summer Resorts. . . .* New York: "Evening Mail" Office, 1868.

Sweetser, Moses F. *Among the Mountains.* "Here and There in New England and Canada" trilogy. Boston: Passenger Department, Boston & Maine Railroad, 1889. Also 1892 ed.

_____. *A Guide to the White Mountains.* Ed. and rev. by John Nelson. Boston and New York: Houghton Mifflin Company, 1918.

_____. *The White Mountains Region of New England.* Boston: Passenger Department, Boston & Maine Railroad, 1890. Also 8th ed., 1893.

Waldron, Holman D. *The Crown of New England.* Boston: Passenger Department, Maine Central Railroad, 1893.

Welch, Sarah N. (Brooks). *Franconia Notch: History and Guide.* Littleton, NH: By the Author, 1981. Printed by the Courier Printing Company.

The White Mountains: A Handbook for Travelers. . . . Boston: James R. Osgood and Co., 1st (1876) ed., 4th (1881 & 1882) ed., 5th (1884) ed. Boston: Ticknor and Co., 7th (1886) ed., and 9th (1888) ed. Boston and New York: Houghton, Mifflin and Co., 10th (1890) ed., 11th (1891) ed., 15th (1895) ed., and 16th (1896) ed.

White & Franconia Mountains: Stork's Grand Ten Day Tour of the White & Franconia Mountains. Baltimore, MD: Stork's Tours, [1880].

The White Mountain Guide Book. Concord: Edson C. Eastman, 1st (1858) ed., 2nd (1859) ed. Concord: Edson C. Eastman and Boston: Lee & Shepard, 3rd (1863) ed., 4th (1864) ed., 5th (1865) ed., 6th (1866) ed., 7th (1867) ed., 8th (1869) ed., 9th (1870) ed., 10th (1872) ed., 11th (1873) ed., 12th (1875) ed., 13th (1876) ed., 14th (1878) ed., 15th (1879) ed., 16th (1881) ed.

White Mountain Hotels and Boarding Houses: How to Reach Them, Their Localities, Accomodations, and Charges. Bethlehem, NH: The White Mountain Echo, n.d.

The White Mountain and Winnepissiogee Lake Guide Book. 1st ed. Boston: Jordon & Wiley, 1846. 2nd ed., Boston: Henry Marsh, 1848.

The White Mountains Described and Illustrated. . . . New York: Alexander Harthill and Co., [1860].

The White Mountains of New Hampshire and Coast and Woods of Maine. Portland, ME: Maine Central Railroad, 1890.

Williams, Wellington, comp. *Appleton's Railroad and Steamboat Companion. Being a Travellers' Guide through the United States of America. . . .* New York: D. Appleton & Co., 1849.

D. Photographic View Books

Album of the White Mountains. Portland, ME: Chisholm Brothers, [c. 1885].

Franconia Notch, White Mountains, N. H.: A view book of Nature's beauty spot in the Switzerland of America. Boston: Published for the Profile and Flume Hotels Company by C. B. Webster & Company, [c. 1910].

Pen and Sunlight Sketches of Scenery Reached by the Grand Trunk Railway and Connections. . . . Montreal: Grand Trunk Railway Company, 1891.

Pollock, Charles. *Souvenir of the White Mountains and Vicinity.* Boston: Charles Pollock, 1892. Varying cover titles.

_____. *White Mountain Scenery.* Boston: Charles Pollock, 1895, 1896 eds.

Scenes and Prominent Hotels of the White Mountains, New Hampshire. Bethlehem, NH: C. G. White & Son, 1903.

Scenic Gems of the White Mountains. Portland, ME: G. W. Morris, [c. 1901, 1903, 1904 eds.].

Sweetser, Moses F. *Views in the White Mountains.* Portland, ME: Chisholm Brothers, 1879. Duodecimo one star (Crawford Notch) edition.

_____. *Views in the White Mountains.* Portland, ME: Chisholm Brothers, 1879. Duodecimo two star (Franconia Notch) edition.

_____. *Views in the White Mountains.* Portland, ME: Chisholm Brothers, 1879. Octavo one star (Crawford Notch) edition.

_____. *Views in the White Mountains.* Portland, ME: Chisholm Brothers, 1879. Octavo two star (Franconia Notch) edition.

_____. *Views in the White Mountains.* Portland, ME: Chisholm Brothers, [c. 1880]. Octavo "omnibus" edition. 1879 copyright.

_____. *Views in the White Mountains.* Portland, ME: Chisholm Brothers, [c. 1881-82]. Octavo "omnibus" edition. 1879 copyright.

_____. *Views in the White Mountains.* Portland, ME: Chisholm Brothers, 1879. Quarto "omnibus" edition.

Views in the White Mountains. Portland, ME: C. R. Chisholm, 1878.

Views in the White Mountains. Portland, ME: Chisholm Brothers, 1896, 1898, 1904, 1908, 1911, 1912, 1917, 1920, 1921 eds.

Waldron, Holman D. *With Pen and Camera thro' the White Mountains.* Portland, ME: Chisholm Brothers, 1896, 1898, 1901, 1902, 1905, 1907 eds.

White & Franconia Mountains. Boston: Charles Pollock, 1895.

The White Mountain Picture Book: Seventy Scenes Among the Granite Hills. Bethlehem, NH: The White Mountain Echo, [c. 1895].

White Mountain Views. Boston: Forbes Albertype Co., [1884].

Wittemann, A. *White Mountains Illustrated, Indelible Photographs.* New York: The Albertype Co., 1889, 1890 and 1891 eds.

E. Carroll and Belknap Counties

Albany, New Hampshire, 1766-1966—Bicentennial Observance, July 2, 1966. Albany, NH: Albany Bicentennial Committee, 1966.

Beals, Charles E., Jr. *Passaconaway in the White Mountains.* Boston: Richard G. Badger, 1916.

Beattie, Gerald. "Crawford Notch: A History," *Granite Monthly* 58, No. 7 (July 1926): 202-208.

Beckman, Jane, et al. *Sandwich, New Hampshire, 1763-1990—"A Little World By Itself."* Portsmouth, NH: Peter E. Randall, Publisher for the Sandwich Historical Society, 1995.

Bennett, Ann. "A Revitalized Tradition: Wentworth Hall's Restoration Project," *Mountain Ear,* June 1983.

Campbell, Catherine H. "Crawford Notch in Fact and Fancy." M. S. thesis, State University of New York of Albany, 1976.

_____. "The Gate of the Notch," *Historical New Hampshire* 33, No. 2 (Summer 1978): 91-122.

Canning, Steven. *Town of Bartlett Bicentennial, 1790-1990*. Bartlett: By the Town, 1990.

Carroll, Aileen M. Bartlett, *New Hampsire ... in the Valley of the Saco*. West Kennebunk, ME: Phoenix Publishing for the Bartlett Public Library, 1990.

————. *The Latch String Was Always Out: A History of Lodging Hospitality and Tourism in Bartlett, New Hampshire*. Portsmouth, NH: Published for the Bartlett Public Library by Peter E. Randall, Publisher, 1994.

Center Harbor, New Hampshire. Center Harbor, NH: Center Harbor Historical Society, 1986.

Commemorative Booklet—Bicentennial of Conway, N. H., 1765-1965. Conway, NH: Bicentennial Committee, 1965.

Conway, New Hampshire. Its Attractions for the Tourist, and its Facilities for Business. Conway, NH: S. A. Evans, 1889.

Cook, Edward M., Jr. Ossipee, *New Hampshire, 1785-1985: A History*. Vol. 1. Portsmouth, NH: Peter E. Randall for the Town of Ossipee, 1989.

Cummings, Karen. "Jackson Landmark is Transformed: Eagle Mountain House Soars Again," *Mountain Ear*, 18 July 1986.

————. "North Conway's Hotel Randall, The Venerable Inn of a Bygone Era," *The Mountain Ear*, 5 July 1985.

Downs, Virginia C. *Life by the Tracks: When Passenger Trains Steamed Through the Notch*. Canaan, NH: Phoenix Publishing, 1983.

Eastman, Tom. "Mountaintop Hospitality of Yesteryear: Recalling the Days of the Chocorua Peak House," *The Mountain Ear*, 21 July 1888, pp. 2, 4, 5, 6.

Emerson, David, comp. *The Conways*. Dover, NH: Arcadia Publishing, 1995. "Images of America."

Garey, Carl B. "The Kiarsarge House," Unpublished ms., Conway Public Library (NH), n.d.

Garland, Margaret B. *Yesterdays: Lodging Places of Jackson and their Recipes*. Jackson, NH: Jackson Historical Society, 1978.

"The Good Old Days" (A Pictorial) In the Conways of N. H.: Nostalgic Glimpses of Another Era. Fryeburg, ME: Saco Valley Printing, 1969.

Haynes, George H. *East Side of the White Mountains*. No. Conway, NH: Board of Trade, 1892.

Heard, Gordon Tasker. *The Hotels of Intervale, New Hampshire, 1850-1890*. Winchester, VA: Wisecarver's Print Shop, Inc., 1994.

Horne, Ruth B. D. *Conway Through the Years and Whither*. Conway, NH: Conway Historical Society, 1963.

Hounsell, Janet M. "Auction, Flames Ended Crawford House's 183-Year Life," *The Valley Visitor*, 23 June 1988, p. 5.

————. "Eagle Mountain House Firmly Rooted in Jackson's Past," *The Valley Visitor*, 6 October 1988, pp. 4-5.

————. "Eastern Slope Inn's Roots Deep in North Conway," *The Valley Visitor*, 9 June 1988, pp. 3-4.

————. "Gone 10 Years, Jackson Falls House Still Recalled," *The Valley Visitor*, 8 December 1988, p. 5.

Hurd, D. Hamilton. *History of Merrimack and Belknap Counties, New Hampshire*. Philadelphia: J. W. Lewis & Co., 1885.

Johnson, Clarence. "Center Harbor," *Granite Monthly* 23, No. 3 (September 1897): 164-172.

Johnson, Richard D., comp. *Around Jackson*. Dover, NH: Arcadia Publisher, 1995. "Images of America."

Kantac, Robert. "The Eastern Slope Inn," *Outlook: The Magazine of the White Mountains Region of New Hampshire* 9 (Fall 1987): 36-38.

"Lake Winnipiseogee," *Granite Monthly* 3, No. 9 (June 1880): 370-400.

"Land sale marks the final chapter in the story of historic Gray's Inn," *Northern Light*, 19 September 1988, pp. 1, 2.

Lewis, Bea. "Jackson's Wentworth Hotel Recalls Another Era," *The Valley Visitor*, 23 June 1988, p. 3.

Merrill, Georgia Drew, ed. *History of Carroll County, New Hampshire*. Boston, MA: W. A. Fergusson & Co., 1889. Facsimile reprint, Somersworth, NH: New Hampshire Publishing Co., 1971.

Morey, Florence. "Abel Crawford and his Mount Crawford House," *Appalachia* 30, No. 1 (June 15, 1954): 1-9.

————. "One Hundred Years of Crawford House," *Appalachia* 32, No. 3 (15 June 1959): 421-23.

Nevins, Winfield S. *The Intervale, New Hampshire*. Salem, MA: Salem Press, 1887.

Nickerson, Marion L. *Bearcamp River House*. Ossipee, NH: n.p., [1985].

Nickerson, Marion L. and John A. Downs. *Chocorua Peak House*. Center Conway, NH: Walker's Pond Press, 1977.

North Conway and Vicinity. North Conway, NH: North Conway Board of Trade, c. 1891.

Nute, Helen. "Eastern Slope Inn: Its History Goes Back to 1864 As The Randall House," *The Irregular*, 14 December 1976, pp. 2-3, 16-17.

O'Meara, Kathy. *Remember When ... A Collection of Old Photographs of Wolfeboro, N. H.* Wolfeboro, NH: Wolfeboro Chamber of Commerce, 1976.

On the Eastern Slope of the White Mountains, New Hampshire. Conway, NH: Conway Chamber of Commerce, [c. 1925].

Parker, Benjamin F. *History of Wolfeborough (New Hampshire)*. Wolfeborough: By the Town, 1901.

Parsons, Thomas W. *The Willey House and Sonnets*. Cambridge, MA: John Wilson and Son, 1875.

Perry, A. Bernard. *Albany's Recollections*. Albany, NH: n.p., 1976.

Pinkham, Charles H. "North Conway: Famous White Mountain Resort." Unpublished ms., Conway Public Library (NH), [1961].

Randall, Harry H. "The Randall Hotels." Unpublished ms., Conway Public Library (NH), [1958].

Randall, Katherine M. Odell. *Forget Not Your Heritage*. No. Conway, NH: By the Author, 1971.

Reminiscences of Jackson, 1900-1950. Jackson, NH: Jackson Conservation Commission, [1950].

"Thorn Mountain House and Cottages, Jackson, N. H. for Gen. M. C. Wentworth, William A. Bates, Architect," *American Architect and Building News* 18, No. 520 (12 December 1885): 282; Supplement, op. p.3.

Trainor, Michael L. "100 Years' history at Eastern Slope," *Valley News*, 27 January 1981.

F. Grafton County

Bean, Grace H. *The Town at the End of the Road: A History of Waterville Valley*. Canaan, NH: Phoenix Publishing, 1983.

Bethlehem and Points of Interest. New York: Commercial Publishing Co., 1896.

Bethlehem, New Hampshire, In the Heart of the White Mountains. Bethlehem, NH: Board of Trade, [c.1921 ed]; [c.1922 ed.]; [c.1925 ed.].

Bicentennial Commemorative Booklet of the Town of Lincoln, New Hampshire, 1764-1964. Lincoln, NH: n.p., 1964.

Bixby, Roland. *History of Warren.* Crawfordsville, IN: R. R. Donnelleys and Sons, 1986.

Blaisdell, Katherine. *Over the River and Through the Years.* Book Five. Bradford, VT and Woodsville, NH: The Journal Opinion, 1983.

Bolles, Rev. Simeon. *The Early History of the Town of Bethlehem, New Hampshire.* Woodsville, NH: Enterprise Printing House, 1883.

Campton [N. H.] Bicentennial, 1767-1967—Commemorative Booklet. Campton, NH: Campton Bicentennial History Committee, 1967.

Caswell, C. E. *Business Directory of the Town of Warren, N. H.* Warren Summit, NH: The Messenger Office, [1890].

Child, Hamilton, comp. *Gazetteer of Grafton County, N. H., 1709-1886.* Syracuse, NY: Syracuse Journal Co., 1886.

Clay, Paul R. *Picturesque Littleton and the White Mountains.* St. Johnsbury, VT: C. T. Ranlet, 1898. Reprinted, with additions, 1968, by the Littleton Area Historical Society.

Colby, John H., ed. *Littleton: Crossroads of Northern New Hampshire.* Canaan, NH: Phoenix Publishing, 1984.

Conrad, Justus [Woodbury, Elmer E.]. *The Town of Woodstock and Its Scenic Beauties.* Woodstock, NH: n.p., n.d. [c. 1935].

_____. "The Town of Woodstock," *Granite Monthly* 23, No. 1 (July 1897): 11-23.

Curtis, Percy (Mrs. William N. Cox). *The Profile House.* Boston: Andrew Graves, 1872.

Emery, Samuel. "Lisbon, New Hampshire," *Granite Monthly* 10, No. 3 (March 1887): 95-103.

Goodrich, A. L. *The Waterville Valley: A History, Description and Guide.* Waterville, NH: n.p., 1904. 2nd ed.

Goodrich, Nathaniel L. *The Waterville Valley: A Story of a Resort in the New Hampshire Mountains.* Lunenburg, VT: The North Country Press, 1952.

Hancock, Frances Ann Johnson. *Saving the Great Stone Face: the Chronicle of the Old Man of the Mountain.* Canaan, NH: Published for the Franconia Area Heritage Council by Phoenix Publishing, 1984. Edited by Ruth Ayers-Givens.

Jackson, James R. *History of Littleton, New Hampshire.* 3 vols. Cambridge, MA: Published for the Town by the University Press, 1905.

Jailer, Mildred. "Welcome to the Profile House." *Royale Forum* 113 (13 December 1965): 3-7.

Kilbourne, Frederick W. "A Closed Chapter of White Mountain History: The Franconia Notch as Summer Resort," *Appalachia* 16, No. 2 (February 1926): 298-313.

_____. "Moosilauke: The Story of a Mountain," *Appalachia* 23, No. 2 (December 1940): 147-158.

Little, William. *The History of Warren: A Mountain Hamlet, located among The White Hills of New Hampshire.* Manchester, NH: William B. Moore, Printer, 1870.

A Little Pathfinder to Places of Interest Near North Woodstock, N. H. North Woodstock, NH: North Woodstock Improvement Association, 1912.

Littleton, New Hampshire: The Business Center of the White Mountains. Littleton, NH: Littleton Chamber of Commerce, [1925].

March, Arthur F., Jr., comp. *Littleton, New Hampshire.* Dover, NH: Arcadia Publishing, 1995. "Images of America."

Moses, George H. "Lisbon," *Granite Monthly* 20, No. 5 (May 1896): 311-324.

_____. "A Lost Town: A Sketch of Bethlehem," *Granite Monthly* 17, No. 1 (July 1894): 16-33.

_____. "On the Ammonoosuc: A Sketch of Littleton," *Granite Monthly* 17, No. 3 (September 1894): 165-194.

Mudge, John T. B. *The Old Man's Reader: History and Legends of Franconia Notch.* Etna, NH: The Durand Press, 1995.

Murray, Hon. Amelia M. *Letters from the United States, Cuba and Canada.* New York: G. P. Putnam & Co., 1856.

Nicol, John L. *Thumbnail History of Warren, New Hampshire.* Warren, NH: By the Author, 1963.

Pearson, H. C. "The Warder of the Pass: A Sketch of Franconia," *Granite Monthly* 21, No. 2 (September 1896): 148-162.

Pickwick, Hazel Ash, Mabel S. Jesseman and Barbara Jesseman. *Lisbon's Ten Score Years, 1763-1963, Plus One Score More, 1963-1983.* Lisbon, NH: Friends-in-Council Civic Committee, 1983. Reprinted. Originally published in 1967.

Speare, Eva A. Twenty *Decades in Plymouth, New Hampshire, 1763-1963.* Plymouth, NH: Bicentennial Commission, 1963.

Stearns, Ezra S. *History of Plymouth, New Hampshire.* 2 vols. Cambridge, MA: Printed for the Town by the University Press, 1906.

Sugar Hill, New Hampshire: A Glimpse Into the Past (1780-1986). 2nd ed. Sugar Hill, NH: Harrison Publishing House, 1986.

Sweet, William B. *Adventures of a Deaf-Mute.* Boston: Boston Deaf-Mutes' Mission, 1874.

Taylor, Hattie Whitcomb. *Early History of Bethlehem, N. H.* Bethlehem, NH: n.p., 1960. Reprinted, 1980.

Views of Bethlehem and Vicinity. Portland, ME: Chisholm Brothers, [c.1885].

Vincent, Jane, et. al. *Sugar Hill, New Hampshire—A Glimpse Into the Past (1780-1986).* Sugar Hill, NH: Harrison Publishing House, 1986. 3rd. ed. 1st ed., 1976, ed. by Alice C. Nelson. 2nd ed., ed. by Jane Vincent, et. al.

Welch, Sarah N. (Brooks). *A History of Franconia, New Hampshire, 1772-1972.* Littleton, NH: Courier Printing Co., 1972.

Whitcher, William F. *Some Things About Coventry-Benton, New Hampshire.* Woodsville, NH: News Print, 1905.

Wilson, Gregory C. *Bethlehem, New Hampshire: a bicentennial history.* Bethlehem: By the Town, 1974.

Woodstock Bicentennial Pictorial. Woodstock, NH: Bicentennial Pictorial Committee, 1976. 2nd ed.

G. Coos County

Ahearn, Mary. "Life at the Glen House," *Mount Washington Observatory News Bulletin* 8, No. 1 (March 1967): 2-4.

A Book of Bretton Woods in the White Mountains. Bretton Woods: The Mount Washington and the Mount Pleasant, [c. 1910].

Brandt, Del. "Tip-Top House Has Always Led a Charmed Life," *The Valley Visitor,* 23 June 1988, p. 6.

Bray, Donald H. *They Said it Couldn't be Done: The Mount Washington Cog Railway and its History.* Dubuque, Iowa: Kendall/Hunt Publishing Co., 1984.

Bretton Woods Hotels. Bretton Woods, NH: The Bretton Woods Hotel Company, [c. 1919].

Burt, F. Allen. *The Story of Mount Washington.* Hanover, NH: Dartmouth Publications, 1960.

Center, Gilbert S. "A History of the Town of Colebrook, New Hampshire." M. A. thesis, University of New Hampshire, 1950.

Chamberlain, Allen. "Historic Landmarks at the Mount Washington Summit," *Appalachia* 15, No. 3 (December 1922): 263-265.

Cooper, J. M. "Jefferson," *Granite Monthly* 25, No. 2 (August 1898): 64-78.

Cross, George N. *Randolph, Old and New: Its Ways and By-Ways.* Randolph, NH: By the Town, 1924.

Dickey, Thomas A. "The Flying Bunkhouse," *Mount Washington Observatory News Bulletin* 2, No. 3 (September 1961): 5-7.

Dodge, Barbara Derrington. *The Dodge Family and Their Hotel.* Littleton, NH: Courier Printing Co., 1973.

Dodge, John B. and F. Schuyler, Jr. *100 Years of Gracious Hospitality: The Story of the Dodge Family of Mountain View House of Whitefield, New Hampshire.* Whitefield, NH: n.p., 1965.

Early, Kevin. "The Grand, Old Hotel Enjoys a Renaissance," *Northern Light,* 6 August 1985, pp. 1, 4, 7.

Emerson, Arthur William. *A Yearbook of Bretton Woods.* New York: Charles Francis Press, [1909], [1910] eds.

Evans, George C. *History of the Town of Jefferson, New Hampshire, 1773-1927.* Manchester: Granite State Press, 1927.

Fabyan, Horace. *Mount Washington House, White Mountains, N. H.* New York: Baker, Goodwin & Co., 1852.

Ford, Daniel. "The Life and Hard Times of the Sports Village at Bretton Woods," *Country Journal* (May 1977): 33-34, 36-37.

Gifford, William H. *Colebrook: "A Place Up Back of New Hampshire."* Colebrook, NH: The News and Sentinel, Inc., 1970.

The Glen House and Its Attractions. Concord, NH: Edson C. Eastman, 1872.

Glimpses of Gorham, New Hampshire, 1836-1976. Gorham, NH: Gorham Bicentennial Committee, 1976.

Gosselin, Guy. "Zadoc and Ezra—Two Journals," *Mount Washington Observatory News Bulletin* 25, No. 2 (Summer 1984): 27-29.

Gregory, Jane. "The Shingle Style," *Down East* 32, No. 7 (February 1986): 49-51, 69, 71, 110.

Harnett, Lynn. "The Grand Hotel," *New Hampshire Profiles* 35, No. 12 (December, 1986): 36-41.

Historical Memories of the Town of Jefferson, New Hampshire, 1796-1971. Jefferson, NH: Anniversary Committee, 1971.

"History of The Balsams and Environs," *The Balsams Guest Directory.* Dixville Notch, NH: The Balsams Corporation, 1991.

Hitchcock, C. H. and J. H. Huntington, et. al. *Mount Washington in Winter....* Boston: Chick and Andrews, 1871.

Hoik, Daniel B. "The Protected Valley of the Bretton Woods Resort," *Outlook, The Magazine of Northern New Hampshire* 4, No. 1 (Spring 1978): 24-27.

Holt, Rachel, et. al. *History of Dummer, New Hampshire, 1773-1973.* Dummer, NH: Dummer Bicentennial Committee, 1973.

Jordon, Charles J. "The Mountain View and How It Grew," *Coos Magazine* 1, No. 2 (July 1989): 24-26.

Kenney, Charles. "Grand Hotel in the Wilds," *The Boston Globe Magazine,* Sunday, August 31, 1980, pp. 14-18.

Kidder, Glen M. *Railway to the Moon.* Littleton, NH: Courier Printing Co., 1969.

Leavitt, Richard F. *Colebrook Yesterday: A Picture Visit Through the Old Home Town.* Colebrook, NH: Colebrook Public Library, 1970.

Lehr, Frederic B. *Carroll, New Hampshire: The First Two Hundred Years.* Carroll, NH: Carroll Bicentennial Committee, 1972.

Leich, Jeffrey. "Possession of the Summit: 'A Prolific Subject of Contention,'" *Mount Washington Observatory News Bulletin* 31, No. 2 (Summer 1990): 31-38.

Maynard, Fred B. "Skyline Fireworks," *Appalachia* 28, No. 1 (June 1950): 40-47.

McAvoy, George E. *And Then There Was One: A History of the Hotels of the Summit and the West Side of Mt. Washington.* Littleton, NH: The Crawford Press, 1988.

McGoldrick, Linda C. "Dixville Notch: Up-Country Success Story," *New Hampshire Profiles* 33, No. 11 (November 1984): 50-53.

McIntyre, C. Douglas. "The History of Whitefield." M. A. thesis, University of New Hampshire, 1942.

McKinney, Gordon B. "The History of Whitefield." B. A. thesis, Bates College (Lewiston, ME), 1965.

_____. "The Land No One Wanted: An Economic History of Whitefield, New Hampshire," *Historical New Hampshire* 28, No. 4 (Winter 1972): 185-209.

[Merrell, Margaret]. *Shelburne, New Hampshire, Its First Two Hundred Years.* Shelburne, NH: Bicentennial Committee, 1969.

[Merrill, Georgia Drew]. *History of Coos County, New Hampshire.* Syracuse, NY: W. A. Fergusson & Co., 1888. Facsimile reprint, Somersworth, NH: New Hampshire Publishing Co., 1972.

Milliken, Charles. *The Glen, White Mountains, N. H.* Boston: Robinson Engraving Co., 1891.

_____. *The Glen House Book, White Mountains.* Cambridge, MA: John Wilson and Sons, 1889. Also 1891 ed.

Mitchell, Walter J., Jr. "The Mount Washington Summit House," *Mount Washington Observatory News Bulletin* 6, No. 4 (December 1965): 5-7.

Moses, George H. "Gorham," *Granite Monthly* 20, No. 4 (April 1896): 234-247.

Nilsen, Kim R. *A History of Whitefield, New Hampshire, 1774-1974.* Whitefield, NH: Published for the Town, 1974.

Peabody, Mrs. R. P. *History of Shelburne, New Hampshire.* Shelburne, NH: Mountaineer Print, 1882.

Randolph, N. H., 150 Years. Randolph, NH: Sesquicentennial Committee, 1974.

Roberts, Guy, and Frank H. Burt. *Mt. Washington.* Whitefield, NH: Guy Roberts, 1927. 4th ed.

Smith, Alan A. "Sign of the Times," *Mount Washington Observatory News Bulletin,* No. 1 (March 1966): 5.

Somers, Rev. A. N. *History of Lancaster, New Hampshire.* Concord, NH: The Rumford Press, 1899.

Stevens, John Calvin II, and Earle G. Shettleworth, Jr. *John Calvin Stevens, Domestic Architecture, 1890-1930.* Scarborough, ME: Harp Publications, 1990.

Stillman, Damie, et. al. *Architecture & Ornament in Late 19th-Century America.* Newark, DE: Department of Art History and the University Gallery, University of Delaware, 1981.

"Tip-Top House," *Mount Washington Observatory News Bulletin* 4, No. 2 (June 1967): 8-9.

Tolles, Bryant F., Jr. "The Mount Washington Hotel at Bretton Woods: Resort Jewel of the White Mountains," *Mount Washington Observatory News Bulletin* 34, No. 4 (Winter 1993): 99-110.

True, Nathaniel Tuckerman, M.D. *History of Gorham, N. H.* Gorham, NH: The Mountaineer, 1882.

Walbridge, J. H. "Whitefield, New Hampshire," Special Illustrated Edition of the *White Mountain Times*, 1898. Whitefield Publishing Co.

Westhall, James E. "The Renaissance of Bretton Woods," *New Hampshire Echoes* 3, No. 3 (August 1972): 25-31.

II. *Newspapers*

The principal newspapers for source material on the hotels are *Among the Clouds* (1877-1917), published for much of its history on the summit of Mount Washington, and *The White Mountain Echo* (1878-1927), published in Bethlehem, NH. No complete run of either title exists in a single repository. Portions of each may be found at the Appalachian Mountain Club (Boston), the Dartmouth College Library (Hanover, NH), the Bethlehem (NH) Public Library, the North Conway (NH) Public Library, and the New Hampshire Historical Society.

Ammonoosuc Reporter (Littleton); *Among the Clouds* (Mount Washington); *Bath* (ME) *Daily*; *Berlin Independent*; *Berlin Register*; *Boston Globe*; *Boston Post*; *The Bugle* (Mount Washington Hotel, Bretton Woods); *The Colebrook Sentinel*; *Concord Monitor*; *Coos County Democrat* (Lancaster); *Coos Republican* (Lancaster); *Hanover Gazette*; *Haverhill* (MA) *Gazette*; *The Idler* (North Conway); *Industrial Journal* (Bangor, ME); *The Irregular & Mount Washington Valley News* (North Conway); *Laconia Democrat*; *Lewiston* (ME) *Evening Journal*; *Lisbon Courier*; *Littleton Courier*; *Manchester Union (Union Leader)*; *Manchester Weekly Mirror*; *Mountain Ear* (North Conway); *The Mountaineer* (Gorham); *New Hampshire Sunday News* (Manchester); *New Hampshire Sunday Times* (Manchester); *The News and Critic* (Laconia); *The News and Sentinel* (Colebrook); *New York Times*; *North Conway Weekly* (North Conway); *North Conway Daily Sun*; *Northern Light*; *The Northern Sentinel* (Colebrook); *People's Journal* (Littleton); *Plymouth Record*; *Portland* (ME) *Press Herald*; *Portland* (ME) *Sunday Telegram*; *Portland* (ME) *Transcript*; *Profile Events* (Profile House, Franconia Notch); *The Reporter* (North Conway); *Sunday News* (Manchester); *The Valley Visitor* (Laconia, NH); *Waterville* (ME) *Morning Sentinel*; *The Waumbeck's Penny Daily* (Waumbek Hotel, Jefferson); *Weirs Times and Tourist Gazette*; *White Mountain Banner* (Littleton); *The White Mountain Clarion* (Sugar Hill and Franconia); *The White Mountain Echo* (Bethlehem); *White Mountain Life* (Littleton); *White Mountain Republic Journal* (Littleton).

III. *Magazines and Journals*

Appalachia (A. M. C.); *Coos Magazine*; *Granite Monthly*; *Granite State Magazine*; *Historical New Hampshire* (N. H. H. S.); *Magnetic North*; *Mount Washington Observatory News Bulletin*; *New Hampshire Echoes*; *New Hampshire Profiles*; *Outlook*.

Index

Abbott, Frank H., 129, 197
Abbott, Karl, 128, 129, 162, 177, 200-201
The Alpine (Hotel Alpine), 166, 168, *168*, 169, 178
Alpine House, the first, 50, 71,
Alpine House, the second, *46*, 50-51, 71
Amster, Nathan, 88
Anderson, John, 122, 214-215
Astor House, 18
Atlantic and St. Lawrence Railroad, 47-49, 51, 64, 225

The Balsams, 16, 20, 22, 24, 26, 164, 175, 189, 191, 197, 198, 202, 213, 223-235, *224*, *225*, *226*, *227*, *228*, *229*, *230*, *231*, *233*, 236-237, *238*
The Balsams Corporation, 237
Barron, Asa T., 58, 73, 90, 114
Barron, Merrill, and Barron Company, 58, 116
Barron, Oscar F., 58, 90
Barron, Oscar G., 90, 114
Bartlett, NH, 42, 123, 147-148
Batchelder, James H., 168, 178
Bates, William A., 84-85, 87-89, 155
Bay of Naples Inn, *187*, 187-188, *188*
Beal, Ezra, 50, 71
Beecher, Henry Ward, 91, 116
Bell, John, 166
Bellows, John, 51-52
Bemis, Dr. Samuel A., 31, 43
Bethel, Maine, 50
Bethlehem, NH, 42, 92-94, 124-125, 136, 144, 159, 177, 197, 201
Boston and Maine Railroad, 71, 73, 75, 110, 114, 146, 175
Boston, Concord and Montreal Railroad (B., C. & M.), 40, 48, 68, 75, 90, 100, 101, 109, 110, 112, 114, 136
Bowles, Henry H., 131-132
Bowles, Levi, 165
Bowles & Hoskins Company, 131-132
Breezy Hill House, 139, 160, *160*
Bretton Arms, 221, *221*, 236
Bretton Woods Company, 122, 222
Bretton Woods Conference, 222
Bretton Woods, NH, 16, 20, 22, 24, 26, 29, 116, 118, 145, 213, 222-223
Brown, George T., 38
Brown, O. H., 99
Burrowes, John W., 119, 182

Cabot, James Elliot, 32, 33, 38, 44
Carlton House, 165
Carrere and Hastings, 22, 97-98, 106-107, 119, 214
Catskill Mountain House, *17*, 18-19
Cave Mountain House, 148
Center Harbor, NH, 40-41, 48, 110, 171
Chadbourne, Orin N., 153
Chadbourne, Marcia G., 153
Chandler, Charles A., 51
Cobb, Albert Winslow, 21, 182
Cocheco Railroad, 48
Coffin, Ira, 38

Colebrook House, 165
Colebrook, NH, 107, 165, 171, 181-183, 191, 223, 225, 236-237
Colonial Arms, 22
Concord & Montreal Railroad, 117, 136-137, 145-146
Connecticut Lake House, *246*
Conway House, 62-63, *62*, 66, 74
Conway, NH, 42, 47-48, 62-63, 147-148
Coombs, George M., 22
Crawford, Abel, 29, 31, 35
Crawford, Ethan Allen, 30, 32-33, *35*, 37, 44, 60
Crawford, Thomas J., 35, 55
Crawford House, the first, *55*, 55-56, *56*, 66, 69, 72, 171
Crawford House, the second, 19, 23, 41, 56-60, *57*, *58*, *59*, *60*, 66, 69, 72, 90-91, 114, 116, 136, 145, 152, 171
Crawford Notch, 19, 29, 47, 60, 78, 91, 110, 116, 136, 145, 214, 218, 220
Cruft, Isaac, 124-127, 159
Cummings Construction Company, 229-231

Davis, John, 34
Davis, Nathaniel T. P., 31
Deer Park Hotel, 166, *166-167*, 168, 169, *174*, 174-176, *175*, 178, 186
Dix House, 189, 225, 226
Dixville Notch, NH, 164, 223, 225, 233
Dixville Notch Corporation, 229-231
Dodge, Frank Schuyler, 205-207
Dodge, Frank Schuyler, Jr., 207
Dodge, John B., 207
Dodge, William F., 202-204, 207-208
Doudera, Frank, 231-232
Dow, Edward, 115
Dudley, James W., 160
Dunn, E. D., 111
Durgin & Fox, 93-94
Dwight, Reverend Timothy, 29

Eagle Hotel, 71
Eagle Mountain House, the first, 123-124, *124*, 151, 153
Eagle Mountain House, the second, 24, 74, 148, 151-154, *152*, *153*, 176, *179*
Eastern Railroad, 79, 110, 136
Eastern Slope Inn, 24, 84, 105, 148, 150. *See also* Hotel Randall, the third.
Eastman, Cyrus, 55-57
Eastman, Ebenezer, 55
Elliott's Hotel, 170-171
Elliott, Silas B., 170
Elliott, J.R., 102, 167
Emerson, William Ralph, 182

Fabyan, Horace, 30-31, 34, 43, 74, 110-111
Fabyan House, the first, 110, *111*
Fabyan House, the second, 17, *108*, 110-114, *111*, *112*, *113*, 116-117, 135
Fairview House, 166, 169, *169*, 178
Farr, George A., 134-135
Fassett & Stevens, 118, 214

[261]

Fassett, Edward F., 118, 120
Fassett, Francis H., 118-121, *119*, 181, 190, 192-194, 208, 214
Flagler, Henry M., 22, 97, 214-215, 229
Flume and Franconia Hotel Company, 65-66
Flume House, the first, 64-65, *65*, 74, 129, 139, 249
Flume House, the second, 129-130, *130*, 135, *141*, 145, 167, 178
Forbes, Barton A., 153
Forest Hills Hotel, 159-163, *160*, *161*, *162*, 197, 201
Franconia House, the first, 159
Franconia Inn, 131, 160
Franconia, NH, 159, 197, 201
Franconia Notch, 38, 45, 48, 64, 66, 90, 128, 145, 166, 168, 197, 201-202, 209
Frank Abbott & Son, 129, 201

Gale, Arthur P., 148, 151-153
Gale, Cyrus E., 123-124, 176
Gale, Eugene, 107, 204-206, 210
Gale, Marcia P., 123-124, 153
Gale Family, 153
Giant's Grave, 30-31, 36, 44, 110, 111, 214
Gibb, Major Joseph L., *35*, 36, 38, 55-56, 72
Gibb, Stephen C., 38
Gibson, Harvey Dow, 105, 150
Gifford, Charles Alling, 214-215, 217-218, 235
Glen Ellis House, 105, 123
Glen House, the first (Pinkham Notch), 19, 41, 51-55, *52*, *53*, *54*, 66, 68-69, 110, 171
Glen House, the second (Pinkham Notch), 20, 26, 118, 145, 147, 152, 175, 188, *190*, 191-197, *192*, *193*, *194*, *195*, *196*, 208, *210*
Glover, George, 206
Goodnow, Eliot H., 131
Goodnow House (Franconia , NH), 130-131, *131*, 139 160
Goodwin, Charles B., 127
Gorham House (Gorham, NH), *50*, 51, 71
Gorham, NH, 42, 47, 49, 50, 51, 52, 61, 136, 164, 196
Grand Trunk Railway, 47, 50-51, 225
Grand Union Hotel (Saratoga Springs, N.Y.), *16*, 19
Granite Hotel (Littleton), 42, 45
Gray, Charles W., 51, 154-156, 158-159, 176
Gray's Inn, the first, *142*, 148, *154*, 154-156, *155*
Gray's Inn, the second, 156, *156*
Gray's Inn, the third, 22, 156-158, *157*
Gray's Inn, the fourth, 22, 158, 158-159, 177
Greeley, Nathaniel, 170
Greenleaf, Colonel Charles H., 45, 65-67, 74, 196-201

Hale, Henry S., 189, 223, 226, 231, 237
Hampshire House, 16, 22, *230*, 230-231, *231*
Hampshire Inn, 165
Hayes, Margaret, 50
Hiram Noyes & Sons, 163-164
Hitchcock, Colonel John R., 50, 61
Hodgdon, A. W., 99
Hoskins, Seth F., 131-132
Hotel Alpine (The Alpine), 166, *168*, 168-169
Hotel Lookoff, *14*, 131, 160, 163-164, *163*, 167, 177, 197
Hotel Randall, the first, 123, 148
Hotel Randall, the second, 84, 148, *149*
Hotel Randall, the third, 105, 148-150. *See also* Eastern Slope Inn.

Howard, Henry, 124-125
Hunt, Herbert, 162
Huntress, James L. & Son, 171

Intervale House, 80-82, *81*, *82*, 123, 148
Iron Mountain House, the second, 148, *150*, 150-151, *151*

Jackson Falls House, *63*, 63, 74, 123, 237
Jackson, NH, 63, 84, 123, 147, 148, 150-151, 154-155
Jefferson Hill House, 98-99, *99*, *100*, 100
Jefferson Hotel and Land Company, 97-99
Jefferson, NH, 95-97, 130

Kallman, Alvin and Zara, 232
Kearsarge House, 62, 76, *78*, 78-82, *79*, *80*, 104, 110, 123
Kearsarge Tavern, 61-62, 78, 104
Kellogg, Harold Field, 201-202
Kilbourne, Frederick W., 31, 192
King, Thomas Starr, 32, 95-96
Knight's Tavern, 38

Lafayette Cottage, 39, 200
Lafayette House, 38, 38-39, *39*, 45, 64, 69
Lancaster House, the first, 64, *64*, 74
Lancaster House, the second, 74, 165, *165*
Lancaster, NH, 64, 78, 109, 165
Lannin, J. J., 231, 233
Lary House, , 42, *42*, 45
Leavitt, Franklin, 51, 55, 66, 191
Leavitt, John T. G., 116, 123
Libby & Sons Company, 196, 209
Lincoln, NH, 166
Lisbon, NH, 130, 139, 159, 160, 197
Littleton, NH, 42, 48, 56, 63-64, 68, 71, 134-135, 139, 144, 159, 223
Loring and Phipps, 69
Lowe, E. M., 88-89, 159

Maine Central Railroad, 117-118, 120-121, 136-137
Mallett, Ernest J., Jr., 90
Maple Villa, 148
Maplewood Casino, 127-128, 136, 138, 140, 159
Maplewood Cottage, *125*, 125, 128
Maplewood Hall, 127, *128*, 138, 159
Maplewood Hotel, 19, 124-128, *126*, *127*, 135-136, 138, 159
Maplewood House, *125*, 125
Marino, Michael, 153
Marsh, Sylvester, 44, 110-111, 136
Martineau, Harriet, 38
Mason, H. E., 148
Mason, Nathaniel R., 62
Mason's Hotel, 82, 104, 123
Merrill & Cutler, 170, 173
Merrill, Captain Edward, 50
Merrill, C. H., 58, 90
Meserve, James M. and W. A., 150-151
The Metallak (The Nirvana), 22, 26, 171, 175, *180*, 181-183, *183*, *184*, *185*, 185, *186*, 187-189, 191
Milliken, Charles R., 51, 53, 55, 191-196, 208
Milliken, Weston F., 51, 53
Mohonk Mountain House, 22

INDEX

Moosilauke Inn (Breezy Point House), 169-170, *170*, 173, 178
Morgan, Sylvanus D., 61, 106, 129, 146, 159, 163, 177, 196-198, 202, 215, 228
Moss, Frank T., 128
Moulton House, 45
Mountain View House, *21*, *22*, 26, 152, 164, 175, 189, 191, *202*, 202-210, *203*, *204*, *205*, *206*, *207*, 209-210
Mount Crawford House, 31-32, *32*, *33*, 38, 43
Mount Lafayette House, 45
Mount Madison House, *49*, 51, 71, 164
Mount Monadnock Mineral Springs and Land Company, 181-183
Mount Pleasant Hotel Company, 117, 215-216, 236
Mount Pleasant House, *19*, 22, 114, *116-117*, *119*, 116-123, *120*, *121*, *122*, *123*, 135, 137, 145, 188, 193, 197, 214
Mount Washington Carriage Road, 44, 52, 196
Mount Washington (Cog) Railroad, 90, 110, 114, 117, 137, 145-147
Mount Washington Hotel, 16, 20, 22, 24, 26, 118, 145, 175, 189, 197-198, 201, *212*, 213-223, *214*, *216*, *217*, *218*, *219*, *220*, *222*, 230-232, 234-236
Mount Washington Hotel Company, 111, 116
Mount Washington House, 30-31, 34-43, *55*, 110-111, 136
Mount Washington, NH, 52, 60, 79, 91, 111, 114, 116, 123, 144-145, *145*, 175, 191, 196, 203, 214
Mount Washington Railway, 61, 96, 109-110, 114, 144, 146-147
Mount Washington Summit House, the second, 114-115, *115*, 177. See also Summit House, the second.
Mount Washington Summit Road, 77

New Hotel Randall, 148, *149*
New Profile House, 26, 39, 128, 145, 162-163, 175, 177-178, 189, 191, 196-202, *197*, *199*, *200*, *201*, *205*, *211*
New York and New Haven Railroad, 48
New York, Hartford and Springfield Railroad, 48
The Nirvana. See The Metallak.
North Conway House, 62, *62*, 73, 79
North Conway, NH, 42, 61, 78, 79, 80, 82, 107, 110, 123, 136, 144, 147-148, 150
Northern Railroad, 48, 71
North Woodstock, NH, 48, 68, 110, 130, 166, 168-169, 178
Notch House, *35*, 35-36, 44, 55
Noyes, Hiram, 163-164

Oak Hill House, *134*, 134-135, *135*, 140, 159
Old Moosehorn Tavern, 30, 31, 37-38

Parsons, George, 225-226
Pavilion Hotel, 45, 110
Peckett, John Wesley, 131, 139
Peckett, Robert, 131, 139
Peckett's-on-Sugar-Hill, 139
Pemigewasset House, the first, 39, *40*, 40-41, 45, 49, 63
Pemigewasset House, the second, 100-103, *100*, *101*, *102*, *103*
Pemigewasset House, the third, 107
Pemigewasset Valley Railroad, 166
Perkins, Marland A., 196
Piper House, 148
Pitman Hall, 148, *148*
Plaisted, Benjamin H., 95-96
Plumer & Porter, 97-98
Plymouth, NH, 39, 48, 100, 110, 166
Poland Spring House, *18*, 21, 189, 201

Portland and Ogdensburg Railroad, 58, 110-112, 116, 136, 214
Presidential Inn, 148
Preston, William G., 161-162
Price, John D., 122
Priest, Harry W., 160
Profile and Flume Hotels Company, 196
Profile and Franconia Notch Railroad, 68, 110, 136
Profile House, the first, 19, 27, 38-39, 41, 66-70, *66*, *67*, *68*, *69*, *70*, 74, *75*, 90, 110, 130, 152, 171, 196-198
Profile House, the second, 20. See also New Profile House.
Profile House, the third, 16, 201-202
Purdon, James, 206

Randall, Harry H., 84, 148, 150, 176
Randolph, NH, 164
Ravine House, 164, *165*
Reynolds, Foster F., 122, 222
Rogers, Isaiah, 18
Rosebrook, Eleazar, 29-31
Rosebrook Place, *28*

Sanborn, Hermann W., 167-168
Sanderson, Edward Thornton, 127, 140
Sawyer, Albert W., 169, 178
Seuter, Col. Samuel, 41
Senter House, the first, 39-41, *41*, 110, 171, 178
Senter House, the second (New Senter House), 171-175, *172-173*, *174*, 179
Shelburne, NH, 52, 164
Shute, F. F., 99
Sinclair House, 92-94, *93*, *94*, 124, 159, 163
Sinclair, John H., 92-93, 106, 125, 159
S. Mudgett & Sons, 81
Spalding, Randall E., 24
Spaulding, John H., 33
Spaulding, Samuel, 60
Stevens, John Calvin, 21, 118, 137, 180-182, *182*, 183-189, 208
Stickney, Carolyn Foster, 222
Stickney, Frederick W., 171, 173-174
Stickney, Joseph, 117-122, 213-216, 221-223, 236
Sugar Hill, NH, 130-131, 139, 159-160, 163, 167
Summit House, the first, 60-61, *61*, 114, 216, *250*
Summit House, the second, 21, 50, 60, *115*, 114-116, 137, 145
Summit House, the third, 145-147, *146*, *147*, 175, 198
Sunset Hill House, 131-134, *132*, *133*, 163-164
Sunset Pavilion, 79, 82-84, *82*, *83*, 176

T. J. Rowen & Company, 165
Taft, Richard A., 38, 64-69, 74
Taft & Greenleaf, 67, 130
Tamworth, NH, 107, 147-148
Thayer, Henry L., 63
Thayers Hotel(Inn), 63-64, *64*, 66, 74
Theobald, George A., 99
Thompson, Joseph M., 51-53
Thompson, Samuel W., 61, 78-79
Thorn Mountain House, 84, *84*, 88, 90, 105, 148
Tillotson, Neil, 232-233
Tilton, Henry L., 116
Tip-Top House, 50, 60-61, *61*, 73, 114, 116, 146, 175, *250*

[263]

THE GRAND RESORT HOTELS OF THE WHITE MOUNTAINS

Tremont House, 18
Trickey, Joseph B., 63
Trickey, W. H. H., 80-81
Twin Mountain House, *90*, 90-92, *91*, *92*, 106, 109, 114, 116, 136, 210

Uplands (Upland Terrace Hotel), 125-129, *129*, 128, 135, 138, 159, 163, 197, 201

W. F. Dodge & Son, 204-205
Walker, Frank P., *225*, 236
Washington House, 42, *45*, 79
Waterville Inn, 170-171, *171*, 178
Waumbek Hotel, 22, 95-100, *98*, *100*, 106, 109-110, 119, 164, 188, 210
Waumbek Hotel & Cottages, 97, *97*, *99*
Waumbek House, , 91, *95*, *96*, 96
Webster, Col. David, 40

Wentworth, General Marshall C., 84, 88, 105
Wentworth Hall, 87, 88, *90*,
Wentworth Hall and Cottages, 20, 24, 74, 84-90, *85*, *86-87*, *89*, 105, 155-156, 159
Whitcher, Chase R., 230-231, *232*
Whitefield & Jefferson Railroad, 106, 110
Whitefield, NH, 109, 136, 152, 165, 202, 206
White Mountain House, 30, *36*, 36-38, *37*, 44, 114, 128
White Mountains Railroad, 48, 109
White Mountain Station House, 49-51, 66, 71
Wiggin House, 148
Willey House and Hotel, 31-34, *33*, *34*, 44, 145
Willey, Samuel, Jr., 33
Winslow, Wetherell and Bradlee, 83, 104
Woodward, N. C., 50
Wright, Frank Lloyd, 217-218

Mt. Pleasant House, Carroll (Bretton Woods), NH. *Engraving from booklet* Mount Pleasant House (Bretton Woods, NH: n.p., [c. 1896]). *Based on sketch by E. Eldon Deane. Author's collection.*

THE ASQUAM HOUSE

on SHEPARD HILL, HOLDERNESS, N.H.

L. H. CILLEY, PROPRIETOR

CRAWFORD HOUSE,
White Mountains, N. H.

This famous Summer Resort is only 80 rods from the celebrated White Mountain Notch. Stages run daily between this and all the Mountain Houses; they also connect with the Mount Washington Railroad

A. T. & O. F. BARRON, Proprietors.

The Ridge,

KEARSARGE, N. H.

A NOTE ON THE AUTHOR

Bryant F. Tolles, Jr., is Associate Professor of History and Art History, and director of the Museum Studies Program at the University of Delaware, where he has been since 1984. Previously he served as executive director of the Essex Institute, Salem, Massachusetts, and assistant director and librarian of the New Hampshire Historical Society, Concord. He received B.A. (American Studies) and M.A.T. (History) degrees from Yale and a Ph.D. (History) from Boston University, and has published extensively on New England architectural and general history, including two books, *New Hampshire Architecture* (1979) and *Architecture in Salem* (1983).

A NOTE ON THE TYPE

The Grand Resort Hotels of the White Mountains was set in Monotype Bell, a traditional face related to the French designs of Didot and Fournier. It was first cut in 1788 by Richard Austin, a professional engraver, and issued by John Bell of London, a publisher, bookseller, typefounder and printer whose avowed ambition was "to retrieve and exalt the neglected art of printing in England." Recut for the Monotype Corporation of London in 1930 under the supervision of Stanley Morison, the type used in this edition was digitally augmented by Bruce Kennett to add the warmth caused by ink spread lost in the digital version.

Printed and bound by Thomson Shore, Dexter, Michigan

Designed by Bruce Kennett and Eugene Kuo

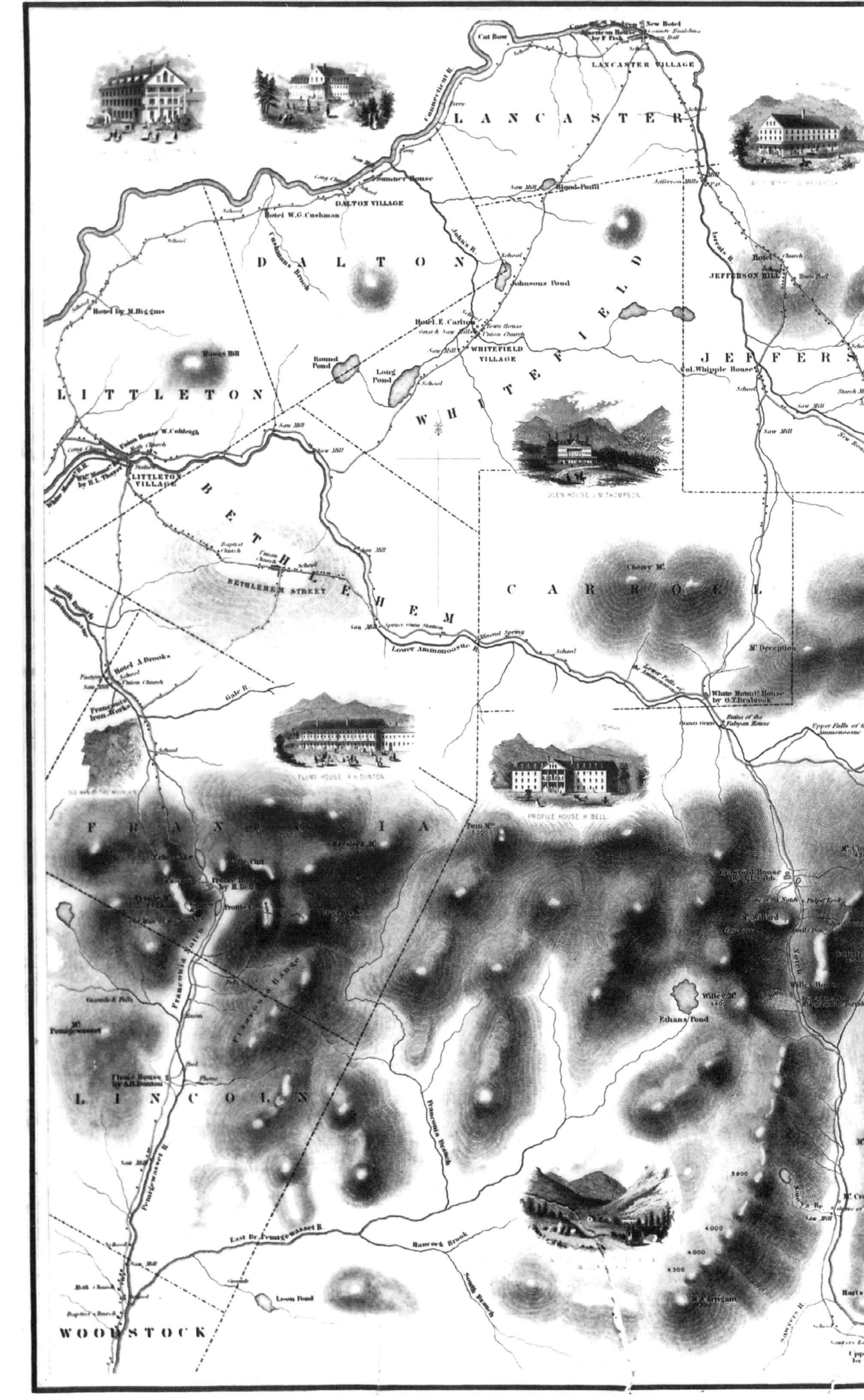